Rethinking Iranian Nationalism and Modernity

Rethinking Iranian Nationalism and Modernity

EDITED BY KAMRAN SCOT AGHAIE

AND AFSHIN MARASHI

University of Texas Press ⟵⟶ Austin

Requests for permission to reproduce material from this work should be sent to:
Permissions
University of Texas Press
P.O. Box 7819
Austin, TX 78713-7819
http://utpress.utexas.edu/index.php/rp-form

∞ The paper used in this book meets the minimum requirements of ANSI/NISO
Z39.48-1992 (R1997) (Permanence of Paper).

Library of Congress Cataloging-in-Publication Data
Rethinking Iranian nationalism and modernity / edited by Kamran Scot Aghaie and
Afshin Marashi. — First edition.
    p.   cm.
Includes bibliographical references and index.
ISBN 978-0-292-75749-3 (cloth : alk. paper)
ISBN 978-1-4773-0751-9 (paperback)
1. Nationalism—Iran.   2. Nationalism—Religious aspects—Islam.   3. Islam and
state—Iran.   4. National characteristics, Iranian.   5. Iran—Civilization.   I. Aghaie,
Kamran Scot, author, editor of compilation.   II. Marashi, Afshin, author, editor of
compilation.
    DS266.R47   2014
    320.54′0955—dc23

                                                                        2013038464

doi:10.7560/757493

This book is dedicated to James Gelvin, our professor and mentor, who trained both of us as historians and who started us on the path of exploring and studying nationalism.

Contents

Introduction

KAMRAN SCOT AGHAIE AND AFSHIN MARASHI

The study of Iranian nationalism has undergone significant changes during the past decade. As older paradigms of culture and society have given way to new critical and theoretical insights, a new generation of scholars of modern Iran has begun the task of questioning the received historiographical tradition long defining the history of modern Iran. Marked primarily by a shift away from perspectives that reified its object of knowledge, shared its self-same assumptions, and had traditionally written from within the ideological parameters of nationalism, the newer approach to the history of Iranian nationalism has instead sought to engage theoretical, conceptual, and comparative perspectives derived from the wider fields of nationalism studies, social history, literary theory, and postcolonial studies. The result is a nascent approach within the field of Iranian studies that has already shed new light on the making of modern Iranian nationhood. This volume brings together scholars broadly engaged in this new scholarship. The goal is to undertake innovative research, study previously understudied subjects, chart new areas of analysis, do comparative studies, and collectively *rethink* the historiography of Iranian nationalism and modernity.

Orientalism, Modernity, and Historiography

Part 1 of this volume begins this process of *rethinking* with a series of articles that critically engage and collectively problematize the conventional analytical vocabulary employed in the historiography of Iranian nationalism. Looking broadly at the encounter with European systems of thought—be they the European orientalist tradition, the European philosophical tradition, or the tradition of European social science itself—these papers question the often unspoken and undertheorized appropriations that have traditionally been employed from these systems of thought in thinking about Iranian history and society.

Afshin Marashi's article begins by questioning the "universalist" claims of European social science, as that tradition has been used to think about Iran's history of nationalism and modernity. Observing that much of what can now be called the "classical social-science tradition" of nationalism studies has been theorized from empirical cases drawn narrowly from the experience of the polyglot Austro-Hungarian polity of Central Europe, the nationalizing monarchies of nineteenth-century imperial states, a highly idealized understanding of the Habermasian "public sphere" of the eighteenth century, or a subaltern and postcolonial studies tradition that emphasizes the centrality of the *colonial presence* in the nation-building process, Marashi observes that, while these traditions of social science must be positively and productively engaged, Iran's historical experience does not conceptually conform to any of these classical paradigms. The challenge that Marashi poses, and which all of the contributors to this volume likewise pose, is the challenge of how to engage with the great tradition of the European social and human sciences without falling victim to the distortions and elisions that an uncritical engagement with that tradition might produce.

As Ali Anooshahr's, Afshin Matin-Asgari's, and Wendy DeSouza's articles suggest, the tradition of Iranian historiography is rife with examples of perilous and uncritical appropriations from European systems of thought. As Anooshahr describes, the political and ideological context of early twentieth-century European fascism came to shape understandings of Safavid historiography in surprising and still largely unacknowledged ways. Matin-Asgari finds a parallel process at work within Persian-language historiography produced by Iranian expatriate scholars in Berlin during and after the First World War who were profoundly shaped by currents of thought circulating within the German intellectual tradition. DeSouza sees a similar process at work in the cultural and national reconceptualization of Persian mystical poetry that grew out of the dialogic interaction between the European orientalist tradition and the tradition of Iranian nationalist historiography. As Anooshahr, Matin-Asgari, and DeSouza argue, definitions of culture, nation, and modernity, which were peculiar and specific to the context of the nineteenth- and early twentieth-century European cultural, literary, and philosophical traditions, came to define a broader European historiographic understanding of Iran, as well as an Iranian intellectual tradition's understanding of itself.

Imagining Iran: Land, Ethnicity, and Place

The articles that comprise Part 2 of this volume continue these themes by focusing broadly on evolving notions of Iranian belonging, as those notions took shape as a result of the rapid crystallization of the *nation-form* over the course of Iran's modern history. In particular, categories such as land, ethnicity, and place became increasingly charged and contested categories as Iran's history entered the age of the international system of nation-states. This new international system embroiled Iran not only within the familiar forms of political and economic—and broadly understood "imperial"—power, but also in new definitions of selfhood and belonging. The rigidly territorialized understandings of the modern nation-state demanded by the rapidly crystallizing international state system of the eighteenth, nineteenth, and twentieth centuries came to also demand increasingly formalized, legalized, and reified *imaginings* for Iranian selfhood.

The articles in this section explore the multifarious ways in which imaginings of Iran were transformed as a result of these processes. Mana Kia and Brian Mann consider the problem of territorialization in two very different, and yet profoundly interconnected, contexts. Kia explores the geocultural meanings of "Iran" in the early modern period through a careful reading of an eighteenth-century compendium of Persian poets. Significantly, as Kia argues, in this prenational age, the sense of belonging, and the meanings associated with notions of land, geography, and "place," followed strikingly different trajectories than those dictated by the later rigidly territorialized global mapping of nation-states. Brian Mann's contribution, by contrast, looks at the notion of Iranian belonging and placehood through a critical analysis of ethnicity and regionalism in the Khuzistani "secessionist" movement of the mid-twentieth century, a period in Iranian history when notions of ethnicity, territory, and land had already become formally *nationalized* but, as Mann suggests, still contested. Firoozeh Kashani-Sabet and Camron Michael Amin look at the question of an evolving Iranian understanding of selfhood and place through the surprising lens of U.S.-Iran relations. While the history of U.S.-Iran relations is usually told from the vantage point of international relations and imperial *high politics*, Kashani-Sabet and Amin's approach is to look at this encounter through the prism of cultural history. What they each discover—though looking at very different sources—is how profoundly formative the experience of "the other" has been as a constituent element in the formation of Iranian selfhood. As all the articles in this section suggest, the transformations engendered by the modern international system produced more than just political consequences for Iran's modern history; rather, these transformations came to shape Iranian nationalism and modernity in ways that are only now beginning to be understood.

Religion, Nationalism, and Contested Visions of Modernity

The chapters in this section explore five broad themes or methods. First is an exploration of the complex and nuanced relationship between religion and nationalism. Second includes the ways in which ancient civilizations and pre-modern cultures were appropriated for the purpose of constructing modern nationalisms. Third includes the study of diverse arrays of competing and contested nationalisms in Iran that defy simple categorizations like "civic nationalism" or "ethnic nationalism," and which continue to evolve to the present day. The fourth theme includes the dynamics of "East vs. West" or "indigenous/authentic vs. foreign" ideals, including alternative visions of modernity, that underpin these nationalist projects. The fifth, which is more of a method than a theme, is to study Iranian nationalism either in a comparative fashion or to broadly contextualize it beyond Iran.

These papers demonstrate that religion has played an integral role in the development of nationalisms in Iran, Egypt, Israel, and the broader Middle East. These studies challenge the idea that Iranian nationalists up until the late Pahlavi period universally downplayed Islamic history and stressed Iran's pre-Islamic heritage, and that this was followed by a reverse trend after the revolution. Instead, Vejdani, Aghaie, Hammad, and Siavoshi argue for nationalists who embraced both Iran's Islamic and pre-Islamic heritages, and did not always label Islam as "Arab" and a source of Iran's decline. In some cases, this was done by stressing the Iranization of Islam, through a focus on Shiʿism, or on non-ethnic Islam, or even by stressing how Iranians played a prominent role in the development of Islam. In other cases, it was done by Islamizing Iran to construct a religious nationalism in which Islamic values were treated as the core constitutive elements of the nation. In the former case, Iranian culture transformed or absorbed Islam, while in the latter Iran's core nature was transformed and subsumed by Islamic concepts and ideals. Either way, the two became inseparable, and were combined in the narratives of the Iranian nation. Within this context, Atabaki and Siavoshi also show how ethnicity proved to be problematic in government discourses about the nation following the Islamic revolution. These studies also demonstrate that the patterns of religious nationalism are not restricted to Iran. Rather, similar patterns can be seen in Egypt, Israel, Turkey, and many Arab countries, as is shown by Ram, Aghaie, and Hammad. Aghaie goes further, arguing for a generalized theory of religious nationalism that puts religion at the center of some nationalisms, and which can be usefully applied beyond Iran to other nationalisms in the Muslim Middle East, as well as to cases of religious nationalisms in other parts of the world.

The above points do not, however, imply that the pre-Islamic heritage of Iran did not play a critically important role as well. These papers demonstrate how ancient symbols and narratives were appropriated in the construction of the modern national narrative. Further, Ram and Hammad show how this pattern correlated in interesting ways with the dynamics within Egyptian nationalism and Zionism. In particular, in the Egyptian and Iranian cases, nationalists "remembered" pre-Islamic civilization, culture, and religion (i.e., Pharaonic and Zoroastrian) selectively, to push modern qualities back in time to the early history of the nation they envisioned, while at the same time claiming an ancient, indigenous origin for many traits of their modern nation. Vejdani shows that during the Pahlavi period Iran's Islamic heritage was not systematically excluded or downplayed in favor of its pre-Islamic heritage, and Aghaie shows that Iran's pre-Islamic heritage was not rejected or downplayed by Islamists in favor of a universalist, or antinationalist, Islamism. Atabaki further shows how efforts were made to include Turks/Azeris as prominent players in Iran's pre-Islamic and Islamic history. Similar patterns can also be seen in an analogous form in Israeli Jewish nationalism or Zionism, as is demonstrated by Ram's article comparing Zionism and Islamism.

In all of the chapters in this section, nationalism is treated as a set of contested visions of what the nation should be. For example, Grigor shows how artistic representations of the nation have evolved from avant-garde in the Pahlavi period, followed by a kitsch style after the revolution, which was in turn challenged by the reemergence of a new avant-garde style. Siavoshi explores the competing and contested visions of the Iranian nation by comparing the discourses of the Islamic regime, the reformist opposition, and monarchists. Aghaie explores the domestic religious nationalist discourses within Iran. Atabaki shows how ethnic identity markers such as Turk/Azeri and regional histories related to alternative narratives of the nation. And Ram explores similar issues in relation to Israeli nationalism and its relationship to Iran.

These papers also demonstrate how the positioning of the nation's civilizational and moral context or affinity is both arbitrary and important. Thus, the nation was coded or defined as either Western or Eastern, and in either case the pattern was to define the nation as an indigenous phenomenon, and to exclude or rationalize foreign or alien elements and qualities that either were part of the nation, or which influenced it. In the case of Iran, the debate tended to center around how to negotiate the apparent foreignness of Islam. In the case of Egypt and Iran, efforts were made to find a local, non-Western basis for nationalism, while in the case of Zionism, the approach was to define Israel as being solidly part of the Western or Judeo-Christian civilizational sphere, and distinctly not associated with the Islamic Middle Eastern "other."

These studies also demonstrate that there were broadly similar patterns of evolution among these different nationalisms, rather than each case being unique. Hammad's paper shows how Iranian and Egyptian nationalists directly influenced one another and worked to define a "local" and "authentic" nationalism, and Ram's paper shows how Zionism and Khomeinism share many important qualities, despite their mutual antagonism and condemnation. He also shows how Israeli views of Iran are inextricably connected to the complexities of domestic ethnic and religious politics and to diverse and evolving conceptions of the Jewish state, and how the same is true of Iran and its views of Israel.

Collectively, the themes outlined in this book by no means exhaust the possible range or trajectories for rethinking Iranian nationalism and modernity. Indeed, if the chapters in this volume can be said to revolve around the broad themes of Iran's modern intellectual encounter with European thought, its new imaginings of territory and place, and the contested nature of debates surrounding the notion of Iran's national "heritage," then the chapters in this volume can in fact be said to merely initiate a selective process of conceptual rethinking. While themes of ethnicity, regionalism, and gender, for example, make their appearance in this volume, the larger questions that these and other themes pose can certainly lead to yet further trajectories of *rethinking*, and it is hoped, more concentrated reflections on these issues. What this volume does hope to accomplish, however, is therefore not an exhaustive exercise of problematizing the historiography of Iranian nationalism and modernity, but rather an initial exercise of collectively juxtaposing innovative, experimental, and alternative perspectives that it is hoped will in turn lead to new perspectives and possibilities in thinking about Iran's modern history.

Rethinking Iranian Nationalism and Modernity

PART 1

ORIENTALISM, MODERNITY, AND HISTORIOGRAPHY

CHAPTER 1

Paradigms of Iranian Nationalism: History, Theory, and Historiography

AFSHIN MARASHI

The history of nationalism has increasingly come to occupy a central place in the study of modern Iran. Since at least the mid-1990s, the growing number of conference papers, articles, and monographs examining various aspects of Iran's experience with the nation-form suggests that there has emerged a confluence of interest among specialists in examining Iran's *national question*.[1] This focus spans both the literary-cultural tradition of Iranian historiography and Iranian historiography's social scientific tradition. The result has been a productive body of recent scholarship whose emergence can only be explained by understanding changes within both the field of Iranian studies and in the wider domain of the humanities and social sciences.

It is perhaps a fortuitous coincidence that, at the precise moment during which the 1979 Iranian revolution had engendered a critical reassessment of Iran's modern history, new understandings of culture and society were simultaneously reshaping the entire analytical vocabulary of the humanities and social sciences. The 1980s and 1990s were a time when an older paradigm of "modernization theory" had already been eclipsed, and newer analytical frameworks rooted in literary theory and postcolonial studies were posing tantalizingly suggestive alternative methods for investigating the processes that constitute knowledge, culture, and the nation.[2] Likewise, within the social sciences, the collapse of the Soviet Union in 1991 and the concern over the uncertain future of the former Soviet republics also brought renewed focus to neglected strands of the "historical sociological" school of comparative nationalism studies and the writings of Karl Deutsch, Miroslav Hroch, Ernest Gellner, and Jürgen Habermas, as well as new works in this tradition by Eric Hobsbawm, John Breuilly, Benedict Anderson, and many others.[3] It is within this intellectual climate of a radical rethinking of the traditional disciplinary paradigms of the humanities and social sciences, and a coterminous reassessment of Iran's modern history, that the beginnings of a new historiography of Iranian nationalism can be situated. By the mid-1990s, the intellectual cross-fertilization between Iranian studies and new paradigms of nationalism studies were yielding historiographical results.

And yet, while certain currents in Iranian historiography have followed these larger meta-changes in the disciplines, there has at the same time been surprisingly little self-conscious discussion of these theoretical and disciplinary shifts within the field of Iranian studies. In part, the dearth of reflexive discussion may result from the organic utilization of the assumptions and categories of cultural theory and comparative nationalism studies without much self-conscious reflection of the analytics of that appropriation. Conversely, the dearth of discussion may also result from a well-heeled self-confidence in classical frameworks of knowledge, be they orientalist hermeneutics, positivist social science, or unreconstructed Marxism; or it may perhaps be the result of a defensive retrenchment into these selfsame conceptual and analytical paradigms. Whatever the reason, the result of this partial engagement with new theorizing has been an uneven transformation and a still-emerging critical reflexivity within Iranian historiography.

The time for an initial assessment of Iranian historiography's encounter with the shifting boundaries of the humanities and social sciences is, therefore, perhaps overdue. Conducting this kind of assessment requires a careful review of the broad outline of developments in the field of nationalism studies, and analytically assessing how Iran's modern history adds to, or complicates, the still tentative conclusions of this theorizing. This approach can potentially not only add to the empirical body of knowledge on which theories of nationalism have been based but can also complicate those theories. A reflexive engagement with theories of nationalism can likewise suggest new questions and methods of reasoning inspired by the experience of nationalism elsewhere, which, in turn, may lead to new insights into Iran's modern history. The enrichment of both our theorizing and our knowledge of Iran's modern history can, in short, best be pursued by a self-conscious and reflexive analysis of the relationship between nationalism theory and Iranian historiography.

Historical Sociology and Iranian Nationalism

The tradition of scholarship in nationalism studies that poses the broadest implications for understanding the history of nationalism and the nation-state in Iranian history is the tradition that is generally referred to as "historical sociology." At the most basic level, the literature on the historical sociology of the nation-state represents the first move away from an older, *primordialist* understanding of nationalism and toward a view which emphasizes the social, economic, and historical origins of the nation as a global phenomenon tied to changes engendered in the modern era.[4] Further, the historical-sociologist school of nationalism studies is, by design, focused principally on the macro-level historical changes that define the transition from agrarian societies with lower levels of political, social, and economic centralization, to the emergence of large-scale urban-industrial societies with high degrees of social and political consolidation and interconnection with the global economy. According to this tradition of scholarship, *the nation-state*—and its accompanying forms of nationalist politics—is one of the principal historical by-products of this large-scale transition to modernity. Analyzing the specific and varied historical experiences of different societies and regions of the world as they made this macro-historical transition is the principal preoccupation of the comparative historical sociology of nationalism.

The proliferation of new works in this tradition during the 1980s and 1990s played an important role in spurring a rethinking of Iran's transition to the nation-state form. Perhaps most influentially—in Southeast Asian studies—the specter of unexpected "national wars" among self-described Marxist states led Benedict Anderson to reevaluate the "national question" as something more complex than either the simple atavism of "primordial" identities or, conversely, as a dismissive expression of "false consciousness." Anderson's work, and the work of numerous others during this period, was part of a critical tradition of historical sociology that produced a new comparatively oriented and theoretically aware analysis of the modern world system of nation-states that grew out of—but also challenged—the established assumptions of both Marxian and Weberian social science.[5] From the point of view of critically minded younger scholars in the field of Iranian historiography, the surprise of the Iranian revolution seemed analogous to the unexpected national wars in Indochina in revealing the limits of conventional historical and sociological theories, and in a similar manner spurred a basic rethinking of long-held assumptions in the field. As the new conceptual and comparative literature in the newly christened field of "nationalism studies" came to proliferate during the 1980s, it produced a veritable toolbox of new analytical methods and categories, which very quickly made an impression on those engaged in rethinking Iran's modern history.

Among the most ubiquitous analytical approaches in the comparative nationalism literature is the approach that seeks to highlight the specific social origins of popular nationalist movements in societies making the transition to modernity. According to this approach—most authoritatively represented by

Karl Deutsch, Miroslav Hroch, Eric Hobsbawm, Michael Hector, and Ernest Gellner—nationalism is principally understood as a type of popular social mobilization that expresses the interests of certain coalitions of social groups during a particular moment in the process of industrial modernization.[6] Those classes and groups who find themselves on the periphery of economic changes during the formative moment of the initial transition to capitalist industrialization commonly use the language of ethnolinguistic solidarity to mobilize against the bourgeois-aristocratic classes who are perceived to have socially and economically benefited from the process of industrialization. Nationalism, according to this analytical formulation, represents a *new style* of politics that uses a cultural-national language, which, as Ernest Gellner states, "enables them to conceive and express their resentments and discontents in intelligible terms."[7] These "resentments and discontents" generally crystallize along social and cultural fault-lines within a given polity making the transition from agrarian social formations to modern industrial-capitalist ones.

In evaluating this particular analytical approach for the history of Iran's national experience, we encounter certain key issues. First, it is very clear from the work of most of the key theorists of this tradition that they are generalizing from the experience of national politics in the context of east-central Europe in the nineteenth century. Deutsch, Hroch, Hobsbawm, and Gellner were all explicitly focused on east-central Europe and the social origins of nationalist movements during the period of the Austro-Hungarian Empire's rapid disintegration. This particular historical context lent itself well to highlighting the relationship between social forms of popular mobilization and the specifically ethnolinguistic languages of protest.

Second, this literature is also premised upon the key variable of the uneven spread of industrialization. Nationalism, according to this formulation, is understood as a political form that grows out of industrialization's expansion from a single industrial core region to an ever-expanding concentric process affecting other regions, first within Europe and then the rest of the world. This uneven spread of industrialization is seen in classical *historicist* terms as both a temporal and spatial sequence beginning in Western Europe in the eighteenth century and spreading to Germany, Italy, the Austro-Hungarian Empire, Iberia, Ireland, Scandinavia, Japan, and the colonial and semicolonial domains. The particular form of national politics is therefore determined not by generalized economic conditions, but by economic conditions producing a specific social *awareness* of inequality at a key moment in the macro-historical transition to industrial modernity.[8] Theorizing from the experience of east-central Europe, the temporal and spatial pattern of unevenness produced an awareness of differential social-economic transformation which, in turn, took shape as a political consciousness on the part of those who found themselves disadvantaged by the pace and sequence of modernity's unevenness. This political sensitivity usually manifests itself not as crude class-consciousness, but along ethnolinguistic fault-lines separating those city-dwellers who benefit from industrial modernity's *forward march* and those town and village dwellers on the temporal and spatial margins of this process who do not.

Finally, the social origins of nationalism theorizing pay particular attention to the role of the intellectual vanguard of these national-popular movements. This vanguard class is analyzed less for its particular ideological or "discursive" character than for the key social-cultural role that it played in the process of popular mobilization. As the interconnected processes of uneven development, state-formation, and educational expansion spread across the regions of east-central Europe during the nineteenth century, more and more strata of society entered into the domain of formal politics. Among these newly educated social actors entering into the social-cultural domain of modern-urban politics were those described by Deutsch, Hroch, Elie Kedourie, and others, as "the marginal men"—newly educated and underemployed town dwellers who, because of their contact with the modern-urban sector, understood the instruments of formal politics and modern communication and were able to make use of them in order to give voice to the social frustrations of those coalitions of groups and classes who were losing out during the epochal transition to industrial modernity.[9] The position of these "marginal men" as social-cultural *intermediaries* and *interlocutors* between the newly crystallizing domain of modern-urban politics and the rapidly disintegrating world of agrarian-traditional life made them ideal as political vanguards able to use an ethnolinguistic language to mobilize their marginalized social-national compatriots—consisting of the newly urbanized underclass, the socially insecure town dwellers, and an increasingly frustrated peasantry—into popular movements challenging the ascendant urban bourgeois-aristocratic industrial elites.

In considering the relevance of this "social origins of nationalism" paradigm for understanding the modern history of Iranian nationalism, a number of conceptual problems immediately present themselves. If, as the east-central European paradigm suggests, the emergence of national-popular social movements is a political outcome produced by the social-economic dislocations of the early stages of industrialization, we would expect to observe that the use of the national form of politics in Iran *followed* the early history of Iran's industrialization. On the contrary, the exact opposite appears to be the case. Iran's industrialization was notoriously late, coming only well into the twentieth century, at least two generations after the early use of nationalist language and popular mobilization in Iranian politics.[10] Further, in contrast to east-central Europe, the language of ethnolinguistic nationalism was not used as the basis of social-popular movements targeting emerging economic and industrial elites in Iran during the early history of industrialization. Instead, the language of nationalist politics was first used by state elites and modernizing literati with access to transnational intellectual discourses. Rather than for popular mobilization, the early use of the language of nationalism by these literary and intellectual elites was generally for social-cultural *reform* projects.[11]

Further, the paradigmatic "marginal men" using an ethnocultural national language to voice the social-economic frustrations of town dwellers and peasantry simply did not materialize during the early history of Iranian nationalism. The political-intellectual vanguard of Iranian nationalism was indeed "marginal," but its marginality was expressed in terms of its culturally liminal position between Iran's literary-philosophical tradition and the new transnational discourses of modernity and the Enlightenment. Iran's nationalist vanguard can best be described as *marginal elites* who were political-intellectual elites within Iran while also being socially and discursively situated as marginal or peripheral with respect to Euro-modern cultural forms. Very rarely during the early history of Iranian nationalism did members of this nationalist vanguard find themselves as the organic spokespersons of town dwellers and peasantry decrying the social-cultural status of Iran's bourgeois-industrial elites. The record of popular-social mobilization in nineteenth and early twentieth century Iran—such as the movement challenging the 1871 Reuter Concession, the 1891–1892 Tobacco Protest, and other such early social-popular movements—were instead proto-Islamist movements that used a religious language and were led by what may be termed a "clerical vanguard." The 1905–1911 constitutional movement, by contrast, may be described as representing a broader coalition of social strata and ideological languages, including those espousing an overtly nationalist language; but the popular-social constituency of the constitutional coalition was likewise grounded in proto-Islamist language, and led by "marginal men" in the form of popular preachers and newly politicized segments of the formal clerisy.[12]

These conceptual problems do not suggest that the paradigm of east-central European popular nationalism is without use in thinking about modern Iranian history. On the contrary, when adjusted for the differences attributable to local circumstances, some of the parallels are in fact illuminating. While Iranian industrialization did not in itself operate as a key variable in Iran's political development until comparatively late, the social-economic effects of integration into the world economy did begin to shape the course of Iran's social history already in the nineteenth century. The penetration of foreign commercial goods into certain regions of Iran, and the coterminous process of commercialization of agriculture, did produce social dislocations analogous to those observed in the east-central European paradigm of nationalism studies.[13] The key distinction to be made, however, is that the social dislocations were felt to be caused not by local bourgeois-aristocratic proto-industrial elites of the city who spoke a different regional language or dialect than the town dwellers or peasantry—as was the case in the paradigm of east-central Europe—but rather, by global-imperial economic penetration into Iran. The nature of this particular form of social-economic dislocation produced, in turn, a particular form of social-popular protest. Within this distinctively Iranian paradigm of popular mobilization, it can be argued that Islamic language played the role of a surrogate protonationalism, and it was the politicized segments of the clerisy who played the role of a surrogate nationalist vanguard.

The east-central European paradigm of nationalism studies can, therefore, be useful in illuminating certain aspects of Iran's modern history. Taking into account the disparities of context and the distinctions of time and space, this literature does highlight some important comparative parallels. Other elements of Iran's history of nationalism, however, remain unanalyzed and unexplained. While helping to explain the social and economic context of popular mobilization at certain moments of Iran's modern history, this literature does not begin to explain the cultural history of national identification in Iran's nineteenth and twentieth centuries. The articulation of these forms of national identification represent another basic dimension of Iran's experience with the nation-form in the modern period and requires the exploration of other categories of analysis.

Nationalizing States and the Practice of "Cultural Representation"

The study of nationalism also underwent a considerable shift in the 1980s, coinciding with the larger cultural or linguistic *turn* in the humanities. As these meta-changes took place, new understandings of the processes by which "the nation" came to be conceived as a cultural category also emerged. Looking beyond the social and economic origins of popular mobilization, this new *culturalist* approach to the history of nationalism looked more closely at the disciplinary processes that worked to normalize certain understandings of the nation. How exactly were notions of "national identity" constructed and articulated? How did these new narratives and understandings circulate within a given polity? What were the techniques involved in these processes of construction, circulation, and normalization?

In asking these questions, the scholars in the cultural history of the nationalist tradition assumed—along with their historical-sociologist colleagues—that nationalism was something more than an inert and ahistorical quantum of force to be activated and deactivated depending on particular circumstances. The cultural theorists of the nation shared with the historical sociologists a deep skepticism of nationalism's self-declared primordialist credentials. And yet, unlike the historical sociologists—who understood the culturalist language of nationalist movements as primarily instrumental—the cultural theorists argued that the "the nation" did have a cultural history worthy of study. From the point of view of the cultural historians of nationalism "the nation" was understood as a highly flexible, dynamic, and amorphous symbolic system that could be made and remade to signify a wide array of cultural meanings and symbolic associations. The great emphasis in this tradition of theorizing is in highlighting the distinctively modern processes that work to make, shape, or construct a particular constellation of symbolic associations comprising a national identity. These processes of cultural construction consist of the analysis of nationalism's narrative forms, the work of intellectuals in shaping these new narratives, and the analysis of the institutional practices—schools, commemorations, ceremonies, etc.—through which a novel scenario of national identity becomes normalized within a given polity. The role of the cultural historian of nationalism is, therefore, to document these practices of cultural construction, and to explain how certain representations of the nation achieve dominance at particular historical moments.

Perhaps the most prolific body of literature that has grown out of this *culturalist* tradition—which in turn may be potentially useful for understanding Iran's history—is the writing that has analyzed the experience of eighteenth- and nineteenth-century European monarchies as they made the transition from premodern dynastic orders reigning over loosely organized territorial realms to modern national states within a global system of nation-states. This history of monarchical *nationalization*, spanning roughly from the late eighteenth century to the eve of the First World War, is generally analyzed as a politically conservative effort on the part of dynastic elites who were seeking to articulate a new ideology of "the nation" for the purpose of retaining monarchical legitimacy during a period of political threat to the authority of the old elites engendered by newly emerging popular movements. In practice, these nationalization efforts produced new understandings of sovereignty on the part of these struggling monarchical states that invoked notions of "a people" with a shared history and culture, while also projecting the image of the monarch as central to "the national polity." In order to retain the loyalty of the masses, the conceptual price that was paid by these monarchies was to cede to the idea of *national sovereignty* an implicit understanding that the source of the monarch's authority no longer resided "outside" or "above" the realm, but that instead the new *national monarch* was an organic part of the national community. This ideological concession to "the people" made the theoretical basis of the monarch's sovereignty now inherently much more fragile, as it implied that the monarch's status as the organic embodiment of the nation could be rejected through a demonstration of popular-national will. Nevertheless, the cultural and institutional labor that went into producing this new notion of *monarchical nationalism* has been the focus of cultural historians who have studied the history of European monarchies during the turbulent period of the transition from traditional understanding of sovereignty to a new understanding embodied in the modern politics of the nation-state.[14]

To what extent is this literature useful for understanding Iran's history of nationalization? In a number of key ways, Iran's cultural and political structures seem remarkably analogous to those of early modern Europe during the critical moment on the eve of nationalization. Despite a tendency on the part of Iranian nationalists and sympathetic historians to exaggerate the continuity of Iran's monarchy, it is nevertheless true that the monarchical institution had deep—if discontinuous—roots in Iran's history. Further, at the beginning of the nineteenth century, after a long period of political decentralization following the collapse of the Safavid order (1501-1722), Iran did emerge with the newly established Qajar dynasty (1796-1925) heading the now-restored monarchical state. In addition, despite the tenuous and diminishing quality of its control over territory—not least because of the territorial losses incurred during the early nineteenth century to an ascendant Russia—the Qajar dynasty could nevertheless claim some degree of sovereignty over a loosely demarcated territorial zone that included the core region of the Iranian plateau. The preponderance of Shi'ism as the almost universal religious affiliation within the core region provided another key element of religio-cultural continuity that likewise made Qajar Iran analogous to some of the nationalizing monarchies of early modern and nineteenth century Europe. Given these factors, we can conclude that, on the eve of modernity, Iran did have some institutional preconditions analogous to those of the paradigmatic European polities at their comparable initial stages of nationalization.

And yet, these apparently analogous preconditions can also be misleading. Most importantly, while the principle of monarchy—now in its Qajar form—was an established principle in Iran's history, the existence of the monarchical institution should not be casually conflated with the institutional structure and conceptual presence of a modern state. In the case of the analogous European monarchies, the transition from premodern forms of monarchical sovereignty to the new notion of *national monarch* was accompanied by a robust effort of modern state-building. These state-building efforts unfolded gradually over the course of the eighteenth and nineteenth centuries and were generally enabled by the technological innovations made possible by industrialization; state-building efforts such as urban rebuilding, road construction, and rail service, as well as the authority that accompanied the new proliferation of government-issued legal documents, postal service, policing, and conscription, were among these common state-building efforts of this period. The cumulative result of these state-building efforts was not only "administrative centralization," as classical modernization theory would suggest, but, more importantly, a new conceptual and semiotic understanding of *the state*. The increasingly visual, and even tactile, reminder of the state's presence in the quotidian affairs of the population worked to give life to "the state" as an autonomous *social category*, which now came to occupy a permanent place in the conceptual vocabulary of a given population. The changing notions of national-monarchical sovereignty in nineteenth-century Europe only had real political power when accompanied by the newly felt physical and conceptual presence of *the state* within nationalizing polities.

The same pattern cannot as readily be discerned for the case of the Qajar state. While state-building efforts did begin in the same period, they were by contrast piecemeal, intermittent, and comparatively minimal when measured against the state-building efforts of the nineteenth-century European monarchies, or even against the efforts of Qajar Iran's immediate Middle Eastern neighbors, the "Ottoman state" or the "Egyptian state" of Muhammad Ali and his heirs.[15] A cultural shift did take place in the ideology of Iranian monarchy in this period, analogous to the more public role for monarchy played by the European dynasties; however, this ideological shift, and the new public projections of sovereignty, took place without the accompanying technical and administrative formalization that would make the Qajar monarch the embodiment of a more abstract category of "the state." This key difference from the classical European paradigm of monarchical nationalism may play an important role in understanding Iran's history of nationalism. We cannot assume, as the comparative-nationalism literature might lead us to, that the abstract category of "the state" was an already established presence in the social imaginary of the Iranian polity. As with the social effects set in motion by Iran's belated industrialization, the belated crystallization of the Iranian state as a technical-administrative presence, and hence as an autonomous conceptual category, would have to wait until the twentieth century.[16] The case of Qajar Iran's history of monarchical nationalization therefore poses to the comparative-nationalism literature this analytical problem: What kind of historical evolution can we expect in a polity that acquires a modern cultural understanding of *national monarchy*, but which has yet to actualize the conceptual presence of a *national state*? The answer to that question might rest in understanding Iran's modern history.

Habermas and the Iranian Public Sphere?

In addition to the problem of *the state*, there is another problematic point of comparison in using the culturalist tradition of nationalism studies for understanding the history of Iranian nationalism. In explaining the origins of nationalism within a given polity, the theorists of nationalism have generally assumed the presence of a broader cultural universe that has already been shaped by post-Reformation and post-Enlightenment cultural systems. Nationalism, according to the cultural theorists, is a form of political consciousness that is naturally connected to the secular ontology of Enlightenment modernity, and is necessarily a historical phenomenon that has emerged after, in Benedict Anderson's words, "the dusk of religious modes of thought."[17] The history of nationalism in those polities still defined by a premodern ontology is an issue on which the cultural theorists of nationalism remain silent. The reason for this theoretical silence is, once again, that our more generalized assumptions about the history of nationalism are based on a limited range of empirical cases drawn largely from the historical experience of early modern and modern Europe. This, by itself, does not invalidate this tradition of theorizing for understanding Iran's history of nationalism. To the contrary, by carefully evaluating the comparative similarities—and differences—between the assumptions of the European paradigm and the Iranian case, we can expand our understanding of both.

Drawing largely upon the work of Jürgen Habermas, the cultural theorists of nationalism have argued that the historical prelude to "the nation" is the formation of the so-called public sphere—defined as an autonomous social and cultural communicative space situated *beneath* the authority of government and *above* the social space occupied by the general populace.[18] This autonomous domain—represented physically through institutions such as the coffee house, the tavern, civic clubs, the theatre, the press, and libraries, among other eighteenth- and nineteenth-century examples of an emerging European urban culture—became the arena for debate and discussion, as well as the location where we can begin to identify the formation of a socially consensual public opinion. It is in this social space, according to the cultural theorists of the nation, that protonationalist intelligentsia came to experiment with new cultural constructions of community, and in the process redefined the oral tradition of rural life as *national folklore*, redefined traditional storytelling as *national literature*, and redefined the amorphous heritage of the past as *national history*. The formation of the public sphere in the Europe of the late eighteenth and early nineteenth centuries, therefore, produced an arena where the protonationalist intelligentsia could emerge to culturally and discursively define the nation and claim to speak in its name. As Benedict Anderson has noted, building upon the work of Habermas, the boundary of a given public sphere was "inherently limited" by the geographic parameter of a given vernacular language and the marketplace of "print-capitalism" that accompanied this linguistically defined *public*.[19] Specific linguistically demarcated cultural-national communities thus came to be imagined, once they were socially *enabled* by the crystallization of their respective public spheres.

Significantly, however, this version of the early history of nationalism assumes a universe of culture where the philosophical assumptions of the post-Reformation and post-Enlightenment tradition had already been established. In Habermas's—and Anderson's—highly idealized and historicist version of the eighteenth and nineteenth centuries, the formation of the public sphere expanded the arena of communication and cultural discourse, thus making possible new configurations of identity and community. What the public sphere also did, however, was to institutionalize a limited range of discursive possibilities that extended *only* within the philosophical range of assumptions tied to post-Reformation and post-Enlightenment ontology. Coming *after* the eclipse of religious modes of thought, the social crystallization of the public sphere in the late eighteenth and early nineteenth centuries thus ensured that the consensually determined culture to emerge from the debates within this nascent domain would by its nature lead to a culture that shared the assumptions of the Reformation, Enlightenment, and a secular political modernity.

For the history of nationalism in Iran, this rendering of the historical sequence in the evolution of the public sphere and "the nation" again proves problematic. As with the problems of sequencing relating to the patterns of industrialization and popular mobilization discussed above, and as with the problematic sequencing relating to new notions of sovereignty and the administrative formalization of the modern state, the crystallization of the public sphere also creates *sequencing* problems for thinking about Iran's history. A public sphere analogous to that described by Habermas and Anderson did also take shape in the Iran of the late nineteenth and early twentieth centuries. The new circulation of newspapers, the proliferation of a novel print-culture made possible by emerging print technologies, and the energetic quality of the literary-polemical discourse of the years surrounding the constitutional revolution, all testify to the formation of an *Iranian public sphere* that was capable of giving form to a *generalized opinion* claiming to speak for the national community.[20]

However, in contrast to the idealized paradigm described by Habermas and Anderson, the public sphere that took shape in Iran did not crystallize in an Iranian social and cultural universe already defined by the philosophical ontology of the Reformation and the Enlightenment. At the moment of its crystallization, Iran's public sphere was, by contrast, a philosophically mixed communicative space in which a secularized Iranian modernist discourse shared the same public sphere with the Shi'a religio-political tradition. In contrast to the historical sequencing described by Habermas and Anderson, the Iranian public sphere did not crystallize *after* the philosophical and ontological victory of a still nascent and fragile Iranian Enlightenment—such a discursive hegemony, in fact, never took place. The formation of an Iranian public sphere, therefore, did not predetermine the emergence of a "secular-national" cultural-ontological consensus in the new discursive arena. On the contrary, the formation of a public sphere within Iran's historical sequence *enabled* a much larger array of cultural possibilities and narrative forms to circulate and contest for hegemony. Iran's experience with the public sphere, therefore, had the effect of expanding the definition of *the political* into forms that did not follow the classical historicist assumption of Habermas and others who follow this line of argumentation.[21]

As the above discussion suggests, this tradition of theorizing—like the theorizing of the social origins of the nation, and the theorizing of the nationalizing state—cannot be mechanically applied to the Iranian case. However, when the comparisons are critically engaged, with an emphasis on highlighting the points not only of similarity but also of contrast, then the resulting theorizing yields analytical possibilities that can contribute to larger comparative-theoretical debates.

Postcolonial Theory and the Historiography of Iranian Nationalism

The theories of nationalism posed thus far represent theoretical paradigms of the nation-form rooted in the historical experience of European nationalism. As already noted, this European-centeredness of nationalism theory poses conceptual problems for thinking about Iran's experience of national formation. While Iran's history shares broad similarities with some of the classical cases of Western European nationalization, in other respects Iran's history of nationalism must be understood as emerging out of the specific context of Iran's position as a semicolonial Asian state in the world system of the nineteenth and twentieth centuries. Any sophisticated analysis of Iran's history of nationalization must, therefore, also take into account the specifically extra-European circumstances that shaped the history of Iranian nationalization, and consider this question: Does the Iranian case approximate the classical paradigms of European nationalization, or should Iran's experience of nationalization be situated within a comparative typology alongside the history of nationalism in the colonial context of Asia and Africa?

The historiography of South Asia—specifically, the traditions of subaltern studies and postcolonial theory—has made the most valuable contributions in theorizing the specifically extra-European contexts that have shaped the history of nationalism outside of Europe. This tradition of theorizing has produced a number of key ideas that can be useful for purposes of comparison with the history of Iran.

Perhaps the most important idea to emerge from the subaltern studies group are those that critique the traditional historiography of the independence movement in colonial India. As Ranajit Guha has argued in one of the seminal essays of the subaltern-studies group, the conventional historiography of India's nationalist movement was for a long time dominated by what he calls an "elitism" that reflected the perspective of the British colonial class and the bourgeois-nationalist Indian elite. As Guha has argued, this elitist cultural, political—and ultimately historiographical—perspective "originated as the ideological product of British rule in India."[22] Among the historiographical assumptions that were implied by this perspective were that the masses of India's subaltern classes were docile participants in the nationalist movement, that the consciousness of Indian nationalism was principally shaped by the Indian modernist-nationalist elite, and that ultimately it was this Indian nationalist elite that led the masses "from subjugation to freedom."[23]

The intention of Guha and the subaltern-studies theorists in highlighting the "elitist" assumptions of the traditional historiography of the Indian nationalist movement is grounded in something more than the impulse of the social historian to include the histories of those who have traditionally been marginalized in conventional accounts of the past. Instead, the intention of the subaltern-studies group is rooted in a Marxian dialectical impulse intended to analyze the revolutionary tactics and social dynamics that enabled the Indian modernist-nationalist elite to successfully forge a political alliance with the subaltern masses and achieve the political goal of independence. How was it possible for an elite nationalist class, whose philosophical and ontological worldview shared so much more with the British colonial elite than with the "mytho-religious" consciousness of the Indian subaltern masses, to make a plausible claim of speaking for *the nation* and mobilize a broad-based movement of independence? This question—or what Guha refers to as the problem of the "structural dichotomy" of elite and subaltern in India[24]— serves as a point of departure for the subaltern-studies group; the answer lies at the center of the similarities and differences marking the national histories of India and Iran.

As Ranajit Guha, Partha Chatterjee, and others have argued for the Indian case, following the ideas of Antonio Gramsci, the Indian nationalist elite's great tactical success was in its ability to *temporarily* claim the right to speak for the masses.[25] The transitory viability of this claim was only achieved within the highly volatile context of a movement that had as a common objective the removal of the *external* presence of the colonial state. The common political and discursive opponent shared by the subaltern masses and the national-ist elite allowed for a Gramscian "passive revolution" and "war of position," in which the bourgeois-nationalist elite was able to articulate a language of opposition to the Raj which simultaneously reflected the political aspirations of the nationalist elite and the "mythic" consciousness of the subaltern.[26] This moment of political and discursive *correspondence* between elite and subaltern was viable only in the presence of—and in opposition to—the colonial state. It was, for this same reason, a highly fleeting moment that assured the national-ist elite would have great difficulty maintaining its hegemony once the exter-nal presence of the colonial state had disappeared in the post-independence period. At the moment of the revolution, however, the correspondence be-tween the bourgeois-national elite and the subaltern masses was enabled by the stark presence of the colonial state. As Guha states, "such effort when linked to struggles which had more or less clearly defined anti-imperialist ob-jectives . . . produced some splendid results."[27]

When this history is compared with the experience of Iran, a number of key points of comparison present themselves. In the broadest sense, Iran's his-torical transformation in the modern era is distinguished by the lack of a "pas-sive revolution" as described by Guha and Chatterjee. What we might term *the missing passive revolution* and the accompanying failure of the bourgeois-nationalist elite in modern Iranian politics to achieve hegemony can be ex-plained in large part by the fundamentally different political terrain in Iran in comparison to the national movements emerging in societies that had had the long presence of a colonial state. Iran's historic experience, as one of the few regions in Asia and Africa that never experienced a direct colonial pres-ence, produced a set of fundamentally different political, ideological, and so-cial alignments, which in turn would come to profoundly shape the material nature of its politics in the modern era. Iran's lack of an *external presence* in the form of a colonial state made the task of forging a historic bloc of bourgeois-nationalists and Iranian subalterns immeasurably more difficult. Iran's nationalist elite, like that of India, shared more of its ontological and philosophical assumptions with European post-Enlightenment modernist rationality than it did with a mytho-religious ontology of the Iranian subaltern. In contrast to India, however, there was no external colonial presence that could help forge a *transitory correspondence* between elite and subaltern in the name of a social movement seeking national liberation. The missing colonial state made the discursive and political divide separating the nationalist elite and the Iranian subaltern much more challenging to overcome.

What made the possibility of temporary correspondence between elite and subaltern even more difficult to forge in the Iranian case was not only the absence of a colonial state but also the prescriptive character of the Pahlavi state itself. The Pahlavi monarchical state had monopolized the discourse of modernity and nationalism in the decades preceding the 1979 revolution, and had in effect become the political hegemon on the terrain of Iranian politics, with a self-described modernization program that took the form of a civilizing mission that borrowed heavily from the discourses of nineteenth-century positivism and colonial science.[28] Within the terrain of an Iranian politics that lacked a colonial history analogous to the Indian case, the Pahlavi state thus came to play the role of a *surrogate colonial state*, and in turn came to take on the political character of an external presence against which discursive and political forces came to position themselves. On such a political terrain, the bourgeois-nationalist stratum was subsumed within the class and cultural configurations of *Pahlavi modernist-rationality*, and had very little opportunity to speak on behalf of the Iranian subaltern. When Iran's social movement of liberation came, therefore, it did not take the form of the bourgeois-nationalist revolution that had enabled the Indian modernist class to rise to power in the post independent period. Instead, the revolution overthrowing the Pahlavi state took a much more *populist-subaltern* form, invoking a mytho-religious consciousness in the form of Shi'ism and led, not by nationalist intellectuals, but rather by a vanguard of Iranian 'Ulama and religious "organic intellectuals."

Further, Shi'ism's ideological function in this context should not be understood only in terms of the theological-political evolution of classical Shi'ism, as is usually done in explaining the Iranian revolution; rather, the role of Shi'ism can also be interpreted within the political configuration of what might be termed Iran's *semi-postcolonial position*.[29] When modernist nationalism became the official ideology of the Pahlavi state during the middle part of the twentieth century, it came to monopolize the public discourse of Iranian society. As Chatterjee argues with respect to India, it was the culture that was preserved within the "private domain" of domestic space that became the culture of resistance used to confront the *external* presence of the state at the moment of the revolutionary struggle.[30] In the case of India, the external presence was the British colonial state and the so-called ideology of the Raj; in turn, the "spiritual principle" retained within the private sphere of Indian life came to be an Indian national culture. It was this inner domain of national culture preserved within domestic space that became mobilized as the culture of national difference in opposition to the Raj. In the case of Iran, the public space was dominated by the modernizing-positivist culture of *Pahlavi nationalism* for much of the twentieth century. The domination of the public domain by Pahlavi nationalism in turn led to a political configuration where the "culture of difference" took the form of the culture of Shi'ism preserved within the private-spiritual domain of the Iranian subaltern. As Pahlavi nationalism came to dominate the state-dominated public domain, this inner spiritual domain of religion—and its accompanying class and political alignments—came to play the role of "national" culture when the moment of the revolution came.

These basic structural configurations of Iran's political terrain—and the similarities and differences shared with the experience of South Asia—worked, in part, to produce the outcomes of Iran's modern historical experience. The missing external presence of a colonial state, and its substitution by a Pahlavi state espousing nationalism and scientific modernity in the public domain, came to configure the basic social and discursive alignments of Iran's modern political development. These alignments, in turn, enabled the use of Shi'ism as a surrogate ideology of *difference*, and precluded the national-modernist elite from forging a social-discursive alliance with the Iranian subaltern. As with the comparisons with other traditions of theorizing, thinking about Iran's modern experience through the conceptual lens of subaltern studies and postcolonial theory reveals key differences that can be illuminating in thinking analytically about Iran's national question.

Conclusion

As the foregoing might suggest, engagement with the comparative study of nationalism and the broader currents of theorizing in the humanities and social sciences is by its nature a tenuous and tentative enterprise. The simple appropriation of the language of theorizing, or the mechanical application of categories and vocabulary from paradigmatic models derived elsewhere, can each by itself work to obscure more than it reveals. And yet, the impulse to steer clear of these dangers and pitfalls can also work to restrict the conceptual range of historiography in a field. The changes in the humanities and social sciences over the past three decades—in particular, the changes that have re-shaped our understanding of the global history of nationalism—have clearly posed new possibilities for Iranian historiography. Despite the dangers and pitfalls, a careful and critical engagement with new theorizing has already produced positive results for both Iranian historiography and comparative nationalism studies.

While the above survey of the different paradigms of nationalism studies does not claim to be comprehensive—in fact, the range and proliferation of scholarship in the related fields surveyed here shows no sign of abating—what even this limited survey does suggest is that a critical engagement with comparative nationalism studies may be fruitful in suggesting new avenues of investigation. At the very least, even this limited survey of the possible ques-tions that these traditions of theorizing may yield for Iranian studies sug-gests that Iran's history of nationalism does not fit neatly within the estab-lished typologies. Conforming to neither the classical European paradigms of nationalization and national politics, nor to the historical terrain of other extra-European contexts of national politics, Iran's history seems to reveal to theories of nationalism the limits of the established paradigms of national-ism. At the same time, however, these established paradigms of nationalism yield remarkable echoes in Iran's modern history, and therefore demand our engagement with this tradition of theorizing. Recognizing these conceptual limits and theoretical echoes is the result of a critically engaged approach to Iranian historiography. This critical engagement can in turn help us to ask new questions, form new analytical perspectives, and pose new understandings of both theory and Iran's modern history.

Notes

1. Early articles and monographs include the two special issues of *Iranian Studies*, vol. 26, nos. 3–4 (Summer/Fall 1993) and vol. 29, nos. 1–2 (Winter/Spring 1996), and the articles therein. Mehrzad Boroujerdi, "Contested Nationalist Constructions of Iranian Identity," *Critique: Journal for Critical Studies of the Middle East*, 12 (Spring 1998): 43–56. See also the key monographs by Firoozeh Kashani-Sabet, *Frontier Fic-tions: Shaping the Iranian Nation, 1804–1946* (Princeton: Princeton University Press, 1999) and Mohamad Tavakoli-Targhi, *Refashioning Iran: Orientalism, Occidentalism, and Historiography* (New York: Palgrave, 2001). Other early works include Mostafa Vaziri, *Iran as Imagined Nation: The Construction of National Identity* (New York: Para-gon House, 1993).

2. In addition to the debates surrounding Edward Said's *Orientalism* (1978) and the increasing availability of Foucault's works in English translation, the influence of Terry Eagleton, *Literary Theory: An Introduction* (London: Blackwell, 1983) can also be taken as a popular measure of a decisive shift in the humanities during this period.

3. See the concise edited collection of excerpts from this tradition in John Hutchinson and Anthony D. Smith, eds., *Nationalism* (London: Oxford University Press, 1994).

4. Among the classic works in this tradition, Elie Kedourie, *Nationalism* (Oxford: Blackwell Publishers, 1994 [1960]) is perhaps the most noteworthy of the early post-primordialist sociological critiques of nationalism. Charles Tilly, ed., *The Formation of National States in Western Europe* (Princeton: Princeton University Press, 1975) is another major early work of the historical sociology of nation-state formation in the modern era.

5. Benedict Anderson, *Imagined Communities: Reflections on the Origins and Spread of Nationalism* (New York: Verso, 1991 [1983]). The other self-consciously comparative and critical work of this period is John Breuilly, *Nationalism and the State* (Chicago: University of Chicago Press, 1982).

6. Karl Deutsch, *Nationalism and Social Communication* (Cambridge: MIT Press, 1969 [1953]); Miroslav Hroch, *The Social Preconditions of National Revival in Europe* (New York: Columbia University Press, 2000 [1969]); Otto Bauer, *The Question of Nationalities and Social Democracy* (Minneapolis: University of Minnesota Press, 2000 [1907]); Eric Hobsbawm, *Nations and Nationalism Since 1780* (Cambridge: Cambridge University Press, 1990); Ernest Gellner, *Nations and Nationalism* (Ithaca: Cornell University Press, 1983); Michael Hechter, *Internal Colonialism: The Celtic Fringe in British National Development* (Berkeley: University of California Press, 1975). See also the lucid contextualization of this tradition in Geoff Eley and Ronald Suny, eds., *Becoming National: A Reader* (New York: Oxford University Press, 1996), 3–18.

7. Gellner, *Nations and Nationalism*, 62.

8. The most concise statement about the problem of "unevenness" can be found in Ernest Gellner, *Thought and Change* (London: Weidenfeld and Nicholson, 1964), 166–171, but see also his *Nations and Nationalism*. See also Anthony Smith's discussion in Anthony Smith, *The Ethnic Revival in the Modern World* (Cambridge: Cambridge University Press, 1981), 26–29, and Tom Nairn, *Faces of Nationalism: Janus Revisited* (London: Verso Books, 1997), 50–52. For a critique of the historicist assumptions in this tradition, see Dipesh Chakrabarty, *Provincializing Europe: Postcolonial Thought and Historical Difference* (Princeton: Princeton University Press, 2000), 11–16.

9. The term "marginal men" is originally Elie Kedourie's. See Elie Kedourie, *Nationalism in Asia and Africa* (London: Weidenfeld and Nicolson, 1970), 27. For Hroch's analysis of the social composition of the nationalist *intelligentsia* of Central Europe, see Hroch, *Social Preconditions*, 14–17.

10. On the slow pace of industrialization in nineteenth-century Iran, see Charles Issawi, ed., *The Economic History of Iran, 1800–1914* (Chicago: University of Chicago Press, 1971); Nikki Keddie, "The Economic History of Iran 1800–1914 and its Political Impact," *Iranian Studies* vol. 5, no. 2 (1972): 58–78; Ahmad Ashraf, "Historical Obstacles to the Development of a Bourgeoisie in Iran," *Iranian Studies* vol. 2, no. 2 (1969): 54–79; Willem Floor, *Industrialization in Iran: 1900–1941* (Durham: Durham Centre for Middle East and Islamic Studies, Occasional Papers Series, No. 23, 1984).

11. On the literary-intellectual articulation of Iranian nationalism in the nine-

teenth century, see Mohamad Tavakoli-Targhi, *Refashioning Iran*; Mohamad Tavakoli-Targhi, "Refashioning Iran: Language and Culture during the Constitutional Revolution," in *Iranian Studies* vol. 23 (1990), 77–101. See also Afshin Marashi, *Nationalizing Iran: Culture, Power, and the State, 1870–1940* (Seattle: University of Washington Press, 2008), 49–85.

12. The key scholarship on these issues include Nikki Keddie, "The Origins of the Religious-Radical Alliance in Iran," *Past and Present* 34 (July 1966): 70–80; Nikki Keddie, "Pan-Islam as Proto-Nationalism," *Journal of Modern History* vol. 41, no. 1 (March 1969): 17–28; Nikki Keddie, "Religion and Irreligion in Early Iranian Nationalism," *Comparative Studies in Society and History* vol. 4 (1962): 265–295; Nikki Keddie, *Religion and Rebellion in Iran: The Tobacco Protest of 1891–1892* (London: Frank Cass, 1966); Hamid Algar, *Religion and State in Iran, 1785–1906: The Role of the 'Ulama in the Qajar Period* (Berkeley: University of California Press, 1969).

13. John Foran, *Fragile Resistance: Social Transformation in Iran from 1500 to the Revolution* (Boulder: Westview Press, 1993); Willem Floor, *Guilds, Merchants, & 'Ulama in Nineteenth-Century Iran* (Washington, DC: Mage Publishers, 2009).

14. The most concise statement of this idea is in Eric Hobsbawm, *Nations and Nationalism*, 80–100. See also David Cannadine, "The Context, Performance, and Meaning of Ritual: The British Monarchy and the 'Invention of Tradition,' c. 1820–1977," in Eric Hobsbawm and Terence Ranger, eds., *The Invention of Tradition* (Cambridge: Cambridge University Press, 1983), 101–164; Anderson, *Imagined Communities, 83–112*; Daniel Unowsky, *The Pomp and Politics of Patriotism: Imperial Celebrations in Habsburg Austria, 1848–1916* (West Lafayette, IN: Purdue University Press, 2005); Matthew Truesdell, *Spectacular Politics: Louis-Napoleon Bonaparte and the Fête Impérial, 1849–1870* (New York: Oxford University Press, 1997). For a similar and slightly earlier formulation of this idea, see Reinhard Bendix, *Kings or People: Power and the Mandate to Rule* (Berkeley: University of California Press, 1978).

15. For attempts at administrative reform in the nineteenth century, see Shaul Bakhash, *Iran: Monarchy, Bureaucracy, and the Reforms under the Qajars, 1858–1896* (London: Ithaca Press, 1978); Guity Nashat, *The Origins of Modern Reform in Iran, 1870–80* (Urbana: University of Illinois Press, 1982); A. Reza Sheikholeslami, *The Structure of Central Authority in Qajar Iran, 1871–1896* (Atlanta: Scholars Press, 1997); Abbas Amanat, *Pivot of the Universe: Nasir al-Din Shah and the Iranian Monarchy, 1831–1896* (Berkeley: University of California Press, 1997). See also Stephanie Cronin, ed., *The Making of Modern Iran: State and Society under Riza Shah, 1921–1941* (London:Routledge/Curzon, 2003), 1–11.

16. The classical Weberian definition of "the state" as linked to bureaucratic rationalization and the monopoly of violence does not capture the semiotic notion of the state that I have in mind. The state, as I understand it, is not a single institution or practice but is, rather, the *cumulative presence* produced by these institutions and practices. The creation of this type of "state" and its cumulative presence (through a standing army, regularized policing, national taxation, universalized legal codes and adjudication, national schooling, public health infrastructure, and visual representations of the state) would wait until the twentieth century to take on a decisive modern-national scale.

17. Anderson, *Imagined Communities*, 11. While there is not a universal agreement on this point, the emergence of modern nationalism as one of the forms of post-

Enlightenment culture in Europe is a broad theme that recurs in the literature. See, e.g., Elie Kedourie, *Nationalism*, 12–23; George Mosse, *Crisis of German Ideology: Intellectual Origins of the Third Reich* (New York: Grosset and Dunlap, 1964), 13–30; Omar Dahbour and Micheline R. Ishay, eds., *The Nationalism Reader* (Atlantic Highlands, NJ: Humanities Press, 1995), 22–57.

18. Jürgen Habermas, *The Structural Transformation of the Public Sphere: An Inquiry into a Category of Bourgeois Society* (Cambridge, MA: MIT Press, 1991 [1962]). See also Craig Calhoun, ed., *Habermas and the Public Sphere* (Cambridge, MA: MIT Press, 1992); Geoff Eley, "Nations, Publics, and Political Cultures: Placing Habermas in Nineteenth Century Germany" in Craig Calhoun, ed., *Habermas and the Public Sphere*, 289–339; Geoff Eley and Ronald Suny, *Becoming National*, 23–25.

19. Anderson, *Imagined Communities*, 70–78.

20. The classic statement on this can be found in E. G. Browne, *Press and Poetry of Modern Persia* (Los Angeles: Kalimat Press, 1983 [1914]). See also the discussions in Janet Afary, *The Iranian Constitutional Revolution, 1906–1911* (New York: Columbia University Press, 1996), 116–142; Firoozeh Kashani-Sabet, *Frontier Fictions*, 101–143; Shiva Balaghi, "Print Culture in Late Qajar Iran: The Cartoons of 'Kashkul,'" *Iranian Studies* vol. 34, nos. 1–4 (2001), 165–181; Negin Nabavi, "Readership, the Press, and the Public Sphere in the First Constitutional Period," in Houchang Chehabi and Vanessa Martin, eds., *Iran's Constitutional Revolution: Popular Politics, Cultural Transformations and Transnational Connections* (London: I. B. Tauris/Iran Heritage Foundation, 2010), 213–224.

21. For a similar line of argument, see Dipesh Chakrabarty's argument in *Provincializing Europe*, 14, regarding a form of politics in India which, as he states, "called upon gods, spirits, and other spectral and divine beings"; see also Ranajit Guha, *Elementary Aspects of Peasant Insurgency in Colonial India* (Delhi: Oxford University Press, 1983). Babak Rahimi makes a similar argument for Safavid Iran. See Babak Rahimi, *Theatre State and the Formation of an Early Modern Public Sphere in Iran* (Leiden: Brill, 2011). On the role played by nineteenth-century print technologies in empowering a "printed economy of enchantment," see Nile Green, *Bombay Islam: The Religious Economy of the West Indian Ocean, 1840–1915* (Cambridge: Cambridge University Press, 2011), 90–117.

22. Ranajit Guha, "On Some Aspects of the Historiography of Colonial India," in Ranajit Guha and Giyatari Spivak, eds., *Selected Subaltern Studies* (New York: Oxford University Press, 1988), 37.

23. Guha, "On Some Aspects," 38.

24. Ibid., 42.

25. Partha Chatterjee, *Nationalist Thought and the Colonial World* (London: Zed Books, 1986), 44–52. This idea is also further elaborated in Ranajit Guha, *Dominance without Hegemony: History and Power in Colonial India* (Cambridge: Harvard University Press, 1997).

26. Chatterjee, *Nationalist Thought*, 48–49.

27. Guha, "On Some Aspects," 42.

28. On this issue, see Cyrus Schayegh, *Who Is Knowledgeable Is Strong: Science, Class, and the Formation of Modern Iranian Society, 1900–1950* (Berkeley: University of California, 2009).

29. The most comprehensive religio-theological interpretation of Shiʿism and Ira-

nian politics is Said Amir Arjomand, *The Shadow of God and the Hidden Imam: Religion, Political Order, and Societal Change in Shi'ite Iran from the Beginning to 1890* (Chicago: University of Chicago Press, 2010 [1984]).

30. Partha Chatterjee, *The Nation and Its Fragments* (Princeton: Princeton University Press, 1993), 6.

CHAPTER 2

Franz Babinger and the Legacy of the "German Counter-Revolution" in Early Modern Iranian Historiography

ALI ANOOSHAHR

The conventional narrative of the rise of the Safavid Empire runs as follows: A twelve-year-old boy rose up in revolt and declared his intention to unleash the apocalypse. Bands of Turcoman tribes (Qizilbash) fully devoted to the mystical doctrine of their semidivine king marched to battle at his call and willingly sacrificed themselves for him. The combination of the boy Ismail's charisma and the devoted and disciplined militancy of his Qizilbash gave birth to a new empire that ruled in present-day Iran and the Caucasus in the early modern period. The Safavids are generally viewed as the founders of what eventually became modern Iran. The advent of the empire is often referred to as a "revolution."[1] Of course, "revolution" implies a major socio-economic transformation, and yet surprisingly, the field suffers from a dearth of economic explanations (as opposed to religious/psychological ones) for Ismail's uprising. What is the reason for this?

Much of this conceptualization was first formulated immediately after the end of World War I by a German Orientalist named Franz Babinger (1891–1967), perhaps the most famous scholar of the Ottoman Empire from the foundational period of the early twentieth century. In addition to publishing numerous articles, Babinger wrote the still standard work of bibliography on Ottoman historians,[2] composed the only biography of the Ottoman Sultan Mehmed the Conqueror,[3] and contributed to the founding of the Department of Turkology at the University of Munich. It is less known, however, that soon after his return from military service in the Ottoman Empire during the First World War, Babinger composed an early article that touched on the origins of the Safavid Empire.

Babinger explicitly rejected the usefulness of a historical-materialist analysis for understanding the rise of the Safavids, focusing primarily on spiritual (*geistig*) explanations, and connecting the dynasty to Anatolian religious up-heavals (whereas his British contemporary Edward Granville Browne pri-marily described the reign of Shah Ismail and his successors in terms of Per-sian dynastic history). As such, Babinger projected tropes from the German Counter-Revolution of the post–First World War era (i.e., the reaction of the German right against two Communist revolutions in the country) into the subject matter about which he wrote, and his perception of the Safavids has continued to be influential to the present day.

In 1919, Babinger joined and fought alongside the protofascist militias, the *Freikorps*, who overthrew the Munich Soviet Republic and committed many atrocities in that city, killing hundreds of noncombatants. Some of the Mu-nich *Freikorps* then got involved in politics. The Nazi movement subsequently arose in Munich among the very men who were in, or had led, Babinger's unit (such as Ernst Röhm and Franz Ritter von Epp). In other words, I contend that our perception of Safavid origins as an ideological revolution, fought by fanatical warriors, and led by a charismatic leader, actually owes a great deal to the experiences of the German *Freikorps*, including Babinger himself. This is, of course, not to say that there exists an easy one-to-one correspondence between Babinger's medieval Anatolia and Iran on the one hand, and early twentieth-century Germany on the other (though Babinger explicitly claimed that a connection did exist).

To argue this and to trace the legacy of the German Counter-Revolution in Safavid historiography, this article will first compare and contrast the rele-vant writings of the British Orientalist E. G. Browne with those of Babinger. There are some crucial differences between the two. Next, Babinger's scholarly compositions will be analyzed, then compared to one of his political writings in order to show the presence of a common set of ideologically derived motifs and tropes in both texts. Third, Babinger's views will be briefly contextualized in postwar Germany. Further, Babinger's direct and indirect influence will be traced in the works of scholars such as Walther Hinz, Vladimir Minorsky, and Roger Savory. Finally, the article will close by providing some sugges-tions that run counter to the strand of Safavid historical scholarship that is traced here. This article is, therefore, primarily interested in historiography. However, my intention has been not to merely review a number of important works or statements, but rather to historicize what seems to be a key juncture in this scholarly trajectory.

The Foundational Works of Browne and Babinger

E. G. Browne and Franz Babinger wrote about the rise of the Safavids at roughly the same time, but without knowledge of one another. Babinger's article was published in 1921, while the fourth volume of Browne's *Literary History of Persia* was released in 1924. Both men influenced Safavid historiography in important ways, though Babinger's contribution was indirect and less well known. A comparison of the two authors is instructive, as both drew on similar sources (such as the reports from Italian travelers).

Browne understood the formation of the Safavid Empire in terms of both Iranian nationalism and dynastic history. He believed that the rise of the Safavids signaled the re-creation of Persian nationality after eight-and-a-half centuries of subjugation by Arab, Turkish, and Mongol invaders and dynasties.[4] The phenomenon was basically comparable to a restoration of the Sasanian Empire: "self-contained, centripetal, powerful and respected."[5] However, Browne was fully aware that there existed few direct parallels between sixteenth- and twentieth-century "nationalisms." This was so because he believed that for the Safavids, modern issues such as language and race were secondary to religion,[6] and much of Safavid "propaganda" was in any case undertaken in Anatolia, rather than in Iran proper.[7]

As for the Safavid leader Shah Ismail, Browne tried to portray him in a balanced way, describing the young monarch's good and bad qualities: On the one hand, he was ruthless and bloodthirsty; on the other, he was handsome and noble.[8] Here Browne relied on Italian sources, one of whom even described Ismail as "amiable as a girl." Browne did not try to reconcile these conflicting characteristics of his subject, but simply listed them all in order to show the "strangest blend of antithetical qualities" that formed Ismail's personality.[9] Clearly, the British Orientalist was not at all interested in creating either a hero or a villain out of the young shah.

The intensity of the relationship between Ismail and his followers (who, according to one Italian traveler, perceived him to be divine, and willingly risked their lives for him) got its due space in Browne's narrative. Interestingly however, Browne did not believe the spiritual devotion of the Qizilbash to have been exclusively responsible for the early success of the shah, and instead posited the breakdown of Aqquyunlu authority as the most pertinent cause.[10] By implication, Ismail was thus a successful opportunist. Particularly significant was how Browne deemed it relevant to include reports demonstrating the financial aspect of the Safavid victory, noting how many individuals not belonging to the Safavid order flocked to Ismail in hopes of receiving money.[11] How did economic matters contribute to the rise of Shah Ismail? Browne did not pose the question, but at the same time, he did not find it necessary to suppress any evidence indicating the materialist aspirations of an evidently religious movement.

At the time of writing his thoughts on the Safavids, Browne was unaware of a monograph in German that had been published a few years before. In fact, the general neglect by Safavid scholarship of Franz Babinger's *Schejch Bedr ed-din, der Sohn des Richters von Simaw: Ein Beitrag zur Geschichte des Sektenwesens im altosmanischen Reich* continues to this day, a fact no doubt brought about in part by the author's reputation as primarily an Ottomanist. In any event, Babinger's work can be contrasted with Browne's in a number of significant ways. While Browne understood the early Safavid period in terms of Persian dynastic history, Babinger analyzed it as an extension of Ottoman history. Moreover, Babinger introduced to the early Safavids the concept of the *Männerbund,* or "society of males," which was in vogue as an intellectual as well as social phenomenon in interwar Germany. Third, Babinger's portrayal of Shah Ismail was not intended to show the latter's personality contradictions, but rather to elevate him to a heroic position. Lastly, whereas Browne quoted his Italian sources to hint at the worldly and acquisitive nature of the Safavid movement, Babinger explicitly distanced himself from materialist explanations and focused exclusively on spiritual ones.

With the exception of the first, all of Babinger's contributions listed above stem from a political ideology which he shared with many other young veterans of the First World War: German fascism.[12] This claim demands a detailed investigation of Babinger's writings, both academic and political. Therefore, a major portion of the present article will now be devoted to teasing out the fascist or protofascist metanarrative in two of Babinger's articles.

Who was Franz Babinger? He was born on January 15, 1891, in Weiden in der Oberpfalz, in eastern Bavaria, to a family of high-ranking civil servants, and was baptized in the city's Catholic church four days later.[13] He attended a *Gymnasium* (high school) in Würzburg, where he showed exceptional aptitude in languages.[14] When the First World War broke out, Babinger volunteered in the imperial army and was sent to the Ottoman Empire as a lieutenant in an artillery regiment.[15] In 1917, he was transferred to Syria, where he was wounded three times.[16] Within a year after the defeat of Germany, Babinger had returned to academic pursuits and published a number of important works that established him as a prominent scholar in his field.

However, the activities of the young Orientalist in those early postwar years were not limited to the halls of academia. As stated above, Lieutenant Franz Babinger was swept up in the violent political storm that broke out on the scene in Germany roughly between November 1918 and June 1919. In the spring of 1919, Babinger joined the ultra-right-wing volunteer force, the *Freikorps* Epp, and took part in the conquest and subduing of Munich communists during a bloody five-day period generally referred to as the "White Terror."

The political background is as follows: After Germany's defeat in the war and the Kaiser's abdication, a number of successful leftist revolutions shook the country. The first culminated in the Spartacist "January rising" of 1919, which unfolded mainly in Berlin and was wrongly blamed on Rosa Luxemburg (1871-1919) and Karl Liebknecht (1871-1919).[17] The second to take place in Bavaria also began in November of 1918 and was led by the Socialist Kurt Eisner (1867-1919) against the Bavarian monarchy. Following Eisner's assassination by Anton Graf Arco-Valley (1897-1945), a coalition of revolutionaries proclaimed the Bavarian Soviet Republic, headed by Eugen Leviné (1883-1919), which lasted until May of that year. The reaction to both revolutions was swift and brutal. Gustav Noske (1868-1946), the Social Democratic defense minister, called on volunteer militias, the *Freikorps*, which were made up in part of recent veterans who operated all along Germany's new borders in the east as well as inside the country. The new force in Berlin defeated the revolution and murdered Luxemburg and Liebknecht, among others. In Munich, the "White Terror" of the *Freikorps* claimed the lives of several hundred people, most of whom were noncombatants.

It is difficult to say what exactly Franz Babinger might have done in Munich, or how much he might have ideologically shared with his comrades and superiors. The leader of his specific unit, Colonel Franz Ritter von Epp, later Nazi governor of Bavaria, had taken part in the Namibian genocide of 1904,[18] and roughly one out of every ten other *Freikorps* Epp members, such as Babinger's friend Ernst Röhm as well as Rudolph Hess and Karl Brückner, subsequently filled the ranks of the SA and the SS.[19] Nevertheless, the fact remains that the young Orientalist projected onto his study of the Ottomans and Safavids a perspective formed by the experiences of the reactionary Counter-Revolution. Babinger's activities are relatively well known in scholarly circles, but few people have investigated the potential relationship between his political activities and his scholarly pursuits.[20]

As stated above, Babinger's scholarship constitutes a very different conceptualization from Browne's, insofar as the German author treated Safavid history as an extension of Ottoman history. Babinger's main thesis was that, following the defeat of the Ottomans by Timur (Tamerlane) in 1402, massive social upheavals broke out in the Balkans and Anatolia, beginning with the revolt of Schejch Bedr ed-din (Turkish Sheyh Bedreddin), and ending with the Safavid uprising about a century later. To better understand these events, Babinger wanted to concentrate on mental/spiritual (*geistig*) aspects of that history while excluding economic approaches. He wrote:

> The impetus for the present essay was provided by a recommendation from Carl Brockelmann who suggested that I should turn my attention to the dervishes of Mount Stylarios [*die Stylariern*]. Some weeks earlier Richard Hartmann ha[d] recommended that I "examine the economic origins of the Dervish uprisings in Asia Minor." Yet, the more I investigated the subject, the more I realized that a portrayal of the spiritual (*geistig*) movements in the Ottoman Empire was among the most essential tasks of any historian who turns his attention to these people."[21]

Right at the beginning, Babinger had decided to focus only on religious causes and overlook economic ones. The intentional exclusion of historical-materialist explorations into the background of the Safavids has its roots here.

Babinger was by no means alone in this. In the postwar period, a generation of young German scholars considered the defeat of their country as a symptom of the failure of the old imperial culture that included (for some) its scholarly aspects. For instance, in the field of archeology, the dominant classical humanism of the German academy lost a great deal of prestige in the wake of the war, and those scholars interested in the non-Hellenic "barbarian" peoples (such as enthusiasts of Germanic antiquities) began to gain a firmer foothold in universities.[22] Others, such as young classicists who were veterans of the recent war, advocated a stronger focus on spirituality in Greek history.[23] The spirit of these young scholars also found expression in Oswald Spengler's *Decline of the West* (1918), in which the author criticized the obsessive fixation of European intellectuals on progress.[24] Franz Babinger was part of this scholarly cohort. His comments further down in his essay make these connections much more concrete. For instance, he considered the worship of the leader (*shaykh* or *imam*) by Muslim mystics and the followers of the Shi'a sect essential to explaining the phenomenon he was studying:

> Already in earlier descriptions, above all in those of R. A. Nicholson's, one sees a glimmer of what the divine veneration of a master means. So for example it was neither the comforting doctrine of the Safavid Ismail, nor his good-natured chubbiness, that called forth that powerful religious movement, and gave it its uncanny driving force and attraction. It goes without saying that this idolatrous veneration of the living master could easily draw

on the Imam-centered enthusiasms of the Shiʿa. . . . The connection between the Dervishes and Shiʿa is, therefore, in no sense coincidental, but has clear psychological origins.[25]

In order to fully understand this bizarre social and spiritual phenomenon, with its hero worship, fanaticism, and the company of male ascetics and mystics (dervishes), Babinger said that he drew inspiration from the works of Heinrich Schurtz and especially Hans Blüher—the scholar who popularized the concept of the *Männerbund* or "male organizations."[26] Blüher's work ties neatly into the turmoil of postwar Germany. Basing his studies on anthropological research on "primitive" societies, the experience of the German youth movement (the *Wandervögel*), and Freudian theories of sexuality, Blüher rejected the bourgeois notion of the heterosexual family as the foundation of society and instead posited male fraternities involved in hero worship and religious mysticism as the basis for state formation.[27] Blüher was strongly anti-modernist. He considered the nineteenth-century and early twentieth-century prevalence of utilitarianism, corporations, and the growing prominence of women to be a cause of social sterility and superficiality.[28]

Babinger made explicit and implicit connections between his contemporary Germany, with which Blüher's work was primarily concerned, and premodern Iran and Anatolia. And in those passages at the beginning and end of the narrative (where the problem is first stated and a solution is offered) contemporary references abound. A typical passage runs as follows:

And so it seemed to me to be a fruitful undertaking, precisely at the present moment, to turn my attention to those strange social movements that threatened to shake the foundations of the young, hardly yet consolidated Ottoman Empire, and which show in more than one regard *remarkable correspondence with phenomena of the present day* [italics added], when changes in public sentiment and desires are taking place which fall completely out of the framework of straightforward progress. Any long-term pressure on the popular soul creates tensions which must eventually be released with enormous force and which, in their blind fury, cannot be guided by any rational calculations. . . . The tremendous upheavals of the early fifteenth century, the assault of the Mongols under Tamerlane and the civil wars, were not just a struggle of raw power; rather, the misery of the times, hunger and despair had called forth in the Ottoman people a spiritual division, which led eventually to those fateful consequences. After all, no one knew whether the field they had so laboriously tilled one day would, on the following day, be trampled by the horses of the plunderers. Indeed no one could even be clear as to what state they belonged to, since the territories of the princes were constantly changing.[29]

There are a number of important clues here. The "strange social movements" have been compared to Germany in 1919. In both regards, the events seem to run counter to the ideas of historical progress or development, a viewpoint apparently shared by the author and Oswald Spengler. The enormous pressures on the souls of the people (such as the Mongol invasions, civil war, and random raids of plunderers) are posited as the causes of these revolutions. The contrast between the tilled fields (order) and trampling by soldiers (chaos) sums it up neatly. What did all this misery lead to? The revolt led by the religious leader Sheyh Bedreddin. But this was no mere uprising. Babinger specifically describes Bedreddin's teaching as communism. "The most striking feature," he wrote, "is the unmistakable communist course that this doctrine appears to have adhered to."[30] Nor did Babinger's contemporaries miss the analogy. In this light, it is by no means a mere coincidence that when another Turcologist, Friedrich Giese, reviewed Babinger's monograph, he referred to the disturbances in the Ottoman Empire as a "Communist putsch."[31]

But how did it all come to an end? The revolt was put down and the rebels were slaughtered. However, out of this death and destruction rose a new hero, a savior-man, who restored order and prosperity. "It is hardly surprising then that in those days of hunger and distress a man should arise who believed that he could, with his teaching and with his influence, steady them, that another should be added to the number of true and false prophets. . . . [Verse] *Against the dark background of the time, an enterprise of bold daring and a rash adventurer present themselves.*"[32] The situation could only be salvaged by a bold hero who was a kind of prophet. The concept of the "man," the savior and hero, was a common motif among young German writers and soldiers of the postwar years. For *Freikorps* writers (to whose company Babinger belonged),[33] the "man" was the abstraction of a leader, or *Führer*, who would come and save his soldiers, leading them to victory.[34] The poem cited is from a play by Schiller entitled the *Wallenstein*—a historical drama set in the seventeenth century, from which the term *Freikorps* had been adopted.

Now, who was this strong leader in Anatolia and Iran? After the failure of Bedreddin, Babinger claimed that the principles of his teachings were kept alive and were finally propagated successfully by the Safavid order, most effectively by the young Shah Ismail.[35] Babinger, drawing primarily on the narratives of Italian travelers, found in Shah Ismail a good, strong, and charismatic leader.

[According to Spandugino], in the eyes of Ismail and his followers money and status counted for nothing. All that mattered was devotion to the new faith. They performed their military duty *"senza stipendio alcuno,"* without any pay at all. Ismail represented the needs of the most basic common life and generous almsgiving. He rejected the Sunni prohibition on drinking wine and eating pork, because Ali, his idol, could not have countenanced it; he himself led by example and ate pork. It seems to me to be highly probable that Ismail adopted not only old Persian ideas but also a number of Christian practices, naturally in altered forms appropriate for his goal.[36]

Ismail here is down-to-earth and cares for the poor. Moreover, he combines Christian and old Persian customs with Islam, a practice that the author seems to approve of overall, perhaps reflecting the viewpoint of his source, which he takes at face value. In other words, Babinger did not consider the possibility that Ismail may have been purposefully provocative and antinomian, assuming of course that the descriptions of his actions were not rooted in anti-Safavid polemic, or in Spandugino's zeal to portray the shah as a possible partner in a potential alliance of Christian powers against the Ottomans. To Babinger, such qualities showed Ismail to be a kind-hearted and earthy leader who was, moreover, highly charismatic. Again, relying on Italian travelers, Babinger further described Ismail as a man who could win the hearts of thousands, who was worshipped by his followers almost as a God, and espoused a life of poverty and simplicity.[37] Thus, while Babinger was drawing on the same sources as Browne, his Shah Ismail is decidedly unsullied by violence (the description of his ruthlessness is excluded), unchallenged in his masculinity (his portrayal as an amiable girl is expunged), and most importantly, he remains untainted by money (the mention of soldiers joining him in search of money is omitted).

In sum, in his first major monograph on the Safavids, Franz Babinger described certain religious upheavals in Anatolia that eventually paved the way for the genesis of the Safavid Empire. He specifically compared the state of affairs with contemporary events, and described the occurrences as an outbreak of religious disturbance (which, however, smacked of communism) caused by war, brought to an end by violence, and finally restored to order by a charismatic leader. In the years to come, Babinger momentarily left fifteenth- and sixteenth-century Anatolia and turned his attention for a while to writing his early masterpiece *Die Geschichtsschreiber der Osmanen und ihre Werke* and spent the 1920s teaching at Berlin. However, following the victory of the Nazi party in the elections of 1933, things began to change for him. A series of events forced Babinger to publicly recall his service with the *Freikorps* in Munich, and the resulting remembrances bear a number of interesting similarities to his article on the Safavids.

Babinger's Political Writing

Soon after the Nazi victory of 1933, German universities began to expel Jewish professors from their academic positions. As it turned out, Franz Babinger's maternal grandmother had been Jewish by birth, although she had been baptized in the Catholic Church, and so Babinger's career was suddenly in danger. The issue, it seems, was first brought up during the search to fill a chair at the university. The Iranist Hans Heinrich Schaeder wrote a scathing review of Babinger, pointing out, among other things, that his Aryan descent was to be doubted. Babinger's friend, the Egyptologist Baron von Bissing, personally wrote to Franz Ritter von Epp, the new Nazi governor of Bavaria, reminding the General of Babinger's role as a *Freikorps* soldier in the "liberation" of Munich from communists, and stating that Babinger had assured von Bissing that the legal restrictions against the Jews did not apply to him.[38] Babinger himself undertook a literary campaign. In response to an anonymous attack on him, he wrote to the newspaper *Der Stürmer*, run by the early militia the Sturmabteilung, or SA, assured the readers of his Aryan descent, and reminded them of his friendship with SA leader Ernst Röhm.[39] He also published a four-page newspaper article describing his *Freikorps* service under Epp and Röhm. The purpose of the latter article was obviously to remind the authorities of the author's sacrifices in the service of the fascist cause. Thus, considering these circumstances, the views expressed by Babinger about the events must be taken with a grain of salt, to say the least.

The goal here is not to put Babinger on trial posthumously and judge the genuineness or extent of his fascist sympathies. Rather, the point is to show that, no matter how Babinger truly felt about the "White Terror" in Munich, he certainly fell back on a storytelling technique that he had already used in 1919. Indeed, the same overarching pattern evident in Babinger's "Schejch Bedr ed-din" is present in his memoirs recalling his *Freikorps* activities. Here too, the state of affairs is presented first as a moment of chaos unleashed by a population pushed to the breaking point by war and violence. A communist revolution follows. Then, through the efforts of a strong hero, the day is saved, and law and order is resumed. In other words, I suggest that the similarity of the two texts under analysis here derives from the projection of the events of 1919 onto Safavid/Ottoman history. Babinger's remembrances start as follows:

In the first days of April 1919, the situation in Bavaria was extremely confused. One rumor followed another, and nothing is more revealing about the state of affairs in those days than leafing through the pages of a newspaper from 1919. While one could maintain cooler consideration in the north of the country, the south was all topsy-turvy. There, foreign agitators were at work, riling up the people who had been especially worn down by war and revolution, taking advantage of people's desperation. The general strike in Augsburg on April 4th was the prelude to an alarming intensification. The chief troublemaker Dr. Wadler openly stated the immediate objective to be the elimination of political parties, the unification of the entire proletariat, a general strike, and the proclamation of a soviet state, declaring fraternal links with the Russian and Hungarian proletariat. Everyone knew that the formation of a Bavarian Soviet Republic would happen soon. The city of Würzburg, where I was at that time, was thrown into a flurry by the most implausible reports. The future soviet leaders were working feverishly on a list of hostages, whom they intended to take into custody immediately, and in general on a list of people whom they wanted to get rid of on April 6th. A former servant of one of my brothers (both active officers of the old army) brought word that an officer of our name would be shot. It could not be determined which one of us three was meant. The passiveness to which the bourgeoisie of Würzburg was condemned had paralyzed every individual. On Saturday, one of my brothers and I, along with four likeminded persons, resolved to proceed from Würzburg surreptitiously and struggle along to *Freikorps* Epp at Ohrdruf.[40]

The mood of the opening lines is one of disorder, confusion, and vulnerability caused by the amount of information and the speed at which it is delivered. Babinger knows that the news coming out of the city is unverifiable, but he nevertheless accepts the reports that war has led to a riotous condition and that evil alien intruders are taking advantage of the people. He then manages to take control of the situation and establish some facts. Next, the story becomes personal, and the sense of disorder and vulnerability returns. Again, the maddening influx of information creates great agitation (*Aufregung*), and this escalates to the point where the author begins to be gripped by fears of an attack on his life. The threat is very personal. It is *his* life that he is anxious about: "It could not be determined which one of us three was meant," meaning: *it could be me*. The brothers are not even named. The sense of alarm is increased when Babinger realizes that the men around him are impotent, literally passive and lame. Of course, the city could not have been both passive and also have fallen into a state of flurry. The agitation is Babinger's and his fellow soldiers.' In any event, the useless paralysis of the middle classes causes Babinger and his brother (still unnamed) to run to the company of fighting men, the ultra-right-wing Epp *Freikorps*. Some assertiveness is recovered in this escape. The men "resolve" to go, and their escape is described somewhat forcefully: "*durchschlagen*." Next, Babinger recalled how he secretly made his way to Ohrdruf, dressed as a civilian but carrying his military gear with him, and eventually registered with the commander of the *Freikorps*, Franz Ritter von Epp, who stands in sharp contrast with the lame bourgeoisie of Würzburg. "The robust and upright nature of Colonel von Epp captivated all who encountered him, and I still remember quite clearly the enthusiasm that was already prevalent then."[41] Of course, in line with what is expected of the *Führer*, Babinger's leader Franz von Epp finally leads the invasion of Munich and returns order to chaos.

> Thus, against the will of the government, the Bavarian capital was at least partly liberated in the afternoon of May 1st, 1919. In Munich the judiciousness and vigor of our *Führer* [Franz von Epp] blossomed, supported by superb colleagues, among whom his later chief of staff Captain Röhm played the most outstanding role; the forces under his command were skillfully deployed to eliminate the possibility of the resurgence of Spartacist despotism once and for all. We were dispatched to particularly threatened quarters of the town. A strict police curfew (entering the streets was forbidden to the population after dark) created a certain degree of order even at night. Already, in the first days of May, thanks to the tirelessness of our *Führer* [Franz von Epp], foreign riffraff such as Russians and other shady aliens were ruthlessly expelled, a civil guard was formed, and in short, Munich was again a city of law and order (*Ordnung und Ruhe* lit. "order and calm"). . . . To have been an eyewitness to these *Freikorps* days, and especially having been in Orhdruf, will remain a dear memory for each member for his whole life.[42]

Babinger's remembrances of the events of 1919 share a number of curious similarities with the events of late fifteenth-century Iran and Anatolia. In both situations, a population is driven to despair and violence as a result of the pressures of wars and political instability. The people break out in a communist revolt, but are brutally suppressed. Eventually, a charismatic leader arises who brings about order and stability. Although Babinger's political writings indeed date from over a decade later, the similarities between his two articles (one written in 1919 after his participation in the "White Terror," and the other written about it) suggests that he drew on the tropes of the Revolution and the Counter-Revolution to describe his subject of study: the rise of the Safavids.

The Legacy of the "German Right" in Walther Hinz

Still, Babinger's foundational contribution to Safavid studies influenced the field indirectly. This was because the work of Babinger on Shah Ismail was tangential to his Ottoman studies. Soon after his dismissal from the university and his move to Romania, however, another German scholar picked up Safavid history where Babinger had left it off and incorporated his conceptualization into the historiography. This scholar was Walther Hinz, and in 1936 he published his *Irans Aufstieg zum Nationalstaat im fünfzehnten Jahrhundert*, which he had completed under the supervision of Babinger's colleague and nemesis Hans Heinrich Schaeder. Hinz's book was the first monograph-length study on Safavid origins in a Western language, and therein he combined material from a variety of narrative sources originally in Persian, Turkish, Georgian, or Italian to give the most thorough analysis of the fifteenth-century background to date. He combined the two approaches to Safavid history as embodied by the works of Browne and Babinger. Hinz explicitly followed Edward Browne in his portrayal of the Safavids as a continuation of Persian dynastic history and as the manifestation of Iranian nationalism. In other words, in his configuration the Safavid period marked a success in a millennia-old struggle of the Persian people in overthrowing a foreign yoke and establishing a national state. Moreover, Hinz adopted from Babinger the concept of the Safavids as a *Männerbund* that was led to victories by a superhero. Also like Babinger, Hinz primarily analyzed the relevant events in terms of religious causes and at the expense of historical-materialist ones. Finally, Hinz shared with Babinger an affiliation with the German right, and like Babinger, Hinz projected onto the early Safavids the political rhetoric of his contemporary Germany in the 1930s. What is especially interesting is that in Hinz's work, Safavid history has been changed, or updated, to reflect the transformation of the ideology of Germany's political right from militant fascism to National Socialism. Thus, if Babinger's Shah Ismail recalled the *Freikorps* Counter-Revolution of 1919, in Hinz's book the founders of the sixteenth-century dynasty recalled the SS and Nazi racial ideology.

Walther Hinz was born on 19 November 1906 in Stuttgart. He pursued a doctorate in the field of Russian history, but in the early 1930s, while completing his doctorate in Leipzig, he encountered Hans Heinrich Schaeder, who drew him to Iranian studies. Hinz followed Schaeder to Berlin in 1931, composed a book on the Safavids, got a job at the Ministry of Education, and ended up teaching at Göttingen, beginning in 1937.[43] Hinz joined the Nazi Party early on and acted as the representative of the regime in his administrative functions.[44] During the war, he joined the German military intelligence, and spent some time after the war in a British internment camp,[45] though he later completed a denazification program and returned to academia. In the 1930s, when he was working on the Safavids, Hinz appeared to be fully committed to the National Socialist ideology, and in any event, his *Irans Aufstieg zum Nationalstaat* certainly echoes the vocabulary of the party.

Hinz was clearly aware of Babinger's article on Bedreddin, but he was quite circumspect in referring to him directly. For instance, he remarked, "That in the fifteenth century Asia Minor found itself in a condition of religious fermentation, which was strengthened by ceaseless military complications and the resulting economic hardship, is a matter treated several times by German research."[46] The absence of direct reference to Babinger becomes even more noticeable when one combs through Hinz's bibliography and discovers that he had obtained copies of Ottoman manuscripts from Babinger personally.[47] The connection between the two scholars was indeed stronger than the cryptic references in Hinz's book would seem to indicate, as he and Babinger had composed a pamphlet in May of 1933 to help Oriental studies in Nazi Germany. It seems that Babinger's absence from the canon of modern Safavid historiography is partially a result of Hinz's cautious distancing of himself from his friend in *Irans Aufstieg*.

Nevertheless, Hinz borrowed Babinger's conceptualization of the early Safavids as a tightly knit spiritual male organization. "The Iranian national state of the Safavids," he wrote, "owes its emergence to a *Männerbund* built on a religious foundation."[48] But Hinz's contribution consists of more than a mere combination of his two predecessors. Indeed, Hinz added a Nazi tinge to the Safavids by using party terminology to describe the well-disciplined structure of the Safavid order and racializing the Safavid movement.

An example of the former innovation is provided in cases in which Hinz discusses the strictness of the order's followers and their absolute loyalty to their master. For instance, he wrote, "Regarding the blind devotion with which Safavid Sufis obeyed the master of their order, one gets a revealing impression from later descriptions when the young disciples had already developed into combat units."[49] While there is no doubt that devotion played an important role in the structure of sixteenth-century Sufi brotherhoods, Hinz's understanding is specifically modern and National Socialist. The word "combat unit" (*Kampfgemeinschaft*) was a Nazi term referring to an idealized community of soldiers in battle, as well as the political fighters of the party before 1933.[50] It had military revolutionary connotations used, for instance, by the Nazi ideologue of the 1920s, Otto Strasser, who stressed the importance of military service for the formation of a new elite in the second revolution, the war being the first revolution.[51] The ideas go back to *Freikorps* members and writers such as Ernst Röhm and Manfred von Killinger, who were friends with Otto Strasser and his brother Gregor.[52] As a party member, Hinz could not have been unaware of the political significance of this term. What is interesting is that his use involves the progression of the idea from revolutionary *Freikorps* days to the strict discipline of the party after its capture of the German state. In fact, the very idea of blind devotion and its connection to bravery gain significance in the context of the disbanding and purging of the unruly SA and its replacement by the SS, a militia responsible to Hitler alone. The motto of the SS was after all "Meine Ehre heißt Treue" or "My honor is loyalty" [to the *Führer*], and the recurrence of this same sentiment in Hinz's book is certainly suggestive. "Their bravery, which arose from their most faithful devotion to the master of their order, soon became proverbial in the East as well the West";[53] or the Sufis "simply await the orders of their 'perfect master'";[54] or "the basis for the characteristic and incomparably effective cohesion of the combat units formed under Shaykh Haidar [Shah Ismail's father] remained the inner bond of the members with their master."[55]

Moreover, in addition to emphasizing the discipline and loyalty of the Safavids, Hinz added a clear ethnic and "racial" element to their history. And here, his concept of ethnicity is very different than Browne's, for the English scholar had believed that ethnic identity was not really part of the consciousness of sixteenth-century people. Quite the contrary, Hinz firmly believed that the Persians were an Aryan *volk*. He stated that the Safavids had paved the way for "the national rebirth of Iran and the consequent cultural creativity of the Aryan Persians."[56] The adjective "cultural-creative" is a telling qualifier, because the concept is tied to Nordic racial ideology, the most recent expression of which had been formulated by Hans F. K. Günther of the University of Jena,[57] basically stating that only Nordic people (i.e., Aryans) were truly creative and dynamic in world history.[58] Now, since Hinz had portrayed Shah Ismail as the hero of Iranian nationhood, it was important that the Safavid leader be of Aryan stock. "The founder of the first Iranian national empire after nearly nine centuries—to which race did Ismail, whom one tends to generally regard as a Turk, actually belong?"[59] And the answer, "[I]n pseudo-Angiolello, it is said: 'This Sophi (Ismail) is very handsome, *fair*, and very delicate; his facial hair is of a *reddish hue*, though he only wears a mustache.' According to these descriptions, a Nordic extraction seems to be present" [emphases in the original].[60]

Thus, Hinz's work was a continuation and development of both Browne's and Babinger's. He saw the Safavids in terms of Iranian nationalism, male fraternities, superheroes, and religious causes. But he also updated the projection of German history into "Iranian" history (defined as such, even though the early Safavid movement was decidedly Anatolian and Caucasian) and added racialism and the importance of party discipline to the historiography. In sum, as the German right developed from a *Freikorps* phase to a National Socialist one, so too did Safavid history.

Vladimir Minorsky and Roger Savory

Although Hinz's book was never translated into English, his contributions were publicized in the Anglo-American world by the works of Vladimir Minorsky. Minorsky had read and favorably reviewed Hinz's *Irans Aufstieg* in 1937, and found it to have been an improvement over Browne and Babinger.[61] He did, however, disagree with Hinz, and modified his statements a bit. Most importantly, Minorsky stated that the Safavids could not be placed in a direct line of Persian history, but rather as a continuation of Turcoman dynasties of the Qaraquyunlu and Aqquyunlu, which ruled western Iran and eastern Anatolia during the fifteenth century. Minorsky did, however, believe that, by separating Iran from the rest of the Muslim world, the Safavids were indeed responsible for the creation of the modern Iranian state.[62] All the same, Minorsky incorporated some of Hinz's ideas into his own influential compositions on the Safavids, such as his translation and commentary on the administrative manual entitled *Tadhkirat al-Muluk*, completed in 1943.[63] It is perhaps odd that in a commentary on a handbook of fiscal administration, Minorsky proposed a description of the early Safavids that was peculiarly antimaterialist and much more focused on spiritual and racial explanations. The exuberant devotion to Shah Ismail was not just one aspect of Safavid propaganda, but the symptom of a new phenomenon. "Towards A.D. 1500, the royal power was reborn with the full prestige of its magic origins. Even European contemporaries were aware of the supernatural prerogatives of the Shahs. . . . To become operative, this religious conception of kingship required the credulity of the semi-nomad Turcoman tribes, which carried the Safavids to the throne."[64] Here, the numerous cash-deprived soldiers rushing to the Shah Ismail, of whom Browne had written, have completely disappeared. Nor was the success of the shah placed within the context of the unpopular crackdown on the extortionist powers of the Aqquyunlu military at the end of the fifteenth century (a potential source of recruitment for Ismail), on which Minorsky later wrote so expertly. Instead, we have sorcerer-kings and semi-nomadic adulators posing as historical cause. Moreover, the spirit that defined Safavid beginnings also served as their essential core identity, and the fortunes of the dynasty rose and fell in direct relationship with its adherence to it. Thus, a major cause of Safavid decline almost two hundred years after Ismail's death was "the complete disappearance of the basic theocratic nucleus round which Shah Ismail had built up his state, without the substitution of some other dynamic ideology."[65] This is none other than an "origins and essence" argument, similar to the "ghazi thesis" employed by Minorsky's colleague at SOAS, the Ottomanist Paul Wittek, who defined the essential characteristic of the Ottoman Empire to be holy war, or "ghaza."[66] The further a state deviates from its principal defining ethos, present at its beginning, the more it devolves into a cycle of decline. Thus, Minorsky was defining the rise of the Safavids in a manner quite similar to those conservative/romantic formulations of his German and Austrian colleagues.

But in addition to its charismatic spiritual essence, the Safavid state was also marked by a clear racial characteristic. As we saw earlier, Browne had downplayed the role of ethnicity. But for Minorsky, the players on the historical stage belonged to four distinct ethnic groups: Turks, Tajiks, Arabs, and Georgians, and this ethnic identity had unmistakable "racial" connotations, for Minorsky had understood it in terms of "blood."[67] The ethnic divisions ran through every strand of Safavid polity. For instance, in the Safavid army, the *Qurchi* represented "the old tribal cavalry . . . doughty Turcoman warriors . . . qïzïl-bash," while the *tufangchi* [musketeers] "were recruited among sturdy peasants and consequently represented the pure Iranian element";[68] elsewhere we have "Native Iranians . . . and Turk invaders";[69] and finally Minorsky's famous dictum "[l]ike oil and water, the Turcomans and Persians did not mix freely."[70] In sum, Minorsky's Safavids had been fully transformed from Browne's dynastic, vaguely Persian (in political and decided nonethnic terms) polity into a charismatic, spiritual, and racial entity.

One need not look far for a major source of this conceptualization in Minorsky's work. The inspiration and even vocabulary had come from Walther Hinz:

The curious office of *KHALIFAT AL-KHULAFA* [deputy of the Safavid king] is a survival of a basic organization of the early Safavids, *very similar to the single party of a modern totalitarian state.* . . . Under Shah Ismail's grandfather Junayd extreme Shiʿa ideas had crept into the organization, and the new sect doctrine promoted the successors of Shaykh Safi to the position of living embodiment of the godhead. This evolution further consolidated the order and resulted in the political triumph of Ismail. . . . *As the supreme heads of their original order, they claimed the blind obedience of the Sufis.* . . . [A]s soon as internal crisis broke out the Safavids appealed to the feelings of "Shahisevani" [love of the king] of their adherents, and *the conflict was settled in the atmosphere of the superior discipline of the single party.* The office of the Khalifat al-Khulafa served as a special secretariat for Sufi affairs.[71] [Italics added]

Hinz is in the footnote to this curious passage, and actually his language regarding devotion, obedience, and discipline is echoed here. More recently, Roger Savory has noted, without expanding his argument, that Minorsky's rhetoric recalls the Soviet Union. But this sentence is much more ambiguous. If Savory implied that Minorsky was projecting contemporary politics into early Safavid history, then terms such as "single party" and "modern totalitarian state" could just as easily have applied to Fascist Italy or Nazi Germany. What is significant, however, is that the fascist roots of this conceptualization (blood and spirit) and comparison (single-party state) were being covered over. Without knowledge of the influence of Hinz, and indirectly of Babinger before him, Minorsky's passage could be taken as a random analogy detached of its actual historical parent: German fascism. As such, modern scholars continue to see the Safavids in terms initially defined by Babinger and Hinz, but, unaware of the historical root of these terms, they simply update the analogies to various contemporary revolutions.

Roger Savory, for instance, in his "Some Reflections on Totalitarian Tendencies in the Safavid State," stated that he was inspired by Minorsky's comment regarding the similarity of the Safavids with modern single-party totalitarian states. However, writing during the Cold War, Savory took it for granted that it was the Soviet Union that had provided Minorsky with his "single-party" model.[72] Thus, Savory called the Safavids a revolutionary movement comparable to the Bolsheviks,[73] dubbed the inner circle of the Safavid movement the "politburo,"[74] concurred with Minorsky that the Sufi beliefs of Shah Ismail's followers were political ideology,[75] equated the magnetic charisma of Ismail with Lenin's,[76] linked the disciplined marginalization of the Qizilbash with Stalinist purges,[77] and compared Soviet class struggle with ethnic struggle between Turks and Tajiks (Persians). The irony of this careless comparison with a modern Marxist revolution lies in the fact that Savory, like his predecessors, still failed to consider possible materialist causes of Safavid victory. What we have here, then, is not a rigorous comparative analysis (which might be of dubious value, due to its anachronism), but the persistence of the counter-revolutionary romanticism of 1919 (charisma and ideology) and racialized statism of 1934 (purges, discipline, ethnic struggle), overlaid by Cold War rhetoric. This model possessed such a pervasive influence that Savory could easily apply it again within a few years, and this time to a "conservative revolution." He wrote in 1986 that the Islamic Revolution of Iran led by Ayatollah Khomeini was indeed none other than the reappearance of a Safavid precedent, albeit in modified form. Needless to say, the Islamic revolution of Iran was also seen by him as a primarily idealist endeavor led by Shiite clerics "representing . . . millenarian ideal of the utopian government of the Mahdi [apocalyptic figure in Islam]."[78]

Other contemporary scholars continue to refer to the Safavid movement as a "revolution." For the most part, they seek spiritual and religious causes for the success of the movement. But even the few, such as Jean Aubin, who have investigated certain economic aspects of this history, do not seek materialist explanation for the success of the Safavids. To end this article, then, two alternative ways of looking at this history will be proposed. These are mainly drawn from scholarship that do not directly address the early career of Shah Ismail, but can nevertheless be used to problematize the causal explanation associated with the scholarship of the German right.

Some Alternatives

It would be useful to place the Safavid uprising within the context of administrative or fiscal reforms that took place in the second half of the fifteenth century by the Ottomans, the Aqquyunlu, and finally the Timurids. The Ottomans undertook a number of fiscal reforms, which, although ultimately unsuccessful,[79] particularly hit hard and upset the old frontier *begs* (lords) and *ghazi*s (raiders) in Anatolia.[80] This is, of course, where Shah Ismail's father and grandfather, Junayd and Haydar, who are known for militarizing the order, began to acquire recruits. Moreover, Haydar and Junayd led their followers in *ghazas* in the Caucasus, which suggests that one of the immediate goals of the movement involved religiously sanctified plunder. No doubt, this would be quite attractive to cash-deprived military men. By the time of Ismail, the social situation in the Aqquyunlu domain had changed considerably. As Minorsky has demonstrated, from 1488 on, powerful viziers undertook wide-ranging centralization policies in the name of Islamic law (sharia). These "back to Islam" policies involved a crackdown on public drinking and the confiscation or abrogation of land grants (*suyurghals*).[81] These reforms especially targeted the Turcoman emirs, as well as a number of rich *'ulama* and Sufi hospices, along with their destitute dependents.[82] In the 1490s, Ahmad Beg Aqquyunlu continued these policies (which had been reversed for a brief time), and in this he seems to have been particularly keen on curbing the power of the military. According to a later historian, Hasan Beg Rumlu, himself a Turcoman emir, "[I]nstead of orders, [Ahmad Beg] wrote letters (*kitâbat*) to Maulana Jalal al-din Davani and Mir Sadr al-din Muhammad and on the verso apposed his seal. Thus it was that he introduced the law of justice to make the Turks withdraw their hands from the heads of the lowly and the peasants. Therefore the Turks, although outwardly obeying his orders, in their hearts opposed (*'indd*) him."[83] Here, "the Turks" refer to the army whose predatory powers were being targeted in the name of Islamic "orthodoxy." A closer look at these events would shed a great deal more light on Ismail's revolt. The combination of disenchantment among Turcoman emirs and leaders of Sufi hospices would already explain much about the composition of the inner core of the Safavid uprising. One might even go so far as to say that the antinomian behavior of Ismail, as noticed by Babinger and Browne, might make more sense in this context. If the oppression of the "state" is enforced in the name of "orthodoxy" or "back to sharia," it stands to reason that the opposition should assume the rhetoric of "heterodoxy" or "away from sharia." If the drinking of wine is banned by the government as a cover for its reforms, the public drinking of alcohol is espoused by a man who claims to have direct access to God, and thus does not need to follow the law. As Jean Aubin has argued, following Petrushevskii, the early Safavid state in Anatolia and Western Iran (former Aqquyunlu territory) engaged in no restructuring of *suyurghals*.[84] In other words, the new Safavid government of Shah Ismail was the first in over a decade that avoided centralization reforms. Ismail's attitude toward land grants after the capture of Khurasan is consistent with his actions in Persian Iraq. Maria Subtelny has shown that centralization policies, similar to the ones in the Aqquyunlu domain, were undertaken by some of the administrators of the Timurid ruler Husayn Bayqara in Khurasan. Here too, the battle cry of the viziers was a "return to sharia," and here again the main targeted groups included the powerful Turkic emirs.[85] In this light, it is crucial to note that, upon Ismail's conquest of Herat, most of these policies were reportedly reversed. According to Amini-e Haravi, the author of an early history of Shah Ismail called *Futuhat-e Shahi* or "royal conquests," after the fall of Herat, Ismail received those whose property had been taken by the central administration (*divan*) and returned their lands to them. These included the author himself. Moreover, Ismail appointed a local to oversee the matter of *suyurghals*, because he did not want Iraqis ignorant of Khurasani rules to interfere.[86] It seems then, if the anachronistic label "conservative revolution" must be applied to the early Safavids, it should refer as much to the fiscally conservative impulse of the landed elite (emirs, Sufis, and some *'ulama*).

Such an approach to Safavid history actually eliminates the need to overanalyze the structure of the Sufi order of Ardabil and its in-house propaganda as the main *cause* of Shah Ismail's successes. In another words, the reasons for the triumphs of the Safavids might be much more related to broad social patterns in the region and have less to do with military discipline or Messianic aspirations of the core Qizilbash. By concentrating on these socioeconomic factors, we might begin to move beyond the legacy of the German Counter-Revolution in the field.

Notes

1. Most recently by Roger Savory, *Iran under the Safavids* (Cambridge: Cambridge University Press, 1980); Jean Aubin, "Révolution chiite et conservatisme. Les soufis de Liahejian, 1500-1514," *Moyen Orient & Océan Indien* 1 (1984): 1–4; Kathryn Babayan, *Mystics, Monarchs and Messiahs: Cultural Landscapes of Early Modern Iran* (Cambridge: Harvard University Press, 2002); and Colin P. Mitchel, *The Practice of Politics in Safavid Iran: Power, Religion and Rhetoric* (London: I. B. Tauris Academic Studies, 2009).

2. Franz Babinger, *Die Geschichtsschreiber der Osmanen und ihre Werke* (Leipzig: O. Harrassowitz, 1927).

3. Franz Babinger, *Mehmed der Eroberer und seine Zeit: Weltenstürmer einer Zeitenwende* (München: F. Bruckmann, 1953). Translated into English by Ralph Manheim, *Mehmed the Conqueror and His Time* (Princeton: Princeton University Press, 1978).

4. E. G. Browne, *A Literary History of Persia: IV. Modern Times (1500–1924),* (Cambridge: Cambridge University press, 1929), 3.

5. Ibid., 4.

6. Ibid., 12.

7. Ibid., 20.

8. Ibid., 22.

9. Ibid., 62.

10. Ibid., 50–51.

11. Ibid., 62.

12. There is a huge literature on Fascism. I mainly follow Robert O. Paxton, *The Anatomy of Fascism* (New York: Knopf, 2004).

13. Gerhard Grimm, "Franz Babinger (1891–1967): Ein Lebensgeschichtlicher Essay," *Die Welt des Islams* 38 (1998), 293–294.

14. Gerhard Grimm, "Franz Babinger," 296, 298.

15. Gerhard Grimm, "Franz Babinger," 306–307.

16. Karl Süssheim, *The Diary of Karl Süssheim (1878–1947): Orientalist between Munich and Istanbul*, Barbara Flemming & Jan Schmidt, (Stuttgart: F. Steiner, 2002), 226.

17. Eberhard Kolb, *The Weimar Republic*, trans. P. S. Falla and R. J. Park (New York: Routledge, 2004), 14–21.

18. Andreas E. Eckl, *S'ist ein übles Land hier: Zur Historiographie eines umstrittenen Kolonialkrieges* (Köln: Köppe, 2007), especially 217–293 for Epp's journal of the campaigns.

19. R. G. L. Wait, *Vanguards of Nazism* (New York: W. W. Norton, 1969), 85.

20. In a striking case of oversight, or worse, Gerhard Grimm overlooks Babinger's own statement that after leaving his unit on a mission to Berlin, he returned just before the assault on Munich began. Dan Prodan, in his *Franz Babinger en Roumanie,*

1935–1943: Étude et Sources Historiques (Istanbul: Les Editions Isis, 2003), devotes a single sentence to Babinger's *Freikorps* days, but gives a whole chapter to the claim that the scholar might have been acting as a Nazi spy while in exile in Romania.

21. Babinger, "Shejch Bedr ed-din," 1.

22. Suzanne Marchand, *Down From Olympus: Archaeology and Philhellenism in Germany, 1750–1970* (Princeton: Princeton University Press, 1996), 308.

23. Marchand, *Down From Olympus*, 330.

24. Marchand, *Down From Olympus*, 306.

25. Babinger, *Shejch Bedr ed-din*, 3.

26. Heinrich Schurtz, *Alterklassen und Männerbünde* (Berlin: G. Reimer, 1902); Hans Blüher, *Die Rolle der Erotik in der mänlichen Gesellschaft* (Jena: E. Diederichs, 1919) and *Familie und Männerbund* (Leipzig: Der Neue Geist Verlag, 1919).

27. Hans Blüher, *Family & Male Fraternity: [A Theory of the Eros]*, trans. Heinrich Hoffstiepel (Paris: Dioscures, 1994), 59.

28. Blüher, *Family*, 60.

29. Babinger, *Shejch Bedr ed-din*, 7, 8, 10.

30. Ibid., 65.

31. *Orientalistische Literaturzeitung* 9, (1922), 363–364.

32. Babinger, *Shejch Bedr ed-din*, 18.

33. See the analysis of his political article below.

34. Wait, *Vanguards*, 51.

35. Babinger, *Shejch Bedr ed-din*, 78, 85.

36. Ibid., 87, 88.

37. Ibid., 88.

38. Gerhard Grimm, "Franz Babinger," 319, 317.

39. Ludmila Hanisch, "Akzentverschiebung—zur Geschichte der Semitistik und Islamwissenschaft wahrend des 'Drittes Reiches,'" *Berichte zur Wissenschaftsgeschichte*, 18 (1995), 219.

40. Franz Babinger, "Einer von Vielen," *Das Bayernland* 44/19 (October 1933), 601.

41. Ibid., 601–602.

42. Ibid., 604.

43. Rüdiger Schmitt, "Hinz, (A.) Walther," *Encyclopedia Iranica* (online version at www.iranica.com).

44. Ludwig Paul, "Göttingen, University of, History of Iranian Studies," *Encyclopedia Iranica* (www.iranica.com).

45. Rüdiger Schmitt, "Hinz."

46. Walther Hinz, *Irans Aufstieg zum Nationalstaat im Fünfzehnten Jahrhundert* (Leipzig: Walter de Gruyter & Co., 1936), 119.

47. Ibid., 153.

48. Ibid., 12.

49. Ibid., 16.

50. Michael Burleigh (ed.), *Confronting the Nazi Past: New Debates on Modern German History* (London: Collins & Brown, 1996), 184.

51. Barbara Miller Lane, Leila J. Rupp (ed. and trans.), *Nazi Ideology before 1933* (Manchester: Manchester University Press ND, 1978), xix–xx.

52. Ibid., xviii–xix.

53. Hinz, *Irans*, 16.

54. Ibid., 98.

55. Ibid., 80.

56. Ibid., 124.

57. Hans F. Günther, *Rassenkunde Europas* (München: J. F. Lehmanns, 1926); *The Racial Elements of European History*, by Hans F. K. Günther; trans. from the 2nd German ed. by G. C. Wheeler, (London, Methuen, 1927).

58. Michael Hau, *The Cult of Health and Beauty in Germany* (Chicago: University of Chicago Press, 2003), 153–155.

59. Hinz, *Irans*, 74; abridged.

60. Ibid., 75.

61. Vladimir Minorsky, Review of *Irans Aufstieg zum Nationalstaat im Fünfzehnten Jahrhundert* by Walther Hinz, *Bulletin of the School of Oriental Studies*, (9, 1:1937), 239–243.

62. Ibid.

63. Vladimir Minorsky, *Tadhkirat al-Muluk, a Manual of Safavid Administration (circa 1137/1725)*, (London: E. J. W. Gibb Memorial Series, 1943).

64. Ibid., 12–13.

65. Ibid., 23.

66. Paul Wittek, *The Rise of the Ottoman Empire* (London: The Royal Asiatic Society, 1938).

67. Minorsky, *Tadhkirat*, 14–15.

68. Ibid., 32.

69. Ibid., 187.

70. Ibid., 188.

71. Ibid., 125.

72. Roger Savory, "Some Reflections on Totalitarian Tendencies in the Safawid State," *Der Islam* (53, 1976): 226.

73. Ibid., 226.

74. Ibid., 228.

75. Ibid., 228.

76. Ibid., 232–233.

77. Ibid., 235–236.

78. Roger Savory, *Studies on the History of Safawid Iran* (London: Variorum Reprints, 1987), xii.

79. Oktay Özel, "Limits of the Almighty: Mehmed II's 'Land Reform' Revisited," *Journal of the Economic and Social History of the Orient* 42, 2 (1999), 226–246.

80. Halil İnalcık, "How to Read 'Ashik Pasha-Zade's History," *Essays in Ottoman History* (Istanbul, Eren: 1998), 37.

81. Vladimir Minorsky, "The Aq-qoyunlu and Land Reforms (Turkmenica, 11)," *Bulletin of the School of Oriental and African Studies*, 17.3 (1955), 451, 453.

82. Ibid., 453, 454, 456.

83. Ibid., 460.

84. Jean Aubin, "Études safavides. I: Shah Isma'il et les notables de l'Iraq persan," *Journal of the Economic and Social History of the Orient*, 2 (1959), 50–52.

85. Maria Eva Subtelny, "Centralizing Reform and Its Opponents in the Late Timurid Period," *Iranian Studies*, vol. 21, no. 1/2 (1988), 123–151.

86. Ibrahim b. Mubarak Jalal al-Din Amini, *Futuhat-e Shahi* (Tehran, Anjoman-e Asar va Mafakhir-e Farhangi: 2004), 358–359.

CHAPTER 3

The Berlin Circle: Iranian Nationalism Meets German Countermodernity

AFSHIN MATIN-ASGARI

Among the least studied features of Iranian modernity are its links to German intellectual traditions, in particular the so-called Countermodernist trends prominent between the two world wars.[1] This chapter will argue that key characteristics of modern Iranian nationalism, during the Pahlavi monarchy and persisting under the Islamic Republic, are traceable to a decisive encounter with interwar German intellectual trends. These include: First, the German Countermodernists' negative or ambivalent stance toward modernity, seen as a condition of crisis, a challenge that needed to be met and surpassed. Second, perceiving the crisis of modernity as a crisis of "the West," defined as a decadent and predatory global civilization dominated by the United Kingdom, France, and the U.S. Third, the Countermodernist depiction of Western civilization as bound up with an evil triad of soulless "materialism," exploitative capitalism, and the deceptions of liberalism and socialism posing as popular sovereignty. Significant too was the idea of Germany offering an alternate normative model to the modern world, hence the notion of German "countermodernity." Assuming "spiritual leadership" on a global scale, Germany would overthrow both modernity and the West. This was because Germany possessed a unique "culture," neither Western nor Eastern, but somehow placed in "the center."

Countermodernity was intimately linked to an evolving historical construction of German identity, defined as standing between the two poles of the East (Orient) and the West (Occident). For reason of geographic proximity, the Orient for Germany was largely linked to Islam and the Islamic world. German-speaking communities had fought in the Crusades and later against the Ottoman Empire's expansion in central Europe. However, by the eighteenth century, the ebbing of the Ottoman threat coincided with the Enlightenment's more positive appreciation of non-Christian and non-

European cultures. Here, an important distinction between culture and civilization began to shape an emerging modern German historical consciousness. French-inspired universal notions of civilization allowed the absorption of people from diverse ethnic and cultural origins into a "higher" (European) civilization. In contrast, nineteenth-century German notions of culture (*kultur*) saw group identities as insular, confined to particular ethnic communities, and sharply differentiated by historical, linguistic and racial boundaries.[2]

The German cultural-national philosophy of history was powerfully articulated by Herder (1744–1803) in terms of the organic cycles of birth, maturation, and decline of self-contained cultures. In Herder's developmental narrative, history was born in the Orient, matured in Greece and Rome and, after ebbs and flows during its westward march, achieved rebirth with the rise of the German people. Drawing on the Roman historian Tacitus, Herder depicted Germans as warlike people who carried the torch of civilization from Asia to defend Christian Europe against Oriental invaders. He also believed that, unlike Western Europeans such as the modern French and ancient Romans, Germans did not conquer and dominate others, but achieved greatness through "self-cultivation."[3]

In Herder's scheme, the earliest civilizations had been Asian, primarily Indian but also Iranian. Ancient India froze in time, stagnating under the yoke of Oriental despotism, but the greatness of ancient Iran survived until the Arab invasion. Privileging pre-Islamic Iranian culture, Herder nevertheless found positive values in Islamic Iran's Persian literary masterpieces, especially in the works of Sa'di. Considering "national literature" as the core of national identity, Herder thus "opened up the gate of Persian poetry to German literature," setting a romantic Orientalist trend depicting Iran primarily through the glorification of Persian literature. This trend culminated in Goethe, who was a champion of pristine national cultures, urging his followers to "compare them with themselves, respect them in their own context, and forget that Greeks and Romans ever existed." Goethe also found positive affinity with Iranian Islam, and presumably with Shi'ism, for its purported qualities of tolerance, sophistication and esotericism.[4]

German cultural and linguistic nationalism became more entangled with Oriental origins with the discovery of Sanskrit as the common root of Indo-European languages. During the nineteenth century, as notions of Indo-European linguistic affinity morphed into racial theories, Germans were tied to an ancient "Aryan" race, originating somewhere in the Orient, i.e., the Caucasus or north India, and linked also to Iran, a term equated with "the land of Aryans." The cultural achievements of Iranians, it was now alleged, were due to their Aryan racial origins, something that made them superior to Semitic Arabs. As a recent study concludes, the association of Iran and Iranians with the discourse of the Aryan race became "a fundamental pillar" of Iranian nationalism.[5]

By the century's turn, the German critique of the modern West, and its concomitant selective appreciation of things Oriental, became more pronounced. Schopenhauer had studied Hindu and Buddhist doctrines, and his 1818 *The World as Will and Idea* pitted the Orient's mystical wisdom against Enlightenment rationalism. In *Thus Spake Zarathustra*, Nietzsche chose an Iranian sage as the voice denouncing Europe's "decadent" Christian bourgeois civilization. Pessimistic views on modern Western civilization can be found in numerous influential German language works, including Freud's *Civilization and Its Discontents*, Albert Schweitzer's *The Decay and Restoration of Civilization* (1923), and contemporary German literary productions—for example, those by Thomas Mann. A landmark culmination of such trends in German thought was Oswald Spengler's *The Decline of the West*.[6] Highly influential on twentieth-century historians like Toynbee and others, Spengler depicted global history as a stage where numerous "cultures," defined by their most vital values and ideas, competed and clashed, thus giving shape to the chaos around them. There was no stability or permanent equilibrium in this scheme, since every culture inevitably passed through childhood, youth, maturity, and old age. "Civilization" corresponded to the old age and declining phase in the life cycle of a culture.

Spengler called modern European civilization "Faustian." Like Goethe's hero, Western civilization had sold its soul in a diabolical bargain. It had sacrificed all values to a relentless pursuit of secular knowledge serving material gain and universal domination. Like Marxists, Spengler saw capitalist imperialism as the highest stage of Europe's expansionism, as well as the beginning of the West's winter season of decline and decay. Yet he differed sharply with Marxists in finding redemption in German culture rather than in universal revolutionary transformation. While England, France, and the U.S. were dragging Western Civilization into the abyss of destruction, Germany would rise to lead a new and different cycle of global regeneration.[7] Spengler thus created a powerful image of the West, or modern Europe, as a decaying civilization, condemned to self-destruction because of its obsession with materialism, capitalist greed, and universal domination.

Imperial Germany's Alliance with Iranian Nationalism in the First World War

The nineteenth-century German obsession with cultural nationalism and authentic national identity took a sharply political turn with the emergence of Imperial Germany. Chancellor Bismarck's "Blood and Iron" unification project meant the new German nation-state was born a militaristic empire, geared to authoritarian modernization, technological and economic supremacy, war, and conquest. By the mid-1880s, Bismarck had launched a project of maritime expansion, with the overland route of German expansionism focusing on the Orient, starting in Eastern Europe and passing through Crimea, the Balkans, the Caucasus, and the Near East, to reach India. The Berlin-Baghdad Railway mapped the direction of this project, whose political expression was the alliance Imperial Germany forged with the Young Turks upon their coming to power.

Grieved by long-term Russian, French, and British imperialist impositions, the Ottomans were Germany's natural allies. A somewhat similar development took place among Iranian nationalists who saw the Constitutional Revolution's aspiration to national sovereignty betrayed by the 1907 Anglo-Russian agreement leading to imperialist military intervention and eventually the occupation of Iran during the First World War. Insufficiently studied by historians, the impact of the First World War and its immediate aftermath were crucial to the formation of modern Iranian nationalism. Though pioneered by thinkers like Fath Ali Akhundzadeh (1812–1878) and Aqa Khan Kermani (1853–1896), a distinctly Iranian nationalist ideology and discourse, anchored in a fairly comprehensive modern worldview, found articulation only in the two decades following the 1906–1911 Constitutional Revolution.[8]

Inspired by Orientalist scholarship and Aryan race theorists such as Gobineau and Ernest Renan, nineteenth-century thinkers had glorified pre-Islamic Iran as the golden age of "national" grandeur, unsullied by the intrusion of Arabs and other non-Aryans. However, when it came to popular mobilization in support of a nationalist agenda, Islam and the moral-political authority of Iran's Shi'i 'ulama could not be ignored. The protonationalists thus developed a strategy for using Islam and clerical authority to advance secular agendas. During the 1890s, this strategy was deployed by Jamal al-din Asadabadi (Afghani) in the Tobacco Protest movement, while Malkom Khan's newspaper *Qanun* (*Law*) advocated a parliamentary system whereby the 'ulama would join political reformers, making laws in accordance with the sharia.[9] Despite a clerical backlash against secular nationalism and constitutionalism, the instrumentalist approach to Islam and the Shi'i 'ulama persisted among two more generations of secular reformers, including social-ists and even communists.[10] Thus, a fundamental problem of modern Iranian nationalism—i.e., direct and critical engagement with Islam and clerical au-thority—remained to be addressed in the late twentieth century, after the in-auguration of the Islamic Republic. It is here that revisiting the 1920s Berlin Circle of Iranian intellectuals clarifies the origins of peculiar entanglements between modern Iran's discourses on nationalism, Islam, and national identity and their relation to a global entity called the West or Western Civilization.

During the First World War, German propaganda focused on the Unity of Islam, calling on Iranian, Turkish, Arab, and Indian Muslims to join Germany against the imperialist Entente allies. An often-missed point in relation to the effectiveness of German propaganda was the blending of socialist themes into its appeals to Islamic, anti-imperialist, and nationalist sentiments.[11] In the Iranian case, many pro-German nationalists—for example, leaders of the alternate government formed in 1915 as the National Defense Committee—were members of the (Social) Democrat Party.[12] As early as 1914, German authorities had focused on the Democrat Party and contacted its prominent leader Hasan Taqizadeh, who was then in New York. During the Consti-tutional Revolution, Taqizadeh had forged close ties with British Oriental-ist E. G. Browne and, through him, with leftist and liberal circles in Lon-don. When the war broke out, it was clear that Browne and his allies could not alter Britain's imperial policy in Iran. By this time, Taqizadeh, then in exile, apparently was searching for support elsewhere, hence looking to the United States. In 1915, however, he arrived in Berlin on an official government invitation, immediately calling on Iranian nationalists in Europe to join him in a German-sponsored committee opposing the Anglo-Russian occupation of Iran. A group of prominent intellectuals responded positively, gathering around Taqizadeh to launch the so-called Berlin Circle of Iranian national-ists. According to Taqizadeh and the famous fiction writer Mohammad-Ali Jamalzadeh, German authorities initially financed the circle's activities and even paid living stipends to its members.[13]

Lasting slightly more than a decade (1915 to the mid-1920s), the Ber-lin Circle brought together the most influential members of the post-Constitutional era's political and cultural elite. These included Hasan Taqiza-deh (1878-1970), Hasan Kazemzadeh-Iranshahr (1883-1961), Mohammad Qazvini (1877-1949), Mohammad-Ali Jamalzadeh (1891-1997), Ebrahim Purdavud (1895-1968), Abdol-Hosein Sheybani (1873-1963), Moretza Moshfeq-Kazemi (1902-1977), Taqi Arani (1903-1940), Sadeq Rezazadeh-Shafaq (1895-1971), Mahmud Afshar (1894-1924), Gholam-Reza Rashid-Yasami, Heydar Amuoghlu (d. 1921), Esmail Amirkhizi, Abolhasan Alavi, and Abbas Eqbal-Ashtiani (d. 1955). The ideas formulated by the Berlin Circle, and disseminated widely through the influential Persian-language periodicals *Kaveh* (1916–1922), *Iranshahr* (1922–1927), and *Nameh-ye Farangestan* (1922–1927), had a profound impact on modern Iranian nationalism and political culture.[14] As we shall see below, and though insufficiently noted by the only existing study of the subject, the Berlin Circle was deeply influenced by interwar Germany's intellectual and political milieu.

From *Kaveh* to *Iranshahr*: The Shifting Foundations of Nationalism and *Weltanschauung*

The Berlin Circle's official organ *Kaveh* was published between 1916 and 1919 (52 issues) and resumed in a second series from 1920 until 1922. Though remaining intensely nationalistic, the journal's politics and worldview changed significantly during these years. Published mainly during the war, the first series mixed nationalism with support for Germany's war goals, Pan-Islamism, and mildly social-democratic sentiments. Initially, Imperial Russia and Britain were equally condemned and attacked as Iran's enemies, but in 1918 Russia suddenly turned into a friend and possibly an ally of Iranian nationalism, when the Bolsheviks denounced Tsarist treaties and then officially endorsed Iran's independence via the Brest-Litovsk Treaty. By 1919, *Kaveh*'s pro-German position collapsed as a defeated Germany embarked on an unpredictable path of revolutionary change. Thus, *Kaveh*'s articulation of Iranian nationalism had to navigate a global scene that had changed rapidly and drastically between 1915 and 1919.

As in politics, *Kaveh* began by openly embracing German intellectual authority, especially in Orientalist scholarship. Explaining its name, the journal's first issue featured an article entitled "Kaveh and His Flag" written by professor Oskar Mann, on whose authority Kaveh suggested Iran change its official Lion-and-the-Sun emblem. Deemed problematic due to alleged association with Seljuk Turks, the latter needed to revert to "the form closer to historical truth," which, according to the *Shahnameh*, had consisted of red, yellow, and purple colors.[15] Similarly, the broad worldview sustaining *Kaveh*'s nationalism openly deferred to Imperial German power. Issue no. 2, for example, called for the establishment of a modern Iranian army staffed by German officers, featuring also a piece on the Kaiser's birthday celebration: "The victory of Germany and its allies being our greatest goal and in our best interest, we Muslims pray to God on this day of His Majesty Wilhelm II's birthday, asking for long life and reign for his majesty the beloved German Emperor, as well as for the final triumph of German armies, joined by the first independent Muslim monarchy, i.e., the great Ottoman government."[16] Barely noted by historians, *Kaveh*'s socialist tendency also had a bearing on the development of Iranian nationalism, as well as on events affecting Iran's national independence during the war and its immediate aftermath. In 1917, *Kaveh* reported extensively on Iranian participation at a peace conference the Socialist International was trying to organize in Stockholm. Officially representing Iran, Taqizadeh and Sheybani travelled to Sweden to negotiate with international socialist leaders, who, according to *Kaveh*, represented "the world's greatest power," possibly on the verge of becoming "the future rulers of the globe."[17] Though the conference could not actually convene, Taqizadeh and Sheybani met with socialist leaders from various countries, including representatives of revolutionary Russia's workers and soldiers, getting the latter's promises of support for Iran's independence and liberation from tsarist impositions. These contacts started a process that soon led to Bolshevik renunciation of tsarist treaties with Iran, followed by the joint Soviet-German recognition of Iranian independence and territorial integrity in the 1918 Brest-Litovsk Treaty. Entitled "A Promise of Life," a January 1918 *Kaveh* editorial enthusiastically welcomed the Brest-Litovsk negotiations, calling for a "day of national celebration" marking the end of nine years of Russian occupation in Iran. The article also noted how the December 1917 Bolshevik exposure and denunciation of secret Entente treaties helped counter Anglo-Russian plans for Iran's dismemberment.[18] Consequently *Kaveh* became more vociferous in its call for the British to evacuate their armies from Iran.[19]

The above developments were crucial in preserving Iran's postwar national independence. Even forty years later, Taqizadeh still saw the Russian Revolution as "the greatest historic event affecting Iran during the past one hundred and fifty years. Without a doubt, if not for the Russian Revolution neither Iran nor Turkey would have existed after WWI."[20] Imperial Germany's commitment to Iranian sovereignty became null with the fall of the Second Reich. But the Soviet pledge at Brest-Litovsk was reiterated by Lenin several times, and eventually reaffirmed in the 1921 Soviet-Iranian Treaty. *Kaveh*'s second series published the entire text of the 1921 treaty, praising it as a highly positive change, in contrast to tsarist policies toward Iran.[21] The new Soviet-Iranian relations were notable also in their contrast to the postwar settlement Britain was trying to impose on Iran. The Allies did not allow Iran to officially participate at the Versailles Conference, while the British continued their occupation, trying to turn Iran into a semiprotectorate via a 1919 treaty proposal that was highly detested and ultimately rejected by Iranian nationalists, who received backing from the Soviet Union.

Back in 1919 Berlin, *Kaveh*'s socialist leanings found new impetus when the German Reich was replaced by a social-democratic republic. *Kaveh* then began to exhibit a new ideological eclecticism that foreshadowed the future confluence of Marxism and Iranian nationalism. The rhetoric of its 1919 articles, for example, combined homage to French socialist leader Jean Jaurès with praise for Sa'di and Zoroaster.[22] Two long articles on Bolshevism in ancient Iran depicted pre-Islamic religious reformer Mazdak as a champion of socialism, citing the Shahnameh's allegedly similar approval of Mazdak.[23] Another article was devoted to Marx, highly praising his intellectual contribution.[24]

Thus, by the time *Kaveh*'s first series unfolded, members of the Berlin Circle had observed firsthand and reacted in writing to some of the twentieth century's most dramatic and fateful political and ideological upheavals. They witnessed the unfolding of the Russian Revolution, the collapse of the German and Ottoman empires, and revolutionary upheaval in Germany and Central Europe. With great anxiety, many of these men have described how Europe's three powerful empires (Germany, Russia, and Austria-Hungary) collapsed, while worker-soldier soviets fought moderate socialists in Berlin and other capitals. Even the less political Mohammad Qazvini would write: "Now is the turn of the socialists. . . . Europe's three emperors are destroyed, while Bolshevism is spreading everywhere like an oil stain."[25]

With the German, Russian, and Ottoman empires mired in civil war and revolution, members of Berlin's Iranian nationalist circle had to quickly rethink their global alliances and, literally, their worldview. While their nationalism faced a powerful new challenge from socialism, they were forced to look either to the Soviet Union or the U.S. as possible allies preventing Iran's total domination by British imperialism. It was in such radically changed circumstances that *Kaveh* launched its second (1920–1922) series, displaying a new nationalist *weltanschauung*, which, in Taqizadeh's (in)famous first-issue editorial, called for "The unqualified acceptance and promotion of European civilization, i.e., absolute surrender to Europe and the adoption of its customs, traditions, order, science, industry, lifestyle, in totality, with the sole exception being language."[26] By this time, Taqizadeh had become a strong advocate of an American presence in Iran. In 1921, he wrote: "For reforms to take their proper course, the main point, in my view, is attracting the Americans to Iran and handing them the administration of affairs. Utmost efforts must be made to draw the U.S. into Iran. Concessions should be given to the U.S. and American advisors must be hired for financial and public affairs, agriculture, trade, roads, telegraph, and American schools must be given full support."[27] Taqizadeh's blatant advocacy of "absolute surrender" to Western civilization, and his concomitant call for placing Iran's "administration of affairs" in American hands, appear diametrically opposed to the axiomatic convictions of modern Iranian nationalism. By the mid-twentieth century, even the most pro-Western politician or intellectual could not openly talk or write this way of Iran's relation to Europe or the United States. During the early 1920s, however, Taqizadeh was far from alone in associating such views with nationalism. According to Jamalzadeh, members of the Berlin Circle "unanimously agreed that, except in religion and language, Iranians must follow Europeans in every other way."[28] At the time, Taqizadeh's call was merely the forceful outcry of an intellectual generation not yet equating "the West" with imperialism, materialism, moral decadence, and an overall predatory intent toward Iran. In a 1918 *Kaveh* article, which seems to both anticipate and respond to Edward Said's arguments in *Orientalism*, Taqizadeh answered the would-be critics of his emerging position of surrender to "Western" intellectual-cum-political authority:

> Some have argued that those who study the nations of Asia and Africa do so with the political motives of the European powers. . . . [But] Some of them [i.e., Orientalists] have been heroes of the weak nations and done great service to them against the interests of their own nations. They have rescued objects by archeology . . . manuscripts have been edited and published . . . all of this has helped the nations of the East to *regain their identity . . . they know more about our history and culture than we do.* . . . Not one Iranian knows Pahlavi . . . it is only because of Europeans who deciphered the old scripts of Avestan, Sanskrit, and Pahlavi that today we know about our kings and ancestors. . . . Iranians must become aware of their ancient culture and their thinkers, artists, and kings *so that they will be aware of their great nation in the past before Islam and of what race they derived from,* how they have reached their current condition, and how *to regain their original greatness as a nation.*[29]

Kaveh's second series then began to introduce a kind of nationalism informed by what the journal itself called a "Western Worldview." A 1921 article entitled "Indian and Greek Worldviews" introduced *Kaveh*'s choice of the Persian term *binesh* for "worldview," corresponding to *"conception du monde"* in French and *"weltanschauung"* in German. The article contrasted "the different worldviews of Western and Eastern nations since ancient times." While the "Western" worldview was secular, materialistic, and rational, the worldview tied to "Eastern philosophy" was spiritual and metaphysical: "Finding these two types in India and Greece respectively, we might call Eastern ways and notions an 'Indian worldview,' while Western forms of reasoning and ideas can be called a 'Greek worldview.'"[30] According to this article, the Indian worldview had shaped Eastern (Asian) cultures, whether Aryan or Semitic, whereas the Greek worldview shaped Europe's Roman, Germanic, and Latin cultures. In modern times, the Indian/Eastern worldview was subjugated to the material superiority of Britain's Western worldview. Iran's "misfortune" was the Indian "origin and essence of its civilization and worldview." Despite their Aryan racial origin, argued *Kaveh*, Iranians had lost contact with the Western worldview, i.e., "the fountainhead and sun of universal knowledge and cultivation." Though originally an Eastern Semitic religion, Christianity had adapted to Greek culture, thus contributing to the progress of European civilization. Unfortunately for Iranians, centuries of unceasing wars against Christian Europe had cut them off from Greek culture during both pre- and post-Islamic eras.[31] Though rudimentary, this paradigmatic articulation of an epistemological chasm between the East and the West provided intellectual underpinnings to *Kaveh*'s urgent call for the adoption of European civilization.

Toward the end of its run, *Kaveh* began referring vaguely to an "Iranian Spirit," which was barely alive and in need of revival through the adoption of Western civilization. This, however, appeared to signal an important transition to the different nationalist politics and worldview soon to be articulated by *Kaveh*'s immediate successors, *Iranshahr*.

Iranshahr: The Spirit of Iran, Critiquing the West and Looking to the East

While *Kaveh* saw Iran's national salvation in the wholesale adoption of Western civilization, a very different view of Iran's relation to the West soon began to take shape in the pages of *Iranshahr*, the Berlin-based periodical that replaced *Kaveh* in 1922. Though sharing certain principles with its predecessor, *Iranshahr* marked a clear departure toward the construction of an Iranian national identity independent from, and even opposed to, Europe. Referring to a folk-heroic leader of an uprising against royal tyranny, the title *Kaveh* hinted at mixing nationalism with socialist tendencies. In contrast, the title *Iranshahr* (Imperial Iran) announced romantic nationalist nostalgia for a lost golden age of pre-Islamic imperial glory. *Iranshahr* published forty-eight issues (1922–1927) under the editorship of Hosain Kazemzadeh (1883–1962), who also changed his own last name to Iranshahr. Born in Tabriz, Kazemzadeh had studied in Istanbul and then resided in France, Belgium, and England. During the First World War, he joined Taqizadeh to write for *Kaveh*. In addition to Kazemzadeh, who wrote almost all editorials, *Iranshahr*'s staff included Rashid Yasami, Taqizadeh, Abbas Eqbal, Moreteza Moshfeq Kazemi, Taqi Arani and Ahmad Farhad. When financial difficulties forced *Iranshahr*'s closure, Kazemzadeh became the supervisor of Iranian students in Germany and eventually settled in Switzerland, where he became preoccupied with theosophical pursuits until the end of his life in 1962.[32]

The worldview that soon emerged in *Iranshahr* clearly reflected intellectual trends then on the rise in Weimar Germany. Briefly, these included a vague metaphysical disposition and attraction to Eastern spirituality; the rejection of materialism and purely secular rationality; belief in racial characteristics and a primordial "national spirit"; dedication to nation-building via the educational cultivation (*bildung*) of "authentic" national culture; and, last but not least, an attempt at formulating a nationalized conception of religion (Islam). First articulated in *Iranshahr*, these notions became axiomatic in early Pahlavi-era nationalism and political culture, though tempered significantly by countervailing authoritarian positivist tendencies.[33]

The opening sentences of the first issue's editorial declared *Iranshahr*'s adherence to a new style of romantic nationalism as the path of Iran's salvation in a world deeply mired in crisis and decline:

We start publishing this magazine at a time when the whole world, and Germany in particular, is shaken by an economic and social crisis and while everyone is trying to save themselves from this backbreaking crisis. . . . Iranshahr magazine will strive to prepare the grounds for the cultivation of the spirit of young and free Iran. It will strive to create the free and pure conditions for the spiritual growth of a new Iranian race. It will expose the secrets of European nations' progress and explain what Iran really needs from European civilization.[34]

In the same issue, a lead article entitled "Orientalism and Occidentalism" marked a departure from *Kaveh*'s defense of a nationalist perspective sustained by Orientalist scholarship. According to this article, while serving Europe's domination of eastern countries, Orientalism had produced an enormous body of knowledge indispensible to humanity for centuries to come. However, and in a reversal of *Kaveh*'s perspective, the article argued for an epistemological break with Orientalism and the construction instead of an "Eastern perspective," which it called "Occidentalism" (*Gharbshenasi*).[35]

Iranshahr's third issue began changing the debate on what Iran needed to take from Europe by focusing instead on which European features were to be rejected. Appropriately titled "Science and Morality," a lead article warned Iranians seeking modernity (*tajadod*) that without "a reform of social morality," the mere adoption of European science and technology led to their further ruin. This was because European civilization itself suffered from a growing malaise of moral decay: "Today, no European nation considers itself fortunate, no one being content with the life they live. Misery and discontent with life are epidemic diseases, while moral corruption is fast spreading among all these nations. . . . Unless their governments find a solution, European nations will fall into conditions similar to those in Iran, because science and technology will not be able to contain 'moral decline.'"[36] Issue no. 4 focused on "Iranian character," claiming each nation had certain fixed characteristics related to both race and culture, i.e., inherited social behavior. Citing the authority of French sociologist and race theorist Gustav Le Bon, it was then argued that Iran needed a cultural and spiritual revolution rather than a political one. This cultural transformation could only come through the deliberate forging of a new, yet authentic national identity:

> To shake up the sleepy and depressed Iran, to make it understand it is still alive and not condemned to death, and to give it a new spirit, making warm and young blood circulate in its veins, we must inject a powerful life-giving messianic elixir into its social body.
> . . . The pages of history and the experience of various nations prove that the only powerful inspiration and ideal for the Iranian nation is indeed "nationality." This means all efforts, thoughts, powers and ideals of the Iranian nation must be focused on the single point of nationality.[37]

However, according to *Iranshahr*, the cultivation of an Iranian "national culture" could be accomplished primarily through a comprehensive project of national education. This approach differed from the soon-to-be-dominant project of forcible nation-building from above under a modern "enlightened despot." Nevertheless, *Iranshahr* shared the nationalist elite's consensus on Iran's need for a newly formed strong centralizing state. Kazemzadeh's editorials, for example, endorsed Reza Khan's anti-Qajar republican campaign.[38]

Meanwhile, *Iranshahr*'s preoccupation with crafting an authentic national culture was taking an increasingly metaphysical turn. By 1924, articles on neo-mystical themes were introducing subjects such as "occult sciences," "animal magnetism," "personal magnetism," "hypnotism," "clairvoyance," and "spiritism." Another area of interest was the blending of modern scientific knowledge with "insights" gleaned from ancient Eastern religions and mysticism. Thus, *Iranshahr*'s increasingly vociferous criticism of Western "materialism" was coupled with a growing appreciation of an ostensibly "spiritual" East, particularly India, as the font of a perennial (mystical) wisdom. This orientation then led to the journal's definition of Iranian national identity as a composite construction whose constituent elements were to be chosen from both Eastern and Western cultures. Significantly, too, this new Iranian national culture was in need of a strong religious dimension, something that *Iranshahr* believed a reformed and modernizing Shi'ism might provide. In an article on "Religion and Nationality," Kazemzadeh already had declared: "In my view, the Shi'i religion has two distinct attributes making it capable of adopting all features of modernity and civilization. First, the openness of the gate of *ijtihad*. . . . Second, for over a thousand years Islam has become an Iranian religion, with its Shi'i form evolving into an Iranian national religion, showing the imprint of the Iranian spirit."[39] The same article made a definitive break with *Kaveh*'s wholesale embracing of European civilization: "We have said repeatedly that Iran should not become Europeanized, in essence or appearance, nor should it remain in its present unfortunate state. Instead, it must make progress, creating the kind of civilization that can be called Iranian."[40] Finally, in a striking passage anticipating the Iranian debates in the 1960s and 1970s on "Westoxication," religion, and national authenticity, Kazemzadeh wrote: "We must scrutinize both Eastern and Western civilizations, adopting their life-giving laws and percepts to create a new civilization, designated as 'Iranian.' This new civilization needs a philosophical foundation. It must be called the 'Philosophy of Unitarianism (*Tawhid*),' incorporating the merits of both Eastern and Western philosophies of civilization."[41] *Iranshahr* also published, more or less regularly, a series of articles on women, a few of which were also by women. The journal's view on the so-called "Woman Question" was the classical conservative nationalist position, soon to be repeated by thinkers like Ahmad Kasravi and modern Islamists. It was summed up in Kazemzadeh's dictum: "Women must remain women!" Basically, women's role and place in the new Iranian nation was to perform their threefold "natural" duties, i.e., being mothers, homemakers, and comforters of men. These "sacred duties" gave women a very high social standing, related to women's "natural" characteristics, such as emotionalism, kindness, and attractiveness.[42]

Conclusion: The Berlin Circle, Authoritarian Nationalism, and the Critique of Europeanism

By the end of the 1920s, most members of the Berlin Circle returned to Iran, where some pursued political careers, while others focused on cultural production. One group, joined by the French- and U.S.-educated Ali-Akbar Siasi

(1895–1990), had already formed the Young Iran Society in 1921. Their program was close to Taqizadeh's vision, calling for a strong secular government, railroad construction, income and property taxes, free elementary education, women's "progress," and adopting "the best features" of Western civilization. Early in his political career, Reza Khan met them, promising to implement what they proposed. But the Young Iran Society soon dissolved, as it became obvious that Reza Shah's modernizing model had no room for independent political organizations. Nevertheless, key proposals of the Berlin Circle remained axiomatic among the nationalist elite and gradually were implemented during the 1930s.[43]

While the cultural nationalism of both *Iranshahr* and *Kaveh* emphasized education, in the German *bildung* tradition, the dominant and official trend of Reza Shah-era nationalism was more positivist, preoccupied with building the nation's material infrastructure, and the forcible transformation of a highly diverse population into uniformly regimented subjects of a modernizing state. The latter trend found exemplary articulation in the ideas of Ali-Akbar Davar (1885–1937), architect of Pahlavi Iran's legal system. A Swiss-educated student of Wilfred Pareto, Davar advocated the forceful implementation of European modernity's material, economic and juridical infrastructure, flatly rejecting the primacy of cultural modernization via education. According to him, "The roots of Western civilization are not schools, libraries and scientists. These are its leaves and branches. The civilization of those who are superior to us is rooted in the railroad."[44]

Davar's authoritarian positivist brand of nationalism also had a precedent in the 1920s Berlin Circle, particularly in *Nameh-ye Farangestan* ("Western Letter"), a periodical published in only 12 issues during 1924 and 1925 and edited by Morteza Moshfeq-Kazemi, who also wrote for both *Kaveh* and *Iranshahr*. However, *Nameh-ye Farangestan* lacked *Iranshahr*'s critical stance toward modern European civilization, and its metaphysical and racialist tendencies. Instead, like *Kaveh*, it was for the wholesale adaptation of European modernity, but in a forcible manner, inspired by fascist Italy. Thus, the first editorial of *Nameh-ye Farangestan* declared: "Let us prepare Iran for a moral revolution changing us from medieval beings into twentieth-century humans. . . . We want to make Iran European. We want to flood Iran with modern civilization. . . . Iran must become Europeanized in body and spirit."[45] Disagreeing with both Nazi and Bolshevik political models, Moshfegh-Kazemi nevertheless rejected modernizing reforms and nation-building via a parliamentary system, advocating instead a "radical" course in the manner of Fascist Italy. He wrote:

by chance I read in the press how Mussolini has accomplished great reforms in Italy, putting an end to that weak country's deplorable conditions; thus gradually I came to believe that in Iran too the only solution is to start by shaking things up by the strong arm [of a leader] knowledgeable both of world affairs and Iranian conditions. . . . Influenced by such ideas, I wrote in [Nameh-ye] Farangestan of the need for an enlightened dictator, familiar with world affairs, who could save Iran.[46]

Authoritarian positivist nationalism, however, did not enjoy total sway under Reza Shah. The views of Ahmad Kasravi (1890–1946), arguably Iran's most original thinker during the 1930s and 1940s, were also linked directly to the mainstream of the Berlin Circle. Directly building on ideas first proposed in *Iranshahr*, Kasravi's critique of "Europeanism," as well as his project of reconstructing religion as nationalist ideology, are arguably the "missing link" between 1920s debates on Iranian national identity, the "Westoxication" discourse of the 1960s and 1970s, and the dominant ideology of the Islamic Republic.[47]

Notes

1. A number of studies in German have covered aspects of this topic, but they remain virtually unnoticed by scholarship outside Germany. See, for example, Ahmad Mahrad, *Die Deutsch-Persischen Beziehungen von 1918–1933* (Frankfurt: 1974), and Bahman Nirumand and Gabriele Yonan, *Iraner in Berlin* (Berlin: Die Ausländerbeauftrage des Senats, 1994). The best and virtually only study in Persian is Jamshid Behnam, *Berlaniha* (Tehran: Farzan, 2000), whose author cites the above works but says he has not used them, 224. On "counter-Enlightenment" and Iranian modernity, see Ali Mirsepassi, *Political Islam, Iran, and the Enlightenment: Philosophies of Hope and Despair* (Cambridge: Cambridge University Press: 2011). For a recent study in German see Hamid Tafazoli, *Der deutsche Persien-diskurs: Von der frühen Neuzeit bis in das neunzehnten Jarhundert* (Bielefeld: Aisthesis, 2007).
2. Todd Kontje, *German Orientalisms* (Ann Arbor: The University of Michigan Press, 2004), 4, 7. On the concept of "culture" in modern German thought see, e.g., Michael C. Carhart, *The Science of Culture in Enlightenment Germany* (Cambridge, MA: Harvard University Press, 2008), and Harold Mah, *Enlightenment Phantasies: Cultural Identity in France and Germany, 1750–1914* (Ithaca, NY: Cornell University Press, 2003).
3. Kontje, 64–77.
4. Ibid., 64–77, 82–83, 121. See also Rudi Matthee, "The Imaginary Realm: Europe's Enlightenment Image of Early Modern Iran," *Comparative Studies of South Asia, Africa and the Middle East* vol. 30, no. 3 (2010), 449–462, quoted on p. 457.

5. This is the conclusion of Reza Zia-Ebrahimi in "Self-Orientalization and Dislocation: The Uses and Abuses of the 'Aryan' Discourse in Iran," *Iranian Studies* vol. 44, no. 4 (July 2011), 445–472; quoted on p. 445. See also Matthee, "The Imaginary Realm," 459. On the Aryan discourse, see Kontje, *German Orientalisms*, 108–109, and Raymond Schwab, Gene Patterson-Black, and Victor Reinking, trans., *The Oriental Renaissance: Europe's Rediscovery of India and the East, 1680–1880* (New York: Columbia University Press, 1984).

6. Although the first volume of Oswald Spengler's *The Decline of the West* appeared in 1918, Spengler had finished the book's first draft by 1914. Arthur Herman, *The Idea of Decline in Western History* (New York: The Free Press, 1997), 241–242.

7. Ibid., 236–240.

8. Afshin Marashi, *Nationalizing Iran: Culture, Power and the State* (Seattle and London: The University of Washington Press, 2008), 53.

9. Fereydun Adamiyat, *Ideolozhi-e nehzat-e mashrutiyat-e Iran* [The Ideology of Iran's Constitutional Movement] (Tehran: Payam, 1976), 30, 32.

10. Adamiyat, 274–281. This point is argued most forcefully by Mashallah Ajudani, *Mashrute-ye Irani* (Tehran: Akhtaran, 2004).

11. On this generation, Behnam, *Berlaniha*, writes (61), "Most of the first generation stayed social democrats committed to Enlightenment ideas. They had come to Berlin as nationalist and constitutionalist followers of a Social Democratic party. Their cooperation with Germans was for the cause of Iranian freedom and not German expansionism."

12. The exact membership of the National Defense Committee is not clear. See Ervand Abrahamian, *Iran Between Two Revolutions* (Princeton: Princeton University Press, 1982), 111, and Abdol-Hosein Sheybani, *Khaterat-e mohajerat* (Tehran: Shirazeh, 1999), 22–23, and the documents cited on 708–713.

13. Behnam, *Berlaniha*, 12, 41–42.

14. On this generational change, Behnam writes: "Most of the first generation stayed social democrats committed to Enlightenment ideas. They had come to Berlin as nationalist and constitutionalist followers of a Social Democratic party. Their cooperation with Germans was for the cause of Iranian freedom and not German expansionism." 61.

15. *Kaveh*, series 1, vol. 1, no. 1, 4. 24 January 1916.

16. *Kaveh*, series 1, vol. 1, no. 2, 8. 8 February 1916.

17. *Kaveh*, series 1, vol. 2, no. 22, 15 August 1917. 2. Sheybani had an official assignment from the Tehran government. See the document cited in Sheybani, *Khaterat-e mohajerat*, 725.

18. *Kaveh*, series 1, vol. 2, no. 24, 15 January 1918. On the significance of Brest-Litovsk treaty to Iranians, see Oliver Bast, *Almaniya dar Iran* (Tehran: Shirazeh, 1998), 165–166, 185–186.

19. See, for example, *Kaveh*, series 1, vol. 3, no. 25, 15 February, 1918.

20. Hasan Taqizadah, *Khatabah-e Aqa-e Sayyad Hasan Taqizadah* (Tehran: Mehregan, 1959), 67.

21. *Kaveh*, series 2, vol. 2, No. 8, 6 August 1921, published the entire text of the 1921 Iran-Soviet Treaty.

22. The editorial of *Kaveh*, series 1, vol. 4, no. 34, 1 March 1919, was on "the Victory of Social Democracy/Socialism in Germany" in 1919. It had a brief but fairly accurate

history of the rise of German socialism and of its program, and ended with the fall of the Second Reich, the failure of Germany's socialist revolution, and the emergence of Ebert's Social-Democratic republican regime.

23. *Kaveh*, series 1, vol. 5, no. 3, 21 March 1920 and nos. 4–5, 21 May 1920.

24. *Kaveh*, series 1, vol. 5, no. 7, 17 July 1920.

25. Quoted in Behnam, *Berlaniha*, 52.

26. *Kaveh*, series 2, vo. 1, no. 1, 11 January 1921, 2.

27. Quoted in Behnam, *Berlaniha*, 54.

28. Ibid., 56.

29. Quoted in Marashi, *Nationalizing Iran: Culture, Power and the State*, 81, emphases added.

30. *Kaveh*, series 2, vol. 2, no. 10, 3 October 1921, 1.

31. Ibid., 2–3.

32. Behnam, *Berlaniha*, 89–91.

33. On the rise of a science-based ideology in early twentieth-century Iran, see Cyrus Schayegh, *Who Is Knowledgeable Is Strong: Science, Class, and the Formation of Modern Iranian Society, 1900–1950* (Berkeley, Los Angeles, and London: University of California Press, 2009).

34. *Iranshahr*, vol. 1, no. 1, October 1922.

35. "Today, while Eastern countries need to adopt the complex and multifaceted aspects of Western civilization, we think it's necessary that individuals know the conditions of Western countries and their civilization, having learned of these while traveling or studying abroad, or learning of Western nations." Ibid., 13–14.

36. *Iranshar*, vol. 1, no. 3. December 1922.

37. *Iranshahr*, vol. 1, no. 4. January 1923.

38. *Iranshahr*, vol. 2, nos. 5–6 and 7. February 1924.

39. *Iranshahr*, vol. 3, no. 1, October 1924 3.

40. Ibid.

41. Quoted in Behnam, *Berlaniha*, 174.

42. Articles on women began in vol. 1, no. 2, and continued more or less regularly from vol. 2, no. 4 onward.

43. Behnam, *Berlaniha*, 113–115. See also Shahrokh Meskoub, *Dastan-e adabiat va sargozasht-e 'ejtema'* (Tehran: Farzan, 1993), 26–30.

44. Kaveh Bayat, "Andishe-ye siasi-ye Davar va ta'sis-e dowlat-e modern dar Iran," *Gof-o-Gu* no. 2 (1993): 116–133, quote on 122. See also Baqer Aqeli, *Davar va Adlieh* (Tehran: Elmi, 1990).

45. Quoted in Behnam, 97–98.

46. Ibid., 67–68.

47. For the most comprehensive study of Kasravi, see *Iran Nameh*, vol. xx, nos. 2–3 (2002); the article by Mohammad Tavakoli-Targhi notes the significance of Kasravi's "Europeanism" discourse and its impact on Islamist thought. A short article in the mid-1970s had recognized Kasravi as the originator of the "Westoxication" discourse. See Asil, "Kasravi va mas'aleh-e sharq va gharb," *Negin* no. 130 (March 1976), 29–37.

CHAPTER 4

The Love That Dare Not Be Translated: Erasures of Premodern Sexuality in Modern Persian Mysticism

WENDY DESOUZA

Premodern mystical poetry has become subject to a display of puritanical morality.[1] By the late nineteenth century, Iranian and European scholars of mysticism began this process by censoring homoerotic tropes such as the male Beloved, which, despite its varied earthly and ethereal meanings, was either feminized or designated as an "allegory." In the first instance, early European scholars of Sufi poetry translated male Beloveds as female. For example, a "Turk" (a Turkish male slave) was changed to a "blooming maiden."[2] Notable twentieth-century Iranian scholars also objected to the homoerotic content in medieval *ghazals* ("love poetry"), yet because they could not deny its existence through translation, they began to justify its continued presence as a mere "stand-in" for heterosexual practice. Throughout the twentieth century, Iranians were asked to interpret same-sex desire as "allegory" when they encountered erotic references to love between a prepubescent male and an older or socially superior male.[3] And ever since the late nineteenth century, there has been a growing tension in academic writing between modern strategies of defining and restricting sexuality on one hand, and an ambivalence toward homoeroticism on the other.

Mystical poetry thus became central to debates over normative male sexuality, precisely for two reasons. First, a number of Iranian intellectuals perceived the creation of a national literary canon as an important step in nation-building by properly molding citizens to "think modern" and foster national brotherhood. It was also vital to the project of redefining and resuscitating authentic and "native" traditions. In this vein, Iranian intellectuals shared a similar outlook to other nationalist intellectuals in that, in the words of scholar Heinrich Seeba, they believed "a nation's collective sense of imagined history is . . . inscribed in images that evoke historical continuity and social unity."[4] Sufi poetry played a dominant role in that vision, considering that it was produced during the premodern "golden age" of Hafez. Undoubtedly some of the finest works ever to be produced in world literature were penned in Persian. Second, since the ideas inherent to premodern mystical poetry greatly contradicted the moral inclinations of scholars, educators, and translators, discussions ensued as to whether it promoted a positive or negative image of Persian sexuality, and whether it should, if at all, be taught to the next generation.

The following discussion will consider how debates over mysticism become truly a debate over what modern sexuality should be, and little about what premodern sexuality actually was. By considering the trope of exoticism in European literature, I will attempt to demonstrate the various incarnations and distortions of Persian mysticism and "Persian sexuality" as conceived by some of the most gifted scholars in the field of Iranian studies. Furthermore, I will also discuss Iranian scholars' views on modern sexuality and how Persian literature was seen to be the basis for sculpting national morality.

Background

In his seminal work *On Human Diversity: Nationalism, Racism, and Exoticism in French Thought*, Tzvetan Todorov studied notions of the "exotic" in French intellectual thought pioneered by writers like Rousseau and, later, Chateaubriand. Todorov maintained that French writers conceptualized exotic lands as an "othering" strategy to advance a more relevant self-critique of local French politics and society, and foreign societies were a foil for either proving or disproving the merits of French life.[5] Todorov surmised that depictions of foreign lands and peoples in French literature were "less a valorization of the other than an act of self-criticism."[6]

Todorov's discussion of exoticism attenuates the academic study of mysticism emerging in the late nineteenth century. From the Romantic period until the institutionalization of Islamic and Iranian studies by the mid-twentieth century, academic and popular writings on Persian mysticism (Sufism) represented little more than an internal critique of the deficiencies of contemporary Western society. Alternatively, Persian mystical poetry was construed as a portal to a world in which sexual activity for men was unrestricted and unburdened by social mores. French and English writers at the turn of the century considered the sexual practices of Persians, for example, as falling "in a state of nature," and depending on one's outlook, this vice or virtue differed from the Christian morality of continental Europe.

Though for many the "East" was depicted in poetry as a place of sexual excess, it was also seen as exceptionally spiritual and antinomian. Early glosses of Persian poetry, based on Persian translations into Latin in the seventeenth century and later English, French, and German, present a cache of images consistent with post-Enlightenment views of the "spiritual East" as the opposite of the "material West."[7] Seventeenth- and eighteenth-century philologists of Persian, similar to early scholars who wrote on "Hindu" India, conceived of a "Sufi" Persia defined by its poetic tradition. Linguists based in India first coined the term "Sufism" to refer to the dervishes and mystical orders they encountered; later, this term encompassed the poetry of Hafez and Sa'di that was popularized in Europe.[8]

English Persianists such as Thomas Hyde (1636–1703) and Sir William Jones[9] (1746–1794), and the French scholar Barthélemy d'Herbelot, who published *Bibliothèque Orientale* (1697), were among the first European linguists to present "Eastern spirituality" as an exotic ideal. At the turn of the twentieth century, Sa'di's *Golestan* was sharply contrasted with Francis Bacon's *Essays*: ". . . the Englishman is clear, cold and sometimes cynical, while the Persian is more spiritual, though not less acute, and has the fervor of the poet which Bacon lacks, and the religious devotion which the 'Essays' altogether miss."[10] While many writers praised the ethereal qualities of Sufi imagery — not to mention the "marvelous depth, the spiritual insight, the tenderness and power of expression" — Persian literature was still valued for its sensuality, not just for its higher aspirations of union with God.

In the eighteenth century, European writers contributed to the popularity of mystical texts by writing fabricated "eye-witness" travel accounts in the tradition of *The Travels of Sir John Mandeville* or Montesquieu's *Lettres Persanes* (1721).[11] These fictional accounts exploited the public's thirst for the exotic by writing about harems and hypersexualized Persian men. Persian mysticism increasingly became associated with sexual deviance, and began to elicit strong moral opposition. Sufi poetry drew a strong reaction from English religious conservatives who believed its erotic content was harmful to Christianity.[12] Their criticisms, however, could not prevent Baron de Montesquieu, Voltaire, and Victor Hugo from starting what would be referred to as the Oriental Movement.[13] These writers read *Les Mille et Une Nuits* (in English, *1,001 Nights* or *The Arabian Tales*; in Arabic, *Alf layla wa layla*), which informed their views of Eastern and Muslim sexuality. Though *1,001 Nights* was thought to be an authoritative resource detailing Eastern mores, and more specifically, Eastern sexual practice, more recently Sahar Amer has shown how translations were altered to suit a European erotic context (in this specific case, Amer discussed the erasure of lesbian preference in the original story).[14]

Persian intellectuals who began traveling in greater numbers to France in the mid- to late nineteenth century were shocked by Europe's eroticized image of them. The most damaging portrait of Persians was *The Adventures of Hajji Baba of Ispahan* (1824),[15] written by the British writer James Morier (1780-1849). In the mid-twentieth century, both Muhammad Qazvini and Seyyed Hasan Taqizadeh wrote in their memoirs that *Hajji Baba* had distorted European views of Persians. In stark contrast, for the public it was generally believed to be a work based on the writer's firsthand account of actual events, and it became popular "not least for its sexual eccentricity fondly supposed in 1824 to be peculiar to Oriental races."[16]

In nineteenth-century Britain and France, readers did not distinguish between *1,001 Nights*, *Hajji Baba*, and the *Divan* of Hafez—a translation of Arabic and Indo-Persian folk stories, a fictionalized travel tale, and a translation of mystical poetry from Persian, respectively. In terms of the public at large, translations of Persian medieval poetry and fictionalized Oriental tales were conflated. Hafez and Sa'di were found side by side on the same bookshelf as novels like *Hajji Baba*, under the rubric of "Oriental." Based on their common association, one may surmise that the first genre's popularity led to interest in the second, and vice versa. Popular writers stylistically edited and embellished Persian stories, relying on translations, since they had little to no knowledge of the original source language.

The early circulation of Persian texts in Europe and, later, in the United States, contributed to the overall notion of a "spiritual" and "erotic" Persia. Not coincidentally, the interest that mystical texts generated led to a growing curiosity about Persia "as it really is." By the late nineteenth century, the public had greater expectations of writers, who were now supposed to have intimate knowledge of Persians and their "eccentricities," and to write about them with the utmost candor. The British pioneered this genre, due to their increased physical presence in the region, and, as Morier did earlier, they used their alleged regional expertise (which was greatly exaggerated) to sell their views of an authentic Persia.

Though French access to Persia was restricted due to British and Russian control of Central Asia,[17] French scholars began to write about Sufi spirituality in the nineteenth century based on one of two thematic strategies: the erotic or the monastic. The erotic tradition can be found in many translations of the Persian *ghazal* and other "love poetry." John Payne's 1901 complete translation of the *Divan*, for example, presented a Hafez who had lived in the world: "For Payne, Hafiz is the ultimate rebel, drunk continually on the juice of the grape (in a physical sense), a womanizer, a debaucher, a libertine who through his dissipation becomes honest with himself and others and so can see the truth of all that is around him."[18] Payne's translation affirmed Hafez's human qualities as a mystic, and Hafez's bodily pleasures are explicit in this rendition. Similarly, Sir Richard Francis Burton (1821–1890) also celebrated Eastern erotica in his writings. In his rewriting of Sa'di's *Golestan*, circa 1888, he was not shy to note allusions to same-sex practice—in the story of Sultan Mahmud and his love for his male slave, Iyaz, he clarified the gender in a text featuring a nude image of Iyaz: "Joseph is the paragon of male beauty in Persian poetry."[19]

By the late nineteenth century, another textual strategy emerged that was decidedly monastic—avoiding references to bodily pleasure, or at the very least calling it exclusively "symbolic." Interest in Sufism as an alternative spirituality led to a surge in publications throughout Western Europe and the United States. This eventually inspired movements as diverse as English Romanticism, Goethe's Promethean movement against Rationalism, and the American Transcendentalism of Ralph Waldo Emerson and Henry David Thoreau.[20] Nineteenth-century linguists and philologists believed that mystical poetry was tarnished by the erotic tradition, and to rectify this, French and English scholars later emphasized the spiritual aspects of these texts and contemplated the true esoteric meanings—*gnosis*, or the "wisdom of the heart." Renowned translator of Hafez Gertrude Bell (1868–1926) claimed that in Sufism, "the highest good to which the Sufis can attain is the annihilation of the actual—*to forget that they have a separate existence* [my emphasis], and to lose themselves in the Divinity as a drop of water is lost in the ocean."[21] More recently, William C. Chittick, in his translation work on Molavi, mentioned the irreconcilability of man's love and "true love" (*'eshq-e haqiqi* or "love for God") and "derivative love" (*'eshq-e majazi*, "love for anything else.") He stated: "The Sufi has already discovered that there is only one Beloved; he sees all derivative love as cold and unreal."[22]

Scholarly Mysticism

The monastic tradition found its way into the Academy in the mid-nineteenth century. Attempting to separate from the long history of Oriental exotica, scholars based their interpretation of mystical poetry on Christian or secular sensibilities. Often they effaced the identity of the male Beloved, and tropes of male same-sex desire were thereby quietly removed from the arena of contemplative spirituality. Paul Smith, in his detailed survey of gender translations by British scholars of Hafez's *ghazal* (no. 8), noted the transformation of a male Turkish slave into a "lovely maid"; "blooming maid"; "maid" or "nymph"; or

"Turkish maid."[23] Though the Persian language does not have gender desig-
nations, the "Turk" in this particular section of Hafez's poem is commonly
known to refer to a male lover, where terms like *gholam* and *shahed* referred to
male slave boys. According to Dehkhoda, "The use of Turks as sex slaves was
so common that after the tenth century CE, the term 'Turk' became synonymous with the beloved or *shahed*."[24]

Scholars who were disquieted by same-sex eros, or perhaps anticipated
a negative reaction from their readership, not only changed the gender of
the male Beloved but also on occasion removed gender references altogether.
English and French translators sometimes replaced "he" and "she" designa-
tions of the Beloved with "thee" and "thou." The work of Walter Leaf in 1898,
moreover, was deemed a truly "spiritual" translation for removing any references to human desire (i.e., gendered pronouns) in the *Divan*; when male pronouns are used, "He" was preferable to "he." Such so-called "spiritual" translations also imitated Biblical language (e.g., "Thy"). In the process, scholars
insisted on the asexual, genderless Beloved.[25]

Scholarly writings on mysticism clash with the original poetry, revealing a
contradiction between the behaviors of medieval Sufi saints and the modern
need for an asexual piety. In Annemarie Schimmel's book *Mystical Dimensions
of Islam*, she called Louis Massignon's work on the tenth-century mystic al-
Hallaj a triumph for depicting "the mystery of loving union . . . celebrated in
verses *free of any trace of the symbolism of profane love* [my emphasis]."[26] Schimmel's praise of Massignon took for granted that removing references to the
"profane" was an important scholarly objective. Schimmel had also noted that
the early influence of Sir William Jones led to "rather absurd views in wild
confusion" among the reading public. In her assessment, English-speaking
Orientalists took more literal approaches to the text, and thus "Hafiz's poetical imagery—unfortunately mostly taken at face value—has largely colored
the Western image of Sufism."[27] The implication was that English translations emphasized desires of the flesh, which formed the public's overall view
of Persian mysticism as a symbol of hedonism.

Though mystical poetry contained numerous types of lovers, Schimmel
seemed transfixed by the idea that divine love was the only *legitimate* Sufi
desire. She referred to the mystic al-Hallaj as a "model of suffering" and "a
symbol for both suffering and unitive experience, but also for a lover's greatest
sin: to divulge the secret of his love."[28] This is not the first instance in which
modern scholarship on Sufism reproduced the ambiguity of the original text.
But, in other places, Schimmel was open to the idea of earthy desires: "[I]t
seems futile to look for either a purely mystical or a purely profane interpretation of the poems of Hafiz, Jami or 'Iraqi—their ambiguity is intended, the

oscillation between the two levels is consciously maintained."[29] In this instance, Schimmel appeared more willing to acknowledge that both mystical and profane interpretations were valid.

Schimmel also wrote about profane love with regard to same-sex eros. In her lecture series "Deciphering the Signs of God: A Phenomenological Approach to Islam," she asserted that the infamous same-sex romance between Iyaz and Sultan Mahmud served as a *primary metaphor* for man and God throughout the Muslim world.[30] During one of her Gifford Lectures (1991–1992), she explained the Muslim appreciation in premodern writings of male beauty, particularly that of the Prophet Muhammad, whose physical attributes, along with other qualities, became a source of admiration. Incidentally, for premodern writers, in poetic verses, hagiographies, and even art, holy and powerful men are extraordinarily handsome.

While at times openly admitting to the homoerotic tendencies in Sufism, however, Schimmel disavowed this in her discussion on Molavi and his love for Shams: "This was the meeting of two mature men, a friendship that had nothing 'romantic' about it, although there are sweet, lyrical verses addressing Shams—rather, this association was timeless, mythical."[31] While the love affair between Molavi and Shams is generally known among educated Iranians, Schimmel instead argued that theirs was a non-romantic friendship. As a whole, Schimmel's position on same-sex desire was inconsistent.

Modern scholars like Schimmel wanted to distinguish their work from the earlier tradition of erotic poetry by focusing on the question of divine love.[32] Some argued that resolving this question was the goal of Sufism itself. Henry Corbin discussed this idea in his theory of the transfiguration of Eros, an idea inspired by the writings of Russian philosopher Boris Vysheslavtsev in *Éthique de l'Éros*, which Corbin claimed was an ideal process of changing profane love into divine love. Corbin argued that in Sufi literature, it was not only possible but preferable for the wayfarer to transcend his or her own carnal desires toward the ultimate goal of union between seeker and the Beloved.[33] In other words, profane or human love was given a provisional status, since it inhibited a seeker's quest for unity with the Divine.

From the standpoint of translation, in both Schimmel and Corbin's statements there is no explicit justification for removing or "moving beyond" the profane as a necessary step in conveying the Persian text's meanings in English or French. Since the essence of the text is spiritual, one must erase references to human desire, unless they are qualified, or accompanied by a symbolic interpretation.[34]

The emphasis on transcending the mundane world toward a greater, all-encompassing reality, according to McGlathery, "is the identifying stamp of

Neoplatonic criticism."[35] In his exhaustive study of the German artist E. T. A. Hoffmann (1776–1822), McGlathery asserted that Hoffmann found German literature distinctive in its approach to transcendent faith, which had very important implications for modern sexuality. The author's main argument is that Hoffmann wrote about sexual sublimation or "substitution fantasies . . . especially of the sort resulting from persecution complexes related to suppressed sexual guilt." The author situated his writings with the Neoplatonic spiritualism of the Napoleonic period in Germany, an intellectual movement that countered empiricist, rationalist, dualist, and materialist traditions:

> If one asks what major theme or character Hoffmann found in German literature that he did not find in foreign authors, it was a peculiarly Neoplatonic mode of sexual sublimation or the type of the mystical or spiritualistic dreamer. . . . It was largely left to German authors to develop the type of the thoroughly metaphysical dreamer, who transformed desire into a quest for mystical union with nature or transcendent powers. . . . The cultural origin of this new German or Wertherian hero evidently lay partly in a traditional piety, which required that transcendent faith, not "all-conquering Desire," should emerge triumphant at the end of the hero's adventures, as well as in the peculiarly mystical and Neoplatonic bent of German Christianity.[36]

The above insights suggest that the underlying sexual psychology found in German literature in the late eighteenth and nineteenth centuries is informed by modern Christian notions of piety. In the modern period, sexual desire was transformed into a more legitimate and heroic quest for mystical knowledge. The pious German tradition was then contrasted with the licentious French novel, which was seen as a crass "exposure of parts of the body and sexual acts [that were] an element of arousal for the reader."[37] One of the main differences between medieval and modern Neoplatonist thought was the presence or absence of sexual desire in the text. Partly as a consequence of modern sexual ethics, scholars later censured references to bodily pleasure.[38] Foucault's thesis addressed this development in literature, proposing that, by the beginning of the seventeenth century, it was "necessary to subjugate [sex] at the level of language, control its free circulation in speech, expunge it from the things that were said, and extinguish the words that rendered it too visibly present."[39]

The tradition of "divine" and "profane" also figures into religious and secular intellectual trends of twentieth-century Europe, where new concerns over "drunkenness" and alternative sexualities appear in full force. The significant political and cultural movements occurring at the turn of the twentieth century had a palpable impact on the study of Persian mystical texts. In France, this coincided with the decree of 1905, when the government removed financial support for religious institutions and drastically decreased the presence of Catholicism in public life. This, *inter alia*, led to the secular study of religion, which, along with France's heavily invested role in North Africa, led to even greater scholarship on Islam and Islamic civilization. The historian of French Indology Roland Lardinois stated that the most prominent scholars of Oriental religions were intellectuals primarily from Protestant and Jewish backgrounds, or the occasional "reconverted" Catholic like Louis Massignon, who created their own unique spirituality. Incidentally, contemporary scholars within the field of Islamology maintain that the difference between Massignon and Henry Corbin's approaches lay in their personal religious convictions—Massignon was a dedicated Catholic who searched for ecumenical models of tolerance, and Corbin a "mystical philosopher" and "Protestant theologian."

Despite the removal of religion, religious ideas still held sway in the Academy and in the field of mysticism. For instance, Louis Massignon drew many parallels between Christian and Muslim mystics in his scholarship. Moreover, al-Hallaj, the tenth-century mystic and the subject of Louis Massignon's three-volume magnum opus, was for him the spiritual presence that "saved" him.[40] The theme of martyrdom and Christlike suffering also appealed to British scholar Edward Pocock, who was intrigued by 'Attar's description of al-Hallaj as a "model of suffering." Other scholars also cited al-Hallaj by way of 'Attar as a Christlike figure who rebelled against orthodox Islam.[41]

The nineteenth and early twentieth-century comparative study of mysticisms, in the words of Cyprian Rice, "make possible a welding of religious thought between East and West, a vital ecumenical commingling and understanding which will prove ultimately to be, in the truest sense, on both sides, a return to origins, to the original unity."[42] The search for common origins and unity among Europeans who had bitterly fought sectarian wars for centuries and whose religious prejudices continued to seethe below the surface spawned numerous writings on the exemplary moral behavior of the wise Sufi—a model for contemporary scholars. As a matter of course, the invention of exotic spirituality, or "Sufism," in fact clashed with Sufi literature itself, which had numerous references to lewd, embarrassing, or improper moral behavior. To rectify this, scholars of mysticism employed esoteric language for interpreting allegorical meanings.[43]

William Chittick, for example, explained that the trope of drunkenness in mystical texts was deliberately used to shock and confuse readers and audiences, creating skepticism toward officially proscribed moral behavior. In this scenario, the Sufi poet subverted official injunctions against the drinking of wine as a rhetorical device. Here Chittick maintained that poets used "imagery that shocks the conventionally pious and flies in the face of juridical and theological discourse."[44] He also stated that the Sufi was "inwardly drunk with God and outwardly sober with the world. . . . The world is the domain of doing what is right and proper, and this needs to be established in terms of a clear distinction between do's and don'ts."[45] In these above statements, "drunkenness" is emptied of its multiple meanings, and he denied that the poet might have actually sanctioned wine. The problem seems to lie in Chittick's assumption that wine inebriation violates the mystical quest, and that references to "drunkenness" therefore require a highly speculative interpretation. While seeming to celebrate the Sufi uses of drunkenness to challenge the "conventionally pious," he claimed that this boldness did not extend to the alehouse. His position is even clearer in his later statement on 'Attar, Rumi and Jami, poets who "were wholly innocent in their use of dangerous imagery."[46] In this way, Chittick asserted that Sufi poets are, first, naive about the many ways in which their works are read, and second, that their use of the trope of "drunkenness" has no correlation to lived experience.[47]

Ernest Renan (1823–1892), philosopher of nationhood and modernity, blended his role as scholar and preacher by declaring himself a "[missionary] of higher values" entrusted with bestowing a "higher culture" upon the masses, and scholars of Islamic studies in France by the mid-nineteenth century saw themselves in similar terms. Louis Massignon, whose life bespoke a struggle with same-sex desire, is a case study for uncovering attitudes toward normative sexuality at the turn of the century.[48] Rather than simply erase "dangerous imagery," Massignon's unique contribution was to create a way of writing about Persian mysticism that nuanced the original erotic meanings.

Iranians and Iranian Studies

Persian scholars of the nineteenth century were more explicit in their objections to erotic tropes in premodern poetry. Criticisms of Sufism first appeared in the mid-nineteenth century, most notably those of Mirza Fath 'Ali Akhundzadeh and Mirza Aqa Khan Kermani.[49] Though premodern Islamicate writings occasionally associated Sufism with pederasty and opium smoking, in the modern period Kermani continued to claim that "[Sufis'] sonnets about roses and nightingales have encouraged the youth to pursue pederasty and booze . . . it was the otherworldly mysticism and Sufism of Sheikh Iraqi, Maghrebi and others which has produced so many lazy, spineless, passive beggars."[50] In this selection, Kermani not only accused Sufis of immoral behavior tied to "pederasty and booze," but he also connected these practices with modern concerns about decadence. Pederasty and booze had always been prohibited from a religious perspective, and though it was often assumed that the Sufi practice of gazing at male youths was tied to celibacy rituals, Shiʻa clerics often criticized this as sexual transgression, or alternatively, the sin of celibacy, since sacred marriage was preferred to abstinence.[51]

Modern reformers distanced themselves from the ʻulama because of their stance against religious dogmatism, and raised their objections to Sufism from the perspective of wastefulness. Glimpses of a similar critique, according to Babayan, can be seen in premodern literature as early as the Safavid period under Shah Tahmasp, who outlined a moral code that challenged Sufi practices of pederasty or celibacy that "reduced men to a state of inactivity."[52] To modern reformers, these references were not mere allegories but real phenomena, temptations that were encouraged by reading mystical poetry. The logic of the argument, essentially, was that if youth were preoccupied with idle pursuits like reading poetry or excessive sexual activity, they shirked their role in nation-building and halted scientific progress.[53]

The accusation of pederasty had been a rhetorical device used to discredit public and religious figures for some time, but why was poetry also now to blame? It should be noted that there was a general attitude during the late nineteenth century, found in Edward Browne's writings, that most pre-Qajar poetry was "thoroughly decadent."[54] Persian reformists defined decadence as the immorality of court life, such as the laziness, hedonism, and sexual promiscuity of the Qajars. Court poetry was then associated with court excesses.

We can also locate here the logical starting point for modern criticisms of Sufism and Sufi orders, which, along with the ʻulama, became symbols of the ancien régime—in Persia, the collaboration of state and religion. Reformists thus framed their criticisms of religion based on "reason" versus "superstition." In the early decades of the twentieth century, writings on Sufism and sexuality proliferate, and this provides us with a rich body of material for explaining the growing suspicion toward mystical poetry.

The post–First World War generation of Iranian intellectuals publicly confronted the erotic tradition to varying degrees. Among those living in France and Germany, this was the first time that many began to question whether mystical writings deserved to be part of the national literary canon, most notably the statesman-scholar Seyyed Hasan Taqizadeh and renowned historian Ahmad Kasravi.[55] These two prolific writers associated reading Persian ghazals with opium smoking, sloth, premodern backwardness, irrationality, upper-class indulgence, the ignorance of the masses, and male same-sex practice. Of course, as mentioned above, this was not the first time that Sufi orders were accused of same-sex practice (specifically sodomy and pederasty), since it was believed that it was condoned in the homosocial and sequestered space of the Sufi orders (*khaneqahs*). In the modern period, it was now clearly defined as a reason (along with many others) for the dangerous effects of Sufi poetry.

Writing a few decades after Taqizadeh, Kasravi represents another critical position on mystical poetry.[56] In an essay written in 1943 entitled "What is Hafez Saying?" (*Hafez Che Miguyad?*), Kasravi stated that the poetry of Hafez was irrational, nihilistic, and hedonistic. He "demystified" Hafez by saying that all premodern poets wrote their stanzas (*bayts*) based on rhyming couplets, and were not at all trying to form coherent thoughts. Kasravi specifically targeted Hafez because of his popularity among Iranians, which he claimed allowed nihilism and fatalism to flourish in Iran and perpetuated Iran's subservience to the West. Moreover, the problem he had with mysticism's irrationality was combined with his views on certain types of sexual practice. Implicit in his writings is the assumption that reading mystical poetry led to "indulgences" like sodomy. In this regard, Kasravi accused men of being submissive to colonialism: "[European Orientalists] are people who wish ill for the East, and they want all Easterners to be just like Hafez, that is, to be satisfied with a corner in the tavern and spend time in drinking wine and sodomy. . . . They want to make machines for themselves, and have soldiers, pilots and paratroopers from the ranks of the youth, but Easterners like Hafez, Khayyam and Sa'di should do nothing but make speeches and compose rhymes."[57] Kasravi's argument implied that while Iranian men were pursuing pleasure—the kind featured in Sufi poetry—European men were building tanks to crush them. There is an implicit guilt over the pleasure of same-sex practice, which was apparently so enticing that it trumped national duty.

Kasravi's views are not "typical," in the sense that most scholars and reformists by mid-century had not spoken out against male same-sex practice, and were perfectly content with reading Hafez. Kasravi is unique in the way that he extends the criticism of native irrationality to European scholarship on mysticism that took advantage of such indulgent Easterners. In addition, two groups of Iranians were specifically named in his criticism of Oriental studies: those that profited from the notoriety and financial reward European recognition brought, and the other group (which included Forughi, Qazvini, and Ghani), who were duped by European trickery. Over and over again, Kasravi's "What is Hafez Saying?" cited the fatalism of Hafez, Khayyam, and Sa'di as the main hindrance to Iranian development.

An array of different opinions on the usefulness of Sufism can be seen throughout the Arabic-, Persian-, and Turkish-speaking worlds, where greater participation by Middle Eastern intellectuals in European scholarship, long-standing internal debates, and European interest and involvement in Middle Eastern lands created a fertile climate for critical debate and self-reflection. According to Albert Hourani, major figures of the Arabic-speaking intelligentsia weighed in on debates surrounding Sufism and modernity. Among these individuals, 'Abd al-Wahhab and Muhammad 'Abduh were both critical of Sufism; specifically, for 'Abd al-Wahhab, because it was attached to sultanate authority.[58] Turkish reformer Ziya Gökalp was unique in his endorsement of Sufism, which he believed represented authentic, communal Turkish culture, as opposed to the "High Islam" of the tainted Ottoman Caliphate. Numerous Indian scholars of Sufism celebrated Sufism as part of a pan-Persianate (and Muslim) heritage. Alternatively, the famous scholar of Sufism Mohammad Iqbal, who was deeply troubled by the state of Muslims in India, believed that while high Sufism had a place in the modern nation-state, in the face of the colonial threat one needed to guard against the dangers of "false renunciation" of the world and ideas promoting alienation; and, returning to the Iranian case, virtually every major intellectual in the first half of the twentieth century had positioned him- or herself on the Sufism question. Such examples include Sadeq Hedayat, who criticized Sufi sheikhs for their hypocrisy, Mohammad Mo'in, who praised Sufi poetry, which presented an alternative to rampant materialism (a perspective shared among many European scholars of Sufism, too), and Mohammad Qazvini, who called Hafez the greatest literary figure of Iran.[59]

Conclusion

European and Iranian scholars, in the post-Enlightenment tradition of Herder, who regarded literature, art, and language as constitutive elements of "national culture," sought to redefine and, in some cases, repudiate mystical poetry.[60] At the same time, in the late nineteenth and early twentieth centuries, other Iranian academics believed premodern Sufi poetry was representative of the nation's distinguished and unique intellectual heritage, and this view is still widely held today.[61] Early nationalists, who were often *belle-lettrists* and scholars of the highest order, argued that national aims could be realized through literary projects, and so they edited and wrote extensive commentaries on the works of Sa'di, Molavi, and Hafez. In particular, prominent Iranian scholars who were living in exile in France, Germany, and England during the two world wars believed that mystical poetry was the very foundation of Persian civilization.

By the post-Second World War era, a handful of influential Iranian reformists promoted the idea that reading mystical poetry led to same-sex practice. Though the colonial threat gave rise to questions over sexual identity, this was not the first time that political problems were blamed on immoral sexual behavior. Previous writings on antidespotism during the Iranian constitutional period discussed Qajar political weakness within the framework of "decadent" court practices, and mystical literature was said to reflect the promiscuity of the court ruling elite.[62] Though sexuality had been targeted throughout various times and literatures, scholars of mysticism, beginning in the late nineteenth century through the interwar period, were intent on erasing or castigating it. Sexual taboos in mystical literature, which were celebrated as well as denied, became central to debates on national literature and questions over "who we are" as well as "who we ought to be" in order to fight the threat of imperial conquest.

The above discussion allows us to historicize criticisms of alternative sexualities in the field of Iranian studies, and especially Sufism, which led to alternative readings, and even translations, of Persian poetry. This had consequences not only for how we read and understand premodern poetry in a modern context, but, more significantly, it allows us to interrogate sexual phobias underlying official European and Iranian national identities and national literatures. While my treatment of these national and regional histories is only a brief foray, I believe extending this inquiry will indeed unearth greater insights into the nature of modern sexuality and academic writing, as well as into the comparative nature of Iranian and European intellectual milieus in twentieth-century Oriental studies.

Notes

1. Alternatively, wherever it survived it was largely exoticized, with translators such as Richard Burton parading Eastern sexuality for European audiences in the tradition of translating the *Arabian Nights* (*Alf layla wa layla*).

2. For literary uses of the term "Turk," which denoted a male Beloved, see Dominic Parviz Brookshaw, "To be Feared and Desired: Turks in the Collected Works of 'Ubayd-i Zakani," *Iranian Studies*, vol. 42, no. 5 (2009): 725–744.

3. Today, scholars of Sufism continue this pattern by suggesting that premodern poets used same-sex tropes to aestheticize their divine quest. A great many commentaries on Hafez, for example, argue that allusions to carnal desires were expressly for spiritual arousal, nothing more. While this continues to be the common mode of interpretation, by far the most quixotic denial occurs in contemporary art. Since the visual domain allows for less interpretive flexibility, contemporary paintings express carnal longings by replacing the male object of Hafez's affections with women, who are now the sole legitimate object of the male gaze. In book illustrations accompanying Hafez's poetry, the juxtaposition between homoerotic text and heterosexual depictions creates an embattled display of gender politics at work.

4. Heinrich C. Seeba, "Germany: A Literary Concept," German Studies Review, vol. 17, no. 2 (May 1994).

5. See Chapter Four, "Exoticism: On the Proper Use of Others," in Tzvetan Todorov, *On Human Diversity: Nationalism, Racism, and Exoticism in French Thought* (Cambridge, MA: Harvard University Press, 1993), 264–352.

6. Ibid., 264.

7. For an excellent survey of eighteenth-century French literature about the idea of Persia, see Olivier H. Bonnerot, *La Perse dans la littérature et la pensée françaises au XVIIIe siècle: de l'image au mythe* (Paris: Champion-Slatkine, 1988).

8. See Carl W. Ernst's chapter "Between Orientalism and Fundamentalism: Problematizing the Teaching of Sufism," in *Teaching Islam*, ed. Brannon Wheeler (Oxford: Oxford University Press, 2002), 3. The Tasavvof often wrote in Arabic and Persian prose. The Malamati include Hafez, Sanaʿi, and Saʿdi. This tradition began around the ninth/tenth century in Nishapur. See entry on the history of "Malamatiyya" in *Encyclopédie de L'Islam* (Paris: E. J. Brill, 1991), 217–222.

9. Jones witnessed the brief British Battle of Plassey in India (1757), when the British East India Company defeated the Nawab of Bengal's forces, chiefly through bribery and established hegemony over Indian trade. After gaining notoriety for translating Hafez, Jones became one of the first to study the new field of "the Orient" at Oxford.

10. See Richard J. H. Gottheil's introduction to *Golestan in Persian and Japanese Literature 2* (London: The Colonial Press, 1900), 5.

11. Stephen Greenblatt delivers a powerful indictment of the colonial travel narrative, which he presents as an act of literary "deception." His insights on "the text's paradigmatic power of imposition"; the "rhetoric of the 'eye-witness'"; and the "absence of the human in history" have been very helpful to my analysis. See Stephen Greenblatt, *Marvelous Possessions: The Wonder of the New World* (Chicago: University of Chicago Press, 1991).

12. Hasan Javadi, *Persian Literary Influence on English Literature: With Special Reference to the Nineteenth Century* (Costa Mesa, CA: Mazda Publishers, 2005), 48.

13. Bonaparte's invasion of Egypt, and Greece's later war with Turkey, led to the increased fascination with Islam and the modern study of the Orient. Victor Hugo's *Orientales* (1829), following the Greek War of Independence, was particularly influential for shaping European views of Turks and Muslims. According to contemporary scholars, Hugo employed literary conventions from the works of Saʿdi and Hafez in his poetic works. The Oriental movement dominated every facet of European intellectual and culture life. As a result, religious conservatives could not turn back the tidal wave of the literary genre's popularity. Notables of eighteenth-century Augustan England blamed the French for this upsurge, beginning with the translation of *The Arabian Tales*: "No sooner had Monsieur Galland translated the Arabian Tales than the whole French nation ran mad, and would never after read anything but wretched imitations of their most wild extravagancies."

14. See Sahar Amer, "Cross-Dressing and Female Same-Sex Marriage in Medieval French and Arabic Literatures," in *Islamicate Sexualities: Translations across Temporal Geographies of Desire*, eds. Kathryn Babayan and Afsaneh Najmabadi (London: Harvard Middle Eastern Monographs, 2008).

15. *Hajji Baba* was translated into French by Auguste-Jean-Baptiste Defauconpret, and later into Persian in 1905. For a historical treatment of this book, see Christophe

Balay, "Orientalisme et occidentalisme," in *Rêver d'Orient, connaître l'Orient: Visions de l'Orient dans l'art et la littérature britanniques* (Paris: ENS Éditions, 2008). Balay's thesis is that the translation of works such as *Hajji Baba* from English into Persian influenced modern Persian prose. Another literary analysis of *Hajji Baba* has been done by Hasan Javadi, entitled "James Morier and his Hajji Baba of Ispahan," in *Iran Society Silver Jubilee Volume* (Calcutta, 1970), 163–177. Incidentally, *Hajji Baba* imitated pre-existing literary plot structures such as the popular French tale by Alain-René LeSage, *Gil Blas*, which was set in Spain. One contemporary scholar described it as following a predictable narrative structure of a "situation initiale, captivité du héros, libération, hauts et bas de la fortune, retour à une stabilité."

16. See Richard Jenning, introduction to *The Adventures of Hajji Baba of Ispahan* by James Morier (London: Cresset Press, 1950), ix.

17. French scholars either organized archaeological excursions into Persia by securing favorable permissions from the Qajar government, or confined their research to North Africa. As a consequence, French scholars pioneered the philology of old Iranian languages and ancient texts, such as the Avesta.

18. Smith is one of the very few contemporary scholars of mysticism I know of who has carried out a systematic study of gender in translations of Hafez. See Smith, www.hafizofshiraz.com.

19. Sir Richard Francis Burton, *Golestan*, 165. The plate accompanying this reference featured a statuesque naked man with a flower behind his ear, depicted in a harem holding a robe in his hand. After the Obscene Publications Act of 1857 instigated by the Society for the Suppression of Vice, which led to the prosecution of publishers who were accused of publishing pornography, Burton began an underground book society called the Kama Shastra Society, where stories like *The Arabian Tales* or the *Kama Sutra* that were considered "obscene" were circulated among a list of subscribers.

20. When surveying European writings on mysticism, I have also found there to be three major areas where Todorov's self-critique argument could be extended, maybe even challenged: First, how do we understand claims by scholars that they were "changed" by mystical writings? In other words, their study of Persian texts, however personalized it was, and their professional exchanges and casual interactions with Iranians, significantly affected their views beyond the "self-critique." Second, scholars of mysticism often believed they were mystics themselves. These scholars also claimed that their cultural Others, Sufi mystics, were *their* chosen masters who "spoke through" them. How might we understand this inversion of power? Third, in the thinking of European scholars, mysticism connected modern Iranians and Iran to Europe by virtue of a shared Aryan heritage. Though in these accounts Iranians often remained exotic Others, how do attempts to find common ground attenuate our understanding of race and colonialism?

21. See Gertrude Bell, *The Hafez Poems of Gertrude Bell* (Bethesda: IBEX, 1995), 40.

22. William C. Chittick, *The Sufi Path of Love: The Spiritual Teachings of Rumi* (Albany: State University of New York Press, 1983), 200–201. In Chittick's introduction, he explains that Shams-e Tabrizi was a "constant companion," with no references to the nature of their love.

23. I have surveyed a wide range of published translations of Hafez in preparation for this chapter, most of which were available at the James Darmesteter library at the Sorbonne in Paris. I include an abridged list below: A. J. Arberry, *Hafiz, Fifty Poems*

(Cambridge: Cambridge University Press,1953); Gertrude Bell (1897); Hermann Bicknell (1875); Elizabeth (Daryush) Bridges (1921); "H. H." (1786); John Haddon Hindley (1800); Sir William Jones (1771); Thomas Law (1785); Walter Leaf (1898); Richard Le Gallienne (1905); Reuben Levy (1923); John Nott (1787); Edward Henry Palmer (1877); John Payne (1901); John Richardson (1774).

24. Quoted in Janet Afary, *Sexual Politics in Modern Iran* (Cambridge: Cambridge University Press, 2009), 95.

25. Annemarie Schimmel, *Mystical Dimensions of Islam* (Chapel Hill: The University of North Carolina Press, 1975), 8. In the late thirteenth century, the eighth-century mystic "discovered" under Louis IX, Rab'ia, was idealized as a woman-saint and cited in a seventeenth-century French treatise "on pure love as a model of Divine love."

26. See Annemarie Schimmel, *Mystical Dimensions of Islam* (Chapel Hill: University of North Carolina Press, 1975), 65.

27. Ibid.

28. Schimmel, *Mystical Dimensions of Islam*, 64.

29. See I. Parsinejad, "Zeyn ol-'Abedin Maragheh'I," *Annals of Japan Association for Middle Eastern Studies* 2 (1987), 71.

30. Her writings were published after the Gifford Lectures series as a book of the same title: *Deciphering the Signs of God: A Phenomenological Approach to Islam 1991–1992* (New York: State University of New York Press, 1994).

31. Annemarie Schimmel, *I am Wind, You are Fire: The Life and Work of Rumi* (Boston: Shambhala Dragon Editions, 1992), 22.

32. The question of divine versus human love continues to be one of the enduring debates in the study of mystical texts. This question first appeared in French and English literary circles following the Symbolism movement of the 1870s, a movement said to have its origins in Russia. Armand Renaud and Jean Lahor, who incorporated Persian tropes by Khayyam and Hafez in their work, disagreed on the concepts of human and divine love. In contrast to Renaud, Lahor believed human love was both "cruel and exquisite," and human and divine love were inseparable, reflecting one another, and came from the same source. He also believed that "les amours terrestres," or "human love," gave one access to high levels of mystical "intoxication."

33. It is generally accepted that mysticism prides itself on open interpretations, though it would be a mistake to categorize all Sufi texts as permissive with regards to sexuality. Mohammad Ali Amir-Moezzi, the current director of the Centre d'Études des Religions du Livre at the EHESS in Paris, noted the tension among medieval Persian poets, i.e., between more puritanical poets among the Tasavvof school, and in contrast, among the Malamati ("blame") or Iranian school, who often invoked erotic language. Amir Moezzi, who currently occupies the chair Corbin once held at the École Pratique des Hautes Études, Ve Section, stated recently that he believed there was no separation between profane and mystical love in the poetry of Hafez and 'Attar. This is based on a conversation I had with him on 30 October 2009.

34. While nineteenth-century and early twentieth-century scholars asserted the irreconcilability between earthly love and love for God, more recently scholars have offered a more nuanced portrayal of the two spheres. For example, Firoozeh Papan-Matin explained the oneness of "this life" and the "unseen world" in her description of the life of Ruzbehan:

Ruzbehan's mundane life is so intertwined with his visionary experiences that he is left no space for succumbing to the "mundane" wholeheartedly. In fact, in Kashf al-Asrar, Ruzbehan's concerns for this life are always accompanied by elements of the unseen world. In other words, the former are distinct from his direct and immediate relationship with God and the unseen world, *but are not separate from them* [my emphasis]. Papan-Matin's important observation about the dualistic nature of heavenly and mundane is not only important to her work for philosophical reasons, but for the purposes of this discussion, it again raises the question as to why previous scholars relegated this life to a lesser status.

35. Ibid., 27.

36. Ibid., 136–137.

37. Incidentally, famous authors such as Christoph Martin Wieland (1733–1813) were credited during this time for muting the eroticism of French novels in order to create a more childlike and innocent sexuality for a German audience.

38. There really is no precise definition, but for the purposes of convenience I provide Ghulam Abbas Dalal's definition: "The Neo-Platonists believe in the Supreme Good as the Source of all things. Self-existent, it generated from itself. Creation was the reflection of its own Being. Nature, therefore, was permeated with god. Matter was essentially non-existent, a temporary and ever-moving shadow for the embodiment of Divine. The Neo-Platonists believed that by ecstasy and contemplation of the All-Good, man would rise to that Source whence he came." See Ghulam Abbas A. Dalal, *Ethics in Persian Poetry: With Special Reference to Timurid Period* (New Delhi: Abhinav Publications, 1995), 35.

39. Michel Foucault, *The History of Sexuality*, vol. 1 (New York: Vintage Books, 1990), 17.

40. For a more thorough discussion of Massignon, refer to my dissertation "Scholarly Mysticism and Mystical Scholars: Iranian and European Intellectuals at the Dawn of Modern Sexuality and Gender" (PhD dissertation, UCLA, 2010).

41. F. A. D. Tholuck, a German Protestant scholar who claimed he was "not at all prone to mystical ideas," in 1821 wrote the first comprehensive book on Sufism, and later systematized the study of mysticism order to prove the robustness of Christian teachings.

42. Cyprian Rice, *The Persian Sufis* (London: Allen & Unwin, 1964). The study of mysticism also flourished during the Cold War era, when Henry Corbin and Mircea Eliade attracted worldwide attention for their work on the history of religions. This renewed interest appeared amidst the superpower rivalry between ideological poles— neither of which presented a model for contemporary spirituality. As one scholar noted, the most recognized scholars of mysticism "achieved their fame and influence at a time when religion, at least in its public manifestations and its private intellectual forms, seemed most on the wane."

43. What I mean by "silence," for example, is the numerous references, say, in literature about Rumi where there are only vague or oblique references to his male "companion." As a casual observation, in speaking with some friends in Iran, it is generally understood among Iranians that this was a homosexual love affair.

44. See William C. Chittick, *Sufism: A Short Introduction* (Oxford: Oneworld Publications, 2000), 27.

45. Ibid., 37.

46. A. J. Arberry, *Sufism: An Account of the Mystics of Islam* (London: Unwin Paperbacks, 1979), 116.

47. In contrast, A. J. Arberry challenged the exclusively allegorical interpretation of drunkenness by saying, "The allegory of wine raises its own separate problems. There are those who take every reference to the crimson cup as intending spiritual intoxication. . . . But it is a difficult position to maintain consistently . . . it is by no means to be imagined that others employing the language of the tavern did not refer to a literal as well as a metaphorical drunkenness." Arberry had no trouble accepting both literal and allegorical meanings—or, at least, he assumed that such meanings cannot always be determined. More importantly, his commentary suggests that even those scholars who opposed purely metaphorical interpretations of "wine vocabulary" still rarely questioned, if at all, the moralistic bent of its proponents.

48. See DeSouza, "Scholarly Mysticism," ibid.

49. I am indebted to Ali Gheissari and his excellent overview of Iranian intellectual history in the modern period. See Ali Gheissari, *Iranian Intellectuals in the Twentieth Century* (Austin: University of Texas Press, 1998), 15. It should also be noted that Kermani was a self-professed Azali-Babi and supporter of al-Afghani's pan-Islamism. In his work entitled *A'ineh-ye Sekandar*, he called for the overthrow of despotism and the strengthening of national feeling. For a more detailed discussion of Akhundzadeh's rationalist critique of Sufism, see Iraj Parsinejad, *A History of Literary Criticism in Iran, 1866–1951: Literary Criticism in the works of enlightened thinkers of Iran—Akhundzadeh, Kermani, Malkom, Talebof, Maraghe'i, Kasravi, and Hedayat* (Washington, DC: Ibex Publishers, Inc., 2003). Parsinejad looked specifically at Akhundzadeh's essay "Darbare-e Nazm va Nasr" (On Verse and Prose).

50. Quoted in Lloyd Ridgeon, *Sufi Castigator: Ahmad Kasravi and the Iranian Mystical Tradition* (London: Routledge, 2006), 23. This book was published within a year after Afsaneh Najmabadi's work on a similar theme, and Najmabadi had taken on Kasravi's moral bent in her earlier work, though Ridgeon did not seem to be aware of Najmabadi's work.

51. Babayan demonstrated that the push for heterosexual marriage does not originate in the modern period; for example, the criticism of "Sufi excesses" like celibacy and sodomy can be found in a late-seventeenth to early-eighteenth-century text. See Babayan, *Islamicate Sexualities*, 265.

52. Ibid., 266.

53. During the same time period, leading Shi'a clerics also joined reformists in their criticism of Sufism. Hamid Algar mentioned, in particular, Seyyed Muhammad Baqer-e Behbahani, who distrusted their antinomian behavior, and apparently referred to himself as *sufikosh* ("Sufi killer"). Modern *'ulama* had accused Sufi brotherhoods of theological "innovations" (or *bid'a*).

54. It is not clear to what extent Persian writers shared Browne's view of pre-Qajar poetry. See chapter entitled "Hafiz and His Commentators" in Edward G. Browne, *A Literary History of Persia*, vols. 3 and 4, 299.

55. See my unpublished paper, "Colonialism, Masculinity and Anti-Same Sex Practice in the Writings of Sayyed Hasan Taqizadeh," presented at the panel "Queer Domesticities in Art and Literature," at the annual Cultural Studies Association Conference, Berkeley, CA, 2009.

56. *Iran Nameh* featured a special volume on Kasravi: *Iran Nameh* vol. XX, issues 2–3 (2003).

57. Ahmad Kasravi, *Hafez Che Migoyad (What is Hafez Saying?)* (*Tehran*, 1943).

58. Albert Hourani, *Arabic Thought in the Liberal Age, 1798–1939* (Cambridge: Cambridge University Press, 1983).

59. Muhammad Qazvini's, preface to *Bahth dar athar u afkar u ahval-e Hafiz*, by Qasim Ghani, vol. 1 (Tehran: publisher?, 1321/1942) stated that Ghani once pressed him to name the "most poetical of the poets of Persia," upon which Qazvini cited Hafez "as chiefly among them." Arberry once deferred to Qazvini's expertise of Hafez's poetry. (See *Yadgar*, vol. 1, no. 9, 69–78.)

60. Arvidsson's work is especially useful when evaluating the racialist features of Iranian studies in Europe. Refer to Stefan Arvidsson, *Aryan Idols: Indo-European Mythology as Ideology and Science* (Chicago: University of Chicago Press, 2006), 30–31.

61. An entry in the *Encyclopædia Iranica* furthers this belief about the critical importance of Persian poetry to "Iran's cultural distinctiveness": "With a strong tradition of oral literature, particularly poetry, the idea of 'Iran' and its elements in Persian cultural heritage have been widely disseminated to the masses in urban, rural, and tribal areas. There are many illiterate people who know verses from the *Divan* of Hafez and Sa'adi and the *Shahnameh* of Ferdowsi by heart and often refer to them in their daily social discourse." See Ahmad Ashraf's entry on "Iranian Identity, in the 19th and 20th centuries," in *Encyclopædia Iranica*, last updated December 15, 2006, http://www.encyclopediairanica.com (accessed April 24, 2010).

62. Echoes of such accusations date back even further to premodern chronicles that discussed the decline of a king, which often was evaluated in retrospect, as a result of sexual excess or deviance. This insight was provided by Ali Anooshahr, historian of comparative Mughal, Safavid, and Ottoman empires.

PART 2

IMAGINING IRAN:
LAND, ETHNICITY, AND PLACE

CHAPTER 5

Imagining Iran before Nationalism: Geocultural Meanings of Land in Azar's *Atashkadeh*

MANA KIA

Nationalist views of Iran are predicated on "a congruence of state, society and culture," territorialized onto a homeland and sharply delineated from those around it.[1] The scholarship of the last few years has detailed the various ways in which this process of imagining Iran as a national homeland occurred in the later nineteenth and early twentieth centuries.[2] All agree that there were previous notions of a place called Iran, and ways of belonging to it, that were different from what came after. But the question remains, what were these notions? Without specific historicizing, concepts like Iran tend to be read according to modern understandings that are paradoxically predicated on timelessness, even as they argue for radical differences caused by modernity.[3] For Firoozeh Kashani-Sabet, whose work specifically focuses on the importance of land, works of medieval geography describe regions "much like nation-states today." Geographical notions of a large swath of land understood to be Greater Iran were, she argues, "a means of self-definition" shared by "other Iranians" in medieval times.[4] Such a reading creates a premodern period consisting of centuries of static homogeneity, posed in contrast to the radical changes of the modern period. Yet, strangely, a sense of being Iranian seems to have existed throughout nonetheless. Historical contingency is evacuated, obfuscating the important differences in the constitution and narration of geocultural borders of Iran at particular times.[5] It is certainly important to trace continuities in "the long-standing patterns within societies to distinguish between rivals and neighbors by delineating territorial and cultural boundaries," but not without questioning implicit nationalist assumptions as to the congruence of such boundaries.[6]

Even scholarship not directly concerned with nationalism or the modern period is still bounded by nationalist assumptions about how the land of Iran was conceived of and what it meant to be from Iran within the broader geocultural Persianate world.[7] This article seeks to contribute to the question of continuity by outlining what I call geocultural meanings of land in a famous late eighteenth-century poetic *tazkereh* (commemorative compendium), the *Atashkadeh* of Lotf ʿAli Bayg "Azar" Baigdeli (AD 1721-1781/AH 1134-1195).[8] In the present study, I refer to Central Asia as Turan and South Asia as Hendustan and seek to historicize what is meant by Iran in the early modern context, because part of what enables anachronistic conceptual interpretations of the past is the use of anachronistic names. Even in a text like the *Atashkadeh*, where the land of Iran is central to the geographical mapping of Persian literary culture, there are specific perceptions of land and culture, shared with other texts of this period, that distinguish it from modern nationalist concepts. Iran was distinct from, but contiguous in meaning with, the lands around it, and these meanings can initially lend themselves to (proto-) nationalist readings. One difference with nationalism lies in geocultural meanings, the ways in which significance is vested in land through a history of near and far figures and events contained in the corpus of Persianate learning. I use the term "Persians" to refer to a group of people who shared a particular language of learning. Knowledge of Persian was derived from a corpus of well-known texts, and gave rise to shared literary tropes, interpretive paradigms, and representational forms. Persians in Iran, Turan, and Hendustan shared particular understandings of the meaning of geography, and how these meanings constituted bases of origin and community.[9]

The *Atashkadeh* as a *Tazkareh*

The *Atashkadeh* is a *tazkereh*, a commemorative compendium of poets, a rich yet often overlooked genre of source material (beyond literary studies) for eighteenth-century social and cultural history. Understanding *tazkereh*s as commemorative compendiums instead of biographical dictionaries can show us something about the cultural and social contexts of their authors in a way that is less dependent on, but still mindful of, the value of the factual content of the entries. *Tazkereh* authors, as poets themselves, include and represent certain past and present poets as part of an imagined community, a cultural community of ancestors and peers, that transcended shared origins or homelands as they were conceived of in the eighteenth century.[10] This cultural community transcended actual acquaintance, political loyalties, social ties (such as those between teacher and student), and ethnic commonalities (genealogical or broader tribal groupings) to create lineages based on poetic sensibilities, which defined the *tazkereh* author himself.[11] These authors had gone through "a process of moral and intellectual education designed to produce an *adib*, a gentleman-scholar," and thus the constitution of *tazkereh*s as books of ancestors and peers, was "intimately connected with the formation of both intellect and character."[12] Knowledge of poetry and the ability to compose it was one basic feature of this community of peers, who were often well versed in—or even best known for—other things, such as medicine, religious sciences, accounting, political administration, military leadership, and even commerce. Commemoration of friends, contemporaries, and bygone poets created a field of representation in which the poetic self of the author came into being.

Contemporaneous understandings of *tazkereh*s in other types of texts support this understanding. In the early nineteenth century, 'Abd al-Latif Shushtari, when describing his friend Abu Taleb Esfahani, mentioned that he had written a *tazkereh* "from which the amount of his learning and taste is evident (*meqdar-e fahm va saliqeh-ash az an hovayda ast*)."[13] Abu Taleb's learning was evident in his ability to provide biographical information and poetry, but his refinement of taste, also, was demonstrated by his choice of poets and particular selections of their poetry. Shushtari understood the text as demonstrating something about Abu Taleb, indicating that the perception of *tazkereh*s as texts of self partly defined their consumption. Underpinning this expression of self is the possession of specific types of learning, shared by others in a larger Persianate cultural community.

Though it was common to include contemporaries whom the author had never met, the most substantive entries were usually about people with whom the author had a relationship or interaction, since reliability of information was perceived to be derived from personal acquaintance.[14] It was through overt reference to, and specific representation of, the author's social community, political ties, and literary commitments in entries on other poets that the author's character was constructed. Understanding the way in which self-construction was a critical aspect of eighteenth-century Persian *tazkereh*s enables an appreciation of the ways in which social and political ties needed to be expressed in a particular text. Such an appreciation acknowledges the narrativity of the entries, why the author chose to leave out, or foreground, certain facts according to concerns that tell us about the possibilities of Persianate selfhood beyond inscrutable personal idiosyncrasies.

Unlike the *tazkereh*s of previous centuries, eighteenth-century *tazkereh*s were usually not created within the context of court patronage, and had substantial historical and autobiographical narratives that were novel to this genre.[15] The *Atashkadeh* departs from other early modern *tazkereh*s in several ways. Most were organized alphabetically or by *tabageh* (station).[16] In contrast, Azar's *Atashkadeh* maps poets according to origin, an imperfect territorialization that is different from the all-encompassing meanings of territorial origins in modern nationalism. Geographical refiguring, particularly of one's homeland, however it was conceived of, had always been a concern of the *tazkereh* genre, particularly in times of great upheaval.[17] Azar was born in the year the Afghans invaded Iran, laid siege to Isfahan, bringing down the Safavid state and inaugurating a period of political instability only briefly interrupted by Nader Afshar's seizure of the throne. Azar perceived himself as living in a ruined Iran, and the *Atashkadeh* places an overweening emphasis on Persians originating in the former Safavid dominions (*mamalek*) of Iran before Azar's time. A small number of historical poets originating in Turan and Hendustan, as well as a separate category of women, are included at the back. Post-Timurid poets who traveled or migrated to Hendustan are included, but given relatively short shrift. The conclusion is a historically rooted autobiographical narrative that also includes sixty entries on Azar's poetic contemporaries. Though Azar includes contemporaries who migrated to, or originated in, Hendustan, the most substantial of these entries are of those poets who were part of his circle of friends, as is the case with most *tazkereh*s.[18]

Often read as "an early expression of literary nationalism in Iran," linking Persian culture to the land of Iran by omitting large numbers of Persian poets originating in Central and South Asia,[19] the *Atashkadeh* endeavors to do two things that must be distinguished from nationalist concerns. First, it seeks to memorialize a new style of poetics (only later called the *bazgasht*) by refuting the value of the *tazeh gu'i* style (often anachronistically called the "Indian Style," or *sabk-e Hendi*) of the preceding centuries.[20] But in doing so, the *bazgasht* rejected many post-Timurid poets originating in the cities of Iran, as well as from Turan and Hendustan. Second, the text seeks to place Iran (specifically *'Eraq-e 'ajam*) at the center of poetic culture, since it is from there that the new style originated, at a time when Iran was perceived to be in a state of ruin in contrast to its glorified Safavid past. This impulse to recenter Persia in Iran must be understood in a context where the greatest centers of poetic patronage had been in Mughal domains, in the cities of Lahore and Delhi, for the past century and a half. Centers of patronage were also where poetic styles developed and from which they emanated. The *Atashkadeh* was written as an intervention in the style that was current at the time, placing Azar's own Isfahani circle on the larger poetic map by linking it to the old masters originating in Safavid lands and attempting to shift the center of stylistic development back to Iran. The very means by which the *Atashkadeh* distinguished and centered Iran within the larger Persianate world depended on a history and standard of evaluation that was shared with other Persians in Turan and Hendustan. In the text, Iran is central to the Persianate world and foremost in it culturally, but not singular or unique, sharing many overlapping features with Turan and Hendustan. A person's history, language, and community could not be reduced to their birth in the various cities of Iran. Furthermore, a person's origin was also defined by tribe, lineage, or learning in a way that could supersede territorial origin.

Geocultural Persianate Landscapes

The Persianate world included lands where a body of knowledge—geographical, historical, religious, philosophical, and poetic—was dominant among the educated classes, mainly in Iran, Turan, and Hendustan. Ethical evaluations and paradigmatic possibilities were contained in this literary corpus. According to Kathryn Babayan, one prominent feature of the Persianate ethos was a sense of cyclical time and being, exemplified in the *Shahnameh*, where "Iranian society is portrayed as encountering similar ethical dilemmas in different ages. In each era, kings are confronted with analogous situations as they attempt to rule their dominion with justice and to deal with political realities and ethical choices regarding their sons, warriors, subjects and neighbors (Turan, Hind, Rum)."[21] These paradigmatic stories, first told in the *Shahnameh* and more widely dispersed through other texts and genres, underpinned Persianate cultural understandings of ethics, history, and place.

In the context of the Mughal court, manuscripts of the *Shahnameh* were less often patronized.[22] However, widely circulated universal histories contained stories of pre-Islamic Persian kings, alongside pre-Islamic Quranic history, and gave meaning to history and land within the Persianate world. This parallel dual narrative permeated Irani and Hendustani Persian texts up through the early nineteenth century, first through shared Timurid historiographical heritage, then, as it developed, in the closely related Mughal and Safavid historiographical traditions.[23] The hugely influential Timurid universal history, *Rawzat al-safa*, begins with pre-Islamic Quranic creation up through the Flood, including the prophets, patriarchs, and kings of Israel, then continues at length with the history of pre-Islamic Persian kings up to the arrival of Islam. "The termination of both narratives signaled Islam's moral and political superiority," beginning with the birth of the Prophet Muhammad.[24] The narrative of pre-Islamic Persian kings is a prose re-inscription of the epic poem the *Shahnameh*. After the fall of the Abbasids, the historical narrative of Muslim domains becomes increasingly focused on the Persianate Islamic East, and then entirely on Iran and Turan.[25] This format of reconciled, parallel, pre-Islamic, Quranic, and Persian history in the *Rawzat al-safa*, with a post-Mongol emphasis on the Persianate East, became the template for Mughal and Safavid universal histories throughout the early modern period, however much their post-Timurid accounts might have differed.[26] These universal histories circulated widely in the libraries of Hendustani and Irani Persians, Muslim and non-Muslim alike, well through the nineteenth century, as did the *Shahnameh* and its abridged prose narrative retellings.[27]

One of the last *tazkereh*s written in Iran that at least attempts to encompass lands beyond it, the *Atashkadeh* maps poets (excepting princes, nobles, women, and contemporaries) onto a regionally partitioned Persianate world that reflects both the accumulated dual narrative of Perso-Islamic histories and the specificities of Azar's own time and location.[28] A native of Isfahan and the Shamlu *oymaq*, his family fled to Qum for fourteen years after the Afghan invasion (1722), which occurred in the year of his birth. In 1736, Azar's father was appointed governor of Lar and then Fars, bringing the family to Shiraz.[29] After his father's death in 1738, Azar accompanied his uncle on the Hajj, by way of the Shiʻi shrine cities. He ended his pilgrimage in Mashhad, just as Nader Shah's army was returning from Hendustan in 1741. Azar accompanied Nader's army to Mazandaran, Azerbaijan and ʻEraq-e ʻajam, eventually settling in Isfahan. He spent the next years in service to various rulers of the city, frequenting circles of the eloquent and learned, in particular naming his teacher Mir Sayyid ʻAli "Moshtaq."[30] When ʻAli Mardan Khan sacked Isfahan, Azar lost seven thousand verses of poetry and most of his library. "For a time after this crossroads (*rahgozar*) the parrot of speech and the nightingale of my temperament were broken-winged, until with the solicitous care of friends (*beh takallof-e ahbab*) sometimes they [the parrot and the nightingale] would engage in adorning the rose garden of thought."[31] In the years following his friend-assisted poetic recovery, he made enough of a name for himself that *tazkereh*s in Delhi took note of him.[32] Azar later spent time in Shiraz, Karim Khan Zand's capital, before retiring to Qum in the 1760s to take up poetry and write the *Atashkadeh*. He died in 1780.[33]

The geographically organized portion of the *Atashkadeh* is divided into the larger regions of Iran, Turan, and Hendustan. These regions are further subdivided into smaller regional domains, and then into cities. Azar begins with the larger region (*velayet*) of Iran, whose "distinctly temperate climate and the intellect/perception (*edrak*) of the inhabitants of that region (*deyar*) it is not necessary to make manifest," because "all the books of histories speak to this point."[34] Significantly, it is to a presumably common body of historical texts that Azar points to justify his contention about the nature of the land's climate and its inhabitants. These descriptions of larger regions are brief; the smaller domains, Azerbaijan, Khorasan, Tabarestan, 'Eraq-e 'arab and 'Eraq-e 'ajam, and Fars listed under Iran, are described more substantially.

Beginning with Azerbaijan, Azar contemplates the origin of the land's name, its history, and the characteristics of its climate and people. The terms *velayet* and *deyar* refer to Azerbaijan as well as Iran, acting here as a synonym for *mamlakat*, demonstrating the fluid ways in which smaller and larger domains are referred to in context by the same word. The name Azerbaijan "is derived from (*mansub bah*) Azar ibn Amir ibn Asud ibn Sam, who was the son of Nuh [Noah]. Some have written that in the time of Shapur, Azar was the name of a person who claimed to be a prophet and seduced a great number of people into accepting his claim. Shapur seized him and melted metals (*felezzat*) on his chest and he was not injured, causing the belief of people to grow. The flourishing of that region is due to him."[35] The qualification "some have written" precedes the pre-Islamic Persian narrative from the *Rawzat al-safa*, unlike the Quranic narrative, which demanded acceptance as absolute truth.[36] Following the *Rawzat al-safa*, Azar prefaces his inclusion of such popular stories with disclaimers of their veracity, but includes them because of their wide currency. His description of Mazandaran begins with its near past, of Shah 'Abbas, who, on account of his mother's family origin, spent much time there, building gardens and palaces. In providing its geographical details, Azar taps into a far, possibly mythical, past, explaining that one of its impregnable fortresses was a place where

[. . .]during the time of Afrasiab's conquest and the defeat of the Iranis, Manuchehr was besieged. Afrasiab was not victorious in his conquest of the fort. In the end, the great ones of Iran and Turan agreed on this condition for peace, that from the aforementioned fort an arrow should be launched and wherever it hit the ground should be the division of the holdings of Afrasiab and Manuchehr. Arash, one of the great warriors (*pahlavanan*) of Iran, launched an arrow that, after examination, had struck the ground on the banks of the Jayhun [Oxus] river. However much the acceptance of this story is outside the pale of probability, it has been written on account of its great fame (*shohrat*).[37]

These pre-Islamic Persian geographical lineages are viewed with a degree of skepticism, such as the account according to which an arrow could fly from Mazandaran to the Oxus. Yet such accounts are still included in the descriptions of geographical regions, because their fame had come to partially convey the character and meaning of these places.

The context of Azar's composition was the ruin of Iran, a perception that undergirds the *Atashkadeh* as a whole and is an essential part of the rhetorical labor of the text. Khorasan, "a province consisting of old and great cities, is the great cornerstone (*rokn*) of the region of Iran. At this time, like the rest of Iran, it is ruined."[38] More specifically, in describing places such as Kerman and Sabzevar, Azar elaborates that cities and their populations have been much reduced by "the vicissitudes of the times (*enqelab-e zamaneh*)."[39] Azar and many other authors writing in the middle decades of the eighteenth century repeatedly reiterated this perception of the many regions of Iran being ruined, though they differed on its causes.[40] Different views on specific events were, nonetheless, bound up in the shared understanding of the meaning of lands where Iran and Hendustan had contrasting relationships to sacred space and cultural knowledge. Place of origin, direction of travel, and the reason for writing structure meaning within these travel texts.

Though political fragmentation, colonial encroachment, and a decided Iranianization of the Persian language was occurring in both Hendustan and Iran by the nineteenth century, a Hendustani Persian could still narrate places according to this dual Islamic and pre-Islamic Persian narrative.[41] 'Ali Mirza "Maftun," a traveler from Patna through Iran in the early nineteenth century (1826–1828), maps the geographical meaning of Tehran beginning with the older, nearby town of Rayy, figured as Tehran's ancestor.[42]

> It is revealed to those versed in histories that the land of Rayy is in the fourth clime and one of the great old cities of [the province of] *'Eraq-e 'ajam* and there are differing accounts of its building. Some give the credit of its founding to Hushang, some to the prophet Seth, son of Adam.[43] Regarding the flourishing and habitation and spaciousness of it [Rayy] they [the histories] tell stories which are not empty of strangeness (*ghorebet*). For those who depend on proof (*ahl-e khobrat*) it is manifest that the aforementioned land has been wrecked and ruined several times by massacre and pillage and earthquake."

The most spectacular instances of ruination, he notes, were at the hands of Genghis Khan.[44] Maftun demonstrates his knowledge of the dual narrative, though he also expresses skepticism about the veracity of both the pre-Islamic Quranic and Persian distant past. The only history he can be sure of, which has left material evidence and contemporaneous histories, is the more recent history of Rayy's destruction centuries ago at the hands of invaders like Genghis Khan.[45] But, regardless of relative perceptions of reliability, the less reliable distant past still widely marks the geocultural meaning of place.

Art historians have noted that Mughal manuscript traditions included representations of architecture in both image and text, as a way to lend character to a place and commemorate the achievements of rulers.[46] Later paintings presented architectural monuments as the sole subject in more technical and clearly articulated detail, reminiscent of actual architectural plans drawn for functional purposes.[47] These new types of paintings, inserted in Mughal texts re-commissioned in manuscript form in the late eighteenth and early nineteenth centuries, represented architecture as a more integral sign of the achievements of certain rulers.[48] This connection is echoed in Maftun's descriptions of architecture, its patron/ruler, and their links to the history of the city. After mapping out the different gates of Shiraz, Maftun notes that "in the direction of the western gate there are grand structures, exalted palaces without blemish, and gardens pleasing to the heart and without compare and the like, which are the constructions of Mohammad Karim Khan Zand, known as *Vakil*, who at one time was the ruler (*farmanfarma'i*) of the domains of Iran."[49] Shiraz had been the seat of Karim Khan's rule and contemplation of that rule included a careful cataloging of his architectural achievements, both of which Maftun wholeheartedly approved. Maftun describes Karim Khan as "protective of peasants, attending to the comforts of soldiers, the spreader of justice, a guide for manliness/humanity (*moruvvat*), lord of the sword, politically astute," and so much more along these lines that he hardly seems unworthy of taking the throne, a paradox of humility that is precisely the point. Immediately following this, Maftun, as if to underscore these qualities, notes that "his mind inclined greatly to building," and what follows is a detailed description of these structures mapped onto the city of Shiraz.[50] Such connections between rulers and their structures are not limited to Karim Khan, as Maftun limns Isfahan with structures built by the Safavid shahs, Tehran as built by Fath 'Ali Shah, and Mashhad as built by centuries of rulers, particularly the Afsharids. Architecture mapped onto urban space as a sign of political order serves as a vehicle through which Maftun narrates places, as the accumulation of their histories.

The importance of a ruler's architectural contributions to the formation of the character and identity of place is not limited to Indo-Persian contexts. Though only briefly part of Safavid domains, the *Atashkadeh*'s short section on *'Eraq-e 'arab* is included under the larger region of Iran.[51] Azar notes that Baghdad was founded in the year 763/146, close to a garden built at the time of the Persian kings near the palace of Ctesiphon. Thus, the seat of the Caliphate is mapped onto a site defined by the power of pre-Islamic Persian kings. The next mention of architectural contribution is not of 'Abbasids but of the Ilkhanids, and then Shah 'Abbas Safavid, "who built new fortifications around the city after conquering it."[52] This last serves to undergird the region's link to Iran by noting the role of the kings of Iran in the very physical structure of the city.

Though geographically distinct from Iran, Turan is part of the Islamic and Persianate heartlands through its shared pre-Islamic Persian history. Azar notes that "when Faraidun ruled, he divided up the domains of his empire during his life. He gave [the land] from the banks of the Jaihun [Oxus] to Tur, which became known as Turan. He entrusted the region of Rum [one manuscript says Hend][53] to Salm. He gave the domain of Iran to Iraj, who gave his name to Iran. In the end, what happened came to happen and it is fully detailed in [the aforementioned] histories."[54] This story originally appears in the *Shahnameh* and subsequent universal Persianate histories as Faraidun's division of the world. In the *Atashkadeh*, it appears as a history, not as a myth, of the division of the Persianate world.[55] The genealogy of these lands, as once united and then ruled by brothers, however bitterly they may have fought, creates a picture of related regions springing from one origin. The conflict that ensues between the brothers is caused by envy of Iraj's lot, since the throne of Iran is the coveted, choice portion. The land of Iran is connected to, but set hierarchically above, neighboring lands, as the original seat of rule. The resulting envy-fueled aggression on the part of Iraj's brothers and their descendants serves to set them, and thus their lands, ethically lower than Iran.[56] Though sharing common origins with Iran, the relation is one of conflict, where Iran has the higher moral status, due to the more noble behavior of its ruler.[57]

Azar's inscription of pre-Islamic Persian history onto Turan extends to smaller regional and city descriptions.[58] The *Atashkadeh* describes Farghana as the farthest region of Turan, "at the corner of the civilized world (*dar kenar-e maʿmureh-e ʿalam*)."[59] Azar has mentioned other lands, such as Europe (*farangestan*), China (*kheta*) and Syria (*sham*), demonstrating that the term *maʿmur* does not refer to the known world, but the civilized/Persianate world. This specifically Persianate refinement of civilization does not exclude the possibility of civilization in other places, like the Hijaz, which possesses the sacralized history of Islamic refinement. But though the holiest site of Islam, it does not possess Persianate poetic culture and the history in which Iran is the center, a history particularly prominent at a time when Azar was self-conscious of a less exalted present. The inclusion of Hend, even in the reproduction of only some manuscripts of the *Atashkadeh* in the tripartite division of the Persianate world reflects the legibility of Persianized Mughal Hendustan and the decreasing Persianization of Ottoman *Rum* by the eighteenth century, an updated geocultural mapping from the fifteenth century of *Rawzat al-safa*.[60]

This occasional inclusion is precarious, though not reflected in descriptions of the larger land of Hendustan.

In the *Atashkadeh*, Hendustan is outside of pre-Islamic Quranic and Persian history. Azar describes Hendustan as a place where "the customs and etiquettes [. . .] are for the most part in conflict/opposition with [those of] the inhabitants of Iran and even Turan (*rosum va qava'ed-e an ja aksar khelaf-e ahl-e Iran ast balkeh Turan*)."[61] This opposition between the customs defining the societies of the two lands is further underlined by the strangeness of the land itself. "The strange fruits of that place cannot be found in this region [Iran]."[62] Yet, individual descriptions of these smaller regions and cities are far more equivocal with respect to their relation to Iran.[63] Because of its verdant gardens, delightful plains, and the quality of its air and water, Azar describes Delhi as exceptional among the cities of Hendustan. Immediately following is the presumably pertinent history of Delhi, its conquest by Muslim rulers in 1192/588, from which time it was a center of Muslim rule by "dynasties of great nobility."[64] Skipping ahead to the latest of these dynasties, Azar focuses on the architectural contribution of Shahjahan, who filled the gaps in the city's structures, ensuring the city would flourish, which is why it is called Shahjahanabad. "At this time, which is the year 1179 [1765-1766] that which had successively happened, caused by the arrival of Nader Shah Afshar and Ahmad Shah Afghan, has brought extreme disorder and ruin [to the city]."[65] For Azar, Iran was not the only land to have fallen into ruin. Hendustan had also been laid low by invaders and resulting chaos. By this time, many of the literati of Delhi had migrated to other cities, mainly regional centers of Faizabad, Hyderabad and Morshedabad, and were generally in agreement with Azar's assessment.

In the *Atashkadeh*, both the people and land of regions of Hendustan are celebrated. Azar describes Lahore as "a famous city of Hendustan. Even though it is in an area with a warm climate, they say that in the summer snow and ice come to hand and it has good fruits. Its people are clever/shrewd (*zirak*)."[66] This description of Lahore contrasts with the more negative description of the larger land of Hendustan. Even less equivocal, Azar's description of Kashmir is positively glowing, disrupting arguments that the *Atashkadeh* glorifies the land of Iran in contrast to, and to the exclusion of, others, particularly Hendustan.

From the abundance of gardens, trees, the multitude of rivers and streams, the whole city is a portion of the verdancy of heaven (*tamam-e shahr qet'eh-i ast az marghzar-e jannat*).[67] They say that its soil imparts great joy (*farah-*

nak) and its air elicits delight (*'eshrat angiz*). During the reign of Soltan Sekandar the religion of Islam came to prevail. The weaving of shawls is the specialty of that region that they take to all parts of the world. That region yields a great deal of saffron.[68]

The physical character of the land itself is vaunted as heavenly, the very earth and climate inducing joy and delight. In the following section of Kashmir's poets, Azar refers to Binesh as "from that paradisiacal region (*deyar-e khold asar*)."[69] Calling a land "paradisiacal" was generally a form of demonstrating affiliation, a way of declaring home.[70] In some cases, within Persianate geocultural understandings, places like Kashmir were understood to be paradisiacal, whether or not an author had been there, and whether or not the place was within the larger land with which the author was affiliated. Azar also demonstrates familiarity with images of other beautiful green mountainous places to which he has never been, including Badakhshan and Qandahar.[71]

Geography gained meaning according to climes, where domains gained character in a symbiotic relationship between the inhabitants, government, land, and climate. Persianate regions were intertwined in the clime system, though climes did not correspond to larger regions.[72] The middle clime of the seven, the most temperate and thus desirable fourth clime, was not limited to the domains of Iran, but also extends to the regions of Turan and Hendustan, such as Kashmir.[73] Various domains of Iran were also in the warmer, less temperate third clime, such as parts of Khorasan, *'Eraq-e 'arab*, Fars and parts of *'Eraq-e 'ajam*.[74] Though entirely in the third clime, Fars was "the seat of most of Pishdadi and Keyan kings [pre-Islamic Persian dynasties]. They say that Persepolis (*estakhr*) is the first of Irani cities to have been built in the inhabited world (*rob'e maskun*)."[75] In spite of its venerable age and pre-Islamic Persianate history, this integral part of Iran is in the third clime, not the fourth. The northern reaches of Azerbaijan are in the colder fifth clime.[76] The land of Iran is not contained in the central, most desirable fourth clime, which includes portions of other lands. Lands located in the same clime shared similar physical features that corresponded to moral character. These features problematize a reading of the *Atashkadeh* as a text in which the land of Iran is vaunted above all others, per modern nationalist notions that require narratives of radical difference and unique singularity of homeland.

The way the land was depicted geographically, what this meant about the moral constitution of the inhabitants, and how meaning was assigned to a place, are all indicative of a humorial. understanding of connections between land and nature. "Water and air" was an expression used to refer to the means by which land could determine human or cultural disposition. Azar notes that the shoemaker/poet Aqa 'Abdullah "Sha'ef" was from Qom, "but he had an extremely pleasant disposition," a statement that points to a commonly held idea about the dispositions of Qomis.[77] This essence could be altered. The poet "Dami" was the son of a Hamadani, "but he himself was born in Isfahan and [because] the temperate water and air of that paradisiacal region nourished the sapling of his body/form (*qamat*), he knows himself as an Isfahani."[78] Circulating features of the land, such as water and air, could interact with a person's body and transform his nature. Less mutable than people, land nonetheless gained character according to its people, especially its rulers under whose stewardship the flows of people took place.

Origin and Land

Not everyone in Azar's poetic community could be linked to a land, but everyone was born in a place. Azar describes them as "kings and princes of every land (*har deyar*) and commanders of great power of every dominion (*mamlakat*), including Turks and others that in truth are not connected to a [particular] land (*mansub beh-velayati nistand*)."[79] This deterritorialized section provides an alternative view of whom Azar considers part of the Persianate, figures whose ties to lands were multiple and not the basis of their origin. Lineage, tribe, position, and service define the individuals in this section. The kings and princes range from descendants of Soltan Mahmud to Seljuks, Safavids, and Timurids of Iran, Turan, and Hendustan.[80] The most attention is given to the progenitors of the line, as in the lengthy description of the maternal and paternal genealogy of Shah Esma'il Safavid. This shah is most important for who he was, rather than his poetry, most of which was written in Turkish.[81] Azar also provides sizeable entries, mostly historical rather than poetical, for a number of his sons and descendants.[82] This section lists numerous pre-Safavid rulers, such as Sultan Ya'qub, "the son of Hasan Padshah Torkaman [Aqqoyonlu]. [Judging by] that which has been gleaned from histories, there had never been such a king among the Turks (*etrak*)."[83] This ethnicity is a known identity, which defines a specific dynasty, the Aqqoyonlu, who ruled northwestern Iran from Tabriz in the fifteenth century. Among the Timurid princes included are those, such as Homayun and Akbar, who ruled Hendustan. Azar describes Homayun as being "of the sons of Timur Gurkan. After Babor Padshah, he raised the flag of kingship in the domain of Hendustan."[84] The Gurkani rulers of Hendustan were largely defined as originating from the Timurid royal line. At different times, these princes ruled various domains in Iran, Turan, and Hendustan. It is lineage that defines them, as no single place can.

Descriptions of high nobles (*omara'*) focus less on fathers and more on generalized lineages of tribes and ethnically defined groups of people, in service to kings of Turan, Iran, and Hendustan. Azar describes the origin of the poet Bikhvodi not as a place, but as a lineage/tribe, the Rumlu (*aslash az ta'efeh-ye Rumlu*), and that he grew up (*nashv va noma'yafteh*) in Farah.[85] The poet Salim is identified as "from the Shamlu *oymaq* and a resident (*saken*) of Tehran and Qazvin."[86] For men from these Turkomen *oymaq*s, collectively known as the Qizilbash, this tribal identity turned family lineage trumped geographical place as the primary factor of origin. Place merely functions to distinguish them further as individuals. They are residents of cities, sometimes more than one, but do not belong to them like other poets. Azar himself was a Shamlu, and while this heritage no longer meant the same thing as in the first century of Safavid rule in terms of language or military position, it had crystallized into an ethnic identity of origin. When this ethnic identity was taken beyond the borders of Iran, to which the Qizilbash were particular, it became a marker of the specificity of Iran within the larger Persianate world.[87]

Belonging to multiple lands because of political loyalties were other figures, such as Bairam Khan Baharlu'i, who was "of the oymaq of Baigdeli Baharlu'i Turcomans. From the beginning of Homayun Shah's reign, he renounced service to the Safavids (*az dawlat-e Safavi ru gardan shodeh*) and went from Qandahar to Hendustan."[88] Bairam Khan's move from Qandahar to Hendustan occurred in tandem with switching loyalties from one king to another, causing these lands to accrue as part of his identity. But his immutable origin is his Turcoman ethnicity and Baharlu tribal identity, modified by his service to rulers of particular lands. The only sense of belonging to one land or another is his service to kings who rule particular kingdoms. Regardless of the reasons, the lack of centrality of place is the defining feature of origin in the section on kings, princes and high nobles. When included, place is multiple and accumulated in a narrative of origin determined by lineage and service, not a site of origin in and of itself.

For women, lack of fixity to a particular land at first seems to do with the mutability of their primary affiliations, as a daughter, wife, or mother, definitions created according to male relatives, who are themselves assumed to be more geographically fixed.[89] The only information Azar provides for Nur Jahan Begum's origin is that she was "the wife (*haram*) of Jahangir, the king of Hendustan." Her two verses are prefaced with vague vignettes about them being improvised in the context of her interaction with Jahangir.[90] But sons, like daughters, shared the same affiliation with prominent fathers. Nur Jahan is defined according to her husband, a king, not her father, who was less well known. Additionally, her known poetry was composed during her presence at court, a contextual affiliation that would have been mentioned for a male poet as well. Women are thus not alone in being defined by other men, though marriage is one association discussed only in their context. Details beyond links with other men, such as place of origin and other activities in their lives, are included in the biographical information, when available. Mahsati's entry is the longest provided for a woman, and fairly substantial in the *Atashkadeh*, regardless of sex. The only male mentioned in her biography is the Soltan at whose court she enjoyed prominence and patronage. The way in which Soltan Sanjar is narrated in her biography serves to historicize and specify her position, much as it would for any man. Azar's description of Mahsati as noble-born from Ganjah is a marker of origin that could easily be given to any male poet.[91] But unlike a male poet, she is not listed under Azerbaijan's poets. Instead of a poet of Ganjah, Mahsati is a woman poet, who happens to be from Ganjah. For Azar, it is her womanhood, not her location, that is a defining feature of her origin.

Women poets were a particularity, different from the general category of poets who are presumed to be male. This difference is transmitted to Azar in the form of the loss of, and lack of preservation of, women's work, as well as the scanty biographical information available about them. Azar in turn reproduces this particularity in the organizational structure of the *Atashkadeh*. The poet 'A'esha "is from the people of Samarqand (*az ahl-e Samarqand*)." This is the only biographical specific Azar is able to provide, except for what he extrapolates from her poetry, "that her words are sweeter than sugar." Instead of his personal selection, her poetry consists of what remains and he remarks, "though [no] verses besides these two *ruba'i* have reached my consideration, it can be comprehended that she had a pleasant (*khosh*) disposition." It is not that her work has merely failed to circulate, but that "copies of her thoughts have disappeared from among [us]."[92] Even the work of the well-known Mahsati "was lost over time, especially in 'Abdullah Khan Uzbeg's conquest of Herat."[93] Paucity of poetry and biographical source material haunts the *Atashkadeh* as a whole, but overwhelmingly in this section.

Even if the geographical origin of some women is known, their gender, the meaning of their female sex, trumps that location as a definitive source of origin. They are defined by their particularity as women. Azar titles their section "an account of the circumstances [of the lives] and poetry of virtuous women linked to every land who lived in different times and whose words robbed all [others] of eloquence."[94] That this eloquence is in reference to other women poets only is clear when Azar comments that Mahsati "of all the types (*asnaf*) of women, no one with such an exquisite (*deqqat*) disposition has been seen."[95] Women are compared to each other, cordoned off from male poets into their own category, irrespective of different stations and affiliations or geographical and genealogical origins.[96]

This gendered particularity is also constituted by the language and selection of detail of the biographical entries themselves. Though her biographical description and length of poetic selections make her entry like a man's, Mahsati is still only a woman. Azar explains that her name is a compound contraction of *mah* (moon) and *seti* (the name by which female sayyids were called).[97] Grafted onto her genealogy, her gender is modified into a particularity. In another sizeable entry, Azar remarks that Laleh Khatun "pursued rulership in a manly/capable (*mardaneh*) way and ruled the region of Kerman for a time."[98] There is no specific male according to whom her biography gains distinction, but the gendering of the ideals of bravery and strong leadership equate her with masculinity in general, both literally and figuratively.[99] In order to praise her, Azar evokes this abstracted male presence, in contrast to its presumed contemptible opposite, a presence according to which she is defined as an exception. Women are marked as flowers (Laleh) or noted for appropriate qualities, such as chastity ('Esmati).[100] Set apart from all other poets, who are men distinguished by their place of origin, rank, or their temporal proximity to Azar, it is these social specificities of their sex that become most important and that turn female poetry writers into the single category of women poets.

Conclusion

Even in a text such as the *Atashkadeh*, which seeks to map poets onto geography, place has a secondary role as a marker of origin for some people. Outside of such textual labors, a person's alignment with lands was multiple, a multiplicity Azar was able to strip away for most past poets, reducing them to their place of birth, but not when it came to princes and nobles, women, and his contemporaries in the three lands. In order to valorize Iran in that mapping, Azar relies on the overlapping schematics of history and geographical characteristics specific to a still intermeshed social, political, and cultural Persianate landscape. Even many of the poets whom Azar maps onto Iranian cities spent most of their lives elsewhere, as integral parts of Turani and Hendustani social and cultural circles. In the eighteenth century, Azar's valorization of Iran was unable to separate its society, culture and geography from neighboring Persianate lands. It is only within this shared Persianate geocultural context that

Iran as a land could be distinguished, distinctions that defied the exclusivities of nationalism.

Notes

1. Afshin Marashi, *Nationalizing Iran: Culture, Power and the State, 1870–1940* (Seattle: University of Washington Press, 2008), 6.

2. Firoozeh Kashani-Sabet, *Frontier Fictions: Shaping the Iranian Nation, 1804–1946* (Princeton: Princeton University Press, 1999); Marashi, *Nationalizing Iran*; Mohamad Tavakoli-Targhi, *Refashioning Iran: Orientalism, Occidentalism and Historiography* (London: Palgrave, 2001). Marashi focuses on royal ritual and public ceremonies. Tavakoli-Targhi traces the increasing Iranianization of Persian culture, a multifaceted idea of history and a body of knowledge vested in language. Kashani-Sabet argues that the preservation of the land of Iran was the impetus for nationalism.

3. For a discussion of the multiple contextually determined meanings of the term *mamlakat*, for instance, see Mana Kia, "Accounting for Difference: A Comparative Look at the Autobiographical Travel Narratives of Muhammad ʿAli Hazin Lahiji and ʿAbd al-Karim Kashmiri," *Journal of Persianate Studies* 2 (2009), 210–236.

4. Kashani-Sabet, *Frontier Fictions*, 15. I do not challenge the nucleus of her argument, that European colonial threats to the territorial integrity of the Qajar kingdom generated modern nationalist discourse. It is the ahistorical idea of Iran traced over thousands of years that I find problematic.

5. For instance, Kashani-Sabet argues that those described as "Iran's enthusiasts" regarded the Qajars as "heirs to previous emperors" and "dreamed of reconquest and the genesis of a new Persian empire" (4). Late eighteenth- and early nineteenth-century Irani Persian texts see the restoration of Iran as the unification of the specific territories held under the Safavids, not a timeless ancient empire. This distinction is vital for understanding the changing historicity of Iran as an idea, and its political and social significance in the medieval and early modern periods. Kashani-Sabet even notes this Safavid-specific territorial understanding of Iran in her early nineteenth-century sources, but does not comment when she notes changes in this association in late nineteenth-century sources (19).

6. Kashani-Sabet, *Frontier Fictions*, 18.

7. Muzaffar Alam, "The Culture and Politics of Persian in Precolonial Hindustan," *Literary Cultures in History: Reconstructions from South Asia*, ed. Sheldon Pollock (Berkeley: University of California Press, 2003), 131–198; Muzaffar Alam and Sanjay Subrahmanyam, *Indo-Persian Travels in the Age of Discoveries, 1400–1800* (Cambridge: Cambridge University Press, 2007); Ehsan Yarshater, "Safavid Literature: Progress or Decline," *Iranian Studies* 7/1–2 (winter-spring, 1974), 217–270.

8. Lutf ʿAli ibn Aqa Khan Azar Baygdeli, *Atashkadeh*, ed. Hasan Sadat Nasiri, 4 vols. (Tehran: Amir Kabir, 1336–1378 [1957–1999]).

9. For a fuller discussion of Persianate cultural knowledge, see Mana Kia, "Contours of Persianate Community, 1722–1835" (Ph.D. dissertation, Harvard University, 2011).

10. For more on how *tazkerehs* functioned in commemoration of Persian literary

history, and their intervention therein, see Sunil Sharma, "Redrawing the Boundaries of 'Ajam in Early Modern Persian Literary Histories," in *Iran Facing Others: Identity Boundaries in a Historical Perspective*, eds. Abbas Amanat and Farzin Vejdani (New York: Palgrave Macmillan, 2012).

11. Only poetic *tazkerehs* authored by men remain to us. The only *tazkereh* authored by a woman is on Sufis of the Chisti order, *Munis al-arvah* by Jahanara Begum, the Mughal emperor Shah Jahan's daughter. I thank Sunil Sharma for bringing this to my attention.

12. Tarif Khalidi, *Arabic Historical Thought in the Classical Period* (Cambridge: Cambridge University Press, 1994), 85.

13. Mir 'Abd al-Latif Shushtari, *Tuhfat al-alam va zel al-tuhfat*, ed., Samad Muvahhid (Tehran: Ketabkhaneh-e Tahuri, 1363 [1984]), 368. Abu Taleb is the author of the famed travelogue to Europe from Calcutta, *Masir-e Talebi*.

14. This perception is part of the larger Islamicate historiographical tradition. Dwight F. Reynolds et al., *Interpreting the Self: Autobiography in the Arabic Literary Tradition*, ed. Dwight F. Reynolds (Berkeley: University of California Press, 2001).

15. On the development of the *tazkereh* genre, see Sunil Sharma, "Redrawing the Boundaries of 'Ajam"; and "Amir Khosraw, Fayzi and the Geography of Indo-Persian Literature," unpublished papers.

16. Sharma notes that two other geographically oriented *tazkerehs*, Amin Razi's *Haft 'Iqlim* and Taher Nasrabadi's *Tazkereh*, did exist ("Geography of Indo-Persian Literature," 5–7). Azar is aware of them and references them often.

17. Sharma, "Boundaries of 'Ajam'" and "Geography of Indo-Persian Literature."

18. See the section on Azar and the *Atashkadeh* in Edward Granville Browne, *A Literary History of Persia*, vol. 4, intro. J. T. P. de Bruijn (Bethesda, MD: Iranbooks, 1997), 282–284.

19. Tavakoli-Targhi, *Refashioning Iran*, 105. Though they take generic context and literary history more into account, most scholarly treatments of the Atashkadeh assume this protonationalist impulse. Sharma "Boundaries of 'Ajam," 5–9; "Geography of Indo-Persian Literature," 13, 16–18; and Alam "Persian in Precolonial India."

20. Tavakoli-Targhi notes that in the wake of the *bazgasht*, Persian in Qajar Iran was written in a new, simpler style. Tavakoli-Targhi frames this as part of the genealogy of modern Iranian nationalism, but its practitioners, like Yaghma Jandagi (d. 1271/1859) called it *farsi-e baset* (basic Persian) or *sadeh nevisi* (simple prose) (*Refashioning Iran*, 107). The important thing is that at the first half of the nineteenth century it was considered a style of writing, not a practice of national identity. For more on the problematics of Sabk-e Hendi, see Wali Ahmadi, "The Institution of Persian Literature and the Genealogy of Bahar's 'Stylistics,'" *British Journal of Middle Eastern Studies* 31, 2 (2004), 141–152; and Rajeev Kinra, "Make it Fresh: Time, Tradition, and Indo-Persian Literary Modernity," in *Time, History, and the Religious Imaginary in South Asia*, ed. Anne C. Murphy (London; New York: Routledge, 2011), 12–39. For more on Bahar, see Matthew Chaffee Smith, "Literary Courage, Language, Land, and the Nation in the Work of Malik al-Shuʿara Bahar," (Ph.D. dissertation, Harvard University, 2006).

21. Kathryn Babayan, *Mystics, Monarchs and Messiahs: Cultural Landscapes of Early Modern Iran* (Cambridge, MA: Harvard Center for Middle East Studies, distributed

by Harvard University Press, 2002), 29. Persian as a literary language in Rum (Ottoman domains) had declined by the eighteenth century.

22. This does not mean that manuscripts of the *Shahnameh* were not commissioned or circulated in Mughal domains. Emperors treasured copies in their libraries and manuscripts were produced in noble and regional courts. See Sunil Sharma, "The Production of Mughal Shahnamas: Imperial, Sub-Imperial, and Provincial Manuscripts," in Ferdowsi's *Shahnama: Millenial Perspectives*, ed. Olga M. Davidson and Marianna Shreve Simpson (Boston: Ilex, distributed by Harvard University Press, forthcoming 2013).

23. See Shohleh Quinn, *Historical Writing During the Reign of Shah 'Abbas: Ideology, Imitation and Legitimacy in Safavid Chronicles* (Salt Lake City: University of Utah Press, 2000).

24. Tavakoli-Targhi, *Refashioning Iran*, 85. For the medieval development of this dual narrative, see Julie Meisami, "The Past in the Service of the Present: Two Views of History in Medieval Persia," *Poetics Today* 14, 2 (Summer 1993), 247–275. Mohammad ibn Khavandshah ibn Mahmud "Mir Khvand," *Tarikh-e rawzat al-safa fi sirat al-anbeya' va al-moluk va al-kholafa'*, 15 vols., ed. Jamshid Keyanfar (Tehran: Asatir, 1380 [2001–2002]).

25. The third section begins with the birth of the Prophet Muhammad, the advent of Islam, the first four caliphs, and the subsequent history of caliphs and imams until the Mongol invasion under Hulagu Khan. The fourth section covers the history of kings in Persia from Arab to Mongol conquests. The fifth section covers the Mongol empire, particularly Ilkhanid rule in Iran and Mesopotamia. The sixth section covers Amir Timur and his descendants until the year 830/1426, though many subsequent manuscripts extended this coverage, and other court histories sought to write rulers and their dynasties into this narrative frame.

26. As late as the mid-nineteenth century, Reza Qoli Hedayat, a poet, scholar, and official in the Qajar court, updated *Rawzat al-safa*, extending it to Naser al-Din Shah Qajar's time. In 1017/1608–1609, a courtier at the court of Shah 'Ali 'Adelshah of Bijapur wrote *Tazkereh al-moluk*, which was an abridged version of *Rawzat al-safa* and *Habib al-seyar* that included a history of the kings of the Deccan, beginning with the Bahmanis up through the 'Adelshahis, and including accounts of the sultans of Gujarat, Ahmednagar, Golconda and the Mughals. The last section covers the reign of contemporaneous kings, including the Ottomans and the Safavids. The conclusion includes extracts from the *Shahnameh*. Edward Rehatsek, *Catalogue Raisonnée of the Arabic, Hendustani, Persian and Turkish MSS in the Mulla Firuz Library* (Bombay: Managing Committee of the Mulla Firuz Library, 1873), 73–75.

27. Shahjahan's governor of Ghazni commissioned one such prose retelling for Mughal officials who did not have time to read the full poem. The text, *Shahnameh-e Mokhtasar-e Shamshir Khani*, by Tavakkol Baig, was commissioned in AD 1652–1653/ AH 1063. Copies of this text were made well into the eighteenth century and turn up in the libraries of Hendustani Persians in the nineteenth century. In Bombay, the Parsi Mulla Firuz's manuscript copy is dated AD 1716–1717/AH 1129 (Rehatsek, *Catalogue*, 152). The Sikh ruler of the Punjab, Ranajit Singh, presented an 1835 copy in 1841 to the French Lieutenant-General Comte de Rumigny. This copy at least interposes verses from the poem with prose abridgements. "Shamshir Khani: From Pen to

Printing Press, Ten Centuries of Islamic Book Arts," Indiana University Collections, accessed 6/30/11, www.iub.edu/~iuam/online_modules/islamic_book_arts/explore/sh amshir_khani/index.html. For more on this text, see Pasha M. Khan, "Marvellous Histories: Reading the Shahnamah in India," Indian Journal of Economic Social History Review 49, 4 (2012), 527–556.

28. This location is very much 'Eraq-e 'ajam, or west-central Iran. John R. Perry notes that none of the big literary names of the time lived in Afsharid-ruled Khorasan, which he claims stagnated culturally and economically after 1750 (*Karim Khan Zand: A History of Iran, 1747–1779* [Chicago: University of Chicago Press, 1979], 244).

29. Though the Shamlus, as a Qizilbash tribe, had been formally removed from the upper echelons of central Safavid power, they remained locally powerful. Azar's maternal family had ruled Qalamraw 'Ali Shakar region (around Kirmanshah and Hamadan) through Karim Khan Zand's rule (Perry, 20–21). They were not alone among the Qizilbash tribes to retain local power in provincial areas. See Nobuaki Kondo, "Qizilbash Afterwards: the Afshars in Urumiya from the Seventeenth to the Nineteenth century," *Iranian Studies* 32, vol. 4 (1999), 537–556.

30. He also accompanied 'Ali Mardan Khan and Karim Khan Zand on campaign (Perry, *Karim Khan Zand*, 308).

31. Azar, *Atashkadeh*, 4:10.

32. 'Ali Qoli Khan Valeh Daghestani, *Tazkareh-e riyaz al-sho'ara'*, vol. 1, ed. Mohsen Naji Nasirabadi (Tehran: Asatir, 1384 [2005]), 309; and 'Ali Ebrahim Khan Khalil Banarasi, *Sohof-e Ebrahim: Bakhsh-e mo'aseran*, ed. Mir Hashem Mohaddes (Tehran: Anjoman-e asar va mofakher-e farhangi, 1384 [2006]), 48–49.

33. Perry, *Karim Khan Zand*, 244; J. Matini, "Azar Bigdeli," *Encyclopaedia Iranica*, Online Edition, December 15, 1987, available at http://www.iranicaonline.org/articles /azar-bigdeli-hajj-lotf-ali-big. Also see the introduction to the fourth volume, Azar, *Atashkadeh*, 4:7–17.

34. Ibid., 1:101.

35. Ibid.

36. Such stories fit into the larger historical context of the *Shahnameh*, but it is in histories like the *Rawzat al-safa* that they are specifically narrated, animating the basic *Shahnameh* chronology. Shahpur was the son of Ardeshir, the first Sasanian king. See Abolqasem Ferdowsi, *Shahnameh: The Persian Book of Kings*, trans. Dick Davis (New York: Penguin, 2007), 574–576.

37. Azar, *Atashkadeh*, 2:865. In the *Shahnameh*, this story fits chronologically into the wars of Iran and Turan during the Kayanid period (Ferdowsi, *Shahnameh*, 110–141). It is specifically referred to in the Rawzat. Azar echoes Mir Khvand's credulity with regard to the flight of the arrow, but states that he included it because all the other histories have done so as well. Mohammad ibn Khavandshah ibn Mahmud "Mir Khvand," *History of the Early Kings of Persia: From Kaiomars, the First of the Peshdadian Dynasty, to the conquest of Iran by Alexander the Great*, trans. David Shea (London: Oriental Translation Fund, 1832), 172–176.

38. Azar, *Atashkadeh*, 1:212.

39. For Sabzevar, see ibid., 1:397; for Kerman, see ibid., 2:611.

40. Valeh also shares this perception. See, e.g., *Riyaz al-sho'ara'*, 1:147.

41. For more on the Iranianization of Persian in nineteenth-century India, see Sha-

mur Rahman Faruqi, "Unprivileged Power: The Strange Case of Persian (and Urdu) in Nineteenth Century India," *The Annual of Urdu Studies*, vol. 13 (1998), 3–30.

42. Maftun was a poet born in Delhi who later moved to Azimabad (Patna). In November 1825, he undertook the Hajj, traveling to the Hijaz via Calcutta and the Indian Ocean. After performing Hajj, he arrived in the port of Bushihr in November 1826, in order to perform pilgrimage to the tomb of the eighth Shi'a Imam in Mashhad, from where he returned to Hendustan via Central Asia. Maftun's long journey to Mashhad is punctuated by stops in Shiraz, Isfahan, and Tehran, as well as smaller towns. The minutiae about the state of the roads, every halting place and caravanserai, and nearby villages, with information about the quality of available food and water in marketplaces, indicates that he likely wrote the text as a practical manual for future pilgrims and travelers. See Hajji 'Ali Mirza Maftun, *Zobdat al-akhbar fi savaneh al-asfar: safarnamah-e Iran qarn-e nuzdahom-e miladi*, ed. Zakera Sharif Qasemi (New Delhi: Islamic Wonders Bureau, 2003).

43. Houshang was the grandson of Gayomars and an early pre-Islamic king (Ferdowsi, *Shahnameh*, 1–4).

44. Maftun, Zobdat al-akhbar, 110.

45. Maftun cites Hamdullah Mustawfi Qazvini (1281–1350), who wrote epic poems, histories, and geographies focused on Iran up through the Mongol period, in service to the last Ilkhan, Abu Sa'id, to describe the destruction of Genghis Khan (*Zobdat al-akhbar*, 110).

46. Chanchal Dadlani "The 'Palais Indiens' Collection of 1774: Representing Mughal Architecture in Late Eighteenth-Century India." *Ars Orientalis* 39 (2010): 186–187.

47. Dadlani, "The 'Palais Indiens' Collection," 188–189. The difference is that architectural plans served strictly functional purposes and were not drawn with aesthetic concerns in mind. The *Palais Indien* paintings on the other hand were idealized representations drawn with color, flourishes, and materials reminiscent of the works of art.

48. Ibid., 191–192.

49. Maftun, *Zobdat al-akhbar*, 9.

50. Ibid., 10.

51. Such an inclusion could be due to its importance to Shi'i Islam as the resting place of most Imams, its adjacency to 'Eraq-e 'ajam and the shores of Fars. Whatever the reason, it is obviously claiming illegitimacy of Ottoman rule.

52. Azar, *Atashkadeh*, 3:915.

53. Ibid., 4:11. This is a lithographed copy of an Iranian manuscript.

54. Ibid., 4:239.

55. See Ferdowsi, *Shahnameh*, 36–37.

56. Ibid., 37–41.

57. Azar, *Atashkadeh*, 4:239.

58. For Balkh, see ibid., 4:241. For Badakhshan, see ibid., 4:348.

59. Ibid., 4:411.

60. As noted above, Azar draws on and echoes the *Rawzat*. The *Atashkadeh* has a short entry on Mir Khvand, largely because of the *Rawzat*, since Mir Khwand did not have a *takhallos* and only occasionally wrote poetry (Azar, *Atashkadeh*, 4:282).

61. Ibid., 4:417.

62. Ibid.

63. The land of Hendustan consists of the Deccan, Delhi, Sirhend, Kabul, Lahore, and Kashmir. Azar repeatedly admits that his attention to them is scanty because of the paucity of information at his disposal.

64. This was the date on which Delhi was conquered by Muhammad Ghuri.

65. Azar, *Atashkadeh*, 4:423.

66. Ibid., 4:440.

67. Referring to Kashmir as a city is not the only geographical error Azar makes. He calls the Deccan a *velayet*, though from the description it is obvious that he is referring to the city of Hyderabad (or Golconda, as it was known until the late seventeenth century).

68. Azar, *Atashkadeh*, 4:441. Sultan Sikander "*botshekan*" (idol smasher) was the second ruler of the Sayyid dynasty and ruled Kashmir from 1389 to 1413. For an overview of Islam in Kashmir and other regions of Hendustan, see Annemarie Schimmel, *Islam in the Indian Subcontinent* (Leiden: Brill, 1980).

69. Azar, *Atashkadeh*, 4:441.

70. Valeh calls Isfahan "*behesht neshan*" (Valeh, *Riyaz al-sho'ara*', 2:885). Azar calls Isfahan "*khold neshan*" (ibid., 4:590). Both Azar and Valeh were born in Isfahan and considered it their homeland.

71. Ibid., 4:348.

72. Azar cites *Haft 'eqlim* in the geographical section on Sistan, but does not repeat its particulars on Sistan, because Azar says that he has not seen the region and, therefore, cannot verify the text's information. This is one among many signs of his general skepticism of *Haft 'eqlim*, authored by a migrant from Iran at the Mughal court (ibid., 1:420). For more on climes and the *Haft 'eqlim*, see Sharma, "Geography of Indo-Persian Literature," 5–8.

73. For Kashmir, see Azar, *Atashkadeh*, 4:441. Balkh is listed under Turan, but is in the fourth clime (ibid., 4:241).

74. For Ghaznin, see ibid., 2:535, Sistan (included as part of Khorasan), see ibid., 1:418; *'Eraq-e 'arab*, see ibid., 3:921; Fars, see ibid., 4:115. Yazd (ibid., 4:101) is in the same clime as Delhi (ibid., 4:423).

75. Ibid., 4:115.

76. Shirvan (ibid., 1:148) and Ganjah (ibid., 1:204) are also in the fifth clime.

77. Ibid., 4:520.

78. Ibid., 4:495.

79. Ibid., 1:37.

80. For instance, Azar includes sons of Sultan Husayn Mirza Bayqara' of Herat, such as Badi' al-Zaman Mirza (ibid., 1:48). For Akbar, see ibid., 1:52.

81. For the entry, which lists only one line of poetry, see ibid., 1:57–58. Shah Esma'il wrote poetry in Turkish, because this devotional poetry was aimed at his Qizilbash followers, who were mostly Turkish speakers. He named his sons Bahram, Sam, Alqas, and Tahmasp all after figures in the *Shahnameh*, because he hoped to tap into the ideal of kingship it represented, as part of his political legitimacy. Like his contemporaries, Babur and the Ottoman Sultan Selim (who wrote poetry in Persian), Esma'il was bilingual in Persian and Turkish, linguistic identities which, like origins, could and did accommodate multiple features that were deployed according to context. For more

on Shah Esmaʿil as a poet, see V. Minorsky, "The poetry of Shah Ismaʿil I," *Bulletin of the School of Oriental and African Studies, University of London* (1942): 1006a–1053a.

82. See, e.g., the entry on Shah Abbas I, Azar, *Atashkadeh*, 1:76–77; the entry on Shah Tahmasp, ibid., 1:74; and the entry on Shah Esmaʿil II, ibid., 1:75.

83. Ibid., 1:100.

84. Ibid., 1:99–100.

85. The manuscripts differ on the word *taʾefeh*. One only has *"aslash az Rumlu,"* while three others use the word *tabageh* (a class or order of men) instead. See ibid., 1:49 n. 8. The Rumlu were a tribal group who helped the Safavids come to power in Iran and whose membership became fixed around the time the Safavids gained political power. For more on the Qizilbash, see Kathryn Babayan, *Mystics, Monarchs and Messiahs*, 353–366; Masashi Haneda, *Le chah et les Qizilbāsˈ: le système militaire safavide* (Berlin: K. Schwarz, 1987); and Roger M. Savory, "Qizil-bash," *Encyclopaedia of Islam*, 2d ed., eds. P. Bearman, Th. Bianquis, C. E. Bosworth, E. van Donzel, and W. P. Heinrichs. Brill Online. Accessed 24 July 2011 at http://refereneworks.brillonline .com/?fromBrillOnline=true.

86. Azar, *Atashkadeh*, 1:64.

87. The Qizilbash were so integral to Safavid political identity that, even after their putative loss of power on an imperial scale, they were associated with the land of Iran because of their association with Iran's Safavid rulers. In the early nineteenth century, travelers and migrants from Iran to Hendustan call other Irani Persians in Hendustan "Qizilbash." See Kia, "Contours of Persianate Community," 163–170.

88. Azar, *Atashkadeh*, 1:49. This detail is factually incorrect, since Bairam Khan's Baharlu line was actually part of the Qaraqoyonlu confederation that entered Timurid service in the mid-fifteenth century, when the Aqqoyonlu took over Azerbaijan and eastern Anatolia. Bairam Khan followed his father in service to Babur and never switched loyalties. See Babur, *The Baburnama: Memoirs of Babur, Prince and Emperor*, Trans. Wheeler M. Thackston (New York: Modern Library, 2002), 33; 473 n. 71. The veracity of this claim is not important for the purposes of my argument, which has more to do with perception than accuracy.

89. For more on women poets, see Dominic Parviz Brookshaw, "Odes of a Poet-Princess: The *Ghazals* of Jahān-Malik Khātun," *Iran* 43 (2005), 173–195, and Sunil Sharma, "From ʿAʾesha to Nur Jahan: The Shaping of a Classical Persian Poetic Canon of Women," *Journal of Persianate Studies* 2,2 (2009), 148–164.

90. Azar, *Atashkadeh*, 4:452.

91. Ibid., 4:448.

92. Ibid., 4:445. Azar notes a similar paucity of biographical information and availability of work for the poets ʿEsmati and ʿEfati (ibid., 4:446).

93. Ibid., 4:449.

94. Ibid., 4:445.

95. Ibid., 4:448.

96. Their placement at the end of the *Atashkadeh* is indicative of their relative value as a group. Princes and nobles, also distinguished from other poets by their station, come first, followed by the main/male historical poets mapped onto a hierarchically valued geography, with Iran followed by Turan and Hendustan. Women are last, before the author launches into his autobiography.

97. Azar, *Atashkadeh*, 4:448–51.

98. Ibid., 4:446.

99. This equation of valorized behavior with masculinity is also found in Valeh, who praises female poets who write like men (meaning they write well), or defends their poetry as an exception, though they are women. Specifically, women poets who were also rulers are compared to men in order to praise them. See Sharma, "From 'A'esha to Nur Jahan," 8–12.

100. Azar, *Atashkadeh*, 4:446.

CHAPTER 6

The Khuzistani Arab Movement, 1941–1946: A Case of Nationalism?

BRIAN MANN

Many historians have focused on the complex and intriguing Kurdish and Azeri national movements of the 1940s, but the Khuzistani Arabs are conspicuously absent from the historiography of Iran's "decentralization" era, which lasted from 1941 until 1953. When Iranian Arabs appear, they are often dismissed as nothing more than self-serving agents of British imperialism, or proxies for the British military, the Foreign Office, the Government of British India, or the Anglo-Iranian Oil Company (AIOC). This paper challenges these views and conceptions, arguing that the elites of Khuzistani Arab society voiced a unique Arab ethnic national identity, which became the basis for a burgeoning yet short-lived ethnonationalist movement. To say otherwise, one would have to put aside the fact that the Arabs involved said they constituted a nation, a nation based on a shared ethnic identity rooted in shared traditions, rituals, and history, and one located within a defined territorial homeland. This does not discount that British agents, at times, lent support to the movement, but as this paper will demonstrate, often the British acted against Khuzistani Arab interests. Scholars have long recognized Soviet support for the Tudeh Party, the Mahabad Republic, and the Azerbaijan People's Government, but simultaneously stress these movements as genuine and independent. This paper aims to provide the Arabs of Khuzistan the same treatment that has been afforded to other non-Persian ethnic movements and non-state actors.

Background

The Arabs of Khuzistan had long resented the modernization, centralization, and detribalization efforts of the Pahlavi state, and its ethnically Persian-based nationalism. Therefore, following the Shah's abdication in 1941, a number of Arab elites began to formulate and employ an Arab ethnonationalist identity as a means to recoup the socioeconomic standing and political authority they enjoyed during the rule of Shaykh Khaz'al ibn Jabir. This identity allowed these elites to validate their claim to an independent Arab emirate. Appealing to their coethnics, the British, and the Arab states of the newly formed Arab League, these men sought to reverse the setbacks they suffered during the previous decade and a half. Initially, this ethnonationalist rhetoric was employed by only a few elites of a particular tribal group, but as conditions deteriorated due to the war, and because of the Iranian government's often violent response to tribal activities, the rudimentary ethnic identity became more palatable to other Khuzistani Arab elites. The increase in antitribal repression, and the corresponding decline in legitimacy and power of the central government, created a political and socioeconomic atmosphere in which tribal elites who had once held long-standing enmities toward one another were able to unite under the banner of an ethnonational identity.

While tribal cooperation increased between 1941 and 1945, tribal identities were not brushed aside, since many tribal elites may have embraced their Arab ethnic identity but relegated it to a place below the tribal level in the hierarchy of identity. Furthermore, the movement's evolution was hindered by the classic free-rider problem; many tribal elites did not want to risk involvement. Although the movement gained and lost adherents throughout the war years, it took two developments, both of which occurred in the winter of 1945–1946, that would allow the Arabs to begin to effectively transcend tribalism and trend toward nationalism. The first of these developments was socioeconomic. The rapid influx of Tudeh cadres into Khuzistan during 1944 and 1945 resulted in the Tudeh's domination over Khuzistan's trade unions. The communist influence in the province deeply concerned Arab tribal elites and their tribesmen. The Tudeh's socioeconomic system was anathema to the Arabs; it represented the antithesis of their feudal way of life. Furthermore, the nationalism espoused by the Tudeh cadres was viewed by the Arabs as even more ethnocentric than the nationalism of the former Pahlavi state.

Another development that afforded the Arabs the opportunity to embrace nationalism was a change in their organization and leadership structure. In January 1946, the last of the original leaders of the movement, the old tribal elites whom most distrusted for historical reasons, had left the movement (either by co-option or exile). This allowed the Arab ethnonational identity to become more accessible, palatable, and persuasive, but also deprived the movement of the capacity to organize and mobilize its members.

The language used by the leaders of the Arab movement employed the standard devices of an ethnonationalist discourse. They continuously stressed that their ethnicity, language, customs, and history constituted a defined nation that had no place in an ethnically Persian-dominated Iran. The language of the discourse was subject to its audience, the vicissitudes of tribal politics, Western imperial rivalries, and the dynamics of Iranian domestic affairs.

An application of the conventional primordialist and modernist approaches to nationalism cannot adequately explain the Khuzistani Arab movement. However, it is useful to examine Anthony Smith's model, which argues that modern nations formulate identities based on preexisting *ethnies* that utilize the groups' shared memories, myths, and rituals.[1] Smith's ethnosymbolist approach defines seven preconditions required for the emergence of a nation: 1) a fixed homeland, either current or historic; 2) a high level of autonomy; 3) hostile surroundings; 4) sacred centers; 5) a unique language and script; 6) shared customs and rituals; and 7) a shared vision of history. Together, these seven conditions can create a potent mythology, and lead to the coalescence of an *ethnie* and then the creation of a nation.[2] Although this approach cannot be applied to this case *in toto*, it will be demonstrated that the Khuzistani Arabs possessed all of Smith's preconditions. The problem remains, however, that before and after the Arab elites adopted an ethnonationalist rhetoric, they and their respective tribesmen possessed numerous, seemingly conflicting, identities.

The Khaz'als and the Transcendence of Tribal Identity

In the late sixteenth century, Arab tribes from the Arabian Peninsula, in particular the Bani Ka'b, migrated to Khuzistan in search of more fertile agricultural lands.[3] The Ka'b remained the largest and most powerful tribe in the region until the mid-nineteenth century, when the tribe fractured into rival subtribes. The Muhaisin, a section of the Ka'b, emerged from the power struggle as the dominant clan under the leadership of their shaykh, Jabir al-Ka'bi. Due to their numerical inferiority, the Muhaisin's dominance over the Ka'b was not total at this time, and many tribes continued to maintain a firm degree of autonomy. When Shaykh Jabir died in 1881, however, an ensuing power struggle left his son Shaykh Khaz'al Khan ibn Jabir in power and in possession of the title Shaykh of Muhammarah. During his reign, the Muhaisin signed a number of financial and military agreements with British consuls, military commanders, and AIOC officials.[4] With British support, Khaz'al was also able to consolidate and expand the power of the Muhaisin over most of the tribes of Khuzistan. Over a period of twenty years, Khaz'al forced all but one of the Arab tribes to submit to his authority. Many of the Ka'b subtribes that resisted Jabir's coup had joined to form a large tribe, also called the Ka'b. During the First World War, Khaz'al accomplished what his father could not: the complete capitulation of the Ka'b shaykhs and tribesmen. The only tribe to remain relatively autonomous of the Muhaisin was the Bani Turuf. Khaz'al lacked the military strength required to subdue this numerically superior tribe, but he was able to establish an economic hegemony over them. Briefly, the Bani Turuf relied on the Muhaisin for access to trade and to agricultural capital. Recognizing his economic superiority, Khaz'al afforded them virtual autonomy in exchange for a handsome annual tribute.[5] However, when Reza Khan rose to power in 1921, many British officials gradually came to prefer the central-government rule of the new Shah over the autonomous rule of Khaz'al. The shaykh had spent more than a quarter century suppressing the Khuzistani tribes for both the British and his own personal gain. In March 1925, with tacit British approval, Reza Khan arrested Khaz'al and occupied the province with the Iranian military.[6]

The non-Muhaisin tribes resented Khaz'al's rule, and many welcomed Reza Khan as a liberator. Within months, however, the tribes realized that the Shah's antitribal policies were aimed to destroy their way of life. Many tribesmen were forcibly relocated, and their shaykhs were placed under house arrest in faraway cities. Moreover, their land was confiscated with the property deeds transferred to the central government, the Shah's personal estate, or Persian landowners. Every aspect of the Arab tribal identity was under attack as Arabic was banned in print and in schools, a European dress code was strictly enforced, and Persian place names were substituted for Arabic ones. The presence of the Iranian authorities and the establishment of an anti-Arab provincial administration gave the Arabs a common cause to unite, but their history of intertribal warfare, distrust, and conflicting identities hindered such a development.

Shaykh Khaz'al's death in Tehran in 1936 did not signal the end of the Khaz'al family's involvement in tribal or British affairs. Four of the Shaykh's sons, Chassib, Abdullah, Abd al-Karim, and Abd al-Majid, continued to remain politically active. Following their father's death, the sons became involved in litigation over the fate of the family's date gardens, which lay on the Iranian side of the Shatt al-Arab. In 1940, the British had already experienced massive military setbacks in Western Europe. The war provided Chassib Khaz'al the opportunity to offer his support for the Allies, in an effort to reclaim his family's land.

Immediately upon Britain's seizure of Abadan, Ahwaz, and Khorramshahr, Chassib emerged in order to reestablish Arab autonomy. First, he began to circulate pamphlets among Arab tribal leaders in Basra and in Khuzistan. One such pamphlet congratulated the Bani Turuf, Ka'b, and the various sub-tribes of the Muhaisin on the occasion of the defeat of Reza Shah's army. The pamphlets wished the tribes "good luck and freedom," and requested that they support the British who had "entered your country and have purified it from corruption."[7] Although these pamphlets were successful in inducing broad Muhaisin support for Chassib and his efforts, the Bani Turuf or Ka'b remained distant. The Vice-Consul in Khorramshahr began receiving a "great number" of petitions from the Muhaisin tribal shaykhs in his jurisdiction, but not from other Arab tribal elites.[8] Muhaisin-penned petitions also landed on the desk of the Commander of the 8th Indian Division, A. C. Galloway. Most, if not all, of these petitions, signed by Muhaisin tribal leaders, asked that the British agree to have Shaykh Chassib act as their representative in all matters.[9]

Chassib also focused on the British. He commenced a letter-writing campaign to the British Ambassador in Baghdad, the British Embassy in Tehran, and the Consuls at Basra and Khorramshahr. In each, Chassib laid out a historical basis for an independent Arab emirate in Khuzistan. He stated that the "Arabs of Khuzistan are the residents of this country for generations" and that they had enjoyed "independence and freedom" and never had been required "to yield to the Iranian Government." The letters also stated that only after 1925 had the Arabs "suffered oppression, tyranny, and persecution at the hands of the tyrant Pahlavi government, which killed our tribal heads and fathers, photographed our women folk, shed the blood of our children and violated our religion." The letters then concluded with the request that the British intervene on the Arabs' behalf, take them under the protection of the British flag, and treat them like their "Arab brothers in the Persian Gulf, i.e., Bahrain, Kuwait, etc."[10]

To prove his sincerity and his ability to organize the Arabs and thereby maintain security in the region, Chassib formed a political organization named the Arab Elam State Party of Khuzistan. In a letter to the British Embassy in Tehran, a man claiming to be the secretary of the party, known only as Mahmud, made a historical claim to the legitimacy of a Khuzistani Arab nation. He argued that the Arabs had once had a state in the region, with Susa as its capital. Chassib's previous letters to British officials hinted at an Arab presence in Khuzistan dating back to the tribal migrations of the sixteenth century, but now he and his cohorts harkened back to the seventh-century Arab conquest of Persia, and located Susa as the sacred capital of their Arab nation. The Arabs, according to Mahmud, had a genuine historical justification to reestablish "the gallant ancient Arab State of Elam" and since "it would be only in conformity with British justice not to allow [a single race] to impose its own rule upon the others," the British were obligated to establish a British protectorate with "Amir Sheikh Chassib as King."[11]

Chassib ceased reaching out to non-Muhaisin tribal leaders at this time, as he saw no need to include the "lesser" tribes in his campaign, or benefit on doing so. At this time, the ethnonational rhetoric employed by the Muhaisin likely was little more than a political strategy employed to sway British opinion. As long as there remained the possibility of the British installing him on the throne of a quasi-independent Khuzistan protectorate, there was no reason to jeopardize the possibility by including other Arab tribes, especially since their loyalty was questionable. The Muhaisin did not forget that many tribes had turned on Khaz'al in 1925 when they offered assistance to Reza Shah.

Abdullah, al-Majid, and al-Karim Khaz'al, like their older brother, also sought support from their Muhaisin tribesmen, but again worked independently of Chassib. On one occasion, the three brothers and a few shaykhs of the Baghlaniya and Bakhakh subtribes visited the British Consul in Basra. At this meeting on 29 September, they told the Consul "horrible stories of Persian prisons and Gestapo methods" employed by the Iranians. They asked how British war propaganda could claim the British were waging a war to liberate the oppressed, but simultaneously "ignore the claims of the oppressed Arabs of Khuzistan"? They claimed it was illogical and cruel for the British to free them from the rule of tyranny only to return them to slavery.[12]

There was relative quiet in Khuzistan during the next few months until the Turkic Kuhgalu tribe, inspired by the unruly behavior of their Bani Turuf neighbors, set in motion an armed rebellion in late March. The Kuhgalu allied with the Boir Ahmadi to launch attacks in the vicinity of the Gach Saran oilfields east of Ahwaz. The tribesmen blocked roads, stole oil facility material, and forcibly removed security personnel guarding a number of oil rigs.[13] In response, the Iranian military requested British air support to help quell the rebellion. The request caused division between the British military liaisons and the consular officials at Ahwaz. Major Jeacock, the Air Liaison Officer in the region, provided R.A.F. air support, to the dismay of J. G. Baillie, the Consul-General at Ahwaz, who was never informed of the decision. Baillie wrote a letter to the British Ambassador in Tehran formally protesting Jeacock's policy decision. Baillie argued that the British should not take any action that would give the impression that "we are behind the Persian Government in its treatment of the tribes. The time may come when for our own security we may be compelled to deal more directly with the tribes in spite of the Persian authorities in Tehran."[14] Although military cooperation with

Iranian authorities in Gach Saran secured the oilfields, Baillie was concerned with Chassib's renewed efforts among the Arab tribes.

On 9 April 1942, two days before Baillie wrote Tehran, Chauncey, the Consul-General at Khorramshahr, received a petition signed by sixty-five Arab tribal elites offering their assistance to the British in return for Britain's support for their reclamation of their land from the "Persians." Calling themselves "The Arabs of Arabistan," the petitioners claimed they had "suffered at the hands of Persian officials the severest tyranny and all sorts of torment and humiliation after the absence of our esteemed leader, Sir Khaz'al Khan, your loyal friend." The document called for the formation of an "Arab nation similar to those in the Arab world."[15] The petition's ominous language and the names of the signatories worried Baillie and Chauncey. Firstly, the petition contained the threat "God forbid that the Government of His Britannic Majesty neglects us and not grant our demands after all the tokens of loyalty we showed her formerly and presently."[16] Secondly, it was signed not by the Muhaisin alone, but elites representing the majority of the Idris tribe located south of Abadan. It was evident that the Idris, who followed the shaykhs of the Ka'b after the split in the 1850s, were forgoing their historical enmity toward their distant relatives in order to achieve gains for the Khuzistani Arabs.[17]

On 12 April, rumors spread on both sides of the Shatt al-Arab that Chassib was set to launch an assault on Iranian military encampments in Khuzistan. British intelligence officers confirmed that Chassib successfully crossed the border on 1 April and visited Fao Island at the mouth of the Shatt al-Arab to rally the Nassar and Ka'b tribesmen. Furthermore, the British established that Kharriyah, Chassib's sister, had arrived in Khorramshahr on 11 April and confirmed she spent an entire day purchasing an inordinate amount of flour, rice, and ghee. Sources reported that she accumulated a "house full of food to assist attackers."[18] In response, Consul Chauncey asked his colleagues in Basra to detain Chassib, and, on 12 April, the Mutasarrif of Basra and British Col. Sargon notified Chassib that any attack would face staunch Iranian and British opposition. Some of the shaykhs at the meeting protested that the Khuzistani Arabs had been subjected to torture by the gendarmerie: for example, two *sayyids* had been arrested recently and one had had his eyes burned out with a hot iron, and the other had died after his testicles were twisted with a pair of pliers.[19] A few days later, when Shaykh Hajji Ali Faisali arrived with an armed contingent of tribesmen to meet Chassib on the Iranian side of the Shatt al-Arab, not a soul was there.[20] The British intervention was successful, and when the Ka'b received word that the attack had not occurred, several of their shaykhs visited Chassib in Basra to discuss the developments. Chauncey called on a number of these Ka'b elites, but "at no time [did] they deny there is anything in the air: they merely reiterate that they are solely for the British and will do nothing without their orders."[21]

In the aftermath of the aborted revolt, Chauncey grew concerned that the Ka'b were trending toward Chassib, and thus called a meeting with Kharriyeh and several leaders of the Muhaisin, Idris, and Nassar. The Arabs told the Consul that they had sworn an oath on the Qur'an to support Chassib and his efforts, and then pressed Chauncey to accept a new proposal. First, they asked the British to assume control over the administration of Khuzistan; second, they requested that this administration be succeeded by Arab rule; third, they demanded the immediate disbandment of all of the Iranian gendarmeries. Chauncey rejected all three parts of the proposal immediately. An adherent to the previously adopted British policy of not supporting the Arab tribes, the Consul reiterated that the British would only support the Persian administration in Khuzistan, and could not entertain the idea of Arab rule. The Arabs could not maintain security, Chauncey told them, but the gendarmerie had demonstrated its effectiveness.[22] The Consul's stern refusals silenced the Arabs, and rumors of an Arab revolt ceased.

During the following months, the gendarmerie and police used the Arabs' disappointment and inaction against them, and, in response, small bands of Arab tribesmen began to retaliate. Military patrols were attacked, gendarmerie barracks were looted, and trucks convoying material for the AIOC were robbed.[23] The breakdown in security led Iranian officials to plan a new disarmament campaign, which commenced in early November. A force of eight hundred soldiers, backed by armor, attacked villages approximately one hundred kilometers north of Ahwaz near Shush, the location of the capital of the ancient Arab Elam State.[24] The British implored the Persian military to reconsider the campaign, since the raids against the military and AIOC were small in scale and posed no threat to Iranian or British interests. The British also were concerned that Humayun and Zarrabi, both known to exhibit virulent anti-Arab sentiments, "appeared to be desirous of making an attempt when occasion offered to crush the Arabs by force."[25] Regardless of British concerns, however, the military stepped up its disarmament effort and its level of harassment. The previously abandoned European dress code was put back in force, and Arabs seen wearing the traditional headdress were arrested on sight, causing "irritation between the Arabs and the Persians."[26]

Once the disarmament campaign ended in failure, Chassib, still in Basra, went into action. On the night of 5 May 1943 he crossed the Shatt al-Arab with more than fifty armed and loyal Arabs by his side. The following morning, the group attacked and seized the gendarmerie post located inside one of the late Shaykh Khaz'al's palaces at Qajariyeh. Hajji Ali Faisali, Chassib's confidant, travelled to the palace to discern his friend's intentions, and found more than two hundred Iraqi and Khuzistani Arab tribesmen barricaded inside. The Consul in Khorramshahr recognized the seriousness of the situation, since there were "obvious signs of a universal tendency to join Chassib throughout the southern part of the province." Furthermore, he wrote "the moment was well chosen," with the military preoccupied with the Bakhtiyari in the north.[27]

Rumors soon spread that the Ka'b were sending an armed contingent to aid the revolt. While the Ka'b elites were inclined to join, believing the British would remain on the sidelines as long as the revolt stayed clear of AIOC installations, roadways, and communication lines, the Bani Turuf refrained from joining, likely because their close proximity to the Bakhtiyari put them at greater risk of military retaliation. Nevertheless, the potential for transtribal support for Chassib was real, and the British response was to order him to return to Basra immediately, which he did.[28] Aware that without British support the revolt was doomed to fail, Chassib and the Ka'b had miscalculated Britain's position vis-à-vis the Arabs. A number of Arabs, however, remained in the palace at Qajariyah. Iranian aircraft strafed and bombed the palace, killing not only a number of fighters, but also a number of the Bawiya tribesmen living in the surrounding area. In a written complaint to the British, two Bawiya leaders asked why they should exercise restraint when they faced constant danger from Iranian forces.[29] Col. Galloway agreed when he noted that the Iranians possibly targeted the Bawiya because their leader, Shaykh Barak, had offered his life to Chassib's cause during the Qajariyah assault.[30]

Upon receiving the Arab complaint and Galloway's assessment, the British Ambassador in Tehran was livid. In a letter to Prime Minister Ali Soheili, Ambassador Bullard demanded an explanation for the military strike, writing that if the Iranians repeated infractions that resulted in any Arab revolt, the British would leave the "imperial authorities to get out of the trouble themselves."[31] In the meantime, however, Persian workers at the AIOC oil refinery in Abadan, incited by the local police, attacked the company's Arab employees and tossed their headdresses in the river.[32]

On 25 May 1943, Abdullah Khaz'al delivered a new petition to the British and American embassies in Baghdad. Referring to themselves as the "Arabs of Arabistan" who live in "that Arab emirate on the Persian Gulf," the writers of the petition argued the British should assist a Khuzistani Arab national independence movement, just as they have been assisting other Arab and Pan-Arab nationalist movements. After a leveling of their usual indictment against "the foreign Iranic aggression," the petitioners claimed they constituted a unique nation imprisoned within the Iranian nation-state's territorial boundaries. This Arab nation, they said, possessed its own "beloved language," traditions, and rituals. The writers also were keen to make continuous reference to pan-Arabist sentiments, at times calling the land between Egypt and Khuzistan as "the Arab Home," "the Arab nation," and "the Arab country." They also said they would send a delegate of their choosing to the Arab League conference, so they could represent their "portion of the Arab Home" and thus help plot the course of "the future of the Arab Peoples." The petition ended with a plea that the British stay true to their word and help all Arabs of the world obtain "justice and freedom."[33] Upon receipt of the petition, analysts concluded that the Khuzistani Arab movement was spreading beyond the Muhaisin and its allied tribes. British military intelligence learned that the petition was not written by the usual suspects alone, i.e., Chassib and Hajji Ali Faisali, but also by the shaykhs of the Idris and Nassar tribes near Gusbah[34] and, more importantly, Shaykh Maghamis, the head of one of the largest sections of the Ka'b.[35] Days after delivering the petition, a group of Muhaisin, Idris, Nassar and Ka'b elites met to discuss the attack on Qajariyah and their response to the authorities' harassment campaign. Some argued that Arabs should run for a seat on the provincial council during the upcoming elections, but the majority viewed this as an act of collaboration with the Iranian nation-state. Instead, they decided to disseminate pamphlets, written in Arabic, throughout the province. The pamphlets called on all Arabs to boycott the upcoming elections.[36] In response, the new Chief of Police in Khorramshahr, Sarbahr Daulatshahi, ordered his officers to reinforce the European dress code, ordering that Arabs were to remove their *kuffiyahs*, and any clothing deemed "Arab," at gunpoint. The police also began to confiscate Arabic books from shops and residences, and Arabic gramophone records from Arab-owned coffeehouses.[37]

Following this new wave of oppression, British analysts concluded that the Khuzistani Arab ethnonational identity had been embraced by almost all the Muhaisin tribes, and more than half of the Ka'b and Bani Turuf.[38] The only reason a revolt had not transpired was because the British refused to support one. If the tribes were "assured that the British were supporting Chassib or even that the British would remain neutral and refrain from helping the Persian government, the whole of Khuzistan . . . would instantly revolt." Even those who feared a return of a Khaz'al-dominated Khuzistan were openly embracing a pan-Arab identity, stating publicly that the Cairo conference and Arab nationalism would free them from Iranian rule.[39]

A new disarmament campaign in July 1943 pushed many of the Bani Turuf holdouts toward Chassib. Although they handed in weapons, 80 to 90 percent of them could not be fired and dated to the First World War.[40] The token gesture of handing over obsolete weapons occurred while bands of tribesmen engaged Iranian troops. The fighting worsened, and in retaliation the gendarmeries threw Arab corpses into the river and refused to provide proper burials.[41] The Muhaisin were implicated in the Bani Turuf resistance when Hajji Ali Faisali's brother, Abdul Husayn, was arrested during a Bani Turuf-led attack.[42]

The existence of a Muhaisin-Bani Turuf alliance is further evidenced by Abdullah's activities during this period of violence. His network of Arab smugglers obtained and hid hundreds of rifles and more than 180,000 rounds of ammunition at secret locations on Abadan Island.[43] The smuggling operation continued throughout the summer as rumors of another revolt arose after Chassib and an armed band of tribesmen were arrested by the Iraqi Border Patrol. Soon thereafter, many of the Ka'b holdouts traveled to Basra to meet openly with Chassib.

The movement lost some momentum over the next year, however, because the Iranian military and gendarmerie scaled back their disarmament and harassment campaigns as the Iranians now saw tribes with historical enmities forging alliances.[44] However, the peace was short-lived. By March 1944, the hardliners within the Iranian military decided to renew the offensive, and the local police revived the European dress code. Furthermore, Tehran offered Chassib a deal by which government-owned land in northern Khuzistan would be exchanged for the confiscated Khaz'al lands in and around Khorramshahr and Abadan.[45] When leaders of the Muhaisin, Ka'b, and Bani Turuf tribes visited Chassib in Basra, they begged him not to negotiate, but Chassib replied that Arab rule of Khuzistan was a lost cause.[46] Without a leader for the movement, the head of the Khorramshahr gendarmerie, Captain Azadi, issued a proclamation banning Arab gatherings in guesthouses and coffee shops. The Abadan gendarmerie faced little resistance when it stole hundreds of horses from Arab villagers and the military had little difficulty arresting Arab elites on obviously forged charges of brigandage.[47] In early May 1944, Tehran furthered its effort at undermining pan-Arab unity by ordering the Ka'b to sell eighty percent of their crops to the central and provincial governments, with cultivators and landlords to divide the remaining twenty percent. In response, the Bani Turuf entered into a formal agreement with the Ka'b. The accord stipulated that each tribe would provide "mutual aid and cooperation in resisting Iranian government demands."[48] The two tribes then asked the shaykhs of the Muhaisin to join the pact. Many signed on, while some others awaited Abdullah's instructions. Although some of the Nassar and Idris elites refused to join the alliance, the Ka'b, Bani Turuf, and most Muhaisin tribes initiated a coordinated campaign of armed resistance. The Iranians responded with an airstrike, which killed at least sixty Bani Turuf and Ka'b tribesmen and at least two prominent Ka'b shaykhs.[49]

The new alliance was without a recognized leadership, and so the Ka'b and Bani Turuf wrote Abdullah, asking him to lead their political effort to obtain British and American support.[50] Abdullah began to write the British and the Americans. In one letter, he wrote of "the Iranian Government's aim at suppressing our tribes and nationality . . . with a view of seeking vengeance on the already persecuted population of that Arab territory." In another, he argued that the British should allow the Arabs a free hand to seize control of their lands by force. Not once, in any letter, did Abdullah mention his brother, or his family's claims to land. Instead, he stressed that his purpose was to secure "the interests of the people and territory of Arabistan" and to help maintain the survival of his people's "national existence."[51] Abdullah also crossed repeatedly into Khuzistan to meet with tribal elites. These activities caused the Iranian government to believe a revolt was under consideration, and it asked the British for assistance. In response, the Consul in Basra ordered the Mutasarrif to arrest Abdullah.[52] The Iranian authorities, sensing the British had turned on the Arabs, continued the disarmament campaign, but with new methods. In August, two Ka'b shaykhs were executed in Ahwaz for their alleged involvement in a tribal raid. Seven Ka'b and Bani Turuf shaykhs were also hanged for similar offenses in Dizful and Shushtar.[53] The tribal elites, believing the executions were sanctioned by the British, no longer felt they could rely on their former allies for protection against the Iranian government. In addition, the Iranian Department of Finance engaged in what the Arabs viewed as economic warfare. Government agents were sent to Khuzistan to appraise Arab-owned and cultivated date gardens and other agricultural projects for tax purposes. The Arabs, however, believed that the government sought to extort landowners and cultivators.[54] In response, the provincial governors and military and gendarmerie commanders called on all tribes to submit a summary of their affairs. This summary was to include the names of their subtribes, their numbers of families and houses, whether each was sedentary or nomadic, their specific locations, etc. The Bani Turuf shaykhs were also invited to Tehran to negotiate with the government, but while many of them were in transit Humayun dropped pamphlets from planes notifying the now-leaderless tribes that a new disarmament campaign was to begin, and that anyone failing to comply would be "subjected to severe punishment."[55] Beyond the threat of violence, Humayun also demanded more sensitive information from each of the province's tribes. Each shaykh was now required to list the names of each family head, the number of men in each village, the number of weapons each tribesman possessed, and the name of the canal that provided each family with water.[56] With the Bani Turuf leadership held hostage in Tehran, the tribes lacked the leadership to organize a resistance, or to put their alliance with the Ka'b into action. Some Bani Turuf fled to Iraq, while others entrusted their weapons to tribesmen across the river. Although Iranian actions had effectively fractured and disorganized the Khuzistani Arabs, Jeacock noted that the Arabs were growing more independent in their thinking, and more reliant on their ethnonational identity.[57] Following the wave of executions, the beginning of the new disarmament campaign, and the initiation of the information-collection drive, Jeacock found that the Arab elites had stopped asking the British for advice or support. Instead, he witnessed a significant increase in Arabism amongst the shaykhs. Jeacock also noted that the British were no longer asked to arbitrate intertribal disputes over water or land. With pride, the disputing tribesmen took care of the dispute nonviolently, and on their own.[58]

Abdullah wrote a defiant telegram to the British ambassador in Baghdad, in which he said the Arabs would no longer submit to injustice, enslavement, and corruption. "The Arab people of Arabistan," he wrote, "will not be held responsible if we attempt to attain our national rights and struggle against the cruelty of the Persians with armed force if we cannot attain our rights by peaceful means."[59] If the British would not aid the Arabs, the Arabs would act alone. Consular officers and intelligence analysts downplayed the threat. On 19 October 1945, Abdullah visited the British political advisor at the Amara Consulate in Iraq. At the meeting, Abdullah provided the political advisor with a series of documents aimed at convincing the British that he was now the leader of all the Arabs of Khuzistan and demonstrating transtribal support for him and his efforts on obtaining freedom for the Arabs of "Arabistan." After submitting these documents, Abdullah asked for British neutrality in the event of an Arab revolt. He argued that the only reason the Arabs were deterred from revolting was fear of British reprisal; in exchange for British neutrality, he would guarantee the safety and protection of all AIOC oil installations, roadways, and communication lines. The political advisor was noncommittal, saying that he had no authority to make any promises, and that Abdullah should write the embassy in Baghdad for an official response.[60] Abdullah left the meeting disgruntled, but only wrote Baghdad after he made an attempt to enter Khuzistan with a group of armed tribesmen.

Abdullah's letter to Baghdad was even more incendiary. In it, he implicated the newly appointed Consul at Ahwaz, Alan Charles Trott, in the death of his father.[61] The letter written to Baghdad was equally defiant, in which Abdullah attacked "HMG's inconsistent policy," and stressed that the Arabs would not postpone a rebellion to afford the British time to evacuate Iran. If the Arabs waited, Abdullah argued, the Iranians would have time to send reinforcements to prevent a revolt. However, when an independent Arab state was created in Arabistan, he hoped the British would accord it the same relations they maintained with the other Arab emirates such as Kuwait and Bahrain. The British did not respond, and instead notified Tehran of Abdullah's activities.[62]

The Establishment and Abandonment of Khuzistani Arab Nationalism

During the final months of 1945, Abdullah had been in contact with several Arab shaykhs who had decided the time was right to revolt, because the Iranian government had shown its inability to deal with the situation in Azerbaijan.[63] The government's impotence in the north boded well for the Arabs in the south, and if the Azerbaijanis were to defeat the central government, perhaps the Arabs could do the same.

By New Year's Day 1946, the population of Basra was abuzz with rumors that the British were planning to seize Khuzistan to offset Russian successes in Azerbaijan. The gist of the rumor was that Britain would install an Arab regime in Khuzistan, which would then be incorporated into Iraq, or established as an independent Arab shaykhdom.[64] The British had no such plan, of course, but Abdullah tried to force their hand.

On the night of 9 January, Abdullah crossed into Khuzistan with a few hundred armed followers. They immediately headed to Fallahiyah, the former capital and location of three palaces of his deceased father. Within minutes, Abdullah's force disarmed the gendarmerie posts in and around one of the palaces, and quickly seized the other two. After taking the palaces, Abdullah waited for the Arabs of Khuzistan to join his rebellion. Arabs began to flock across the Shatt al-Arab from Iraq, but few Khuzistani Arabs joined, with the exception of some Muhaisin tribesmen. The governor-general of Khuzistan approached the Consul at Khorramshahr, Maj. Andrew Stewart, asking for advice on how to handle the situation. The governor was reluctant to use force to quell the rebellion and wanted to negotiate. Stewart strongly disagreed. He argued that "any hesitation at this stage may be interpreted as a weakness and result in a rally of local tribes to Abdullah's side."[65] The consul was well aware that the Arabs had refrained from rebellion out of fear of British reprisal. If the Iranians did not act soon, the Arabs would believe the British had sanctioned the revolt. The government in Tehran agreed with Stewart. The Prime

Minister's office cabled Col. Afshar in Ahwaz with instructions to "settle with Abdullah once and for all."[66] The colonel's forces arrived at Fallahiyah after dusk on the night of 10 January, but could not launch an offensive in the dark. Abdullah's men blindly fired in the direction of Afshar's troops, resulting in a brief volley of gunfire and a few casualties on each side. During the night, Abdullah sent a message to Stewart, stating that if the Persians attacked, he would not be held responsible for any damage to British interests in Khorramshahr. The consul wrote back immediately with a stern warning. "If, as a result of any action which may bring you into conflict with the authorities of the Persian Government, of whom you are a subject, British lives or property are endangered, then I cannot absolve you from responsibility."[67] It was clear the British would not support the Arabs under any circumstances. Under the cover of darkness, Abdullah fled with most of his men back across the river into Iraq, and then absconded to Kuwait. Stewart commented that the whole situation had demonstrated to the tribes that the British government would never support the Arabs "in an effort to re-establish their old position of semi-independence in Khuzistan."[68]

The problem for the Arabs was that their tribal structure was retarding the emergence of a defined Khuzistani Arab nationalism. Although some of the tribes had accepted Chassib and Abdullah's formulation of an imagined Arab ethnie, the bonds of the tribe hindered a transition to an effectual ethnonationalist movement. These tribal identities, however strong they were, could not withstand the threat the Tudeh Party posed. The communist system was the antithesis of the feudal socioeconomic system of the tribes. As Tudeh Party offices opened throughout Khuzistan in the first months of 1946 and communist propaganda circulated amongst the tribes, the shaykhs recognized the Tudeh as a direct threat to their authority and their people's way of life. The shaykhs ordered their followers not to join the Tudeh and preached of the perils of communism.[69] This fear of a Tudeh coup in Tehran or takeover of the provincial government eventually led the shaykhs of the larger tribes to send a note to the Arab League Council. They pleaded with the Council to aid them against the "Persians and the communists," and asked that the Iranians accord them the same rights they gave to the Azerbaijanis. The Iraqi minister to the League, Tahsin al-Askari, was dissuaded by the British in Cairo from bringing the matter before the Council, although he asked if the Arabs of Khuzistan could receive the same deal that Ja'far Pishivari's movement received in Azerbaijan.[70] In the end, the situation in Khuzistan was not addressed adequately by the League, due to British pressure and infighting related to the League's response to the Palestine issue.

On May Day, the Tudeh Party organized a large rally in Abadan that included chants of "Death to the traitors Abdullah, Nuri Pasha, and the Pahlavi."[71] Other rallies were held in Khorramshahr, Ahwaz, and Dizful. The Tudeh were successful in recruiting some Qashqai and Bakhtiyari tribesmen, but recruitment among the Arab population had failed. Ervand Abrahamian adroitly concludes that three factors contributed to the failure: geography, employment, and ideology. Unlike the non-Arab tribesmen who left their lands and the authority of their khans, the Arabs remained tied to their lands and therefore continued to submit to their shaykh's authority. Furthermore, the Arabs hired by the AIOC were not individual wage laborers. Instead, they were employed by their shaykhs, who received construction contracts from the company. The Tudeh were organizing the wage earners employed by the AIOC, and did not attempt to unionize construction workers employed by Arab contractors. Lastly, the shaykhs viewed the Tudeh ideology as antithetical to their political, social, and economic way of life.[72] An additional factor, however, was the Persian-nationalist tenor of the Tudeh's public statements and activities. Party leaders and propagandists had made anti-Arab remarks at rallies, often in relation to the Arab contract employees, who received from their shaykhs higher levels of pay than the Persian workers received from the AIOC.

The Tudeh's activities and rhetoric in Khuzistan seemed to contradict its policy toward Azerbaijan, which demonstrated divisions within the Party's central leadership. On the one hand, the Tudeh had pledged its support for Pishivari's autonomous movement in Azerbaijan, a movement that was based on Azeri identity. The Firqah-i Dimukrat (Azerbaijani Democratic Party), with Tudeh backing, had demanded autonomy, due to the province's distinct language, ethnicity, traditions, and religious rituals. At the same time that the Tudeh was demanding the nationalization of the oil industry in Khuzistan, it supported the Soviet Union's attempt to attain oil concessions in Azerbaijan on the grounds of "socialist solidarity, internationalism, and anti-imperialism."[73] The Arabs were well aware of the Tudeh and Iranian government's antipodal position toward Khuzistan and Azerbaijan, which was made clear in their letter to the Arab League.

Several Arab shaykhs and Arab merchants in the Ahwaz district responded to the Tudeh threat with the formation of the Hizb-e Sa'adat (Happiness Party), known locally by its Arabic name, al-Sa'adah. In March, the Happiness Party ran a slate of candidates in the provincial elections. When the votes were counted, the party had won all twelve of Ahwaz's seats on the Khuzistan Provincial Council. The validity of the election was disputed by a group of local Persian lawyers, who argued that Iranian law stated that members of provincial councils had to possess "a complete knowledge of the Persian language."[74] Even though three of the Arabs elected had little or no ability to speak Persian, and some others were illiterate, the Governor-General of Khuzistan, Misbah Fatimi, validated the election.[75] Fatimi feared the Tudeh Party as much as the Arabs did. In fact, in a Tudeh editorial, Fatimi was considered "the product of the tribal feudal system," and Col. Sarhang Alborz, the Chief of Police for Khuzistan, was labeled a suppressor of liberal ideas who "surpasses the German Gestapo."[76]

At a meeting of the Provincial Council in June, Arab members learned that Pishivari had signed an accord with Prime Minister Qavam. In exchange for a degree of political and socioeconomic autonomy, the Azerbaijanis agreed to abandon their demand for independence and to transform their parliament into a provincial council in accordance with the Iranian Constitution. The Happiness Party immediately adjourned to write a letter to the Prime Minister demanding that he grant them the same arrangement, making particular reference to the Arabs' linguistic difference from the rest of the country.[77] When Trott confronted the Arabs about the letter, they denied mentioning the Arabic language in it.[78] Trott noted that the Arab movement was initiated by their opposition to the Tudeh, but in reality constituted a genuine "separatist movement." Any agreements the Arabs made with the other Provincial Council members "are only accidental. (They) want autonomy."[79]

Soon after, Ahmad Amiri, a Ka'b and member of the Sa'adat Party, and several Ka'b, Muhaisin, and Bani Turuf shaykhs asked for Britain's support for the formation of an Arab Tribal Union. They complained about Iranian oppression, which had worsened following Chassib's failed revolt in 1943. They also complained that Tudeh union leaders were pressuring the AIOC into handing Arab construction contracts to Persians. Trott was noncommittal to the union proposal.[80] Nonetheless, shaykhs representing a large cross-section of Khuzistani Arabs held many meetings on Abadan Island to discuss measures for collective security against any Tudeh aggression.[81] British support would be beneficial, but was deemed unnecessary. The situation began to deteriorate in June after several strikes occurred at several oil installations, and the Tudeh formed its own vigilante police force. Groups of men wearing Tudeh armbands began to arrest individuals in Ahwaz and Khorramshahr for "crimes" and put them before Tudeh tribunals. Furthermore, the Tudeh launched a campaign of intimidation. Their police officers demanded that local Arab merchants provide goods and services at reduced prices to Tudeh members and Persian AIOC employees.[82] Rumors spread that the Tudeh were planning a coup d'état with the intention of seizing control of the provincial government. In response, Arab shaykhs throughout Khuzistan convened on the night of 12 June in Khorramshahr and Ahwaz and decided to form a transtribal union of Arabs.[83] Two days later, Hajji Ali Faisali approached Stewart in Khorramshahr. He asked Britain to provide financial support for the Tribal Union. The Arabs had weapons and ammunition, but not enough to defend against the Tudeh. Stewart refused to provide money or arms and urged the Arabs to refrain from violence, as they would only "bring trouble on themselves."[84] The Arabs responded with an announcement that they had obtained a house in Khorramshahr to serve as the headquarters of their union, and publicly stated that their aim was to "obtain the same rights for Khuzistanis and Arabs in particular, as Azerbaijanis have succeeded in obtaining from the Central Government." Almost immediately, Arab merchants in Abadan agreed to support the Union with funds.[85] Just days later in Ahwaz, the Union organized a *yazleh*, an Arab ceremonial dance and recitation intended to arouse the participants' emotions.[86] The day after the *yazleh*, Arabs from all corners of Khuzistan gathered in Khorramshahr to formally open the Ittihad-e Ashayar-e Arab (The Union of Arab Tribes) on 24 June. The approximately 12,000 tribesmen in attendance were organized behind flags representing the different tribes that had joined the movement.[87] At the meeting, the shaykhs wrote a manifesto expressing their aims and demands. Their main objective was to "unite all patriotic Arabs . . . (who) will not allow the Tudeh Party to interfere in Arab affairs." The document went on to demand that the central government grant them "the same concessions and reforms which have been granted to the province of Azerbaijan," as well as the teaching of Arabic in schools.[88] Trott noted in a report to Tehran the significance of the meeting. For the first time, the Ka'b, Bani Turuf, and Muhaisin had disregarded all of their differences and historical grievances, and had effectively formed a united front transcending tribalism.[89] Moreover, Chassib was sent by the Iranian government to Ahwaz to meet with the Union chiefs. Not a single Arab shaykh called on Chassib on his arrival.[90]

The Tudeh responded to the formation of the Tribal Union with accusations that the British had been responsible for it. An article in the Tudeh newspaper *Zafar* accused the British and Arabs of attempting to undermine "the democratic organizations in Khuzistan." The article also accused British Intelligence agents of paying each shaykh 50,000 rials to establish the Tribal Union.[91] At Tudeh rallies, speakers accused the Arabs of planning a rebellion. At the same time, however, Tudeh propagandists began to distribute pamphlets written in Arabic, urging the tribesmen to abandon their shaykhs who are "depriving you of your rights. . . . Their only purpose is to master you and plant seeds of enmity between Arabs and Persians."[92]

British complicity in the formation of the Arab Union is unlikely. Although H. J. Underwood, the British Military Attaché attached to the AIOC, supported the Arabs' efforts, there is no indication that any British official paid money to any shaykh. Furthermore, in response to concerns voiced by the Iranian government, Underwood urged the shaykhs to change the name of their organization to the Khuzistani Farmers' Union and the governor and the chief of police at Abadan, both Tudeh sympathizers, threatened the Union with violence if it did not change its name.[93] The shaykhs refused these demands on the grounds that they were Arabs and that most of their members were not farmers.[94] Soon thereafter, groups of Arabs began to attack Persians attending Tudeh rallies near AIOC installations. These melees were controlled by the local police, but the threat the Arab instigators posed to the security of the AIOC demonstrated that the British were not in control of the Union.

In the following weeks, Tudeh propaganda against the Arabs intensified. The Arabs responded by expelling Tudeh representatives from their areas. They also entered Tudeh offices in the smaller towns and villages and ordered the officials to clear the buildings of all propagandist material.[95] Armed contingents of Ka'b tribesmen plundered Persian villages, the Bani Turuf expelled Persians suspected of being Tudeh agents from their territory at gunpoint, and the Muhaisin launched attacks on Persian vehicles travelling on the roadways between Abadan and Khorramshahr. Concerned with the possible success of the Agha Jari workers' strike, and fearing reprisals in the wake of their anti-Tudeh activities, the leaders of the Arab Union moved up the official opening of their Abadan office to 14 July. They had been emboldened when Fatimi's powers were expanded by order of Prime Minister Qavam—powers that included his ability to declare martial law without receiving approval from Tehran. Fatimi did not trust the Arabs, but he was turning a blind eye to attacks on the Tudeh.

On the night of 14 July, aware of the opening of the Arab Union office, the Tudeh sent a parade of picketers toward the ceremony. When the striking workers reached the Arab Union building, shots were fired, and a two-hour riot ensued. The following morning, Fatimi called on a group of Union shaykhs. At the meeting, the Governor-General advised them to burn down the local Tudeh headquarters in retaliation for the murders of their tribesmen.[96] Emboldened by the Governor-General's overtures, tribesmen assembled on the riverbank opposite Abadan, and by nightfall, thousands with rifles, hatchets, and clubs awaited orders to enter the city.[97] Qavam responded by dispatching Muzaffar Firuz, the Deputy Prime Minister, to Abadan to end the strike. Firuz was accompanied by a high-ranking Tudeh official and a national leader of the CCFTU. The Tudeh agreed to end the strike and cease action against the AIOC and the Arabs. In return, the AIOC agreed to the Friday-pay and wage-increase demands. Firuz then had all Persians arrested during the riots released. The Arabs no longer had the assurance of the Governor-General's support. Fearing an Iranian military response, the shaykhs dispersed their tribesmen and no invasion of Abadan occurred.

To appease the Arabs' desire for revenge, the Iranian government immediately established a military tribunal to ascertain the nature of the events on the night of July 14 and to punish those involved. The Arabs, however, viewed the military tribunal as a sham. Instead of bringing the Tudeh agitators to justice, the investigation focused on the alleged ineptitude of the Chief of Police of Abadan, Lt. Col. Le'ali, at preventing the riot in the first place.[98] The tribunal also focused on questionable evidence of Arab arms smuggling and acts of brigandage, all unrelated to the riot.[99] In protest, the Tribal Union sent a number of letters to the *Mihr-i Iran* newspaper, stating that the murderers were not being brought to justice.[100]

The strike and riot, which had demonstrated the enormity of the Tudeh's strength, caused Qavam to shift further to the left. Three cabinet positions were given to Tudeh politicians, as were other posts. The British Ambassador noted eight of the eleven cabinet positions were now in the hands of communists or "fellow travelers."[101] In response, some shaykhs sent word to Abdullah in Kuwait that their situation had grown worse and asked him to travel to Cairo to submit a request to the Arab League for aid. A Reuters correspondent in Tehran got word of Abdullah's plans, and the entire Tehran press corps published articles about the Arab League plan. The front page of *Iran-e Ma* asked, "Are the Imperialists and Shaykh Abdullah joking?"[102] The press questioned not only the authenticity of Arab League venture, but also implied British complicity. The conservative papers attacked the move as well; *Keyhan* published telegrams written by Qavam that called the Arabs "treacherous."[103] With the plan out in the open, Abdullah was unable to leave Kuwait, and a meeting with the Arab League did not take place.

The Qashqai and Bakhtiyari tribes were also concerned about the power of the Tudeh, and in late August signed a pact of mutual defense.[104] Naming themselves "The Resistance Movement of the South," the group issued a manifesto in which they said the Tudeh represented a threat to "our religion, nationality, etc."[105] After changing its name to the Fars National Movement, the group demanded provincial autonomy similar to that afforded to Azerbaijan, and the dismissal of all Tudeh members of the national and provincial government.[106] The British backed the demand with the threat of force, moving an entire division of the Indian Army to Basra and anchoring British battleships at the mouth of the Shatt al-Arab. The Shah, an ardent anti-communist, was dismayed by Qavam's reliance on the Tudeh, as was most of the officer corps. A coup attempt or British invasion was growing more likely by the day, so Qavam dismissed Tudeh officials, reneged on land reform and labor legislation promises, and appointed conservatives to government positions. In Khuzistan, the Arab shaykhs were promised positions in the provincial council and seats in the Majlis, taxes were relaxed, and other financial incentives were provided.[107] By November, a majority of Union members were professing loyalty to Qavam and his *Hizb-e Demokrat* (The Democrat Party).[108]

The Khuzistani ethnonationalist movement disintegrated as quickly as it formed; but why? First, following the disappearance of the Khaz'als from the scene, the Arabs lacked a strong leader who could effectively organize and mobilize the movement. Second, the movement could not acquire the resources required for its survival. Access to money, weapons, human resources, and political capital was available only outside of Khuzistan, and the Arab movement was unable to secure aid from either the British or the Arab League. Third, the Qavam government was able to co-opt many prominent Arab elites by assenting to many of their negotiable demands. After the Khaz'als were removed from the scene, the Arabs of Khuzistan were unable to find a leader for their movement, and once a few shaykhs left the Tribal Union for the safety of Qavam's Democrat Party, hundreds of others followed *en masse*. The Khaz'al brothers had initiated a nationalist awakening, but their very presence had hindered the movement's transition from intranational to protonational. Ironically, just as their absence allowed the Arabs to unite under a single banner, it also deprived the movement of the leadership it required.

Notes

1. Anthony D. Smith, *The Ethnic Origins of Nations* (New York: Blackwell Publishing, 1986).

2. Ibid., 6–18.

3. John R. Perry, "The Banu Ka'b; An Amphibious Brigand State in Khuzistan," in *Le Monde Iranien et L'Islam*, Tome 1 (Geneva-Paris: Librarie Droz, 1971), 131–152; Ahmad Kasravi, *Tarikh-e Pansad Salah-e Khuzistan* (Tehran: Dunya-e Kitab, 2005).

4. FO 460.1-5, *Foreign Office: Consulate, Mohammerah (later Khorramshahr), Iran (formerly Persia): General Correspondence.*

5. WO 33.1074, *Tribal List. Arabistan (Northern & Southern),* 1923.

6. WO 106.5974, *The Sheikhdom of Mohammerah,* by British Military Attaché, September 12, 1926; Michael P. Zirinsky, "Imperial Power and Dictatorship: Britain and the Rise of Reza Shah, 1921-1926," *International Journal of Middle East Studies* vol. 24, no. 4 (November 1992): 639–663.

7. FO 371.27097, *Chassib Khaz'al to "My Esteemed Brothers,"* October 1941.

8. FO 371.27097, *H.Q. 8th Indian Division, Basra to H.Q. Force Iraq, Baghdad,* 7 September 1941.

9. FO 624.23, File 355, *Shaykhs Laftah, Sansur, and 'Abbas to British Ambassador, Baghdad,* 28 August 1941.

10. FO 371.27097, *Chassib Khaz'al to British Ambassador, Baghdad,* October 1941.

11. FO 624.23, File 355, *Secretary of the Arab Elam State Party to British Embassy in Tehran,* 4 October 1941.

12. FO 624.23, File 355, *Consul Basra to Lt.-Col. Galloway,* 29 September 1941.

13. FO 248.1412, *Tribal Unrest in Gach Saran Area,* by Bushire Consulate, 6 April 1942.

14. FO 248.1412, *Ahwaz Consulate to British Embassy, Tehran,* 11 April 1942.

15. FO 248.1412, Khorramshahr Consulate to British Legation, Tehran, 6 June 1942.

16. Ibid.

17. WO 106.5974, *Report on the Arab Tribes of Khuzistan,* 2 May 1943.

18. FO 248.1412, *Combined Intelligence Center Iraq (C.I.C.I.) to Iraq Force H.Q., Baghdad,* 13 April 1942.

19. The torture of the two *sayyids* was later confirmed by the British Consulate in Khorramshahr.

20. FO 248.1412, *Khorramshahr Consulate to British Ambassador, Tehran,* 14 April 1942.

21. Ibid.

22. FO 248.1412, *A.L.O. Ahwaz to C.I.C.I Baghdad,* 16 April 1942.

23. FO 248.1412, *Khorramshahr Consulate to British Legation, Tehran,* 9 September 1942.

24. FO 248.1412, *Ahwaz Consulate to British Legation, Tehran,* 11 November 1942.

25. FO 248.1412, *Ahwaz Consulate to British Legation, Tehran,* 10 November 1942.

26. WO 208.1567, *C.I.C.I., Tribal and Political Weekly Intelligence Summary,* 22 November 1942.

27. FO 371.35078, *Diary of the Consul-General at Khorramshahr,* from 1 May to 15 May 1943.

28. Ibid.

29. FO 248.1418, *Ahwaz Consulate to British Legation, Tehran,* 17 May 1943.

30. FO 40176, *Ahwaz Consulate to British Legation, Tehran,* 28 December 1943.

31. FO 371.35074, *British Ambassador to Prime Minister of Iran,* 2 June 1943.

32. WO 208.1568, *C.I.C.I., Tribal and Political Weekly Intelligence Summary,* 10 May 1943.

33. FO 371.35074, *Petition of Arabistan to British Minister of State, Cairo,* 25 May 1943.

34. FO 371.35074, *Ahwaz and Khorramshahr Consulates to British Legation, Tehran,* 14 October 1943.

35. FO 371.40176, *Ahwaz Consulate to British Legation, Tehran,* 28 December 1943.

36. FO 371.35078, *Diary of the Consul-General at Khorramshahr,* from 15 to 31 July 1943.

37. FO 371.35078, *Khorramshahr Consulate to Tehran,* 11 June 1943; FO 371.35078, *Diary of the Consul-General at Khorramshahr,* from 1 to 15 June 1943.

38. WO 208.1568, *C.I.C.I., Tribal and Political Weekly Intelligence Summary*, 12 July 1943.

39. FO 371.35074, *Notes on Petition from Tribes of Arabistan*, by Foreign Office, 20 August 1943.

40. FO 371.35091, *Diary of the Consul-General at Ahwaz*, from 15 July to 31 July 1943.

41. FO 248.1418, *Khorramshahr Consulate to Tehran*, 11 September 1943, FO 248.1418.

42. Ibid.

43. FO 371.35091, *Diary of the Consul-General at Ahwaz*, from 1 to 15 August 1943.

44. FO 371.40179, *Diary of the Consul-General at Khorramshahr*, from 1 to 15 February 1944.

45. FO 371.40176, *Diary of the Consul-General at Ahwaz for March 1944.*

46. FO 371.40179, *Diary of the Consul-General at Khorramshahr*, from 15 to 28 March 1944.

47. FO 371.40176, *Diary of the Consul-General at Ahwaz*, for April 1944.

48. Ibid.

49. Ibid.

50. FO 248.1453, *The Ka'b Shaykhs to Abdullah Khaz'al*, 7 May 1944.

51. FO 624.36, File 255, *Abdullah Khaz'al to British Ambassador, Baghdad*, 25 March 1944.

52. FO 624.36, File 255, *Basra Consulate to British Embassy, Baghdad*, 22 July 1944.

53. FO 371.40176, *Diary of the Consul-General at Ahwaz for August 1944.*

54. FO 371.40179, *Diary of the Consul-General at Khorramshahr*, from 15 to 30 September 1944.

55. FO 371.40176, *Diary of the Consul-General at Ahwaz for October, 1944.*

56. FO 371.45477, *Diary of the Consul-General at Khorramshahr*, from 1 to 15 December 1944.

57. Ibid.

58. FO 371.40176, *Diary of the Consul-General at Ahwaz for September 1944.*

59. FO 248.1453, *Abdullah Khaz'al to British Embassy, Baghdad*, 20 May 1945.

60. FO 248.1453, *Amara Consulate to British Embassy, Baghdad*, 2 November 1945.

61. Ibid.

62. FO 248. 1453, *Abdullah Khaz'al to British Embassy, Baghdad*, 2 December 1945.

63. FO 248. 1453, *Amara Consulate to British Embassy, Baghdad*, 15 November 1945.

64. WO 208.1570, *C.I.C.I., Tribal and Political Weekly Intelligence Summary*, 31 December 1945.

65. FO 371.52727, *Khorramshahr Consulate to British Embassy, Tehran*, 15 January 1946.

66. Ibid.

67. Ibid.

68. Ibid.

69. FO 248.1468, *Lt.-Col. Underwood to Khorramshahr Consulate*, 1 May 1946.

70. FO 371.52313, *Memorandum on the meeting between Brigadier Clayton, the P.M. of Iraq, and the Iraq Minister in Cairo*, 29 March 1946.

71. FO 371.52321, *C.I.C.I., Fortnightly Intelligence Review*, 9 May 1946.

72. Ervand Abrahamian, *Iran Between Two Revolutions* (Princeton: Princeton University Press, 1982), 363–364.

73. Ervand Abrahamian, *Tortured Confessions: Prisons and Public Recantations in Modern Iran* (Berkeley: University of California Press, 1999), 82.

74. FO 371.52700, *Diary of the Consul-General at Ahwaz for March 1946*.

75. FO 371.52700, *Ahwaz Consulate to Tehran*, 1 June 1946.

76. Rahbar, 5 April 1946; FO 371.52700, *Diary of the Consul-General at Ahwaz for April 1946*.

77. *Keyhan*, 18 June 1946.

78. FO 371.52700, *Ahwaz Consulate to Tehran*, 26 June 1946.

79. Ibid.

80. FO 371.52700, *Diary of the Consul-General at Ahwaz for June 1946*.

81. FO 248.1468, *Lt.-Col. Underwood to Khorramshahr Consulate*, 1 May 1946.

82. FO 248.1468, *Khorramshahr Consulate to Tehran*, 10 June 1946.

83. FO 248.1468, *Ahwaz Consulate to Tehran*, 14 June 1946.

84. FO 248.1468, *Khorramshahr Consulate to Tehran*, 15 June 1946.

85. FO 248.1468, *Khorramshahr Consulate to Tehran*, 18 June 1946.

86. FO 371.52700, *Diary of the Consul-General at Ahwaz for June 1946*.

87. FO 248.1468, *Shakeri to General Staff, AIOC*, 24 June 1946; FO 248.1468, *Tehran to Foreign Office*, by British Embassy, 26 June 1946.

88. FO 248.1468, *Articles and Objects of the Union of Arab Tribes of Khuzistan*, by Lt.-Col. Underwood to General Manager, AIOC, 25 June 1946.

89. FO 371.52700, *Diary of the Consul-General at Ahwaz for June 1946*.

90. FO 248.1468, *Khorramshahr Consulate to Tehran*, 8 July 1946.

91. *Zafar*, 28 June 1946.

92. FO 248.1468, *Important Notice to All the Arab Brothers in Khuzistan*, by Shakeri to General Manager, AIOC, 25 June 1946.

93. FO 248.1468, *Lt.-Col. Underwood to General Manager, AIOC*, 11 July 1946.

94. FO 248.1468, *Khorramshahr Consulate to Tehran*, 25 June 1946.

95. FO 248.1468, *Lt.-Col. Underwood to General Manager, AIOC*, 30 June 1946; FO 371.72700, *Diary of the Consul-General at Ahwaz for June 1946*.

96. FO 248.1468, *Khorramshahr Consulate to Tehran*, Tel. 160, 15 July 1946.

97. FO 248.1468, *Khorramshahr Consulate to Tehran*, Tel. 161, 15 July 1946.

98. FO 371.52700, *Diary of the Consul-General at Ahwaz for September 1946*.

99. FO 371.52711, *British Military Attaché to Foreign Office*, 31 July 1946.

100. *Mihr-e Iran*, 22 July 1946.

101. FO 371.52709, *British Ambassador, Tehran to Foreign Office*, 2 August 1946.

102. *Iran-e Ma*, 25 August 1946.

103. *Keyhan*, 28 August 1946.

104. FO 371.52711, *British Military Attaché to Foreign Office*, 28 August 1946.

105. FO 371.52711, *British Military Attaché to Foreign Office, Appendix A, Proclamation by the Resistance Movement of the South*, 4 September 1946.

106. FO 371.52711, *British Military Attaché to Foreign Office*, 25 September 1946.

107. FO 371.52700, *Diary of the Consul-General at Ahwaz for October 1946*.

108. FO 371.52700, *Diary of the Consul-General at Ahwaz for November 1946*.

CHAPTER 7

"The Portals of Persepolis": The Role of Nationalism in Early U.S.-Iranian Relations

FIROOZEH KASHANI-SABET

In 1746, more than a century before America and Iran would sign a Treaty of Friendship, the *American Magazine and Historical Chronicle* reported on the latest happenings in Persia. The ruthless commander Nadir Shah had routed the Ottoman army and signed a treaty enabling him to occupy Najaf.[1] Nadir had risen from the ashes of the Safavid Empire to rule over Iran and its borderlands. Brief accounts of Persia appeared in other early American periodicals, including excerpts from Montesquieu's *Persian Letters* and excerpts of Persian poetry in English translation.[2] The volume of articles discussing Persian history, culture, and politics increased steadily in the nineteenth century as Americans had better access to the accounts of European diplomats and travelers to Iran. As early as 1816, excerpts of Sir John Malcolm's *History of Persia* were published in the *North American Review*, a Boston quarterly. Malcolm had been sent on a diplomatic mission to Persia to forge relations between Iran and the British Government of India.

Much of this newfound cultural curiosity about the East focused on poetry. In fact, for some Americans the East—"the land where poetry has most flourished"—became synonymous with poetry.[3] American writers closely followed European scholarship on Eastern literature and relied on European translation of Persian epics to familiarize themselves with the themes and styles of Persian prosody. The "piety of Sufis," as reflected in "oriental poetry," piqued the curiosity of certain missionary audiences, but the influence of Sufis, who "flourished chiefly in Persia," was not restricted to American missionary audiences.[4]

In 1849, the *American Whig Review* contained an article entitled "Ferdousi, the Persian Poet," which discussed classical Persian literature and spoke favorably of Iran's poet laureate, who had taken great pains to renew the Persian language through his epic *Book of Kings* (*Shahnameh*) in the tenth century.[5] Another essay provided samples of Persian poetry by focusing on the verses of the fourteenth-century poet Khvajah Shams al-Din Muhammad Hafiz Shirazi. Comparing Hafiz to Homer, Shakespeare, and Corneille, this writer acknowledged the difficulties of rendering Hafiz's verse into English: "[W]e constantly stumble over puns, quibbles, and other facetiae, appreciable, of course, to the natives exclusively."[6] And yet he appreciated the ways in which the "loves of the nightingale and the rose" became enacted in Persian verse to express the connection between the poet and his muse. Translations of Hafiz's poetry continued appearing in other American periodicals. Such journalistic accounts reflected the popular tastes of nineteenth-century American readership. In particular, the prominent Transcendentalist writer Ralph Waldo Emerson became enamored of Hafiz and his poems, which he discovered through reading Goethe's *West-östlicher Divan* (1819). Emerson had copies not only of Goethe's works, but also the translations of Hafiz's poetry completed by Austrian scholar Joseph von Hammer-Purgstall. Emerson relied upon Purgstall's German editions to translate some of Hafiz's poetry into English himself.[7]

American writers of the nineteenth century did not insist on American exceptionalism or cultural superiority in the literary realm. As one writer, John Orr, averred, "The American mind is intensely practical. . . . Its achievements are great in the records of the Patent Office. . . . And yet, some forty years ago, there uprose in New England about the most remarkable manifestation of Idealism that modern history can show. Into this region, Transcendentalism imported its bit of Oriental sky, and called men to admire the constellations it contained."[8] While these forays into Persian poetry by American writers showed the increasing popularity of the classical Persian literary tradition, official channels of direct communication remained limited.

Historians who have chronicled the contact between Iran and America narrate a familiar outline of events: the arrival of missionaries; the establishment of embassies and businesses; the Second World War and the Allied occupation of Iran; the Musaddiq affair; and the hostage crisis. Leading scholars have argued that American pursuit of Middle Eastern oil, and later America's desire to thwart Soviet penetration of Iran, strengthened the diplomatic ties between Iran and America, especially after the Second World War. Most historians of this era also conclude that America's involvement in the 1953 coup deeply altered Iranians' perceptions of the United States and its role in their country.[9] Much of the historiography on U.S.-Iranian relations remains descriptive as it sorts through this sometimes sordid history. The emphasis on diplomatic and economic history outweighs scholarship on cultural contact and ideological nuances. It is a truism, for example, that America's desire to exploit Iranian oil eventually made Iran a desirable partner in the Middle

East in the interwar era, and that Iranian minds changed radically about the United States after the Musaddiq crisis. These analyses—significant though they have been in teaching us about the events and outcomes of certain policy decisions—have not considered the clash of nationalisms (as opposed to the clash of religious ideologies), or the impulse of rival imperialisms in U.S.-Iranian relations.

Persia was no Palestine. Americans travelers and literati attached little sentiment to its history and territory, which they encountered at a moment of transition. In the 1830s, when the first group of Presbyterian missionaries arrived in Urumiyah, the country was reeling from its defeat to Russia. The rout imposed a debilitating indemnity on Iran and emphasized the economic and territorial vulnerability of the country to foreign penetration. As Iran grappled with the reality of Western imperialism, it strove to rewrite its unique history of imperial rule.[10]

To date, historians have written little about the nineteenth-century origins of U.S.-Iranian relations. What exists has focused on the missionary experience, with scant attention paid to other venues of contact. The missionary experience, while formative, informed but one facet of this relationship, one that would wane significantly in the interwar era. Instead, other paths of cultural and political contact gained ascendancy. Persian curiosity about America eventually gave way to a desire to view the United States as an ally, since the United States did not have a history of colonialism in Iran.

Iran formalized relations with the United States in a treaty of friendship and commerce signed at Constantinople in 1856. Through this agreement, the United States initiated contact with Iran and explored the possibility of establishing economic and diplomatic links.[11] In 1830 and again in 1862, the United States also concluded treaties of commerce with the Ottoman Empire, enabling American expansion to the Islamic heartlands of the Middle East.

In 1883, Samuel Greene Wheeler Benjamin became the first diplomatic representative of the American government in Iran. His reception hosted by Nasir al-Din Shah was a majestic and "brilliant pageant." In his meeting with the king, which was conducted in French, Benjamin partook of local favorites, drinking afternoon tea and smoking the waterpipe. At the meeting, the shah reportedly expressed "great satisfaction to see an American legation at Teheran," and hoped that it would be a permanent arrangement.[12] More than a year later, Benjamin reflected upon his experiences and wrote an essay about the city of Tehran in a contemporary American magazine. At a diplomatic dinner marking the shah's birthday, Benjamin was honored; "various national tunes, including the 'Star-Spangled Banner,' were played with spirit and effect."[13]

Who were the individuals disseminating Persian history and culture in America? Both missionaries and scholars filled these ranks, as did American diplomats who had spent time in Iran. The significance of the Protestant missionaries in bridging the linguistic divide between Iran and America should not be underestimated, as they ranked among the earliest Americans to learn the Persian language. Many even translated English-language sources for Persian-speaking audiences. Yet they were few in number, and thus their influence was limited, and eventually American and Persian scholars took the lead in propagating the study of Persian culture and language on the international stage.[14]

American scholars initially relied on European scholarship to learn about Iranian antiquity and philology. Gernot Windfuhr has maintained that Europeans nurtured an interest in Persian, first for "missionary and economic" reasons, and subsequently on linguistic and cultural grounds. One may reasonably argue that American interest in Iran was spurred similarly by missionary and economic considerations, but they would not remain the sole American motivations for exploring Iranian culture and society.[15]

The growth of Oriental Studies in the United States gave rise to specialized disciplines such as Persian Studies, and expertise in fields such as Babylonian Studies and Assyriology.[16] In a fascinating article, Benjamin Foster contends that the development of Biblical Studies marks the origins of Oriental scholarship in the United States during the colonial era. Indo-European philology overshadowed Semitic Studies in the curricula of divinity schools for a brief twenty-year period from 1860 to 1880. Sanskrit and Indic Studies, to which old Iranian languages could be traced, originated with the Transcendentalists.[17] Though Persian Studies in the United States lagged behind Semitic Studies and Egyptology, its origins must be understood within the context of nineteenth-century American Orientalism. Professorships in Sanskrit, and eventually in Persian archeology and linguistics, promoted the study of Persian antiquity.

Persian Studies straddled many academic worlds within the universe of American higher education. On the one hand, it formed a component of religious studies, with American scholars probing the country's experience with Zoroastrianism and Baha'ism.[18] It also informed the fields of Babylonian and Assyrian Studies—the sites of Persia's ancient Achaemenid Empire. As another American scholar in the field, Robert William Rogers, observed: "It was natural that in America, also, men should begin to talk of efforts to assist in the great work of recovering the remains of Babylonian and Assyrian civilization."[19] In 1884, conferences of the American Oriental Society and the Society of Biblical Literature brought together scholars who expressed support for such endeavors. Participants in these conferences joined with the Archaeological Institute of America to raise funds to send an expedition that might uncover excavation sites. Work finally began in 1889, and the University of Pennsylvania expedition continued in 1890 at Nippur.[20] Eventually, these forays enriched American understandings of pre-Islamic history, and contributed to the emergence of Islamic Studies at American universities in the United States.

American academic efforts to study Oriental antiquity were connected to the emergence of archeological discoveries in the Middle East. From the mid-nineteenth century on, Americans, like Europeans, nurtured an interest in displaying the past through the building of museums. The Smithsonian was founded in 1846, while the University of Pennsylvania's Museum of Archeology and Paleontology was founded in 1887. Popular writers partook of this newfound curiosity about Middle Eastern antiquity. For example, one mainstream author, Zénaïde A. Ragozin, published three works on Chaldea, Assyria, and Persia that attracted a broad readership.[21]

The astounding feat of Henry Creswicke Rawlinson and others in deciphering the Babylonian cuneiform inscriptions of Behistun ("bisutun") expanded the field of ancient Iranian studies in the West. Rawlinson set out as a teenager to travel to India as a cadet of the East India Company, and later his travels took him to Iran. Rawlinson had received no formal training in Oriental languages, but showed a facility in picking up Persian. While in Iran, he served as a major from 1833 to 1839, and began working on the inscription of Darius (522/21–486 BC). Rawlinson published the results of his research with rapidity and gained recognition for his achievements.[22]

Three years after having served as the first U.S. minister to Iran, Samuel Benjamin contended that, despite the remoteness of Iran to the ordinary American, "its past history is so inwrought with the march of civilization that all of us are familiar with the name of Persia. . . . The names of Cyrus, of Darius, of Xerxes, are household words."[23] Benjamin reminded his readers that the "immortal portals of Persepolis were reared ages before the Parthenon of Athens." Like his contemporary Iranian hosts, Benjamin recognized that modern Persia was "shorn of some of her vast territorial possessions" and that it had became a minor political force in recent decades, "thus conveying the impression that she is verging on extinction."[24] But Benjamin seemed certain that "the turn of Persia has come," and to make his point, Benjamin proceeded to discuss the richness of its vegetation and habitat.

The impact of Rawlinson's work and that of others went beyond his circle of European Orientalists. It would, however, be decades before an American, Abraham Valentine Williams Jackson, would hazard climbing the Bisitun to

:e first-hand the splendor of the Persian past.[25] As Jackson later de-
tis climb: "It was an exciting experience, therefore, to clamber and
a up by ropes to reach at last the dizzy ledge."[26] Jackson first visited
903, but returned to the country on four other occasions (1907, 1910,
1918, and 1926) before his death in 1937. In 1918, Jackson even received an
honorary degree from the Persian college Dar al-Funun. His travelogues enjoyed popular readership, though Jackson is also remembered for his scholarly
writings on the Iranian prophet Zoroaster and for his studies of the Avestan
grammar. Until his death in 1937, Jackson's findings on Zoroaster and the ancient Iranian religion had remained unsurpassed.[27] More than a philologist of
Indo-Iranian languages, Jackson also nurtured an interest in Persian poetry,
including the classical works of Omar Khayyam and Firdawsi. Jackson, this
American pioneer of Indo-Iranian languages, wrote of Persia in 1906 that of
"all the Eastern countries which came into contact with Greece and Rome,
Persia alone has preserved her independence."[28] For Jackson, Iran's eventual
adoption of a constitution seemed consistent with its ancient history. As he
reminded readers, "It has sometimes been thought surprising that Persia, the
synonym of the abiding East, should be an Asiatic pioneer in adopting a Constitution, for we are likely to forget that Herodotus once said, 'The Persians,
of all nations, are the most ready to adopt foreign customs.'"[29] The road to
Iranian constitutionalism was paved in part by economic pressures, social dis-
contentment, and Western encroachment.

At the same time, others in America were beginning to see the wisdom of
expanding commercial ties with Iran. In 1902, the American naval historian
Alfred Thayer Mahan published a provocative article in *National Review*. He
famously coined the term "Middle East," and labeled the strategic pivot of
its defense the "Persian Gulf." Mahan was among the first American analysts
to appreciate not only the military and economic significance of the Persian
Gulf, but also the instability of the region. In the nineteenth century, Britain had encroached upon the communities of the Persian Gulf littoral—what
some termed, in jest, "the British lake."[30] Mahan viewed the Persian Gulf and
southern Iran as a central point of communication between the East and the
West, and a point of contention in emerging "world politics."[31]

Some American diplomats looked to Iran as a potential commercial partner in the same interval. Lloyd Carpenter Griscom, U.S. Minister to Persia
from 1901 to 1902, undertook a journey in the country during his brief diplomatic stint there. Griscom—described by one reviewer as "a rich man's son,
born with a silver spoon in his mouth"—attended school both in the United
States and abroad in his youth, eventually graduating from the University of
Pennsylvania. He established ties with the U.S. diplomatic corps and landed

a position as secretary (later chargé d'affaires) of the Legation in Constantinople. He then rose quickly to the position of envoy extraordinary to Iran.[32]

Griscom's trip lasted nearly two months, during which he traveled approximately "a thousand miles" through central Iran. In Isfahan, "the great trade centre of Persia," he investigated "the possibility of improving American trade."[33] As Griscom explained, "It was the first official visit to Ispahan ever made by an American Minister and I hope that my conversations with Persian Officials and merchants of all classes and nationalities will have material results in improving the commercial relations with the United States."[34] The potentially lucrative commercial interests of the United States in Iran cannot be underestimated as an impetus for the establishment and expansion of relations between the two states. As the governor of Isfahan, Zill al-Sultan, summed up the situation in a memorandum read to Griscom, "America is so far from Persia that trade between the two countries is almost impossible, but that the opportunity of Americans lies in investing capital in Persia and building factories of all kinds."[35] American diplomats would explore these commercial possibilities in the decades ahead. While in central Iran, Griscom visited the American Mission of Hamadan. According to Griscom, "It was the first time the Missionaries at this place have ever been visited by an American Minister," as they appreciated the Legation's efforts to improve "their relations with the local government officials," which at times appeared harried.[36] Upon concluding his trip, Griscom confessed, "I am very glad to have made this journey as I am enabled better to understand the political, social, and economic conditions of Persia." He expressed satisfaction at having received "the requisite oriental honors" and at having acquired "considerable valuable information" about the country.[37]

Griscom probed into the potential for furthering trade links with Iran in a letter to the Philadelphia Commercial Museum. Griscom readily admitted that the "problem of obtaining a foothold for American Commerce in Persia is difficult but by no means unsolvable." Recognizing the Russian virtual monopoly over the country's northern tier, and Britain's dominance in the south, Griscom identified Isfahan, located in central Iran, as "disputed territory where the two spheres of influence meet." The significance of Isfahan as a potential center of trade likely explains the Legation's courting of Zill al-Sultan during this interval. Griscom advised that American goods entering Iran should avoid the Caspian littoral, as Russia, "with its prohibitive transit duties forms an impenetrable barrier."[38] Rather, he considered entry through the port of Bushehr as a prospect. To emphasize the "unimportant part played by the United States in Persian trade," Griscom appended a list of the prevalent products entering Iran from the Persian Gulf. Although American goods were sold in Iran, their American make was "concealed and a false origin attributed." Griscom estimated that of over three million pounds sterling "imported into Persia by the Persian Gulf, the part emanating from the United States totals 1,578 pounds in value."[39] He ventured that items "finding a ready market" in Iran included sewing machines, shoes, phonographs, agricultural implements, drugs, clocks and watches, carriages, and the like. Anticipating difficulties in the transportation of American goods, Griscom also identified "the dearth of reliable agents in Persia." As he explained, "Native agents are to be had, but they are not familiar with our business methods. The foreigners resident in Persia . . . do not view with any favor the prospect of an 'American invasion.'"[40] In other words, European powers frowned upon American competition.

The paucity of reliable statistics on population and manufacturers within the country created additional obstacles for American diplomats interested in expanding trade in Iran. In fact, when the twelfth census of the United States was published, the interpreter to the Legation, John Tyler, suggested that the complete set be presented to the shah, with "the effect of indicating a direction in which some useful and necessary reforms could be introduced."[41] A reliable census, however, was not to take place during the reign of the last Qajar kings.

Lloyd Griscom's brief sojourn in Iran ended in 1902, when Richmond Pearson succeeded him as Minister. Upon his arrival through the port of Enzali, Pearson received a royal welcome from Iranian courtiers: "[A]s I entered the court yard a brass band of 24 instruments played, and played surprisingly well, the American National air."[42] Justifying his attention to the minutiae surrounding his arrival in Iran, Pearson explains, "I enter thus minutely into details to show the really hospitable intent of the Persian Government, and if their methods are patriarchal and even fatiguing to the recipient, the good feeling which prompts them makes them welcome to the stranger guest."[43] Pearson's Persian audience manifested a similar inquisitiveness about America's new diplomatic officer to the country. The newspaper *Iran-i Soltani* briefly mentioned Pearson's reception at the court of Muzaffar al-Din Shah.[44] On 4 July 1903, commemorating America's independence, the shah sent his hearty congratulations to the members of the American Legation. Pearson noted that "many distinguished visitors called at the Legation . . . to express good wishes for the Government of the United States."[45] It is interesting to note that along with "sherbet, cigars, the Kalian [water pipe] and light refreshments," "champagne" was also served at the celebration.[46]

What can be gleaned from these curious glimpses into the diplomacy of Iran and the United States in its infancy? First, Iran and America displayed a genuine desire to nurture mutually beneficial foreign relations that included both cultural and economic ties. Second, while recognizing that America could not easily forge ties with Iran, given the distance between the two countries, Persian statesmen valued the possibility of involving the United States in the commercial development of the country. For its part, America strove to enhance its presence in the Near East, where it already had the protection of its missionaries in mind. America emerged as a possible third force—a counterweight to the imposing presence of Great Britain and Russia.

While America's initial interest in Iran converged on culture, Iranian fascination with America seemed rooted in empire. One wonders, however, about the ways in which Iranians sated their curiosity about America. After all, how many Iranians knew English? While statistics of this sort are difficult to compile from the Qajar era, historians have nonetheless documented the reform process (*nizam-i jadid*—literally "new order") that prompted the learning of Western languages in Iran, especially French and English. Iran's exploration of the West focused on travel and the establishment of embassies abroad.

In 1815, Mirza Salih Shirazi traveled to Britain to study English, and eventually went on to produce the first newspaper in Iran. Referring to Shirazi, Reverend Justin Perkins observed: "A periodical newspaper has recently been commenced under the auspices of the king, in Muhammedan Persia. It is edited by a native who speaks our language—having been once ambassador to England—and is strongly desirous of introducing European knowledge and improvements among his countrymen."[47] This passing detail sheds some light on the way in which missionaries and Iranians tried to bridge the language divide during the first decades of their encounter in the nineteenth century.

As journalism flourished, Persian newspapers began publishing short pieces on American life. *Ittila'*, a semi-official Qajar journal published under the guidance of Muhammad Hasan Khan, I'itmad al-Saltanah, for instance, discussed happenings in America. Numerous extant nineteenth-century Persian manuscripts describe the geography and communities of disparate American locales, as well. One such source compares the grandeur that Americans attach to Yosemite to the reverence that Muslims harbor for Mecca. "Yosemite," he writes, "is a name that delights. Just as the name Mecca excites Muslims, so too does this name . . . please the inhabitants of 'Yangi Dunya,'" or in other words, America. Yosemite was depicted as the Switzerland of America, a place renowned for its delicate climate that attracted scores of visitors annually.[48] Iranian envoys to the United States in the late nineteenth and early twentieth centuries included Muin al-Saltanah in 1893 and Mirza Ali Aghar Khan Atabak Azam in 1904.

Persian curiosity about things American became reflected in accounts of world fairs that displayed U.S. ingenuity and inventiveness.[49] Iran had a modest presence at the 1893 World's Columbian Exposition. In 1890, the United States Congress approved an act to allow an exhibition "of a national and international character" to mark the quadrennial of the discovery of the New World. Invitations were sent to several nations, among them Iran, and over sixty countries expressed a desire to participate in the program. As preparations were being made for the fair, Cyrus Adler, the U.S. Commissioner of the World's Columbian Exposition to Turkey, Persia, Egypt, Tunis, and Morocco, went to the Middle East shortly thereafter to seek the involvement of those countries in the exhibition.

In addition, the U.S. Minister in Tehran, E. Spencer Pratt, encouraged Nasir al-Din Shah to form a commission and to allot money to cover the cost of mounting an official exhibit and constructing a Persian Pavilion at the Exposition. Although the shah agreed to arrange a commission, the Iranian government did not provide funds to pay for the costs of exhibit—an expense assumed by the exhibitors themselves.[50] As the assistant commissioner for Persia, Clarence Andrews, remarked, "The Persians are a commercial race, but they did not see their way to sending their goods some ten thousand miles away from home, to be carried through their own country on pack animals over the worst roads in the world to the sea coast, whence, having paid an export duty . . . they would sail away in ships to that indefinite country known to Persians as 'Yanki Dunya,' which as far as they know, has no manufactures to send in return."[51] In other words, it seemed that the Iranian government did not initially consider it worthwhile to invest in a venture that lacked explicit commercial profits.

Despite the Exposition's indefinite commercial prospects for Iran, the Persian government expressed an interest in being represented at Chicago, although it did not foot the bill for preparing such a display. An Armenian-Iranian importer, H. H. Topakian, assumed the costs for organizing the exhibit, which showcased various objects of Persian art. The Imperial Persian Pavilion was installed by designs provided in part by the Commissioner-General, E. Spencer Pratt, and a New York architect familiar with "Eastern forms." It was located in the Manufactures and Liberal Arts building at the Exposition.[52] When merchants from Iran showed reluctance to participate in the exhibit, Pratt tried to locate merchants within the United States who imported goods from Iran and elsewhere in the Middle East to fill their place. Mr. Topakian apparently brought in Persian commodities through Istanbul to New York. From there, he transferred some of his goods to Chicago for the Exposition.[53] Although two Armenian-Iranian merchants and brothers, Ershak Khan and Iskandar Khan, had hoped to present their merchandise at the Exposition, they failed to reach Chicago in time for the inauguration of the fair, and thus did not turn a substantial profit from the Exposition—an occasion that, in theory, could have produced lucrative gains for the vendors. The delay, moreover, prevented the brothers from finding a suitable spot for showcasing their goods, and a dispute seems to have arisen between Mr. Topakian and the two brothers, who had hoped to display some of their merchandise in the Persian Pavilion.[54]

A Persian manuscript from the late Qajar period specifically addresses the subject of the World's Columbian Exposition. According to this source, although the Persian Pavilion was mounted in a short period of time (within approximately four or five months), it attracted ample attention at the Exposition, even winning praise from President Cleveland, who visited the display at the start of the fair. Iranian authorities seemed pleased that local American newspapers such as the *Union Post* had commented positively on the Persian exhibit.[55] Among the objects showcased at the Exposition were carpets of high quality, "whose colors and patterns . . . illuminated the eyes of the spectators," and old weapons such as shields and swords. Although in Qajar Iran armor was used more for *taziyahs* in order to depict the tragedy of Karbala and less for warfare, "the armorers of Ispahan are as expert in damascening, engraving, and inlaying gold and silver as in the days of Shah Abbas."[56] Other relics of Persian artistry included waterpipes, basins, and articles of everyday use, as well as papier-mâché boxes and writing cases painted with images of landscapes or battles.[57]

By far the best-selling item at the Persian Pavilion remained the Persian rug.[58] Evidently, the price of one small silk rug with a particular design was 14,000 tomans, or 15,000 dollars, and "most probably in the country of Etats Unis (United States) a rug as beautiful as this has not been found."[59] Clarence Andrews, the U.S. assistant commissioner for Persia at the fair, also endorsed the magnificence of Iranian rugs when he remarked that "it is in their textile fabrics that the Persians have been most famed for so many centuries, and the rugs and carpets still produced by them are the most beautiful in the world."[60] The Persian carpet became a luxury item for affluent Americans and collectors, as seen in the numerous advertisements in American periodicals. P. T. Barnum even dubbed his Connecticut home Iranistan, styling it with domes and arches. Similarly, the painter Frederic E. Church conceived his mansion, Olana, as "a Persianized amalgam of American villas."[61]

Along with select features of Iran's history and culture, the Exposition marketed Persian carpets. Aside from their customary place in the traditional Persian home, Iranian carpets had gained fame and popularity among European and American travelers to the country. Throughout the nineteenth century, new urban workshops emerged, and foreign investment penetrated the carpet industry.[62] America thus provided another market for a thriving Persian export.[63] In short, according to this Persian source, the Exposition enhanced the splendor of Iran as a prosperous and "civilized" society manufacturing high-quality luxury goods, and a society whose security and organization made it a relatively safe spot for travelers to visit.[64] If the Exposition showcased a familiar aspect of Persian culture for American consumption, the country's political upheavals would gradually bring its contemporary history into the American consciousness as well.

George Washington: A Hero of Persian Constitutionalism

Iran experienced economic uncertainty after its military defeats by Russia and Great Britain. To bring in revenue, Nasir al-Din Shah eventually opened up the country to Western economic penetration by embracing the concessions craze. Concessions were agreements that gave outside powers the authority to exploit a country's raw materials in exchange for cash. Among cash-poor states of the nineteenth-century Middle East, concessions to Western powers became the rage. Iran granted a concession in 1890 to a British subject for managing tobacco sale and production. Tobacco was a popular consumer good at the time, one widely enjoyed by people of various classes. Also, tobacco production benefited many economic groups, including merchants and landowners. Discontent over the concession came to the fore in 1891, when agents of the tobacco company came to Iran. The demonstrations, incited by leading religious leaders and the political dissident Sayyid Jamal al-Din Afghani, brought about the abrogation of the concession in 1892.[65]

When the fracas over the Tobacco Régie erupted in 1891, Truxton Beale, the American chargé d'affaires, described the dispute as a religiously driven episode. In fact, as Nikki Keddie has shown in her study of the tobacco monopoly, the popular dissatisfaction with the monopoly stemmed not just from religious reasons but also from socioeconomic ones. Beale's observations supported the pervasive use of tobacco in Iranian life, which the monopoly threatened to disrupt. In Beale's words, tobacco "was almost a necessity in Persian life."[66] The involvement of the Iranian ʿulama in the dispute mobilized the opposition against the Régie by lending it both leadership and credibility. According to Beale, "When the foreign tobacco monopoly commenced its work in Persia, the mollas, Persian priests, announced to the people that tobacco was unclean. They forbid them to smoke while tobacco was handled by foreigners." The affair had heightened tensions between indigenous Iranians and foreigners within the country, and after several protests Nasir al-Din Shah finally agreed to abolish the monopoly.

After the cancellation of the tobacco concession, the king "ordered one of the high mollahs to smoke in the mosque and to state to the people there that since the internal monopoly was abolished tobacco was no longer unclean." However, the mullah refused, and thereafter he was exiled from the country. As the mullah prepared to leave, he was accosted by his students. Once the students discovered the reason for the mullah's departure, they managed to involve the city's bazaars, which closed in protest, and to gather a crowd of supporters that marched to the king's palace. After more disturbances ensued, the king finally caved in and granted not only the complete abolition of the monopoly, but also an amnesty to those involved in the agitations. The tobacco protest left a powerful impression on the mind of the American chargé d'affaires who made these remarks:

> This affair has brought forth a power in this country that the oldest Orientalist and even the Persians themselves did not dream of, to wit, the extent of the power of the mollahs . . . by common consent a body of them came together, carried on negotiations and correspondence with the Shah, made demands and concessions, and concluded an understanding with him. A means was suddenly found for the expression of popular discontent and for the redress of popular grievances. In a despotism more like that of Cyrus and Xerxes than that of any government existing elsewhere to-day, a parliament seems to have risen from the ground."[67]

In 1896, the dramatic assassination of Nasir al-Din Shah, who had ruled since 1848, surprised the world; the shah gained the dubious distinction of being the only assassinated Middle Eastern monarch of the nineteenth century. The king's killer, Mirza Reza Kermani, was a devotee of the pan-Islamist writer Sayyid Jamal al-Din Afghani, who had opposed the autocratic tendencies of the shah. On the whole, His Majesty's image in an American obituary was not a flattering one. Nasir al-Din was depicted as having amassed "pearls by the quart," and having accommodated "800 women in his palace," eighty of whom were concubines.[68]

By contrast, the United States captured the attention of Iranians both for its rapid technological advancement and its military might. Mirza Ali Muhammad Khan Kashani, who edited a Persian newspaper in Cairo, observed in 1899 that "in one hundred years America has progressed and attained material comforts to such an extent that other nations would be hard pressed to achieve similar results in more than a century." Kashani praised

America's victory over Spain, as well as its audacious control of the Philippines and Cuba. President McKinley's expansion of American trade also drew kudos from this editor, who concluded that "we must learn from the experiences of such nations that have thus progressed."[69]

Mirza Ali Muhammad Khan Kashani was not the only Iranian to admire America's successes in the Spanish-American War of 1898, which gave the U.S. control of Puerto Rico, Guam, and the Philippines. As a result of this conflict, America also managed to oust Spain from Cuba, and consented to Cuban independence in 1902. In his first official meeting with the Persian Prime Minister, Richmond Pearson noted that the "Prime Minister who speaks French with ease remarked significantly that he was glad to see that the United States had grown strong enough to make some people behave themselves. . . . The Prime Minister said referring directly to our conduct in China and Cuba that our National strength seemed to be surpassed by our disinterestedness only."[70] America emerged as a source of political inspiration for Iranians hoping to restore the country's former imperial glory.

In 1905, a year before the tumultuous events culminating in Iran's constitutional revolution broke out, a popular Persian newspaper, *Tarbiyat*, serialized a biography of George Washington, the most renowned hero of America's Revolutionary War. Described as a "nationalist" who strived for his country's freedom, George Washington became a political paragon for Iranian reformers. Ranking America first among nations in terms of culture, wealth, and power, this author recalled the country's humble origins in the eighteenth century as a British colony.[71] America's evolution into an independent nation was narrated through the biography of George Washington.

One year later, rioting reached new heights in Tehran as people were killed, including members of the *ʿulama*, who supported the creation of a house of justice (*adalatkhanah*), or parliament. Muzaffar al-Din Shah finally conceded to this demand, and refugees entrenched at the grounds of the British Legation returned to their homes. A committee of legislators assembled promptly thereafter to draw up the constitution.[72] Reporting on the political upheaval in Iran, Pearson voiced pessimism about the efficacy of constitutional rule in Iran, not least because the shah's subjects, according to him, "have no idea of the meaning of 'constitutional government.'" In fact, Pearson averred that the "Persian language contains no equivalent for 'constitution' as we understand the term."[73] More to the point, Pearson concluded that "Islam seems to imply autocracy." Although Pearson acknowledged the participation of the religious classes in the Iranian Revolution of 1906, he speculated that they "will soon return to their traditional support of autocratic ideas."[74]

Pearson's dismissal of the revolution—the first grass-roots movement of its kind in the Middle East—reveals a conception of Islam as a political and ideological system that precludes its compatibility with constitutionalism and the liberal concepts embedded within it. Coming from this perspective, Pearson failed to perceive the significance of the constitutional revolution, which admittedly did not bring the promise of political reform that the Iranian public had hoped. Nonetheless, the revolution popularized new concepts such as citizenship, and introduced a novel political system into the country.

The deteriorating health of Muzaffar al-Din Shah exacerbated the country's political instability. Like native Iranians, American missionaries became attuned to the competing interests of the great powers in Iran. This rivalry even extended to ministering care to Iran's ailing monarch, who "has for some time grown constantly worse." At various points, British, American, and German physicians served the king virtually simultaneously. According to John Wishard, director of the Presbyterian Hospital in Tehran, the "Russians not to be outdone by the Germans have secured a place for their doctor and he sleeps there at night." As Wishard confessed, however, "I do not understand however that he has anything to do but 'report' to his government daily the condition of affairs."[75] In other words, these physicians could offer little professional help to the king; rather, their presence served an informational purpose instead of a routinely medical one.

Wishard described the plight of the constitutionalists with sympathy. As he remarked, "A long-suffering and down-trodden people had surprised the world by suddenly awakening. At first, their demands were confined to reforms, looking to the lowering of the price of bread and meat, and the lessening of graft in public office."[76] But civic leaders and intellectuals persuaded both the demonstrators and the king that the political structure of the country needed to change.[77] Just before his death in January 1907, Muzaffar al-Din Shah approved Iran's first constitution. His successor, Muhammad Ali Shah, proved himself an opponent of constitutional rule, however.

By the end of 1909, the victory of Iranian constitutionalists had made enough of an impression to impel President William Howard Taft to note in his State of the Union message that "Constitutional government seems also to have made further advance in Persia."[78] With the victory of the constitutionalist faction in the Civil War of 1908–1909, certain strands of Iranian nationalism gained prominence, in particular the promotion of the Persian language and identity. It is for this reason that Iranians were willing to approach America, rather than another power, for economic assistance to restructure the country's finances. For America did not have a significant history of colonial involvement in Iran, and did not appear to circumscribe Iran's desire for national independence.

In 1911 a banker from New York named William Morgan Shuster would narrate for American readers the frustrations that Iranian politicians faced in defending their fledgling parliament and embattled territory from foreign intervention. Shuster had been entrusted with the daunting task of reorganizing Iran's finances. Prior to his appointment to Iran, Shuster had served in the customs service of Cuba, and, in 1901, he became the Collector of Customs for the Philippine Islands. Shuster was also a member of the bar of the Supreme Court of the United States.[79] Shuster, along with four other Americans, sailed to Iran in 1911 to improve the fiscal management of the Iranian government. With one exception, the American financial advisors to Iran all had experience working in America's colonial possessions. The arrangement was negotiated through discussions with Mirza Ali Quli Khan, the Persian chargé d'affaires in the U.S. Iran contracted Shuster to serve as treasurer-general for a three-year term. In Shuster's words, "I had never even dreamed of going to Persia before my appointment . . . [but] I finally decided to do what I could to help a people who had certainly given evidence of an abiding faith in our institutions and business methods."[80] On 2 February 1911, the Majlis enthusiastically approved Shuster's contract, and the American advisors arrived there in April 1911.

A Persian newspaper reported on the contract with a mixture of enthusiasm and apprehension. On the one hand, there was hope that the country, though still reeling from its civil war, had begun to think about reconstruction and management of its finances. On the other hand, there was much that needed to be settled. The minister of finance had yet to be named, and the delineation of responsibilities between the finance ministry and the American financial advisors had not yet been laid out.[81]

A newcomer to the country, Shuster offered his assessment of the "Persian people" in the autobiographical account of his ordeal in Iran. He described the population largely as peasants and tribesmen, "all densely ignorant." Shuster, however, continually lauded the efforts and sacrifices of the Iranian constitutionalists in changing "despotism into democracy in the face of untold obstacles."[82] Yet Shuster's policies quickly met with resistance from Russia and Great Britain, although he had managed to win the support of the nationalists and the 'ulama. As Shuster observes in his memoirs: "A boycott was proclaimed by the Islamic priests against Russian and English goods. . . . The Persian Nationalists asked me to allow them to organize a personal bodyguard to protect me against attempts on my life. I consented and from that time on these volunteer protectors never allowed me out of their sight."[83] Although Shuster's mission ended badly, Iranians remember his sympathy for the constitutional cause. An American missionary report from 1911 to 1912 commented on the events surrounding the American financiers. The episode gave Iranians a glimpse of Americans, as "[t]hrough them America and Americans were brought before the public in a conspicuous way and Parliament, the only expression of the constitutional government, was dissolved and the political condition of the country left in hopeless chaos."[84] This missionary report confirmed Shuster's observations that "there were constantly coming reports of massacre and drepedation [sic] from more remote parts."[85] That the fledgling constitutional government had lost considerable steam was poignantly illustrated in the suspension of the parliament. In 1911, Russia issued an ultimatum demanding the dismissal of Shuster. Not only did Shuster summarily vacate his post, Russian troops entered northern Iran, and remained there until the outbreak of the Bolshevik Revolution of 1917.

Conclusion

Between the conclusion of the First World War and the installment of Reza Pahlavi, Iran experienced tumultuous changes. Oil discovered in commercial quantities in 1908 would enable the British to engineer a "state within a state" through the Anglo-Persian Oil Company; women would forcibly forego the veil in 1936; a defiant king friendly to Nazi Germany would be replaced by a young and inexperienced heir unsure of his mission to lead the country. The United States would also broaden its interests in Iran during this time, particularly as American diplomats believed that "of all foreign capital, Persia prefers American." The State Department proposed that "American investments in Persia might cautiously be increased," particularly to improve transportation facilities in the country, such as the construction of highways.[86] As of 1925, forty-two American firms had branches or "maintain[ed] representatives" in Iran, but of these, only two were "engaged in import trade." The others participated principally in the export of carpets, rugs, and other raw materials. A "conservative estimate" of investments of these firms in Iran amounted to approximately $6,000,000 at the time.[87]

As economic connections emerged, so too did cultural ones. Both societies recognized that economic bonds would prove meaningless without some cultural context. In 1925, discussions took place about the formation of an American society in Tehran.[88] There would, however, be no easy way to reconcile America's imperialist ambitions and Iran's nationalist vision. Oil, frontier security, and diplomatic interests made it difficult at times to align U.S.

policies and Iranian interests. For better or worse, American culture pervaded Iranian society, and Iran intruded upon the American consciousness in cultural and diplomatic circles.

At about the same time that Presbyterian missionaries opened up Iran to proselytizing, American academics were showing curiosity about Persian literature and antiquity. Scholars specialized in the languages, archeology, and religion of the ancient Persian empires, and Iranian Studies eventually emerged as a formal discipline at leading American universities. Contact thus occurred on three levels: missionary; diplomatic; and academic. By the turn of the century, as Iran experienced revolution and political turmoil, America emerged as a potential diplomatic ally and partner in the modern, secular transformation of Iran.

Notwithstanding the vastly divergent historical trajectories of Iran and America in the nineteenth century, both countries shared an interest in empire building. Reflecting upon its long history of imperial domination, Iran hoped to reconstitute a modern Persian empire, but it failed to realize its territorial ambitions. In the same interval, America grew from a nation of colonies to a global empire with footholds on multiple continents. Iran's storied imperial past retained its romantic appeal for travelers, diplomats, and academics alike. This point was not lost on the intellectual and diplomatic pioneers of more than a century ago. While Americans—like other Western travelers in Iran—studied the Persian past with subtlety, their views of Iran's contemporary society lacked a similar refinement. Although neither Hafiz nor Emerson ever intended their verses to shed light on U.S.-Iranian relations, their prose and prosody forged a literary link between these distant and seemingly societies.

Notes

1. "Foreign History of Persia" (1746, January). *The American Magazine and Historical Chronicle* (1743–1746), 3, 41. Retrieved 15 February 2010 from American Periodicals Series Online.

2. "Persian Letters," *The Monthly Miscellany, or Vermont Magazine* (1794–1794); Aug. 1794; 1, 5. American Periodicals Series Online, p. 240. Also, "A Specimen of Perform Tales, Exhibiting their Ideas of the Advantage the Women Have in the Next World over the Men," *New York Magazine, or Literary Repository* (1790–1797); June 1795, American Periodicals Series Online, 337. For excerpts of Persian poetry, see "Oriental Poetry," *The Massachusetts Magazine; or, Monthly Museum. Containing the Literature, History, Politics, Arts, Manners, & Amusements of the Age*, Aug. 1795; American Periodicals Series Online, 309; and "The EXORDIUM of JAUMI'S Persian POEM, entitled Eusoof and Zoollikba," *The Massachusetts Magazine; or, Monthly*

Museum. Containing the Literature, History, Politics, Arts, Manners, & Amusements of the Age, Oct. 1795, 7, 7; American Periodicals Series Online, 392.

3. "Eastern Poesy," (1856, November). *Ballou's Pictorial Drawing-Room Companion* (1855-1859), 11(20), 317. Retrieved February 17, 2010, from American Periodicals Series Online.

4. W. R. A. (1854, January). ART. V.—THE PIETY AND THE POETRY OF THE SUFIS. Christian Examiner and Religious Miscellany (1844-1857), 56(1), 117. Retrieved February 17, 2010, from American Periodicals Series Online. This article also cites John Malcolm's account of the Sufis in his *History of Persia*.

5. *The American Whig Review*, vol. 9, no. 13, January 1849, 54-68.

6. "Persian Poetry, with Examples: Hafiz and Sadi. Stanza. Couplet. Distich," *The National Magazine; Devoted to Literature, Art, and Religion* (1852-1858) (February 1855), 6, 119. Retrieved March 28, 2010, from American Periodicals Series Online.

7. Wai Chee Dimock, "Hemispheric Islam: Continents and Centuries for American Literature," *American Literary History* (August 2008), 35-38. Emerson also wrote a preface for Francis Gladwin's translation of Saʿdi's poetry published in 1865. "ART. XI.—CRITICAL NOTICES," (January 1866), *The North American Review*, vol. CII, no. CCX, 260. Retrieved December 29, 2009, from American Periodicals Series Online. For more on Emerson's preface to the Saʿdi *Golistan* collection, see Ali Saleh Pasha, *Cultural Ties Between Iran and the United States* (1976), 61.

8. John Orr, "The Transcendentalism of New England," *The International Review (1874-1883)*, Oct. 1882. American Periodicals Series Online, 381.

9. James A. Bill, *The Eagle and the Lion: The Tragedy of American-Iranian Relations* (New Haven: Yale University Press, 1989); Badi Badiozamani, *Iran and America: Rekindling a Love Lost* (2005); Mohammad Gholi Majd, *Oil and the Killing of the American Consul in Tehran* (2006); Mansour Bonakdarian, "U.S.-Iranian Relations, 1911-1950," in *U.S.—Middle East Historical Encounters: A Critical Survey*, edited by Magnus Bernhardsson and Abbas Amanat (Gainesville: University Press of Florida, 2007); Kamyar Ghaneabassiri, "U.S. Foreign Policy And Persia, 1856-1921," *Iranian Studies*, vol. 35, nos. 1-3, Winter/Spring/Summer 2002; Kenneth Pollack, *The Persian Puzzle: The Conflict Between Iran and America* (2004); Michael Zirinsky, "A Panacea for the Ills of the Country: American Presbyterian Education in Inter-War Iran," *Iranian Studies*, 26:1 (1993); Thomas Ricks, "Power Politics and Political Culture: U.S.-Iran Relations," in *Iran: Political Culture in the Islamic Republic*, edited by Samih Farsoun and Mehrdad Mashayekhi (1992); Matthew Mark Davis, "Evangelizing the Orient: American Missionaries in Iran, 1890-1940," (Ph.D. Dissertation, Ohio State University, 2001); Ali Mujani, *Barrisi-i Munasibat-i Iran va Imrika az Sal-i 1851-1951* (Tehran, 1375/1996). Older studies include the following: Abraham Yeselson, *United States-Persian Diplomatic Relations, 1883-1921* (1956); Ali Pasha Saleh, *Cultural Ties Between Iran and the United States* (1976); Kermit Roosevelt, *Countercoup: The Struggle for the Control of Iran* (1979); Ahmad Mansoori, "American Missionaries in Iran, 1834-1934," (Ph.D. Dissertation, Ball State University, 1986); James F. Goode, "A Good Start: The First American Mission to Iran, 1883-1885," *The Muslim World*, vol. 74, no. 2, 100-118, April 1984.

10. The following studies on Iranian nationalism document Iran's interest in its imperial past during the Qajar era: Afshin Marashi, *Nationalizing Iran: Culture, Power, and the State, 1870-1940* (Seattle: University of Washington Press, 2008); Moha-

mad Tavakoli-Targhi, *Refashioning Iran: Orientalism, Occidentalism, and Historiography* (New York: Palgrave Macmillan, 2001); and F. Kashani-Sabet, *Frontier Fictions: Shaping the Iranian Nation, 1804–1946* (Princeton University Press, 1999).

11. Mu'tamin al-Mulk, *Recueil des traités de l'Empire Persan avec les pays étrangers* (Tehran: Faros, 1908), 19.

12. "An American in Persia," *The Washington Post*, August 8, 1883, 3.

13. S. G. W. Benjamin, "The City of Teheran," *The Century: A Popular Magazine*, December 1885, 170–171. It is worth noting that American presidents were encouraged to exchange telegrams with the Shah of Iran on the occasion of the Persian New Year's Day. In 1902, President Theodore Roosevelt even presented the Shah of Iran, Muzaffar al-Din, and his brother, Zill al-Sultan, with a copy of his book, *Hunting Trips of a Ranchman*, recognizing that hunting was a favorite pastime of the Persian royal family as well. See RG 59, M223, Box 338, Lloyd Griscom to John Hay, Secretary of State, 9 October 1902.

14. On the general subject of U.S.-Middle East relations, the missionary encounter comprises the bulk of recent scholarship detailing America's engagements with the Islamic communities of the Middle East in the nineteenth century.

15. Gernot Windfuhr, *Persian Grammar: History and State of its Study* (1979), p. 12.

16. C. Wade Meade, *Road to Babylon: Development of U.S. Assyriology* (1974).

17. Benjamin Foster, "Yale and the Study of Near Eastern Languages in America, 1770–1930," http://66.102.1.104/scholar?hl=en&lr=&q=cache:2fNgO9wzZAwJ:128 .36.236.77/workpaper/pdfs/MESV5-1.pdf+Benjamin+Foster+Orientalism. Raj Kumar Gupta, *The Great Encounter: A Study of Indo-American Literature and Cultural Relations* (1986).

18. A. V. W. Jackson, "Avesta, The Bible of Zoroaster," *The Biblical World*, June 1893; 1, 6. "The Behaist Movement," *The Open Court, a Quarterly Magazine [Devoted to the Science of Religion, the . . .* Jan. 1905, 19, 584. Accessed through the APS online database.

19. Robert William Rogers, *A History of Babylonia and Assyria* (1900), 1:239.

20. Robert William Rogers, *A History of Babylonia and Assyria*, 301–304.

21. Meade, *Road to Babylon*, 45. Also, "Mission of the Ancient Persian Empire," *New York Evangelist*, 13 March 1873, 44:11.

22. Philip G. Couture, "'BA' Portrait: Sir Henry Creswicke Rawlinson: Pioneer Cuneiformist," *The Biblical Archaeologist*, vol. 47, no. 3 (Sept. 1984), 143–145. Also, Joseph Bonomi, *Nineveh and its Palaces* (1857), 138.

23. S. Benjamin, "Persia and the Persians," *Journal of the American Geographical Society of New York*, vol. 18 (1886), 27.

24. Benjamin, "Persia and the Persians," 28.

25. Lesley Adkins, *Empires of the Plain: Henry Rawlinson and the Lost Languages of Babylon* (2004), 310–311.

26. Columbia University, Rare Book and Manuscript Library, A. V. William Jackson, Historical Biographical Files, Box 148, Folder 4.

27. Ali Pasha Saleh, *Cultural Ties*, 67; Louis H. Gray, "A. V. Williams Jackson in Memoriam," *Bulletin of the American Schools of Oriental Research*, no. 68 (Dec. 1937), 5–7.

28. A. V. Williams Jackson, *Persia, Past and Present* (New York: The Macmillan Company, 1906) 25.

29. A. V. Williams Jackson, *From Constantinople to the Home of Omar Khayyam* (New York: The Macmillan Company, 1911), 94–95.

30. Sir Richard Temple, "Great Britain in Asia," *North American Review*, vol. 170 (1900), 897–898.

31. Alfred Thayer Mahan, "The Persian Gulf and International Relations," *Retrospect & Prospect* (June 1902). Also, Bernard Lewis, *Historians of the Middle East* (1962), 4:1.

32. Samuel Flagg Bemis, Review of *Diplomatically Speaking*, by Lloyd Griscom, *American Historical Review*, vol. 46, no. 4. (July 1941), 951–952.

33. RG 59, M223, Box 338, Lloyd Griscom to John Hay, Secretary of State, 4 June 1902.

34. RG 59, M223, Box 338, Lloyd Griscom to John Hay, Secretary of State, 4 June 1902.

35. RG 59, M223, Box 338, Lloyd Griscom to John Hay, Secretary of State, 4 June 1902.

36. RG 59, M223, Box 338, Lloyd Griscom to John Hay, Secretary of State, 4 June 1902.

37. RG 59, M223, Box 338, Lloyd Griscom to John Hay, Secretary of State, 4 June 1902.

38. RG 59, M223, Box 338, Lloyd Griscom to Director, Philadelphia Commercial Museum, 30 September 1902.

39. RG 59, M223, Box 338, Lloyd Griscom to Director, Philadelphia Commercial Museum, 30 September 1902.

40. RG 59, M223, Box 338, Lloyd Griscom to Director, Philadelphia Commercial Museum, 30 September 1902.

41. RG 59, M223, Box 338, John Tyler to Secretary of State, John Hay, 14 March 1903.

42. RG 59, M223, Box 338, Richmond Pearson to John Hay, 23 May 1903.

43. RG 59, M223, Box 338, Richmond Pearson to John Hay, 23 May 1903.

44. *Ruznamah-i Iran-i Sultani*, no. 5, 2 June 1903, 2. A copy of this edition of the newspaper can be found in the following microfilm files: RG 59, Richmond Pearson to John Hay, 23 May 1903.

45. RG 59, M223, Box 338, Richmond Pearson to John Hay, 6 July 1903.

46. RG 59, M223, Box 338, Richmond Pearson to John Hay, 6 July 1903.

47. Perkins, *A Residence of Eight Years in Persia, among the Nestorian Christians* (1843), 315.

48. "Tarjumah-i Yosemite," unpublished manuscript no. 9485, Kitabkhanah-i Melli-yi Iran, 1–2. This manuscript was completed on 4 Zhul Qa'da 1293/21 November 1876. I am still working on determining the original source and details about the translator.

49. Muhammad Ali, Muin al-Saltanah, *Safarnamah-i Shikagaw* (1900).

50. Clarence Andrews, "Foreign Nations at the World's Fair," *North American Review*, 16:483 (May 1893), 611–613.

51. Ibid., 611.

52. Ibid., 613.

53. "Sharh-e Ekspozisyon," Unpublished manuscript at the Kitabkhanah-i Milli, Tehran, #4952, 10–12.

54. "Sharh-e Ekspozisyin," 14–16.

55. "Sharh-e Ekspozisyon," 12.

56. Andrews, "Foreign Nations," 612.

57. Andrews, "Foreign Nations," 612.

58. For an account of the Persian presence at the World's Columbian Exposition, see F. Kashani-Sabet, "Inside the Looking Glass: A Historical View of U.S.-Iranian Relations, 1893–1979," presented at Penn's Middle East Seminar, September 2004: https://www.sas.upenn.edu/mec/events/2004/september/middle-east-seminar-series -inside-looking-glass-historical-view-us-iranian-rel. For related discussions on the World's Columbian Exposition and Persian rugs, see Charles Kurzman, "Weaving Iran into the Tree of Nations," *International Journal of Middle East Studies* 37/2005, 137–166.

59. "Sharh-e Ekspozisyon," 13.

60. Andrews, "Foreign Nations," 612.

61. Leonard M. Helfgott, *Ties That Bind: A Social History of the Iranian Carpet* (Washington: Smithsonian Institution Press, 1996), 118.

62. Ibid.

63. Jennifer Scarce, "The Arts of the Eighteenth to Twentieth Centuries: Textiles," in *Cambridge History of Iran*, eds. Gavin Hambly et al., (Cambridge: Cambridge University Press, 1991), 7, 956–957. Cf. Edward Said, *Orientalism* (New York: Random House, 1978).

64. "Sharh-e Ekspozisyon," 19.

65. Nikki Keddie, *Modern Iran: Roots and Results of Revolution* (New Haven: Yale University Press, 2006), 61–62. Sayyid Jamal al-Din Afghani (1838–1897) was a controversial intellectual who criticized the autocratic politics of Nasir al-Din Shah. He traveled widely in the Middle East and India and wrote essays articulating his views on Muslim unity and the role of Western imperialist powers in nineteenth-century Islamic societies. For a biography of Afghani, see Keddie, *An Islamic Response to Imperialism* (Berkeley and Los Angeles: University of California Press, 1968).

66. Foreign Relations of the United States (hereafter referred to as FRUS), United States Department of State / *The executive documents of the House of Representatives for the second session of the fifty-second Congress. 1892–1893*, "Persia," Mr. Beale to Mr. Blaine, Tehran, 11 January 1892, 356. Accessed via University of Wisconsin Digital Collections.

67. FRUS, United States Department of State/*The executive documents of the House of Representatives for the second session of the fifty-second Congress. 1892–1893*, "Persia," Mr. Beale to Mr. Blaine, Tehran, 11 January 1892, 357. Accessed via University of Wisconsin Digital Collections.

68. "Facts About the Shah: He Had Pearls by the Quart and 800 Women in His Palace," *The New York Times*, May 18, 1896, 4.

69. *Surayya*, No. 9, 16 December 1899. *Surayya*, No. 11, 6 January 1990, 4.

70. RG 59, M223, Box 338, Richmond Pearson to John Hay, 23 May 1903.

71. *Tarbiyat*, No. 357, 1905, 1771. Two years later, another journal, *Rahnima*, which began publication during the constitutional period, discussed the history and legal framework of the United States: *Rahnima*, no. 4, 27 August 1907, 7.

72. Richmond Pearson to Secretary of State, Tehran, August 12, 1906. http://digital.library.wisc.edu/1711.dl/FRUS.

73. United States Department of State / *Papers relating to the foreign relations of the United States with the annual message of the president transmitted to Congress December 3, 1906. In two parts*: Part II (1906), 1217. http://digital.library.wisc.edu/1711.dl/FRUS.

74. Ibid., 1217.

75. Presbyterian Historical Society, Reel 271, Wishard to Vanneman, Tehran, 27 November 1906.

76. John G. Wishard, *Twenty Years in Persia* (Revell, 1908), 314.

77. For Persian accounts, see Nazim al-Islam Kirmani, *Tarikh-i Bidari-yi Iranian*, edited by 'Ali Akbar Sa'idi Sirjani (Tehran: Intisharat-i Nuh, 1357/1978); M. Malik-zadah, Tarikh-i Inqilab-i Mashrutiyat-i Iran (Tehran: 'Ilmi Press, 1984); F. Adami-yat, *Fikr-i Azadi va Muqaddamah-i Nihzat-i Mashrutiyat-i Iran* (Tehran, 1981); and A. Kasravi, *Tarikh-i Mashrutah-i Iran* (Tehran: Amir Kabir, 1984).

78. William Howard Taft, "State of the Union Message," 7 December 1909.

79. *The New York Times*, "American to Direct Finances of Persia: W. Morgan Shuster Made Treasurer General of Asiatic Nation on Knox's Recommendation. FOUR OTHERS TO BE NAMED Persian Parliament Has Sought Foreign Aid in Putting Its Government on a Modern Basis," 11 February 1911, 3. Retrieved 21 December 2009, from *ProQuest Historical Newspapers: The New York Times* (1851–2006).

80. W. Morgan Shuster, *The Strangling of Persia* (New York: The Century Co., 1912), 4.

81. Junub, No. 23 (1911), "Mustisharan-i Imrikayi," 1. A subsequent article noted that various financial responsibilities had been turned over to the American advisors. *Jonub*, no. 26, 17 June 1911, 5. Another journalist expressed optimism that the Americans might sort out Iran's financial crisis and help the country acquire the funds needed to build infrastructure such as schools and the like: *Parvaneh*, no. 23 (1911), "Mustisharan-i Imrika'i," 5.

82. Shuster, *The Strangling of Persia*, 245.

83. Shuster, *The Strangling of Persia*, 186–187.

84. PHS, RG 91, Box 1, Folder 21, "Report, 1911–1912," 1.

85. PHS, RG 91, Box 1, Folder 21, "Report, 1911–1912," 1.

86. U.S. Department of State 1925, "Furthering American Economic Interests."

87. U.S. Department of State, September 8, 1925, from American Consul in Tehran.

88. Confidential U.S. Diplomatic Post Records, Iran, 1925–1941, Reel 1, W. Smith Murray to Secretary of State, 28 May 1925, "Statutes of 'The Persian-American Relations Society.'"

CHAPTER 8

An Iranian in New York: 'Abbas Mas'udi's Description of the Non-Iranian on the Eve of the Cold War

CAMRON MICHAEL AMIN

Afshin Marashi has noted in reference to the interwar period that diplomatic history played an important role "as part of the emerging narrative of modern culture in the region."[1] I would broaden that assertion to a longer stretch of history—at least as far back as the rise of European hegemony in the Middle East and up to the present day. The nationalist narrative is being continually revised, and global influence is as important as ever. Alongside official and intellectual formulations of specifically Iranian nationalism, many scholars of modern Persian literature and memoirs have grappled with the complex nature of "identity formation," in which a given individual's expression of "Iranianness" blends a variety of global and regional cultural elements with things that are accepted as authentically Iranian—generally as received (or actively extracted) from Iran's cultural past. Locating what is "Iranian" along a spectrum of global practices and ideas has been the project of various reform-minded activists in modern Iranian history;[2] also familiar is the modernist project of purifying Iranian or Islamic culture from foreign elements (Arab/Turkish/ "west-struck"/"superstitious").[3] This implies a certain plasticity in how "the Other" is perceived as part of a project to define "the Self," one that allows favored traits to be claimed and unfavorable ones to be projected outward to a nonthreatening distance.

A text that illustrates this dynamic very well is a travelogue by 'Abbas Mas'udi, the newspaperman and parliamentarian, published in his widely circulated newspaper *Ettela'at* in 1945. This very public text will be examined for its description of modern America before the onset of the Cold War and the watershed in Iranian-American diplomatic relations: Operation Ajax. What was Mas'udi's America and how was it fundamentally different from modern Iran? As a work of journalism by a member of the Pahlavi elite whose very experience of travel was sponsored by the United States Office of War Information (OWI), Masʿudi's travelogue is at once personal and official, independent and compromised by diplomatic pressures. In short, it is an excellent place to observe the interaction of a personal sense of identity and formal expressions of nationalism.[4]

Abbas Milani's succinct biography of Masʿudi notes his political opportunism and penchant for successfully taking advantage of the sort of crony capitalism that was necessary to underwrite the growth of his media empire in Iran.[5] He also liked to travel and use his access to the media to share his reflections on that travel. Milani takes note of Masʿudi's many trips to the Soviet Union (his first in 1930) and his trip to New York accompanying Prime Minister Muhammad Musaddiq in the fall of 1951. But Masʿudi's first trip to America came at the end of World War II, on a junket organized for four Iranian newspaper editors sponsored by the OWI[6] in coordination with the U.S. Embassy in Tehran. The junket was an exercise in damage control, as America's image in Iran had suffered in the wake of the embarrassing end to the financial mission of American Arthur Chester Millspaugh in 1944. Those specific concerns were part of a more general American anxiety about how America was being perceived around the world at the close of World War II. Writing in support of continued funding for the OWI in late 1945 (six months after the OWI-sponsored press junket for Iranian journalists), Assistant Secretary of State for Public Affairs William Benton wrote:

> The American legend is a curious and contradictory mixture. A legend can hardly be otherwise. We are known to be immensely strong. Yet, Axis propagandists found ready belief for the story that good living had made us so weak and spineless we would not and could not fight. We are acclaimed generous and openhanded with billions to spend on lend-lease and rehabilitation—a veritable Uncle Santa Claus. At the same time we are called Uncle Shylock. We believe in freedom of speech for all, yet sinister capitalists are said to control the means of communication. We stand for free enterprise but our critics abroad stress our great combines and monopolies. The Metropolitan Opera House is the goal of all foreign opera stars but we are said to have no music except swing. We believe in due process of law, yet the world pictures the gangsters shooting it out on the streets of Chicago.[7]

So it should be clear to us (as it was frankly represented by Masʿudi himself) that the tour was intended to impress a more coherent vision of a "real" America upon the Iranian public through these four "opinion makers." As we shall see, Masʿudi's impressions of the U.S. were only partially in alignment with the best hopes of OWI messaging. Though Mas'udi was participating in a stage-managed tour that lasted seven weeks (19 April–11 June 1945), he stayed nearly a year in the United States, gaining the kind of experience of the world that had enhanced the stature of Iranian journalists for decades. Contemporary appreciations of Mas'udi reflect that cultural value. Writing in the late 1940s, press historian Mohammad Sadr-Hashemi placed Mas'udi in a longer tradition of cosmopolitan expertise among journalists, in which well-traveled correspondents are valuable because they can explain the wider world to an Iranian audience:

> In recent years, Mr. Mas'udi has visited Europe and America, and because of the length of these visits has been well able to understand the habits and spirit and mindset of Europeans and Americans, and, therefore, is able to explain them to today's young policy-makers. Reliably, after each trip he has written and published detailed and valuable articles about the situation in Europe and America and the morals of the people there. The articles are highly informed narratives of the situation in the world. Mr. Mas'udi's recent trip to America lasted more than a year over the course of 1945 and 1946. After being elected to the fifteenth session of parliament, he returned to his nation to a well-deserved welcome that exhibited the esteem of the Iranian nation for his efforts.[8]

This is flattery to be sure, but it is in a form built on decades of cultural context. From the very first official newspapers of the nineteenth century, alongside other attributes of journalistic culture that are beyond the scope of this discussion,[9] the ideal of explaining the wider world to the reader was a prominent theme[10]—amplified by the success (and celebration) of expatriate newspapers in the late nineteenth century that could report authoritatively from remote locations, often championed political liberalization in Iran, and doggedly outmaneuvered would-be censors in Iran and abroad.

Mas'udi published a serialized account of his visit to America beginning in August 1945, and it focused mainly on the OWI itinerary. The travelogue reappeared in book form in 1949 (unaltered except for the addition of images), joining the list of seven of his other travelogues that were reissued between 1949 and 1973.[11] There are three historiographical contexts in which we might place this journalistic travelogue. First, there is the context of earlier Iranian visitors' published accounts of America. Starting in 1888, the first Iranian ambassador to America, Hajj Hosaynquli Khan Mo'tamed al-Vozara, has left us some of his correspondence with the Foreign Ministry. In addition, Hajj Mirza Mohammad 'Ali Mo'in al-Saltaneh, has left us his travelogue of his visit to the Chicago World's Columbian Exposition in 1893. We also have a travelogue from Iranian businessman Ebrahim Sahhafbashi, who visited the United States at the turn of the century, but whose writing does not seem to have been published until 1979.[12] Second, in addition to the "cosmopolitan" ethos of Iranian journalism, there is a tendency (clearly shared by Masʿudi) to see journalists as not merely public servants seeking to inform and enlighten the masses, but as appendages of the state—ideally, highly respected ones with real influence on policy.

One need only look at a third, and more narrow, context of Masʿudi's body of travelogues published over the course of his career to appreciate how he read the twin roles of statesman-traveler and statesman-journalist into his own public persona. In the English translation of his travelogue to China, the author credit reads "Senator Abbas Massoudi" and the preface notes that the English translation of his journalistic coup (compiled from columns published in 1973) was offered in response to requests from "foreign residents in Tehran to publish my reports at great length and later to publish them in book form."[13] The opportunities Masʿudi took to meet and be photographed with national and international figures—combined with his service as a member of parliament and then senator—convey a concern with establishing an Iranian and global reputation beyond journalism (though always rooted in it). Indeed, that is how one might best understand the triumphant biography (*Victory of a Smile*) published by his son in 1976.[14] In other words, this text emerges at the beginning of a process in which Masʿudi imagines his personal perspective as being influential upon an ever-widening audience and carrying ever more weight with national and international decision-makers.

New York was Masʿudi's first and longest stop in the United States. Although he understood well that it could not represent America in its totality,[15] he devoted the largest chunk of the travelogue to his time there. New York became a yardstick with which he initially measured his own preconceived notions about America and his reflections on New York City became an intellectual point of departure for the rest of his travelogue. At the risk of obscuring some of the complexity of his description of America in 1945, the "real" America that Masʿudi described was an orderly democracy, driven to both productive and wasteful efforts by consumerism, and it was white. He tended not to associate "real" Iran with the first two aspects of "real" America, but he found some common ground with the race consciousness of Americans of Western European origin.

"Come with Me to America"

On 9 August 1945, Masʿudi published the preface to his series on his tour of the United States. The U.S. State Department must have found the introduction pleasing. Masʿudi briefly acknowledged America's official sponsorship of his tour more in the spirit of asserting his journalistic independence. He also implied that his countrymen's reaction to his trip was immature and superficial, filled as it was with speculation about Hollywood and an opportunity to "go behind the scenes of the cinema": "Now that I have returned to my country and visited with my friends, again these words have been repeated, mostly queries about Hollywood and actors. I have met few who would ask me about the great industries, agricultural progress, or culture of America, so that they might be informed."[16]

In other words, Masʿudi wanted to report on the "real" America, not its glamor—though he did visit Hollywood (a lot) and Disneyland before his tour was over.[17] But the America in this preface was no less idealized than a Hollywood movie. Furthermore, the qualities Masʿudi praised were presented as a critique of Iran. It was not just about what qualities America possessed, but also what Iran lacked. That said, what was good about America was often not innate, but a matter of cultivation and effort by American state and society.

But what were these distinctive, if not exclusive, "American" qualities? Masʿudi's America was hierarchical but culturally classless. His best example was the industriousness of students, even wealthy ones, who willingly worked menial jobs as doormen, janitors, and dishwashers, and in unpaid internships, before graduating.[18] The implicit reward was social mobility, but Masʿudi explicitly described industriousness as a cultural value that cut across all sectors of American society, writing, "Life in America begins from childhood with work, struggle (*zahmat*), and earning money."[19]

The second feature of Masʿudi's America was its rational democracy with an electorate that was at once politically active and utterly obedient to the state. Here Masʿudi made explicit and negative comparisons to Iran. First he cautions his readers: "For example, when I talk of American democracy, I consider it superfluous to then go back and compare it with Iran and its democracy. This is because the meaning and understanding of true American democracy will be explained in the daily reports to come. Readers will themselves become conscious of Iran's strange democracy and stunned at the chaotic condition of Iran that may have no parallel or like in the world."[20]

In other words, it is not just that American democracy is exemplary, but that Iran's is defective. Masʿudi's sense of national shame is almost narcissistic; he used a visit with a group of Iranians living in New York to amplify his perspective. A young man with "a Turkish accent" asked him if the horrible stories about Iran's state of affairs were true, characterizing them thusly: "They say Iran is in chaos and insecurity. They say dear Iran is burning in the fire of corruption and that misfortune and hopelessness has set in among the people. No one is thinking of them; they just spin their webs like spiders and facilitate the misfortune for themselves and the people. Look how what people here [America] do. There is so much activity and cooperation."[21]

Mas'udi confirms the young merchant's fears, and then reports this outburst: "How long must we be the most abased and abject of nations? Can you search the countries of the world today to find one that has the situation we do?"[22] This is an altogether astonishing statement, given the state of the world in 1945, with many countries suffering far worse political and economic conditions than Iran. This amplified a point in Mas'udi's preface to the series, in which he described the harmonious and anything-but-Iranian American results of democracy as follows: "In American governance and democracy, people obey the orders of the government. When the government of the day orders that Mondays and Tuesdays be meatless or that meat should not be eaten for two weeks, then, essentially, meat ceases to exist. This order is carried out with peace of mind. There is no need for control . . ."[23]

This strange conflation of wartime rationing with American democratic values also ignores the fact that rationing was a matter of government control. The relatively light presence of the government in business seems to have challenged Mas'udi's expectations. When he asked a representative of the Associated Press about government funding, he was told that AP's efforts "in no way" received state funding. Roosevelt's efforts in response to the Great Depression notwithstanding, Mas'udi noted that the government generally did nothing for laid-off workers. Even postwar plans to combat unemployment were a matter for local councils, not state intervention.[24] Of course, he got that impression after being shown an OWI "documentary" on ordinary Americans in the heartland making postwar plans on the basis of self-reliance and local community spirit.

American Consumerism

As American officials hoped, Mas'udi was suitably impressed with American cities, industries, and institutions. That said, he often remarked upon an underlying consumerism that drove America's industrious culture. As he marveled at the refrigerator trucks delivering perishable produce throughout New York, he digressed to a discussion of ice cream:

Americans eat a lot of ice cream, and they make very good ice cream. They sell ice cream everywhere, from cafés to restaurants to drugstores. After a meal, more than any other dessert, Americans like ice cream. In addition, when you are out on the streets, you will run into folks with something in their hand. What they eat while they walk is big chunks of ice cream on a thin wooden stick. Because they sell it right out of a refrigerator it doesn't melt right away. They eat as they walk![25]

Americans did not just consume treats and luxury foods, but they also consumed large amounts of basic necessities such as water. While visiting the AP offices, Mas'udi was offered water while he waited for his first meeting. This led him to comment: "How much water Dr. Gurney drinks! In every hallway he heads for a water fountain and drinks water. He is not alone. Americans drink a lot of water. This is due to a pronouncement from the most prominent American doctors, who say, 'Drink a lot of water; it is beneficial for health!'"[26]

With this scientific and cultural imperative to drink, Americans have created an entire infrastructure to consume water from mechanical fountains. He notes that Americans developed a paper-cup industry to support serving water at all sorts of establishments without wasting water by having to wash glasses repeatedly. He wrote: "You have to be careful with fountains that have foot pedals and avoid too much pressure. If you press too hard with your foot, your entire face will be soaked. You must place your foot calmly and gently, so that water will flow in such a way as it can be lapped up. There are such things in a mechanical life."[27]

When an OWI employee found Mas'udi reading a letter in a dark room using just one small lamp, she remarked unkindly that it was a wonder he had not gone blind.[28] Her reaction to his frugal use of energy demonstrated how Americans took abundance for granted, even in wartime. His account of a trip to Macy's department store expressed dismay at the indulgent attitude Macy's employees showed toward misbehaving children, but tied it directly to America's finely honed business and consumer culture. "Regarding the greatness of this store, it is enough to note that last year it had sales of 185,000,000 dollars!"[29]

One departure from the rule of American consumerism was his observations about beauty parlors. Here he heaped praise upon American women, and expressly contrasted them with Iranian women. This critique of "beauty culture" was a persistent theme in the Iranian press during and after the Women's Awakening Project of 1936 to 1941, and perhaps old habits died hard. Masʿudi remarked:

> I saw very few beauty salons. An absence of luxuries and a disinterest in a luxurious life has caused American women to go the beauty salon less often than I imagined they might before my trip. It is not that women do not care about beauty: they do, but they avoid luxury and prefer simplicity. This issue of women going every week to the beauty salon and having their hair done is a Hollywood thing for films. In other places in America, interest in these pleasures is rare, even in comparison to some Iranian women. It does not do for a lady of the house or a lady who values work and effort to go to the salon every week to change her hairdo.[30]

American consumerism is redeemed by an entrepreneurial spirit that Masʿudi seems to admire. Even his discussion of worker's unions—which devotes a good deal of time to the service workers associated with the hospitality industry in New York City—notes the endless variety of unionized workers earning money for each discrete service provided. Indeed, the strength of unions seems to balance out the power of business owners, and it appeared to Masʿudi that "every kind of worker belonged to a union or syndicate."[31] His observation that wearing a hat was expensive because of all the unionized hat-check girls in restaurants and other establishments was confirmed by an Iranian living in New York: "Here I remembered something an Iranian friend who had been living in New York City for several months told me. [He said], 'I've spent more on hat-check workers than I did on the hat. Eventually, it wore me down and I took the hat off. I went around without a hat and was relieved of this expense. Most Americans are the same and walk around without hats."[32]

Common Ground for the "Real" Iran and America

How deliberately it is hard to know, but Masʿudi's serialized travelogue does yield a meaningful thematic structure that resonates in later Iranian expressions of the "non-Iranian." The "real" America is not New York because, in addition to being more advanced than the rest of the country (and, indeed, the world as he knew it), it was more cosmopolitan than the rest of the United States. The "authentic" America in New York was diluted by the many different peoples who lived there and by the outsized opulence in which many

of them lived. It does not take long in this segment for an anti-Semitic shoe
to drop:

Americans do not like New York. Some say that America and New York
are not the same or that they consider New York foreign because of its
special position. . . . The presence of two and half million Jews in New
York and their influence in big, important companies and their hand in
the financial power of America is noteworthy. Add to that the several
hundred thousand different merchants from other parts of the world that
have gathered here. In truth, *real Americans* are a minority in New York.
[Italics added][33]

As if that observation were not cringe-inducing enough, it follows from
Masʿudi's earlier ethnography of New York. After noting matter-of-factly
the relative numbers of Italian-, English- and Irish-Americans, he elaborates
for several paragraphs on the unusual number of Jews in New York and the
United States generally. He was not just impressed by their numbers but their
domination of American culture and media: "The financial power of the Jews
of New York is extraordinary because they have controlling interests in large
companies and institutions. Indeed, their propaganda power is of special note.
Because the control of most of the media for propaganda—radio, theater,
cinema and the press—is in the hands of the Jews. Many editors of important
American newspapers and magazines are Jews."[34]

That said, it is only in that cosmopolitan part of America that Masʿudi
finds anything Iranian. He finds "Iran" on exhibit in a museum[35] and in a small
Iranian trade representative office in the Rockefeller Center. "Authentic Iran"
is reduced, without apparent irony or resentment, to relics from Iran's past and
traditional handicrafts.

Modern Iranian cosmopolitans could be found at Iran's embassy in Washington, DC, and also among Iranian expatriates living in the United States.
Iranian expatriates in New York City acted as occasional hosts, translators,
and sources for Masʿudi, but, quite organically, they were assimilating into
America, somewhat like the friend who stopped wearing his hat to avoid
hat-check fees. The embassy staff included one Mohammad Ebrahim Bayg,
who had been assigned to the Iranian embassy for twenty-five years. He had
been posted there after serving as Iranian diplomatic staff in Belgium and
had memories of every Iranian ambassador who had served in that post. Bayg
ensured that Iranian-style hospitality and Persian cuisine were available to
guests of the Embassy. But a good deal of Masʿudi's account of his "one hour
at the Iranian embassy" focused on the comically embarrassing episode that

led to a break in Iranian representation to the United States. Police who did not understand his diplomatic status arrested the former ambassador, Ghaffar Jalal, after a traffic accident on 27 November 1935.[36] The affair played in the American press as an example of arrogant foreigners not observing American laws (without reminding readers of the important consideration of diplomatic immunity). In Iran, Reza Shah took it as a national insult and recalled Jalal on 5 January 1936, and he set sail for Europe two weeks later.[37] No amount of apologizing from the United States for the way things played out satisfied Riżā Shāh, and all Iranian consular offices were closed in March 1936;[38] Turkey handled Iran's interests until 1943. Iranian staffers at the embassy complained to Masʿudi about the inadequacy of their wages. Masʿudi wrote, "When I asked about his salary and compared it, I was embarrassed that it was about the same as that of a common worker."[39] So, the embassy's history and its current state of affairs in Masʿudi's time were not evidence of Iran's long engagement with the modern "community of nations," but evidence of Iran's inability to function well in that community.

Though Masʿudi was in America to observe and report on the state of American progress in a variety of areas, he did not see a modern place for Iran at America's economic table. His desire for Iran's trade mission to have greater visibility in Rockefeller Plaza was to expand the market for Iranian handicrafts and unprocessed agricultural goods, not to expand opportunities for its modern, though British-dominated, petroleum industry. Modernity expressed as industrialization, technical innovation, scientific discovery, or democratic governance was not Iranian. In his series, that sort of modernity was only American.

But, in Masʿudi's travelogue, Iranians and Americans do share something: cultural "whiteness." In one brief moment, Masʿudi strains to find "God-fearing" common ground between Iranian and American culture after attending a Sunday service at St. Patrick's Cathedral: "It should be understood that most Americans are a people of faith . . . [despite a diversity of denominations]. Because they know that the endurance of any country and nation must rest on a religious foundation . . ."[40]

He generalizes from an experience visiting one upscale American Catholic church about an essential religious American character, and universalizes American Christianity to a vaguely defined "religious foundation" that all nations (including Iran) require to endure. One might be inferring too much from this passage alone to say that Masʿudi only had white American Christians in mind as being akin to Iranians in some way. But consider the place of Native Americans and African Americans in Masʿudi's America. He notes both their troubled history and the harsh realities of 1945. Native Americans are "red skins" (*sorkh pust*, contrasted directly with "white skins," *sefid pust* in this travelogue), who were the original rulers of America, disenfranchised and subjugated by European colonizers and, later, the United States government.[41] African Americans are "blacks" (*siyah-ha*) who, despite the success of institutions like the Tuskegee Institute (part of the OWI-devised itinerary) and the end to slavery, were nonetheless under threat from the white supremacist Ku Klux Klan.[42] Mas'udi does not identify with the KKK, but he seems comfortable with a more benign American "whiteness." He repeats classic racial and ethnic stereotypes in his travelogue, notably against African Americans and, as we have seen already, Jews. And he does so in such a way that it is hard to tell if he is simply reporting what he is told (without objecting to it, as he does with other things he disagreed with), or reporting what he actually thought was the case. His ethnography of New York's African Americans begins ominously enough: "This is the situation of poor districts in New York: they are not clean. It is not just their districts that are unclean, but the homes of the people are filthy."[43] And it only gets worse: "The area of Harlem is filthy. In the streets, alleys, stores and restaurants no one can be seen but those with thick lips, curly hair, and white teeth. *Ivāh*! How many kids each family has!"[44]

Conclusion

Should we be surprised by such attitudes in a member of the twentieth-century modern Iranian elite, or that such racism and anti-Semitism might represent an important, narrow patch of common ground among global elites who are nonetheless separated by gulfs of technological sophistication, political power, and wealth? Perhaps not. Iran certainly has its own history of racial bigotry and ethnic tension to draw on. But I think this low moment in Mas'udi's travelogue anticipates the tricky terrain navigated by the Iranian diaspora as it assimilated into American culture later in the twentieth century (witness every attempt to disavow the racist implications of Hajji Firuz[45] and recent efforts to encourage Iranian Americans to not simply check "white" on the 2010 Census but to write in "Iranian-American").[46] It also resonates a bit with the way nearly all shades of Iranian nationalism emphasize Iran's difference from Turks and Arabs,[47] even when not energetically affirming Iran's "Indo-European" ethnolinguistic heritage.

Mas'udi does not associate Iran with the "rational" nature of American democracy, or the entrepreneurial and modernizing (specifically in regard to industrial and technological innovation) effects of American consumerism.

That said, by focusing on the material effects of "American" progress, he left the door open for other nations (including Iran) to acquire those characteristics and, through "hard work," enjoy the material benefits, while avoiding any unwanted consequences. Also, though he does not really dwell on it, his travelogue suggests that religion was neither an impediment to modernization ("Americans are religious"), nor something that a "nation" could do without.[48] Though he reports "real" America as having mixed feelings about its engagement with the wider world (especially in the area of immigration), it is also an undeniable feature of its modern national character. There is an important implication here for Iranian nationalism: for Iran's national character to be modern, it must be open to contemporary influences, even as it attaches itself to a coherent "national" historical narrative that retains a religious character. This conclusion finds echoes in the writings of other commentators in the late 1950s and early 1960s. For all his hand-wringing over the effects of cultural imperialism in *Gharbzadegi* ("West-struckness"), Jalal Al-e Ahmad (1923–1969) frames his 1962 critique of modernization in Iran as one who truly understood "the West" and the essentially material bases of its hegemony. In his radio sermons, cleric Husayn 'Ali Rashed (1905–1980) emphasized the need to understand that the "real" strength of France was in its social progress, industrialization, and high culture, none of which contradicted Islamic teachings, in his view.[49] Visiting the United States some ten years after Masūdi, the Omidvar brothers used the yardstick of receptiveness to global progressive trends to differentiate the truly "modern" parts of the U.S. (i.e., the northern states) from the segregated south, which they described as being dominated by race-obsessed throwbacks to the eighteenth century.[50] The ability to understand and critique the modernity of other nations, national ideologies, or national characters in itself reflects a changing sense of Iran's national character and its place in the modern world. The questions are then, how far does this cultural shift go, and how widely does it propagate in Iranian society over the course of the twentieth and twenty-first centuries?

Masʿudi's travelogue also offers some cautionary notes as we rethink Iranian nationalism. An individual's expression of nationalism is always going to be mediated by personal drives and other aspects of individual identity (most in evidence here are Masʿudi's journalistic and political ambitions).[51] It is simply not the case that the many efforts to formulate and propagate a particular national ideology[52] will translate with any consistency at the individual level due to competing messages (produced inside and outside Iran), competing priorities, changing circumstances, and the psychological uniqueness of each person. That said, elements of formal ideology do seem to circulate, so that ephemeral, like-minded communities emerge and combine in Iran, among the Iranian diaspora, and across those categories. Mas'udi could find Iranians who understood America well and were even assimilating into American society, but still identified strongly with Iran.[53] It is that combination of Iranians visiting America (like himself), Iranians assimilating into America, and Iranians hearing about America, that creates an image of both countries and their "true" national characters. In an age of increasing literacy, increased mobility, and ever-improving mass communications, these temporary and partial alignments of perspective leave their mark on a public record that may influence others. While nationalism, like music or language, may be standardized on a (web) page, it will always be understood and expressed uniquely. And whatever common ground may be found on the landscape of "nationalism," it can only be one cultural force among many that shapes events.

Notes

I wish to thank the organizers of the "Re-thinking Iranian Nationalism" Conference in Austin, Texas, on 2 and 3 April 2010: Kamran Scot Aghaie and Afshin Marashi. A draft of this work was presented there, with the help of funds provided by the Center for Middle Eastern Studies at the University of Texas at Austin. I received many helpful comments from my fellow participants for improving this study, and here I wish to especially thank Mohammad Ghanoonparvar, Touraj Atabaki and, again, Dr. Aghaie. My research efforts were supported by funds from the University of Michigan (OVPR–Ann Arbor), and the College of Arts, Sciences, and Letters at the University of Michigan–Dearborn. The responsibility for any remaining shortcomings in this work is mine, though I continue to blame others in private.

1. Afshin Marashi, "Performing the Nation: The Shah's Official Visit to Kemalist Turkey, June to July 1934," in *The Making of Modern Iran: State and Society Under Riza Shah, 1921-1941*, ed. Stephanie Cronin (London and New York: Routledge, 2003), 99-119.

2. For example, in feminism see Camron Michael Amin, *The Making of the Modern Iranian Woman: Gender, State Policy and Popular Culture, 1865-1946* (University Press of Florida, 2002), 117-118. Iranian marriage practices were compared to those of other countries as a measure of how "civilized" they were.

3. A reference to Jalal Al-e Ahmad's seminal polemic; see below.

4. Lisa Pollard elaborates on Sandra Naddaf's observation that nineteenth-century Egyptian travelers to Europe, such as al-Tahtawi (1801-1873), were looking to find similarities between "West and East" by emphasizing that "The mirror represents not the willingness of an Egyptian to see similarities where Europeans [traveling to the East/South] could only see difference, but rather reveals the exigencies that faced al-Tahtawi as a servant of Mohammad Ali's state. . . . Through 'travel literature,' the

state began to see itself as modern and to envision for itself a position in the modern world." Lisa Pollard, *Nurturing the Nation: The Family Politics of Modernizing, Colonizing, and Liberating Egypt, 1805–1923* (Berkeley: University of California Press, 2005), 46. Mas'udi was operating in a different but comparable context. He was neither a pioneering journalist nor a direct "servant of the state," as al-Tahtāwī was, but he was the most successful newspaperman in Iranian history at that time, and a close ally of the Pahlavi Court for most of his career. He certainly subordinated his editorial judgment to Riza Shāh's Office of Public Enlightenment in the late 1930s, when the state was looking to control its image abroad and the sense of Iran's place in the world to domestic audiences. In other words, he was part of the Iranian state's propaganda efforts, without holding a bureaucratic position that reflected that role. He was a contributor to the formal national ideology, but also free (by virtue of owning Iran's main daily) to propagate a travelogue comparable to the memoirs examined by Nasrin Rahimieh, *Missing Persians: Discovering Voices in Iranian Cultural History* (Syracuse: Syracuse University Press, 2001); thus my assertion that we can view a very public presentation of the "personal" (and more fluid) sense of identity and formal national ideology in his series on America for *Ettela'at*.

5. Abbas Milani, *Eminent Persians*, vol. I (New York: Syracuse University Press and Persian World Press, 2008), 394–398. His profile is rather like that of his competitor Mostafa Mesbahzadeh, ibid., 399–405. Mesbahzadeh was one of the four journalists chosen along with Mas'udi for the Iranian press junket, amid much controversy. A coalition of Iranian journalists objected to the process of selection. The British held up the travel of *Mehregan* publisher Majid Movaqqar, due to their suspicions of pro-Axis sympathies. Even the Press Officer at the U.S. Embassy, T. Culyer Young, did not think the selection of journalists was representative enough. See T. Cuyler Young to Secretary of State, "Iranian Press Mission," 19 April 1945. The details of the trip, and the various parts played by the War Department, State Department, and Office of War Information, are beyond the scope of this study, but make for interesting reading in U.S. State Department Records 891.91211. There was not much U.S. press reaction to the Iranian Press Mission, although the four toured New York, Washington, DC, the TVA, the Tuskegee Institute, New Mexico, and California (including Los Angeles and San Francisco) before ending their trip at a U.S. State Department luncheon on 11 June 1945. See Associated Press, "Iranian Editors to Tour US as Guests of OWI: Coast to Coast Trip Arranged," *Chicago Tribune* (29 April 1945), 5, and "Editor [Mesbahzadeh] Advises US to Watch Near East," *New York Times* (21 July 1945), 6. The journalists stayed in the United States for some time after the official tour. In one notable departure from the official itinerary, two of the journalists—Mas'udi and Abo'l-Qasem Amini, publisher of *Omid*—received permission to tour aircraft factories (Pratt and Whitney; Sikorsky) in early July before returning to Iran. See Rear Admiral Hewlett Thebaud to Secretary of State, "Visit of Iranian Journalists," 11 July 1945, and Secretary of War to Secretary of State, 10 July 1945, U.S. State Department Records 891.91211/7–945 & 7–1045.

6. Mas'udi describes his visit to the OWI's New York office in the installment published in *Ettela'at* 5863 (31 Shahrivar 1324): 3.

7. William Benton, "The Voice of America Abroad," *Journal of Educational Sociology* 19:4 A Free Press for Free World (December 1945): 213.

8. Mohammad Sadr-Hashemi, *Tarikh-e Jarayed va Majallat-e Iran* vol. 1, 2nd

ed. (Tehran: Kamal, 1363 [1984/5]), 209. The entire entry on Mas'udi's newspaper, *Ettela'at*, is on 202–209.

9. For more on this, see Camron Michael Amin, "Selling and Saving 'Mother Iran': Gender and the Iranian Press in the 1940s," *The International Journal of Middle East Studies* 33 (2001), 344–346 and 357–358.

10. Early expatriate newspapermen as diverse as Mirza Malkam Khan and Da'vat al-Islam extolled the virtues of being outside Iran (London and Bombay, respectively), because of the worldly perspective and independence it afforded. In the opening "statement of principles" for his newspaper, Mirza Malkam Khan wore his exile from the Qajar Empire like a badge of honor that qualified him, and those like him, to enlighten other Iranians:

> A great gathering of the people of Iran has been drawn from their familiar homeland for a number of reasons and has been scattered among foreign countries. Among these scattered émigrés those sensible persons who compare foreign progress with the situation of Iran have for years been wondering by what method it could be possible to deliver some assistance to those unfortunates who remain trapped in Iran. After research and thought, they agreed on the belief that for the need of the salvation and progress of the people of Iran, there could be nothing better than a [politically] free newspaper. (Mirza Malkam Khan, *Qanun* 1 [1 Rajab 1307 (21 February 1890)]: 1, in *Ruznameh-'i Qanun*, edited by Homa Nateq [Tehran: Amir Kabir Publishers, 2535 (1976)]).

So, for Mirza Malkam Khan, the "Mecca" of modernity and journalistic independence was London, but sixteen years later, for Mirza Mohammad Amin al-Tojjar, inspiration for his monthly *eslam-nameh* (an "Islam-paper," a deliberate counter to the term *ruznameh* (newspaper, literally "daily paper") came after an extended journey away from his hometown of Isfahan to Mecca and Medina before settling in Bombay. He meant to counter the liberal (and in his view, Christian or Babi) influence in other expatriate newspapers and postrevolutionary domestic newspapers such as *Sur-e Esrafil*. His anticonstitutionalism rested upon a foundation of antimissionary and anti-Babism from his first paper, *Al-Eslam*, published in Isfahan (with state encouragement) in 1903. Despite its pan-Islamist gestures and rhetoric (initially publishing in Persian and Urdu), *Da'vat al-Islam* expressed an outlook tied to political developments in Iran during the tumultuous years prior to the Civil War of 1908–1909. See Sadr-Hashemi I, 233–241, and *Da'vat al-Islam* 1, October 1906, 1–3.

11. 'Abbas Mas'udi, *Ba Man Be-Amrika Biya'id: Sharh-e Haft Haftah-e Siyahat Dar Sarasar-e Keshvarha-ye Mottahed-e Amrika* (Tehran: Sherkat-e Sahami-i Chap, 1949); *Posht-e Pardeh-e Ahanin Cheh Didam* (Tehran, 1952); *Khaterat-e Mosafarat-e Chin* (Taiwan): *Jam'avari Az Ruznameh-e Ettela'at* (Tehran: Edarat-e Entesharat-e efarat-e Kobra-ye Jomhuri-ye Chin, 1955); *Didari Az Shaykh Neshinha-ye Khalij-e Fars* (Tehran: Iran-e Chap, 1966); *Didari-ye Tazeh Az Shaykh Neshinha-ye Khalij-e Fars Pas Az Khoruj-e Niruha-ye Engelis* (Tehran): Entesharat-e Mo'assaseh-ye Ettela'at, 1973). One can see the mix of Cold War politics (e.g., the "Iron Curtain" and Taiwan) and regional diplomatic concerns (the Persian Gulf) inherent in the choices for Mas'udi's travel and travelogues.

12. For a fuller discussion of these three travelers, see Mohammad Ghanoonparvar, "Nineteenth-Century Iranians in America," in *Society and Culture in Qajar*

Iran: Studies in Honor of Hafez Farmayan, ed. Elton L. Daniel (Costa Mesa, CA: Mazda, 2002), 239–247. Moʿin al-Saltaneh's travelogue is also analyzed in Rahimieh, *Missing Persians*.

13. Sen. Abbas Massoudi [*sic*], *China: A Land of Marvels* (Tehran: Ettelaʿat, 1973), ii.

14. Farhad Masʿudi, *Piruzi-i Labkhand* (Tehran: *Ettelaʿat*, 1976).

15. ʿAbbas Masʿudi, "America Cannot Be Understood Based Solely on New York," *Ettelaʿat* 5886 (26 Mehr 1324): 2. This segment was the twenty-fifth installment of the series. Like most of the entries it is meandering and, at times, contradictory. Indeed, the premise of this installment directly contradicts the headlines of two others entitled, "Know America: New York," *Ettelaʿat* 5861 and 5862 (28 and 29 Shahrivar 1324): 4 and 2 respectively. Largely, it reflects an ambivalent attitude of "Americans" toward New York City. We'll return to this installment later.

16. ʿAbbas Masʿudi, "Ba Man Be-Amrika Biyaʾid," *Ettelaʿat* 5852 (18 Shahrivar 1324 [9 September 1945]): 2, Col C (from left).

17. ʿAbbas Masʿudi, *Ettelaʿat* 5924–5931, "We Enter Los Angeles: Our Night Wanderings in the Little City of Vislo; What Did We See in Our First Encounter with [Film] Artists?"; "Our First Day in a City of Work and Industry,"; "We Tour the 'Mickey Mouse' Park—How Did the Park that Keeps Millions People Busy and Amused Each Night Come to Be?" "Again We Tour Hollywood. Where Did it Come From? The Fame and Importance of Hollywood Came from the Will and Decisions of Three Americans Who Became Partners and Created the Greatness of This City and the Film Industry," "In One of the Film Studios," "Everything is Made Up: Everything You See Behind the Curtain is an Industrial Miracle and a Masterpiece of American Innovation," "How Do Actors Live? Our Last Visit to Hollywood. In the Soldier's Restaurant," "We Leave Hollywood and Now Talk of California's Fruit [Industry]," (12 Azar–20 Azar 1324), all on 3.

18. I encountered a similar disassociation of "menial work" from student life in Iran in 2005, when I asked Isfahan Technological University officials what kind work students did on campus for extra money.

19. *Ettelaʿat* 5852, col. D.

20. Ibid.

21. *Ettelaʿat* 5862, col. C.

22. Ibid.

23. *Ettelaʿat* 5852, col. E.

24. ʿAbbas Masʿudi, "What Thought Have You Given to After the War?" *Ettelaʿat* 5889 (24 Mehr 1324): 3. The film seemed to part of an OWI effort to lower postwar expectations for the kind of government interventionism that had characterized both the war effort and New Deal policies.

25. ʿAbbas Masʿudi, "Groceries in the City of New York," *Ettelaʿat* 5874 (12 Mehr 1324, 2), col. B.

26. ʿAbbas Masʿudi, *Ettelaʿat* 5871 "Come With Me to America: One of the Important American News Services" (9 Mehr, 1324), 2, col. C.

27. Ibid.

28. ʿAbbas Masʿudi, *Ettelaʿat* 5873 (11 Mehr 1324), 2, col. E.

29. ʿAbbas Masʿudi, *Ettelaʿat* 5889, 3, col. G.

30. ʿAbbas Masʿudi, "Family Life in New York," *Ettelaʿat*, 5873 (23 Mehr 1324), 3, col. E.

31. ʿAbbas Masʿudi, "Workers' Unions," *Ettelaʿat*, 5885 (25 Mehr 1324), 3, col. D.

32. Ibid., col. D-E.

33. *Ettelaʿat* 5886, col. C. Masʿudi seems to think of the American Midwest as the abode of "real Americans." Traveling through America in the 1950s, ʿIssa and ʿAbdallah Omidvar located resentment of immigrants, and overt racism, in the American South, in contrast to northern states (and generally rooted in lingering resentments of the Civil War). They clearly considered the South to exemplify a premodern version of America—and a shameful one. ʿIssa and ʿAbdallah Omidvar, *Safarnameh-e Baradaran-e Omidvar* (Tehran: Entesharat-i Jomhuri, 1380 [2001/2]), 253–280.

34. ʿAbbas Masʿudi, "A Walk in the Vertical City," *Ettelaʿat* 5865 (2 Mehr 1324), 2, cols. D and E.

35. ʿAbbas Masʿudi, "Ancient Iran in New York," *Ettelaʿat* 5875 (14 Mehr 1324): 2. He toured Arthur Upton Pope's "Ancient Iran Institute," noting Pope's fame in Iran and affirming Talinn Grigor's observations about the impact of the Iran Heritage Society and the Western scholars, like Pope, who mingled with Iranian intellectuals and politicians to reconstruct an Iranian press that could inform modernist constructions of nationalism.

36. "Iranian Envoy Handcuffed in Elkton, Md., After Row in Which Wife Canes Constable," *New York Times*, 28 November 1935, 1.

37. "MINISTER OF IRAN SAILS, No Grudge Against US, says Recalled Diplomat," *New York Times*, 19 January 1936, 28.

38. "Iran to Take Representatives Out of U.S. To Protest Treatment by American Press," *New York Times*, 31 March 1936, 1.

39. ʿAbbas Masʿudi, "An Hour at the Iranian Embassy," *Ettelaʿat* 5894 (8 Aban 1324), 2, col. F.

40. ʿAbbas Masʿudi, "One Sunday at Church," *Ettelaʿat* 5887 (19 Mehr 1324), 3, col. C.

41. ʿAbbas Masʿudi, "The True Rulers of America are Red Skins," "We Enter the Territory of the Red Skins," "Among the Red Skins," "The Red Skin's Skyscrapers," and "An Hour in the Red Skin's Skycrapers," *Ettelaʿat* 5887, 5917–5921 (28 Mehr, 5–9 Azar 1324), 2, 3.

42. ʿAbbas Masʿudi, "Blacks Launched Movements to Make Themselves Equal Partner with Whites," "This Place [Tuskeegee Institute] is the Center of Black Science and Arts," "The Ku Klux Klan: A Terrifying Society [Devoted to] Annihilating Blacks," *Ettelaʿat*, 5907–9 (21–23 Aban 1324), all on 3.

43. *Ettelaʿat* 5865, E and F.

44. Ibid.

45. For a recent discussion of the issue at Iranian.com, see Anahid Hojjati, "To Iranians in Diaspora: Stop Black Facing Hajji Firooz" (page removed). Some of the response posts link to defenses of the black-faced representations, some agree with Hojjati's rejection of it, and, at least one recommended a "green-faced" Hajji Firuz to show solidarity with Iran's Green Movement. Hojjati's 2010 post has been removed but there was an echo of the same debate posted in 2011. See http://iranian.com /main/2011/mar/haji-firooz-amoo-norooz.html (accessed on 3 July 2013).

46. Shireen Meraji, "The 2010 Census: Don't Put Me Into a Big White Box," on NPR, 29 March 2010. See http://www.npr.org/templates/story/story.php?storyId=12 5219716 (accessed on 30 March 2010). As a self-described "Puerto-Iranian," the author recounts her experience with the diversity of actual assimilation trajectories

for the Iranian-American community, notwithstanding the tendency towards the "white=Caucasian=normal" idea in public and private discourse.

47. In Mas'udi 's ethnography of New York, Iranians are not mentioned as Asian immigrants (though Arabs and Turks are). There is not even a sense that the Iranian in New York represents any sort of trend toward immigration to the United States—so they are not even part of that hyphenated-American experience yet. Chinese immigrants and Chinese-Americans are mentioned separately from all other groups.

48. One can, perhaps, see echoes of this thinking in former President Khatami's "dialogue of civilizations" appreciations of America in the late 1990s.

49. "Payeh-e Furhang-e Yak Mellat (The Cultural Foundations of a Nation)," in *Sokhan-rani-ha-e Rashed dar Radyu Iran*, Vol. 16 (Tehran: Ketābfurūshī-e Muhammadi, 1338 [1960/61]), 435–453. The lecture was broadcast on 15 May 1959 (24 Ordibehesht 1338). Rashed began his career as a religious commentator in Mas'udi's paper, *Ettela'at*, in 1940. In the 1950s, he was recruited to serve as a radio commentator and helped facilitate a cycle of lectures by Ayatollah Motahhari (1920-1979) on Radio Tehran from 1958 to 1960. Motahhari, of course, was a confidant of Ayatollah Khomeini, and one of the intellectual architects of the Islamic Republic. Unlike Metahhari, Rashed never had a complete falling out with the Pahlavi regime.

50. Sons of a successful Iranian textile industrialist, 'Issa and 'Abdallah Omidvar have made something of an industry of their world travels from 1954 to 1964. In 2003, they opened a museum in the section of the Sa'adabad Palace Complex in Tehran. See http://www.omidvar-brothers.com/Fa/default.aspx, and, "Omidvar Brothers to Open Museum in Tehran," *Mehrnews.com*, September 26, 2003 (http://www.mehrnews .com/en/NewsDetail.aspx?NewsID=26720; accessed on July 27th, 2011). 'Abdullah Omidvar (b. 1932) met his wife in Chile in 1964, settled there, made his career in film and advertising, and converted to Buddhism. See "Abdullah Omidvar: Viajero agradecido," *Magazine In Vitro* No. 81 (http://www.revistainvitro.cl/contenido.php?art=126 accessed on 27 July 2011).

51. In this essential aspect of having expressions of nationalism mediated through a public persona, Mas'udi is quite comparable to Rabindranath Tagore (d. 1941). See Afshin Marashi's contribution to the present volume. Of course, Mas'udi was cultivating a national persona against a global backdrop, while Tagore had his international persona appropriated by the Pahlavi regime for its constructions of nationalism directed primarily at a national audience. On a different level, contemporary individual artists (and their would-be patrons in Iran and around the world) who are trying to express themselves more universally have to bypass ideological formulations of "acceptable art" informed by the Islamic Republican religious nationalism. See Talinn Grigor's contribution to the present volume.

52. These efforts—using the institutional power of the state and the latest theories and technologies of mass communication—have been joined repeatedly in Iranian history, and with increasing sophistication. See the contributions of Mohammad Tavakoli-Targhi, Kamyar Abdi, and Afshin Matin-Asgari in the present volume.

53. The contemporary engagement of the Iranian diaspora with the Green Movement since the 2009 presidential elections is illustrative of the robustness of that dynamic still. See Sussan Siavoshi and Roxanne Varzi's contributions to the present volume.

PART 3

RELIGION, NATIONALISM, AND CONTESTED VISIONS OF MODERNITY

CHAPTER 9

Islamic-Iranian Nationalism and Its Implications for the Study of Political Islam and Religious Nationalism

KAMRAN SCOT AGHAIE

America was founded as a Christian nation. Our institutions presuppose the existence of a Supreme Being, a Being after the Bible. And we as Americans believe in the God of the Bible. And the fact that somebody comes with what amounts to an alien religion to these shores doesn't mean that we're going to give up all of our cherished religious beliefs to accommodate a few people who happen to believe in something else. You just can't do that.
PAT ROBERTSON, 700 CLUB, 10/05/2000

While nationalism is one of the most thoroughly studied phenomena of modern history, the scholarship on nationalism still struggles with how to deal with the relationship between nationalism on the one hand and religion and secularism on the other. More specifically, it has proven challenging to study cases in which religion and nationalism appear to be either inseparable or one and the same. This is not because there are no examples of religious nationalism in the world. In fact, there are many such examples, both in the developing world and in industrialized western nations, including the above quoted example of Pat Robertson, which should be read within the context of similar statements by numerous American religious leaders, social activists, politicians, pundits, "culture warriors," and even presidential candidates such as John McCain. Rather, it has to do with a set of assumptions by scholars about the innate nature of nationalism, and its relationship—or lack thereof—to religion. Firstly, the nation itself is not always treated as the key constitutive element of nationalism. Secondly, ethnic nationalism is usually accepted uncritically, and most methods for studying nationalism treat it primarily as an ethnic identity. Thirdly, in cases of "civic nationalism," as in France or the United States, nationalism is typically assumed to be necessarily both secular and liberal. Finally, religious beliefs and discourses that are explicitly ideological, social, political, or moral, are usually assumed to be rejectionist (i.e., antinationalist, or at least nonnationalist).

While scholars allow for such religious nationalisms as Zionism or Zoroastrian, Yezidi, Hindu, Muslim, or Armenian nationalisms, they usually only do so because these can also be treated as ethnic identity markers. This unfortunately leaves no room for nationalist movements that use religion as one of their core ideological and symbolic components. This proves problematic when looking at religious movements that certainly are national movements, and in some cases are also nationalist movements. For example, Hizbullah in Lebanon, Hamas in the Palestinian Territories, the Da'wa and Sadr movements of Iraq, the Justice and Development Party or the Gulen movement in Turkey, and the recent incarnations of the Muslim Brotherhood in Egypt, just to name a few, have at different stages in their development, and to varying degrees, been national or nationalistic movements.

This paper seeks to contribute to a resolution of this methodological problem by making a case for "religious nationalism," thereby providing a way to bring our methods and terminology more into line with historical realities. While nationalism in Iran is the focus of this study, it will be contextualized more broadly to explore its implication for our understanding of other religious nationalisms in the Muslim Middle East, and, to a lesser extent, in other regions as well. This particular formulation of religious nationalism will not treat Islam/Muslim as a simple marker of ethnicity or culture that can be synonymous with ethnic nationalism. Nor will Islam be treated as either being a rejection of nationalism or as existing outside of it. Finally, Islam will not be treated as a non-nationalistic set of symbols or ideals that compete with, or are coopted by or subsumed within, nationalism (either consciously or unconsciously). Instead, a case will be made for a variant of nationalism that constructs the nation, its culture, and its citizenry through Islamist symbols and concepts as the core constitutive elements. Thus, in many ways this model of nationalism has more in common with the civic model of nationalism than it does with cases of ethnic nationalism. This approach to studying these cases of religious nationalism will allow us to look at questions from a different perspective and thereby to provide interesting answers to a variety of questions. The most basic concept in this approach is that the key constitutive element of nationalism is actually the nation-state (existing or proposed), with its accompanying construction of nationality, citizenry, and culture, rather than ethnicity, shared language or culture, or a primordialist nature; therefore, the first step in our analysis is to put the nation back at the center of nationalism, where it belongs. Thus, within these diverse discourses, the nation is defined and redefined in a contest between diverse individuals and groups, with overlapping and ever-evolving religious beliefs, values, and symbols. Therefore, preexisting ethnic, cultural, communal, regional, or religious identities are not always centrally important to nationalism (i.e., pre-modern Arab, Kurdish, Tajik, Turk, or Zoroastrian identities, etc.). Instead, nationalism should be understood to include any identity, whether pre-existing, invented, or re-invented, that is articulated as being the basis of a particular nation-state, its culture, and its citizenry. This allows for more identity options, while at the same time restricting the definition to a smaller number of modern examples of identity, which necessarily include the promotion of a nation-state based upon that identity.

It is well established that different nationalist individuals and groups rely on a select set of symbols and ideals to convey their particular vision of what the "nation" and its citizenry represent. The result is an infinite series of definitions of the nation that either coexist or compete for acceptance in the public sphere. For example, the state may promote a more authoritarian conception of the nation with the monarch at the center, as the Pahlavi Shahs of Iran did, while leftists may conceive of the nation as part of a universal struggle of the proletariat against the bourgeoisie, or of the third world against the imperialist powers. Liberal, western-educated elites, and most modern national governments in the Middle East, have also most often chosen to adopt a modular nationalist model in order to modernize through emulation of the West. Similarly, members of a dominant religious group may choose to focus primarily upon religion, thus either negating the role of ethnicity entirely or, more often, making ethnicity a minor component of the national culture, and this need not be a simple survival of prenationalist cultural or ethnic sympathies. For example, some Islamist nationalists in Muslim countries like Egypt, Turkey, Iraq, or Iran consider Islam to be the primary and most fundamental component of nationalism. Understandably, religious minorities such as Copts in Egypt or Armenians, Baha'is, and Jews in Iran tend to have negative, or at best ambivalent, attitudes toward the definition of the nation based on some sort of Islamist ideals. However, it should also be pointed out that in some cases, such as the case of Arab nationalism, non-Muslims have been willing to accommodate Islam as a noncentral component of nationalism, provided it is included only as a cultural component of Muslim civilization, and does not represent an Islamist political vision.

Four Approaches to Studying Religion and Nationalism

There are four primary ways to approach the relationship between religion and nationalism: 1) religion and nationalism as competitors; 2) religion associated with nationalism; 3) religion as ethnicity; and 4) religious nationalism.

The first is the most standard treatment in historical writings from different parts of the world, and does not need to be discussed in detail here. The second approach, which is called here "religion associated with nationalism," is also rather common, and refers to cases of nationalism in which one can find implicit or explicit religious referents that are not central to the nationalist discourse. For example, a cross or crescent might appear on the flag, religious referents might be used in discussing social issues, or a reference to God might appear in the national anthem or on coins. This sort of thing is seen in most types of secular nationalist discourse, and does not fundamentally undermine the secular nature of these nationalist discourses. In this approach, religion is often considered by secular nationalists to be part of their national character by virtue of being part of the national culture. For example, Iranian nationalists sometimes treat Zoroastrianism in this way, and secular Arab nationalists have usually treated Islam in this way (i.e., as Arab culture), Kurds sometimes treat the Yezidi faith in this way, and some Egyptian nationalists have treated Coptic Christianity in this way. Another common form is one in which secular nationalists deliberately (or even cynically) use religious symbolism as a political tactic to appeal to non-nationalistic religious segments of the society. This, too, does not fundamentally undermine the secular nature of the nationalist discourses in question.

The third approach, which will be termed here "religion as ethnicity," treats religious affiliation as the rough equivalent of ethnic identity. This is a very widespread phenomenon, and most scholars who deal with religious nationalism tend to use this approach. Some of the best examples focus on regions that are characterized by religious or sectarian diversity, accompanied by communal conflict and violence, such as South Asia, the Balkans, Lebanon, or Iraq. This is a reasonable approach in some cases, because most religions have historically been roughly synonymous with ethnicity, in that they have constituted identities characterized by a combination of familial decent and shared culture, and in some cases with a shared common language. Classic cases of this sort of nationalism would be Hindu, Sikh, or Muslim nationalisms in South Asia, Armenian or Assyrian nationalisms in the Middle East, secular Jewish nationalism, and Serbian nationalism in the Balkans.

The fourth approach to studying the relationship between religion and nationalism, and the one explored in this paper, is what will be called here "religious nationalism." This is a nationalist discourse that is centered primarily on the nation, with religion being the core sets of ideals and symbols within that discourse. This approach differs from the above examples in three fundamental ways. First, religion is not external to nationalism. Second, religiosity is not an ethnic signifier, or a cultural by-product of ethnicity. Third, religion is central rather than marginal to the case of nationalism under study. Thus, religious nationalism is a symbolic discourse imbued with religious piety, social values, identity, culture, and symbolic referents. Classic examples of this would be many of the Islamist movements of the Middle East, along with religious Jewish nationalism, some forms of Hindu nationalism in South Asia, evangelical Christian nationalism in the United States, and some Islamist movements in Turkey and the Arab world.

Most scholarship of this type focuses on regions in which there is religious and sectarian violence, such as South Asia or the former Yugoslavia, or in which communal religious identities persist, despite the success of nationalism or globalization of culture. Mark Juergensmeyer has been one of the most active scholars in analyzing religious nationalism on a global scale, showing how secular nationalism has been rejected by some in favor of religious nationalism that is both anti-imperialist and focuses on identities that are grounded in a transnational religious civilization. He articulates this as a potential new "cold war" between secular nationalists and religious nationalists.[1] Several scholars have worked on religious nationalism in South Asia, mostly focusing on Hindu, Muslim, and Sikh nationalisms. For example, Peter van der Veer argues against the ideal that religious identities are simply attachments to the past or primordial identities. Rather, they are the product of ever-changing identities. He also explores the important roles that religious organizations and rituals play in nationalism.[2] Ornit Shani interestingly argues that the newly emerging Hindu nationalism is not primarily the result of Hindu-Muslim tensions. Rather, it is the result of intra-Hindu tensions, especially those associated with changes in the caste system.[3] And finally, Catarina Kinnvall explores how Hindu and Sikh nationalisms have emerged in response to globalization.[4]

While a great deal of interesting work has been done on religious nationalism in South Asia and the developing world, scholarship on this phenomenon in Europe and the United States is still underdeveloped, with a few notable exceptions. Philip Barker has written a book about the role of religious nationalism in Europe (focusing on Ireland, Poland, and Greece) to show that religion still plays a pivotal role in some European nationalisms.[5] Genevieve Zubrzycki has written a book analyzing the role of Catholicism in Polish nationalism in post-Communist Poland.[6] Jouni Tilli has written about Finnish religious nationalism.[7] And finally, Betty Clermont, in her book, *The Neo-Catholics: Implementing Christian Nationalism in America*, has undertaken one of the first rare attempts to explore religious nationalism in the United States.[8]

Religious nationalism in the Middle East has been similarly neglected, although there are a few exceptions. Israel, of course, is such an obvious example of religious nationalism that the rich literature on the subject of Jewish nationalism need not be repeated here.[9] However, it is less obvious that Turkey would be the focus of studies on religious nationalism. In the past two decades, scholars of Turkey have begun exploring a shift in the relationship of Islam to Turkish nationalism, beginning in the early 1980s, which they term the "Turkish-Islamic Synthesis." Beginning in the early 1980s, some Turkish intellectuals began to merge nationalism and Islam in creative ways, making the "Turkish-Islamic Synthesis" one of the central tenets of their ideologies and movements.[10]

Gavin Brockett pushes this idea back even farther in history to the years from 1945 to 1954, saying, "The assertion by Turks that Muslim identities are important does not have to constitute religious reaction. Rather, in the decades after World War II, it represented an effort to negotiate a popular national identity that accommodated rather than excluded religious identities."[11] He goes on to talk about Islamic-Turkish identity, focusing on the term *Musulmanlik* (Muslim identity) rather than the ubiquitous term *laiklik* (secularism):

> Indeed, public and political debate in these years [1945–1954] frequently turned to the importance of Islam for the Turkish nation. . . . Infused by a variety of new religious print media that granted importance to Islam, this national print culture offered Turks a breathing space within which they might negotiate identification with Turkey as a Muslim nation. . . . While they did not necessarily promote an Islamist agenda as we understand it today, they did speak to the complexity of Turkish society and the continued importance of religion in daily life. In fact, nation and religion were becoming intertwined: the former had not simply replaced the latter.[12]

The only other scholar to explicitly propose an approach for the Middle East that is similar to the one taken in this article is James Gelvin. In an article in which he proposes ways to classify different types of Islamist movements, he classifies al-Qaeda as "Islamo-anarchist" and then explains that "al-Qaeda stands in opposition to two types of organizations within the Islamic community. One might be called reformist, the other Islamo-nationalist."[13] He then goes on to explain:

> At first, it might seem counterintuitive that groups identifying themselves with Islam should work within the nation-state system. After all, Islam is a universal religion, and the Islamic community stretches around the globe. But when thinking of Islam and nationalism, it is necessary to remember

two things. First, other transnational religions have become the wellspring of territorial nationalisms. One need only think of Catholic Irish nationalists, Hindu nationalists or Zionists. Second, one must remember that no living religion exists outside the history, practices and experiences of its followers. Muslims, like the rest of us, live in a world in which much of their social and political existence has been defined by the modern state and the modern state system. It only stands to reason, therefore, that their Islam would conform to such a world as well.[14]

While religious nationalism in Iran has remained relatively understudied, there are some exceptions. Mohammad Tavakoli-Targhi talks about how nationalists in the early twentieth century debated the role Islam should play in their formulations of secular Iranian nationalism.[15] Several scholars, including Fred Halliday, David Menashri, Ludwig Paul, Haggai Ram, Golnar Mehran, and myself, just to name a few, have shown how aspects of nationalism survived in Iran after the Islamic Revolution took control of the state, and occasionally emerged in broader revolutionary ideologies.[16] Minoo Moallem uses the term "religious nationalism" and provides a theoretical basis for it. She argues in a chapter titled "Cultural Nationalism and Islamic Fundamentalism" that Islamic national identity was constructed by Iranians as part of the Islamic Revolution. This was done by defining the West as an ethnic category and juxtaposing a Muslim cultural identity in opposition to that.[17]

The research project presented in this chapter began with an article published in 2000 under the title "Islam and Nationalist Historiography: Competing Historical Narratives of the Nation in Iran."[18] The material there will not be repeated here, except to summarize the basic argument, which was that most "Islamist" intellectuals in Iran who were active during the 1950s through the 1970s participated in a nationalist discourse in which the acceptance or rejection of the nation, or even of nationalism, was not fundamentally at issue. While some ideologues explicitly claimed to reject nationalism, their actual writings and speeches relied heavily upon nationalist concepts. Thus they were not rejecting the nation, but rather the particular formulations of the nation proposed by royalists, liberals, ethnic chauvinists, leftists, etc. Therefore, religious and secular leaders in Iran have not existed at two opposite extremes along a spectrum with secularists propagating nationalist ideals and religious leaders opposing these ideals. Iranian nationalism during this period was characterized by a discourse in which Iranians of very diverse ideological perspectives participated. While their arguments converged on various points and diverged on others, many of the same assumptions were accepted by most ideologues regarding the primordialist nature of Iran as a twenty-five-hundred-year-old nation. What was actually being disputed was the role of Iran in the postcolonial era, its relationship to the West, the nature of its government and leadership, and finally, the role of religion versus secularism in Iran's national identity. All of the ideologues dealt with in that study accepted Iran's organic existence in history, as well as certain primordial characteristics. However, they disagreed on several other points related to Iran's modernization agenda. The present paper takes these arguments further and contextualizes the case of Iran more broadly by comparing it with other examples of Islamism and nationalism in the Muslim Middle East, up to the present.

Let us begin our discussion of more recent trends in discourse on Islamic Iranian nationalism with a speech given by the supreme leader, Ali Khamenei, in Paveh on October 18, 2011.

What is important is preserving the group identity of a nation (mellat) or human grouping, under whatever name. The Iranian-Islamic identity of our people and our nation, with the blessing of the Islamic Revolution, with the blessing of the presence of the people on the scene and the entrance and participation of the people in the political affairs of the state, is a well-established fact. Today, the world recognizes the nation of Iran as Islamic while being enlightened, knowledgeable, and advanced in different fields; this is not a small thing. Especially today, when Islamic movements have become active in the Islamic World, the nation of Iran can play a role.

Of course, we have no claim on these nations; we do not say "we are your leaders, take your lead from us"; not at all, we do not make any such claims; each nation, with its own potential, with its own characteristics, and its own capabilities, will find its own way and follow it. However, there is no doubt that the people in these countries who have woken up and found freedom, like Egypt and Tunisia, and some other places, and even countries in which arrogant and occupying regimes are in power, but the people have awakened, in all of these countries, they look and watch the nation of Iran, because for thirty years now, this nation has, under difficult circumstances, it has achieved capability and sufficiency. They look to us. We can be a standard and a reliable symbol for all people in these countries who look to us, the nation of Iran.

When we adhere to Islam and Islamic ideals, along with reason, scientific progress, or participation in different fields of knowledge, and social and political matters, this becomes a model (olgu). Nations then look, and benefit from the experiences of this nation; this is both to the benefit of the nation of Iran, and the nations of this region, and God willing, it is beneficial toward establishing a great Islamic ummah, a united Islamic ummah, in the future.[19]

This speech is an excellent, and at the same time typical, example of how the leaders of Iran have claimed to reject nationalism, while at the same time being nationalistic themselves, going all the way back to Imam Khomeini himself. In this speech, Khamenei reified and praised Iranianness, and argued for the preservation of Iranian identity, which he defined as being an Islamic, Iranian, modern, and revolutionary identity. Thus, to be an ideal Iranian is to adhere to Islamic principles and conduct, while at the same time participating in the revolutionary project as a citizen of the Iranian nation. This project, in turn, involves striving to be a modern nation, committed to science and the advancement of knowledge, while at the same time opposing the tyrannies of regional tyrants and the imperialist West.

He also dealt with the often-misunderstood idea of "exporting the revolution." He did not propose expanding the Iranian nation to absorb other Muslim states, nor did he propose replacing the Iranian nation, or any other Muslim nations, with an Islamic 'ummah, as nonnationalist Islamists, like Al-Qa'idah, typically do. Rather, he promoted the Iranian national agenda while relegating the ideal of a greater Islamic 'ummah to the distant and ideal (or even hypothetical) future. This is analogous to how many leftist-nationalists talk about the supposedly nonnationalistic Marxist ideal of eventually achieving a classless and stateless society in some distant and hypothetical future, which is so unrealistic as to be nothing more than empty rhetoric and symbolism. Khamenei proposed that Iran is not even a leader of other Muslim nations. Rather, it is a model of how one nation (Iran) successfully realized its own national aspirations, and that this success is something to which others can similarly aspire, based on their unique potentials, goals, desires, and circumstances.

While nationalism has been widely condemned in Iran over the past few decades by most intellectuals, the use of various forms of the expression "Islamic-Iranian identity" has remained at the center of political discourse and has continued to be used in different ways by different people. These uses of the term have roots in the ideas and symbols that were debated before the Islamic Revolution, by such ideologues as Shari'ati, Al-e Ahmad, and Motahhari, who argued that Islam was the most important component of Iranianness, or that Iranians played critically important roles in the development of Islam.[20] For example, the reformist ex-president of Iran, Mohammad Khatami, in an interview printed in ISNA said "The Iranian nation (mellat) is one of these nations that twice was the creator of a great world civilization; one was prior to Islam, and [again] after that, when Islam arrived and the glorious light of Islam shined on the soul of this nation. Indeed, Iranians accepted the wisdom and truth of Islam, and had a distinguished role in the creation and articulation of the rich Islamic civilization."[21] Another former prime minister, Mir Husayn Mousavi, similarly said, in a speech given in Yazd, "An Iran which cannot preserve its Islamic and Iranian identity can never defend its Muslim brothers in Palestine or Lebanon . . . we need a strong Iranian and Islamic identity in order to [successfully deal with these issues]."[22] He also said, "Our nation (mellat) is always especially sensitive about its Islamic and Iranian identity, and they have considered this issue to be an important issue. . . . Islamic, Iranian identity is critically important to us."[23]

At the opposite end of the political spectrum, the recently retired president of Iran, Mahmoud Ahmadinejad, gave a speech at the twenty-seventh national meeting of the presidents of provincial departments of education in Iran, in which he said, "Education must be able to create an identity based on Godly values and ideals in students, by relying on Islamic and Iranian principles."[24] In a different context, Ahmad Khatami, the conservative cleric who served as the *emam jom'eh* of Tehran, said in a Friday sermon that "Iran discovered its self/identity with Islam, and reciprocally Islam did a great service to Iran."[25] Some of the points raised in the above references are reminiscent of the writings of Shariati and Motahhari.

Abd al-Karim Soroush, similarly, has explored the implications of the idea of "returning to self," which was articulated by Ali Shari'ati and others of his generation. An excellent example of this treatment is a talk titled *Seh farhang* (three cultures), which he gave at Tarbiyat Modarres University in Tehran, in May 1990, and which was later revised and published as a chapter in his book *Razdani va rowshan fekri va dindari*.[26] He starts the talk by saying, "The situation is that we Muslim Iranians, who live in this country, are the bearers and heirs of three cultures, and as long as we do not define ourselves by these three cultures and do not know in what place and in which cultural geography we live, we will be unable to carry out constructive cultural and societal action. . . . The three cultures of which we are the bearers and inheritors include national, religious, and western cultures."[27]

His conception of "national" culture was a variant of typical primordialist and essentialist conceptions of Iran as a community with shared experience, history, culture, language, etc. His conception of Western culture reflected his broader views regarding Iran's and Europe's experiences of modernity. The triple origins of Iranian national culture, he argued, made it impossible and inappropriate to "return to ourselves," as Shariati, Al-e Ahmad, and others had previously proposed. Rather, these three cultures must be fully explored, combined, and adapted to meet the needs of the Iranian nation. He further argued that, contrary to what the vast majority of intellectuals have proposed, none of these three cultures should dominate the other two; when intellectuals have tried to privilege one over the other two, this has led to conflict, confusion, and negative outcomes. He said, "Anyone who says that religious culture should dominate [our] other cultures must clarify what he/she means by religious culture, and what he/she means by dominate. Which parts does he/she accept and which parts does he/she reject?"[28] He also said "We were born in Asia; in the country of Iran, and among the followers of Islam. Thus we are simultaneously Asian, Iranian, and Muslim. Each of these is an aspect of our culture."[29] His speech, therefore, included a clear rejection of the views of most Islamist nationalists in Iran, and of course of the regime itself, who privilege Islam over national identity, even though this privileging is usually only an empty symbolic gesture.

He also discussed more specifically the role of Islam within Iranian national culture, "If we move beyond these two cultures [i.e., national and Western], we reach Islamic culture, which is quantitatively and qualitatively the dominant culture of Iran."[30] As part of his argument against "returning to ourselves," he argued against xenophobic views of culture, which privilege the origin of aspects of culture over their usefulness and benefit to the nation. In doing so, he controversially equated the foreignness of Islamic culture to that of Western culture; thus, if one is accepted, then the other can be as well:

The religion of Islam . . . is part of us, and is part of our national culture, and it has strong and solid ties to our cultural identity. Yes; Islam did not originate in Iran. However, it has been accepted by Iranians; and this acceptance was enthusiastic and voluntary, not acceptance by force or coercion. And for this reason, it quickly became part of our constitution, [and has remained] part of our culture and identity until today.[31]

If we want to reason that everything that has come from outside is not suitable for us, then we would have thrown away Islamic culture, and on this same basis, we must also discard all the science and technology of Westerners, and be in conflict with them as enemies. Those who spread the historicist, deterministic, and decadent term "west-struckedness" among us were themselves basically feeding on the same idea that propagated nationalism, in its anti-religious sense, in our country. . . . And I say that we, more than anything, are struck by the idea that in culture, we bring in the idea of ownership, and instead of talking about building ourselves up, we talk of returning to ourselves, and we have brought up ours and theirs, and we have put these in the place of truth and falsehood, right and wrong, and we have created confusion and problems.[32]

Let us shift our focus now to a recent episode that serves to illustrate the dynamics, key issues, and broad parameters of the current Islamist discourses on Islamic-Iranian nationalism and identity. In a speech given on 5 August 2010, at the closing ceremony of a gathering of expatriate Iranians, Esfandiyar Masha'i, President Ahmadinejad's Chief of Staff, said:

> We must create opportunities for new generations of Iranians to understand with a rational knowledge the honor of this philosophy of Iran, so that they will understand this "School of Thought of Iran" (maktab-e Iran). . . . Some may criticize me, saying, why don't you say the Islamic School of Thought? The Islamic School of Thought has many different interpretations; I made reference to this in a previous talk. The School of Thought of Iran consists of reaching a pure understanding of the truth of faith, the truth of the Divine Unity of God, and the truth of Islam. From now on, we must introduce the world to the School of Thought of Iran. . . . Iran is a place in which faith has appeared; the history of Iran is filled with faith; the land of Iran has always been where faith has appeared. Why? Because it has always been the site in which science and knowledge were manifest.[33]

In this speech, Masha'i articulated a version of Islamic Iranian nationalism that combined spiritual and humanistic ideals in a new philosophy he called "the School of Thought of Iran" (maktab-e Iran). He said, "Yesterday, I said that Iran is a place in which heavenly and worldly ideals converge; God and humanity both have been exalted in Iran."[34] This was not in itself terribly problematic, and in fact, he mostly promoted relatively typical aspects of Iranian religious nationalism. However, there was one atypical and highly controversial idea in his speech. He proposed a shift in the relative status of Islam versus Iran within that nationalism. It is typical for Islamic-Iranian nationalists to praise Iran's past glories, or its contributions to civilization, or a religious equivalent of "Iranian exceptionalism." However, the typical practice is to give Islam, at least symbolically, a superior status to all other aspects of the nationalism being articulated. Masha'i, thus, violated one of the unwritten rules of this discourse, which predictably lead to a harsh backlash from various ideologues, clerics, and government officials. Some defended his views. Notably, the then-president, Mahmoud Ahmadinejad, said in an interview with Mehr News Agency, "I have also said 'Iran is a school of thought,' it has a culture that is sublime and transcends geography and race."[35] He further said

"Mr. Masha'i is my chief of staff, and I have complete confidence in him, and I know him to be a believer in the ideals of the Islamic Revolution of Iran."[36] In fact, Ahmadinejad has also referenced the idea of a "school of thought of Iran." For example, in a speech he said:

Nobody should think that what I say is based on nationalism [melligarayi va nasiyonalism], because today, Iran is not a single geography, a nation, people, or a tribe; rather it is a school of thought and a path. . . . Iran means justice, worship of God, freedom, and the road to freedom. Therefore, if we were to remove Iran from history and geography, nothing would remain of human civilization. And I dare say that the only civilization that rests on Godly and humanistic principles is in Iran."[37]

As previously stated, criticisms of Masha'i's speech were quick to emerge, and were rather harsh. Most denounced Masha'i as a secular nationalist, and said that his speech denigrated Islam by relegating it to a status below that of Iranianness, and betrayed the ideals of the Islamic Revolution, and of Khomeini. Ayatollah Ka'bi, a conservative cleric in Qom, said "People who seek an Iranian Islam, their ideas are deviant. We seek an Iran that is devoted to Islam, not an Islam that is at the service of Iran and is devoted to Iran."[38] He also said "These words [i.e., Masha'i's speech], enable the objectives of the enemies of Iran."[39] Ahmad Tavakkoli, a conservative in the parliament, said, "Is there anyone who is knowledgeable about Iran's history and geography who does not know that what ties the diverse peoples of Iran together is Islam?"[40] Mesbah Yazdi even responded in a talk in Qom, "It is sad that . . . there is a person who, in the name of following [moral] principles and Islam, says that the time for talking about Islam has passed, and instead of propagating Islam, we must praise general humanistic qualities, which are even prevalent among idol-worshipers."[41] And Mortaza Motahhari's son Ali Motahhari characterized the idea of maktab-e Iran as "a wrong and deviant interpretation of the writings of Dr. Motahhari in *Khadamat-e motaqabel-e Eslam va Iran*."[42] The conservative Friday Prayer leader of Tehran, Ahmad Khatami, said in a Friday sermon: "This is that same old God-rejecting nationalism (melligarayi-e sherk alud); the Imam said that nationalism is against Islam, God's law, and the Qur'an."[43] However, he also went on to say "Clearly liking one's nation (eshq-e vatan) is different from nationalism. Nationalism is considering Islam to be incompatible with Iran, and this contradicts the spirit of the Islamic Revolution. . . . We are defenders of Islamic Iran."[44] While the criticisms were at least partly motivated by internal power struggles and factionalism, it is also clear that the most common objections were not that Masha'i promoted what scholars would typically call nationalism, but that he did not place Islam, at least symbolically, in a dominant position above all other aspects of nationalism. Stated differently, rather than articulating a nationalism in which Islam shaped Iranianness, they felt that his vision allowed Iran to shape, or dominate, Islam.

From the examples above, it is clear that heated debates have continued to rage in the Islamic Republic about what the modern nation of Iran is, and what it means to be Iranian. In this discourse, nationalism (*melligarayi*) is roundly condemned. However, upon closer analysis it is clear that what they have really condemned is secular nationalism, in particular anything that is associated with, or in any way resembles, the nationalism of the Pahlavi era, or modular, western-style nationalisms. In reality, what we as academicians would call "nationalism" has rarely been rejected. For example, the primordialist Iranian nation has generally been accepted as real, and its past glories have commonly been praised, including Iran's pre-Islamic heritage. Iranian ethnicity, based on shared language, and often racial traits, have been accepted. Above all, the discourse has centered on differing and competing notions of what constitutes "Islamic-Iran," which is not to be confused with the unpopular term "Iranian-Islam." This includes infusing Iranianness with Islamic ethical values, and defining Iranian cultural norms in according with Islamic social values. In these debates, Islam is almost always given a higher status than other aspects of Iranian national identity, and the "red line" that has rarely been crossed is to claim that Iranian ethnicity, culture, or race are more dominant factors than religion within Iran's nationalism. Ideologues have worked almost exclusively within the framework of the nation-state, and, while they have conceived of Iran as part of a group of Muslim nations, rarely has the idea of the nation truly been challenged in favor of an Islamic *'ummah*. Going as far back as the 1950s and 1960s, this Islamic Iran has generally been described as being built around sacred, divine, and Islamic ideals, with worldly justice as a main tenet, and anti-imperialism or antiglobalism as one of its main goals. This is best thought of as a form of Modern "Islamic Iranian exceptionalism."

Broader Implications and the Usefulness of This Approach

While it is always possible to find new ways of looking at old questions, or, more accurately, variations on approaches to studying any given topic, this is not a useful endeavor, unless the new approach offers different or more useful answers to important questions. Therefore, we must now turn our attention to the question of whether or not this approach to studying religious nationalism is a useful way of looking at Iran and other Muslim societies in the Middle East.

If we assume that all Islamists are nonnationalistic or even counternationalistic, then it necessarily follows that Muslims are relatively unique among human communities in that, over the course of the past century, they have increasingly rejected nationalism. While it is true that in many nations traditionalist alternatives to nationalism have at times played a role in politics, just as postmodern sentiments have sometimes weakened or challenged the more crude forms of nationalism, nationalism nevertheless remains a very strong force in most nations today, and in most nations it remains the single most dominant force. More to the point, it would be empirically wrong to argue that all Islamists are examples of either traditionalist or postmodernist rejections of modernity. Treating many Islamist movements, discourses, and ideologies like that of the Islamic Revolution and the Islamic Republic as nationalisms eliminates this dilemma, by allowing that some Islamist movements are nationalistic, while others reject nationalism or even modernity itself.[45]

This advantage is particularly evident when looking at the so-called "Islamic resurgence" that is widely believed to have taken place in the 1970s and afterwards. While there are many diverse explanations for this long-term trend, most of them revolve around various conceptions of nativism, in relation to westernization and globalization, or rejectionism in relation to nationalism. In particular, many focus on the idea that modernist, westernizing, national regimes failed to deliver on their promises or to satisfy the continually rising expectations of their citizenry. They often point to the Arab defeat in the 1967 war (as do many Islamist leaders themselves), or the overthrow of the U.S.-backed Shah of Iran in 1978 and 1979, as seminal events in this trend. There certainly is truth to these claims, in some cases. However, there is another way of looking at it, as well. The so-called emergence or resurgence of Islamism during this period can also be viewed as a convergence of two long-term trends; first is a challenge posed to secular, westernizing nationalism promoted by the state and the elites by a newer form of religious nationalism that had a more populist base of support, and second is a trend away from anti-nationalist Islamisms of the nineteenth and early twentieth centuries, which often took the form of pan-Islamism, toward a series of nationalistic religious movements across the region. Interestingly, these long-term trends also ran parallel to the same trend in secular nationalism, in particular in Arab nationalism, or the various transnational ethnic nationalisms focused on ethnicities (i.e., Turkic, Persian, Kurdish, Armenian, etc.). As empires, colonies, and mandates evolved into fledgling nations, alternative identities and allegiances were taken more seriously. Over the course of the past century, the peoples of the Middle East lived their lives within the structures of nations, with varying degrees of economic, educational, social, cultural, and political integration. Therefore, it is not surprising that, over time, it became easier for subnational identities and loyalties (i.e., regional, communal, or tribal loyalties), as well as transnational pan-"isms" to become progressively less relevant or viable in the face of nationalistic sentiments. This is, of course, not a universal trend, but it was the most common trend in many of the nations of the region. Therefore, it is more useful to think of the shift toward religious discourses and movements in the past few decades as having multiple causes. While in some cases it was, at least in part, due to the failure of nationalism, it was more often due to the success of national integration over the course of the twentieth century.

Viewed this way, the story of this shift begins with a small group of elite intellectuals and leaders who promoted modular forms of nationalism in newly formed nation-states. These nationalisms were useful to the states, so they also promoted them. However, in the earliest stages, a relatively small percentage of the population in each of these new nations was integrated actively into this project; therefore, other loyalties and identities remained more important for the majority of the population. Over time, as the broader population became increasingly mobilized, due to increased urbanization, education, indoctrination, and integration into the national economy and polity, new voices and perspectives became increasingly influential, in particular the urban poor, new middle classes, and, in some cases, rural communities. Since most Egyptians, Iranians, Iraqis, and Turks, for example, were religious and socially conservative, it is entirely logical that they expected that the nation they envisioned would also be religious and modeled on conservative principles, with regional social and cultural values playing the most prominent role. Therefore, while they did not feel compelled to challenge the notion of Turkey, Egypt, Iraq, Iran, etc., they felt that the nation needed to be reshaped and redefined to more closely match their aspirations. Thus, in such cases, the shift toward religious conservatism was mostly the result of the success of nationalism and nation building, accompanied by a relative failure to sufficiently promote a broad base of support for that nationalism envisioned by the state and by traditional modernizing elites.

Another advantage of stressing the fact that ethnicity and language are not synonymous with nationalism, nor even necessary components of nationalism, is that it makes it easier to deal with ethnicities and religious identities that predate nationalisms, but which were later subsumed within nationalistic discourses, such as Iran, Iranshahr, Farsi, Muslim, Jewish/Judaism, Armenian, Kurd, Tajik, Arab, Azeri, etc. If discourses on the nation are treated as the key element in identifying the origins of nationalism, it is possible to avoid implying that these premodern identities constitute some form of premodern nationalism or protonationalism. In the case of Iran, there is no denying that prenational ethnic identities were important (such concepts/terms as Irani, Tajik, Farsi/Parsi, and Arya'i); that there were various conceptions of Iran, Iranshahr, or Iranzamin; and that for centuries there has been a Persianate culture or "civilization." However, these were not accompanied by conceptions of a nation, with stable borders, a modern national state, a national culture, and a clear articulation or definition of a national citizenry.

One of the most useful results of using this approach is that it allows for more accurate and nuanced treatment of the goals of Islamist movements that are primarily national movements. For example, when Muqtada al-Sadr entered national politics in Iraq following the U.S. invasion of the country, his movement was a nationalist movement from the start. In fact, some of the earlier variants of this movement that were associated with his family and movements like the Da'wa party were trending increasingly toward nationalism over the past several decades. The same can be said for Hamas in the Palestinian territories, the recent incarnations of the Muslim Brotherhood in Egypt, the Gulen movement and the Justice and Development Party in Turkey, and others. Since these movements have largely pursued national agendas, the scholarship on them often either has to ignore their primary agendas in favor of nonnationalist Islamic goals, or they have to say that they are mixing Islam and nationalism. While the first approach is clearly inaccurate, the second poses more subtle and complex problems. Since all Islamist movements are assumed to be antinational in their basic orientation, when in reality they are pursuing national goals, this is often understood to be a contradiction that needs to be somehow explained. The simple and unreflective way to reconcile this apparent contradiction is to say that these movements represent a mixing of two separate and distinct ideologies, or that they are simply exploiting nationalistic sentiments to pursue religious, nonnationalistic goals. However, when scholars talk about the mixing of Islam and nationalism, they do not define either, and they use both terms inconsistently or inaccurately. If, on the other hand, one treats these movements as religious nationalist movements, there is no contradiction that needs explaining. Rather, our terminology comes into line with the reality on the ground, which is that these movements are often nationalist at their core, and a modernist version of Islam is a core constitutive element of their national culture, ideology, and identity.

An excellent example of this dilemma is the treatment of sectarianism in the Iran-Iraq War of 1980–1988. One debate that emerged among scholars studying that long war was why the Shi'is of Iraq mostly did not join the Iranian side against the Iraqi regime, and conversely why the Arabs of Iran did not side with the Iraqis against Iran. Aside from the pragmatic self-interest of these two communities, one of the common explanations was that nationalism trumped ethnicity in the case of Iranian Arabs, and religious identity in the case of Iraqi Shi'is. While this seems reasonable in the case of Iran, a simpler explanation for the latter case is that the Shi'i identity of Iraqi Shi'is was primarily local and national, and thus, Iranian Shi'ism was irrelevant.

This question arose again after the U.S. invasion of Iraq, when many speculated that the Shi'is of Iraq would naturally identify mostly closely with Iran; or, stated differently, that their Shi'i identity would trump their national identity, thus driving them into the arms of Iran. This of course did not happen, but the problem we are interested in here is the idea that Shi'i identity is separate from national identity, or even that Shi'i identity in Iran is the same as Shi'i identity in Iraq, and elsewhere. Thus, one key question for scholars has been to determine in specific cases whether it is the universal Shi'i or the national identity that will prevail. However, the reality is quite different. Following the invasion of Iraq, it was clear that most mobilized Islamist Shi'is in Iraq had no desire to merge with Iran. In fact, it has become increasingly clear that they viewed Iran only as a foreign ally. Instead, Islamists in Iraq worked to create an Iraq that was built around Islam generally and Shi'ism specifically. Similar trends can be observed in other Shi'i Islamist movements, such as Hizbullah in Lebanon.

Objections to the Idea of Religious Nationalism

There are, of course, objections one could raise to the approach advocated here. We need not spend a great deal of time explaining why secular liberalism cannot be treated as an absolutely necessary condition for labeling a discourse, culture, or movement as nationalistic. Suffice it to say that while many of the nationalisms, especially those of Western Europe, were built at least partly on liberal ideals, many others were not, and in the past two centuries many new forms of nationalism have emerged, especially in developing countries, that do not fit that mold. Another objection is to say that ethnicity is not central to these Islamist ideologies. It is true that ethnicity is not always central to Islamist movements, and in some cases it is irrelevant, or even treated as anathema to the nationalism they are trying to promote. However, ethnic identity need not be present for a nationalism to be accepted as such. This is one way in which these Islamist nationalisms have more in common with civic nationalism than they do with ethnic nationalism. Furthermore, just as ethnic nationalisms often incorporate religion as either a "silent partner," or as an unacknowledged component, these religious nationalisms often tolerate or incorporate ethnic identities and sentiments as a noncentral, tolerated component of their nationalism. I propose here that the key constitutive element of nationalism is the nation and nationality, rather than ethnicity. This brings us to another objection, which is the claim that the nation is not central to Islamist discourses. However, this claim has not always been true, especially in the past few decades. Many Islamist movements have increasingly focused on reshaping their nation, its culture, and its citizenry, rather than pursuing pan-Islamist agendas. Therefore, the nation is not only central to their ideals and goals; it is actually the primary framework within which they operate. This being said, movements under consideration not working primarily within a national framework should not be treated as nationalist movements.

One of the more compelling objections is that Islamist ideologues have often explicitly rejected nationalism. However, as demonstrated above using examples from Iran, a close reading of their writings and speeches shows that, in reality, it was not nationalism that they were disputing; rather, it was particular forms of nationalism that they rejected. Thus, secular nationalisms that were liberal, Marxist, ethnic, or authoritarian were being coded as "nationalism." Then, these ideologues went on to articulate an alternative Islamist vision of the nation, its culture, and its citizenry, most often without calling it "nationalism." Furthermore, more recent religious ideologues have tended to reject nationalism less and less in their writings and speeches.

A related objection is that Islamist discourses tend to have a strong internationalist or transnational component, often taking the traditional idea of an Islamic "*ummah*" as their focus or starting point. However, this is problematic on several levels. First, for most religious nationalists in Muslim countries, the concept of the Islamic *'ummah* as a political unit is irrelevant, except as a utopian ideal, not unlike the Marxist ideal of a "classless and stateless society." Instead, they focus on the Islamization of their nation. Second, while some do refer to the *'ummah*, or to Muslims in general around the world, these are abstract statements of sympathy or kinship, not a call to unite all Muslims in one political state based on the idea of an *'ummah*. More importantly, having an international or transnational dimension to one's rhetoric or ideas does not negate the primary emphasis on the nation. For example, in numerous western nationalisms, it is presumed that the nation is part of a larger block of nations that are characterized by liberal values like democracy and economic liberalism. Likewise, socialist nations, to varying degrees, are also engaged in class struggle on an international scale. The same can be said for nations that position themselves in a third-worldist position vis-à-vis the industrialized West. Even ethnic nationalisms often have transnational ethnic components or sympathies focused on such things as pan-Iranianism, pan-Turkism/Turanism, Indo-European or Aryan peoples, the African or Jewish diasporas, pan-Arabism, etc. It would therefore, be illogical to claim that based on the above, that there is no such thing as Turkish, Jewish-Israeli, Iranian, Egyptian, or various European nationalisms. Rather, we should expect to see a transnational or international component in most forms of nationalism.

Conclusion

The case of Islamic-Iranian nationalism is instructive in finding new ways to study the complex and nuanced relationships between religion and nationalism in the Muslim Middle East and elsewhere. If we accept the possibility that many Islamists are nationalists, it becomes possible to better understand how nationalism has continued to evolve into new forms throughout the past century. It allows us to better understand religious movements that work almost entirely within a national framework. It discourages research questions aimed at explaining false contradictions, and instead encourages more precise and nuanced research questions that are more in line with historical and political realities. While the trends identified here are not universal across the nations of the Muslim Middle East, the fact that this trend is common across the region (and in some other regions around the globe) provides opportunities to ask new comparative questions about when, how, and why religious nationalisms have emerged in many countries. This also has implications for our understanding of nationalism as a historical phenomenon, and of how religious people and societies grapple with new challenges posed by their diverse experiences of modernity.

Notes

1. Mark Juergensmeyer, *The New Cold War? Religious Nationalism Confronts the Secular State* (Berkeley: University of California Press, 1993). See also Mark Juergensmeyer, *Global Rebellion: Religious Challenges to the Secular State, from Christian Militants to Al Qaeda* (Berkeley: University of California Press, 2008). Also, Mark Juergensmeyer, *Religion in Global Civil Society* (Oxford: Oxford University Press, 2006).

2. Peter van der Veer, *Religious Nationalism: Hindus and Muslims in India* (Berkeley: University of California Press, 1994).

3. Ornit Shani, *Communalism, Caste, and Hindu Nationalism: The Violence of Gujarat* (Cambridge: Cambridge University Press, 2007).

4. Catarina Kinnvall, *Globalization and Religious Nationalism in India: The Search for Ontological Security* (London: Routledge, 2006).

5. Philip W. Barker, *Religious Nationalism in Modern Europe* (London and New York: Routledge, 2009).

6. Genevieve Zubrzycki, *The Crosses of Auschwitz: Nationalism and Religion in Post-Communist Poland* (Chicago: University of Chicago Press, 2006).

7. Jouni Tilli, "An interpretation of Finnish religious nationalism: the four topoi of theological depoliticisation," *Nations and Nationalism* 15, no. 4 (2009), 597–615.

8. Betty Clermont, *The Neo-Catholics: Implementing Christian Nationalism in America* (Atlanta: Clarity Press, 2009), and Michelle Goldberg, *Kingdom Coming: The Rise of Christian Nationalism* (New York: Norton, 2007).

9. For an excellent example of this scholarship, see Aviezer Ravitzky, *Messianism, Zionism, and Jewish Religious Radicalism* (Chicago: University of Chicago Press, 1993).

10. For examples of studies on the "Turkish-Islamic Synthesis," see Binnaz Toprak, "Religion as State Ideology in a Secular Setting: The Turkish-Islamic Synthesis," in *Aspects of Religion in Secular Turkey*, ed. Malcolm Wagstaff (Durham: University of Durham, 1990), 10–15; Gokhan Cetinsaya, "Rethinking Nationalism and Islam: Some Preliminary Notes on the Roots of the 'Turkish-Islamic Synthesis' in Modern Turkish Thought," *Muslim World* 89, 3–4 (1999), 350–376; and Umit Kurt, "The Doctrine of 'Turkish-Islamic Synthesis' as Official Ideology of the September 12 and the 'intellectuals' Hearth—Aydinlar Ocagi' as the Ideological Apparatus of the State," *European Journal of Economic and Political Studies* 3, 2 (2010), 111–125.

11. Gavin D. Brockett, *How Happy to Call Oneself a Turk: Provincial Newspapers and the Negotiation of a Muslim National Identity* (Austin: University of Texas Press, 2011), 223–224.

12. Brockett, *How Happy to Call Oneself a Turk: Provincial Newspapers and the Negotiation of a Muslim National Identity*, 113–115.

13. James Gelvin, "Nationalism, Anarchism, Reform: Political Islam from the Inside Out," *Middle East Policy* XVII, no. 3 (2010), 124.

14. Ibid., p. 125.

15. Mohammad Tavakoli-Targhi, "Tajaddod-e ekhtera'i, tajaddod-e 'ariyati, va enqelab-e rohani" [Inventing Modernity, Borrowing Modernity], *Iran Namah* (Spring/Summer 2002), xx, 2–3.

16. For representative examples, see Haggay Ram, "The Immemorial Iranian Nation? School Textbooks and Historical Memory in Post-Revolutionary Iran," *Nations and Nationalism* 6, 1 (2000), 67–90; Golnar Mehran, "The Presentations of the "Self" and the "Other" in Postrevolutionary Iranian School Textbooks," in *Iran and the Surrounding World: Interactions in Culture and Cultural Politics*, ed. Nikki R. Keddie and Rudi Matthee (Seattle: University of Washington Press, 2002), 232–253; and David Menashri, *The Iranian Revolution and the Muslim World*, ed. David Menashri (San Francisco, Boulder and Oxford: Westview Press, 1990.

17. Minoo Moallem, "Cultural Nationalism and Islamic Fundamentalism: The Case of Iran," in *Antinomies of Modernity: Essays on Race, Orient, Nation*, eds. Vasant Kaiwar and Sucheta Mazumdar (Durham and London: Duke University Press, 2003), 196–222.

18. Kamran Scot Aghaie, "Islam and Nationalist Historiography: Competing Historical Narratives of Iran in the Pahlavi Period," *Studies on Contemporary Islam*, 2, no. 2 (2000), 20–46. See also Kamran Scot Aghaie, "Islamist Historiography in Post-

Revolutionary Iran," in *Historiography and Political Culture in Twentieth Century Iran*, ed. Touraj Atabaki (London and New York: I. B. Tauris, 2009), 233–263 and 318–322.

19. "Bayanat-e Emam Khameneh'i dar ejtema'e mardom-e Paveh," *Payegah-e ettela'resani-e sepah-e Fajr-e ostan-e Fars*, 29 September 2011/7 Mehr 1390, http://tanvir.ir/print.php?d=sn&id=2858.

20. For a detailed discussion of these trends, see Aghaie, "Islam and Nationalist Historiography," 20–46. See also Aghaie, "Islamist Historiography in Post-Revolutionary Iran," 233–263, 318–322.

21. "Sayyed Mohammad Khatami: Tamaddon-e bozorg-e Eslami yek sakhteman nist keh ba mohandesi amadeh shavad," *Jahan-e Eqtesad*, 9 March 2010/18 Esfand 1388, http://www.jahaneghtesad.com/index.php?option=com_content&view=article&id=2395%3A1388-12-18-07-08-46&Itemid=626.

22. "Musavi dar Yazd: Hefz-e hoviyyat-e Irani va Islami lazemeh-e defa' az Felestin va Lobnan ast," *Khabargozari-e Mehr*, 18 November 2011/27 Aban 1390, http://www.mehrnews.com/fa/newsdetail.aspx?NewsID=881282.

23. Ibid.

24. "Amuzesh va parvaresh bayad hoveyyat-e paydar-e Eslami va Irani ijad konad," *Hamshahri*, 7 August 2010/16 Mordad 1389. http://hamshahrionline.ir/print-113318.aspx.

25. "Khatami dar namaz jom'eh-e Tehran: Iran ba Eslam hoveyyat miyabad/enteqad-e shaded az hanjarshekani-ha dar bahs-e hejab," *Khabargozari-e Mehr*, 6 August 2010/15 Mordad 1389. http://www.mehrnews.com/fa/NewsPrint.aspx?NewsID=1129102.

26. Abd al-Karim Sorush, *Razdani va rowshanfekri va dindari* (Tehran: Mo'assaseh-e Farhangi-e Serat, 1998/1377).

27. Ibid., p. 71.

28. Ibid., p. 82.

29. Ibid., p. 80.

30. Ibid., p. 76.

31. Ibid., p. 79.

32. Ibid., p. 80.

33. "Matn-e kamel-e sokhanrani-e Masha'i dar ekhtetamiyeh-e hamayesh-e Iranian" *Esteqamat, Websayt-e khabari tahlili*, 16 August 2010/25 Mordad 1389 (note the actual speech was given on 14 Mordad 1389/5 August 2010). http://www.esteghamat.ir/pages.asp?id=7691. For another uploaded transcription of the speech, see also Ali Azadi "Andishe-e sabz: matn-e kamel-e sokhanrani-e Masha'i 'maktab-e Iran,'" Last updated 14 June 2011/24 Khordad 1390. http://andishee.mihanblog/post/82.

34. Ibid.

35. "Ahmadinejad: Iran yek maktab ast/beh Masha'i e'temad-e kamel daram," Khabargozari-e Mehr, 11 August 2010/20 Mordad 1389. http://www.mehrnews.com/fa/NewsPrint.aspx?NewsID=1132128.

36. Ibid.

37. "Defa'e ra'is jomhur va Masha'i az maktab-e Irani," *Tebyan*, 6 August 2010/17 Mordad 1389. http://www.tebyan.net/politics_social/politics/domestic_policy/political_terminology/2010/8/8/132994.html.

38. "Tavakkoli: Ra'is jomhur taklif-e khod ra ba Rahim Masha'i moshakhkhas

konad," *Simab: Sayt-e Khabari Tahlili,* 6 August 2010/ 15 Mordad 1389. http://www
.seemab.ir/fa/pages/?cid=38512.

39. "Vakonesh-ha beh 'maktab-e Irani'-e Masha'i," ed. Ata Allah Babapur, *Tebyan,*
7 August 2010/ 16 Mordad 1389. http://www.tebyan.net/Politics_Social/Politics/Do
mestic_Policy/Political_Terminology/2010/8/7/132966.html.

40. "Tavakkoli: Ra'is jomhur taklif-e khod ra ba Rahim Masha'i moshakhkhas
konad," *Simab: Sayt-e Khabari Tahlili,* 6 August 2010/ 15 Mordad 1389. http://www
.seemab.ir/fa/pages/?cid=38512.

41. "Enteqad-e shadid-e Mesbah Yazdi az moruj-e maktab-e Iran," *Shi'eh Onlayn,*
5 September 2010/ 14 Shahrivar 1389. http://shia-online.ir/article.asp?id=13896&cat=1.

42. "Ali Motahhari: 'maktab-e Irani' enheraf ast," *Tabnak,* 14 August 2010/ 23
Mordad 1389. http://www.tabnak.ir/fa/pages/?cid=114026.

43. Ibid.

44. Ibid.

45. This is similar to the argument made by James Gelvin in "Nationalism, Anarchism, Reform: Political Islam from the Inside Out" (http://www.history.ucla.edu
/people/faculty?lid=289).

CHAPTER 10

The Place of Islam in Interwar Iranian Nationalist Historiography

FARZIN VEJDANI

To claim that early Pahlavi nationalist historians considered the spread of Islam in Iran as the source of decline and backwardness has become an un-questioned axiom in the field of Iranian studies. According to this perspective, Iranian historians, particularly from the nineteenth century onwards, articu-lated a tripartite periodization of history: a golden age starting in pre-Islamic Iran, a period of decline brought about by the Arab invasions and the spread of Islam, and a modern age of renewal witnessing the revival of the "authen-tic" ancient nation.[1] The persuasiveness of this account is in many ways inter-twined with a broader cultural explanation of the 1979 Iranian Islamic Revo-lution. Writing a year after the Islamic Revolution, one notable historian of modern Iran wrote, "The modernizing classes tended to adopt a trend in Iranian nationalism that had begun in the late nineteenth century—the glo-rification of pre-Islamic Iran and of Zoroastrianism, with the Arab Muslim invaders seen as causing Iran's decline [,]" adding, "[t]his type of nationalism, which has its parallels in many societies, widened the cultural breach between the devout popular classes and the Westernizing nationalists."[2]

There is a need to revisit the question of the representation of Islam in Ira-nian nationalist historiography independent of broader explanations for the 1979 Islamic Revolution. These explanations consider the Pahlavi state (1926–1979) to have promoted pre-Islamic Iranian history at the expense of a focus on the recent past.[3] This is not to say that the tendency to glorify pre-Islamic history and see Islam in a negative light was entirely absent.[4] Nineteenth-century Iranian intellectuals, such as Mirza Fath Ali Akhundzadeh and Mirza Aqa Khan Kermani, explicitly articulated such views.[5] In the interwar period, literary figures such as Sadiq Hedayat and Zabih Behruz likewise viewed Islam as the cause of Iranian decline.[6] Such readings of history, however, were generally absent in the official Pahlavi historiography found in history curricula and textbooks. Since textbooks, then as now, had a guaranteed readership, they are an important source for understanding the shaping of Iranian historical consciousness among an increasingly literate population.[7] This chapter argues that the majority of interwar Iranian history textbooks neither ignored Islamic history nor claimed that Islam was the cause of Iranian decline.[8] In light of this, an alternative set of questions needs to be posed about the place of Islam in Iranian historiography: how did secular historiography transform the category of Islam and religion more generally? Where did Islam fit into the grand narrative of Iranian historiography? And what more specifically was their reading of Shi'ism and Shi'i history in relation to Iran?

Pre-Islamic Iran and Nationalist Historiography

Nationalist representations of the pre-Islamic past were ultimately concerned with origins. Far too often, scholars assume that by deconstructing how Iranian nationalists represented the pre-Islamic past, they will be able to understand key aspects of nationalist narratives pertaining to race, civilization, and decline. For instance, the early Pahlavi invocation of pre-Islamic Iranian kingship through official historiography, education, and even state rituals such as the 1934 Millenary celebrations for the birth of Ferdowsi, is treated as the central feature of Iranian nationalism to the exclusion of other facets of its cultural policy.[9] The appropriation of the pre-Islamic past, however, was not unique to the modern monarchs: "Islamic" monarchs including the Sunni Ottoman Sultans and Shi'i Safavid Shahs turned to the pre-Islamic past for legitimacy and in "imagining" a pristine past, although the technologies of imagining certainly differed.[10] The inclusion of pre-Islamic narratives of origins in medieval and early modern Islamicate historiography should, therefore, be reason for pause: the quest for an imagined golden age was by no means a uniquely "modern" phenomenon.

The nationalist emphasis on archeology, which constituted the recently discovered "real" history of pre-Islamic Iran, did, however, suggest an increasingly intellectual orientation toward European archaeological findings, Orientalist texts, and ancient Greek sources.[11] The Iranian nationalist "discovery" of ancient Achaemenid history, via Orientalist scholarship in particular, has sometimes been misconstrued as evidence of Iranian nationalism being a derivative discourse.[12] Such arguments deny agency to Iranian nationalists by ignoring their selective and strategic engagement with European scholarship, scholarship that they often also critiqued in the process of engagement.

Beyond the claim that Iranian nationalists emphasized the pre-Islamic tradition of kingship, some authors have also highlighted the nationalist propensity to view pre-Islamic Zoroastrianism as an authentic alternative to Islam. According to this perspective, Zoroastrianism was a moral and ethical religion particularly well suited to modernity.[13] Those who subscribe to both variants of this argument point out, quite rightly, that Iranian nationalists projected modernity back into the pre-Islamic period and viewed it as an "authentic" origin for the modern nation. Certainly interwar nationalists paid a great deal of attention to pre-Islamic Iran, but they did not necessarily assume, when they sat down to write official textbooks, that Islam was the cause of Iranian decline.

Education, the State, and the Writing of History

The conventional view of the early Pahlavi educational system is that it disproportionately promoted pre-Islamic Iranian history. For instance, David Menashri, commenting on early Pahlavi-era curricula, claims "[t]he teaching of pre-Islamic history, mainly of the Achaemenid period, was stressed."[14] But a careful reexamination of early Pahlavi curricula tells a radically different story. In order to understand the Education Ministry's standardized history curricula, we must first examine the institutional contexts out of which they emerged. In spite of the Iranian state's best efforts to produce a centralized educational system, late nineteenth- and early twentieth-century Iranian educational institutions were, for the most part, characteristically decentralized, diffuse, and dependent on the individual initiative of independent reformers.

The first secular school in Iran, the Dar al-Funun, dates back to the mid-nineteenth century and was primarily intended to train military and bureaucratic officials for the state.[15] History was apparently not a part of the early curriculum, although one of the Dar al-Funun's students, the Qajar Prince Jalal al-Din Mirza, produced *Nameh-e Khosravan*, a history of Iran intended as a textbook for children.[16] After a few fitful attempts at opening further secular schools—such as by the reformist Prime Minister Mirza Hosayn Khan Moshir al-Dowleh and later by the independent educator Hasan Roshdiyeh—a more sustained drive at expanding education for the general population occurred during the reign of Mozaffar al-Din Shah (1896–1907).[17] Relying on both state funds and individual patronage, the teachers and principals associated with these new schools produced some of the earliest and most significant history textbooks.[18]

The 1906 Iranian Constitutional Revolution marks the next important turning point in Iranian education. Schools continued to operate but often faced difficulties associated with a revolutionary context, including disruptions to the daily rhythms of classes and lack of funding for schools. In 1911, the Iranian parliament sent abroad a number of Iranian students, many of whom returned to fill important government and bureaucratic positions, including 'Isa Sadiq, who was a key architect of Pahlavi-era educational reforms.[19] Historians continued to write textbooks during the period from 1906 to 1913, often retelling an Iranian grand narrative in light of the Constitutional Revolution. The First World War, however, led to a lull in the printing of Iranian history textbooks, and books in general, most likely because of the high cost of paper and the restricted publishing climate accompanying the British, Russian, and Ottoman occupations of many regions in Iran. Despite these conditions, schools continued to operate.[20]

Reza Khan's rise to power witnessed a move toward the standardization and centralization of the education system; however, there was no radical rewriting of national history, as there was in the neighboring Turkish Republic.[21] In this respect, Reza Shah was no Ataturk: he did not partake in the articulating of a major historical thesis or personally create organizations and conferences on historical themes.[22] Although there was certainly an expansion of the educational system, a standardization of the school curriculum, and the training of schoolteachers during the interwar period, the crafting of Iranian educational and cultural policy as it pertained to nationalist historiography was largely accomplished independently of the monarch's direct interference.

The transformations in the Iranian educational system were much more subtle and diffuse, transformations that defy simplistic reductions to the fiats of a single strong man. Instead, it is more useful to examine the educators and authors involved in the articulation of nationalist narratives in these new pedagogical settings. These authors spanned several generations, political orientations, and socioeconomic backgrounds. Yoav Di-Capua has traced how the emergence of the *effendiyah* class in Egypt, consisting of the new middle class, shaped and reoriented nationalist historiography toward a greater emphasis on the Islamic Arab past.[23] Charles Smith has similarly examined how Egyptian intellectuals' "crisis of orientation" led to a greater preoccupation with Arab Islam instead of with pre-Islamic Egyptian narratives.[24]

Iranians did not experience a similar crisis of orientation, partly because educators and cultural figures such as Mohammad 'Ali Forughi, 'Abbas Eqbal, Hasan Taqizadeh, and 'Isa Sadiq (to name a just a few), were not proponents of an antireligious form of nationalism. Much more remains to be said about the connections between social strata, intellectual orientations, and political objectives in the Iranian context. For instance, the three historians commissioned by the Ministry of Education to write textbooks for the new standardized curriculum in 1928 were emblematic of the diversity among historians. Hasan Pirniya was from a Qajar bureaucratic and aristocratic background that had been co-opted by the new Pahlavi state. Hasan Taqizadeh had received a traditional *madrasah* education but engaged in activism both in Iran and abroad during the early years of the Constitutional Revolution and the First World War. 'Abbas Eqbal Ashtiyani was a product of the new secular schools established in the late nineteenth and early twentieth centuries, although he came from humble origins and lacked the social status of an aristocrat or a constitutional-era dissident.[25] Despite the diversity of their social backgrounds, most Iranian historians had an overwhelming admiration for Islam and Islamic civilization.

Disciplining Time: Periodizing Iranian History in School Curricula

A preliminary study of school curricula both prior to major Pahlavi reforms and after reveals a relative lack of emphasis on the pre-Islamic period of Iranian history. Inspired by French pedagogical models, Iranian schools generally consisted of six-year programs that were often further divided into three-year cycles (*dowrehs*). History curricula followed the periodization established in textbooks, with each year covering a particular historical era. For example, over the course of the first three-year cycle, students spent each year covering the ancient, medieval, and modern periods. The prevailing assumption that Iranian schools disproportionately focused on pre-Islamic history ignores the pedagogical logic behind the periodization of history. In fact, it was often the case that over the course of six years, for either primary or secondary education, pre-Islamic Iranian history was taught for only a year. The vast majority of the lesson plans focused on Iranian and world history after the spread of Islam. As will become clear, this was as true for curricula before and during the reign of Reza Shah.

Shortly before Reza Shah's coronation, the Ministry of Education published a six-year curriculum for middle schools.[26] During the "preparatory year" (*sal-e tahiyeh*) before the six-year cycle, students covered the mythical history of Iran, i.e., "the Pishdadiyans and Kiyanids," albeit "in summary form," before focusing on the history of the Achaemenids and other ancient civilizations of the Middle East and ending with the Greek invasions and the successor states. The first year of the program began with the Ashkanid and Sasanian empires but also included the Arab governments and the rise of Islam, while the second year continued with the Arab governments, the "great men of Iran" before the Mongol invasion (meaning during the 'Abbasid period), the Mongol domination and resulting destruction, and the Timurids. In the third year, the program began with the period between the Timurids and the Safavids all the way to the present Qajar dynasty, which incidentally was to be covered only in "summary fashion."[27] In the same year, the Ministry of Education established the history curriculum for the Women Teachers' Training College. It by and large followed the organization of the middle school's program, with only a slight variation: Students were expected to study the entire scope of Iranian and world history with an overwhelming emphasis on Iranian history after the rise of Islam.[28]

The centralization of the Iranian educational system led to the further standardization of school curricula. To this end, in 1928 the Ministry of Education prepared a six-year middle school program for boys, which included revisions to the history curriculum.[29] The curriculum was further divided into two cycles, the first constituting mandatory courses for all male high school students, while the second had separate tracks for those specializing in literature and the sciences respectively. Within the first three years of the program, all middle-school students studied the entire scope of Iranian history, but in the second cycle Iranian history was renarrated at various levels of detail, depending on the student's academic concentration. For students with a concentration in literature, there were further history classes during their fourth, fifth, and sixth years, in which pre-Islamic history was excluded altogether.[30]

Iranian Islam as Civilization, Shi'ism, and Orthodoxy

Why would Iranian educators want to craft history curricula that emphasized Iranian history after the rise of Islam? Having examined the curricular logic framing the periodization of Iranian history, we must now return to the question of interwar nationalist narratives and the place of Islam. Contrary to the common perception that Iranian nationalists viewed the pre-Islamic period as a golden age followed by a decline brought about by the Arab Islamic invasions before experiencing a renaissance in modernity, interwar Iranian nationalists highlighted historical continuities over ruptures. The implicit logic of including all periods of history—ancient, medieval, and modern—in the curriculum was to emphasize such continuities. This emphasis on continuities was articulated through nationalist narratives of resilience in which Iranians adapted and synthesized new modes of thought even in times of crisis. The historical narratives crafted for Islam illustrate this point most clearly, since

Iranian historians predominantly sought to craft a genealogy for an "authentic" Iranian Islam. But what did this Iranian Islam entail? Based on a survey of interwar Iranian history textbooks, three interconnected representations of Islam emerge: Iranian Islam as civilization, Shi'ism, and orthodoxy.

The notion of civilization (*tamaddon*) was perhaps the most important organizing principle through which Iranian nationalist historians viewed history.[31] Iranian historians were by no means unique in writing about Islam as a civilization. The Arab Christian historian, Jurji Zaydan, wrote a multi-volume work, *The History of Islamic Civilization* (Tarikh al-Tamaddun al-Islami), in the opening years of the twentieth century. His history was a secular appreciation of Muslim contributions to science, the arts, literature, philosophy, and statecraft.[32] Iranians translated this work in the midst of their Constitutional Revolution and against a backdrop of Young Turk-Iranian constitutionalist solidarity in 1911.[33] These transnational literary transactions through translations informed not only the formation of literature as a discipline, but also the conceptual terminology of the emerging field of historiography.[34] Unlike many subsequent Arab nationalist historians who viewed Iranian influence in Islamic history as a cause of decline,[35] Zaydan acknowledged and indeed praised their role in Abbasid administration.[36] When writing about Islamic history, Iranian nationalists viewed the Abbasid period as a golden age. Contrary to conventional wisdom, they were not particularly bothered by the Arab ethnic origin of the caliphs and the predominance of Arabic as the court *lingua franca* at the time.

Iranian nationalists were not fond of the Arab Umayyad dynasty—a dynasty that was notorious for excluding non-Arabs (including Muslims) from sought-after military and administrative posts. They were therefore careful not to conflate Islam with Umayyad policy. For Iranian nationalists, Islam was a positive historical force, one that highlighted the equality of believers, rather than an ethnic hierarchy that elevated Arabs over Iranians. In neighboring Iraq, the legacy of the Umayyads and the Abbasids had sectarian implications in a country with substantial Shi'i and Sunni Arab populations.[37] Iranian nationalists, however, were less interested in the sectarian or ethnic identity of the Abbasids and more interested in the contributions of ethnically Iranian bureaucrats, administrations, and men of letters to its cultural flowering. Historians placed a great amount of emphasis on Iranian bureaucratic and literate families like the Barmakids, who embodied the "Iranian" contribution to the Abbasid court.[38] Ethnically Iranian men of letters, such as Ibn Muqaffa, Al-Baladhuri, Ibn Sina, and Al-Biruni, among others, were likewise praised for their contribution to Arabic historiography, philosophy, science, and translations. Despite the common misperception that the majority of Iranian nationalists were predominantly language purists, many included Arabic-language texts within the Iranian literary canon.[39]

Iranian historians insisted on pointing out that many of the important Muslim poets and philosophers—all of whom were writing in Arabic—were ethnically Iranians. Writing in the mid-1920s and 1930s, ʿAbbas Eqbal Ashtiyani, the author of dozens of history and geography textbooks, articulated a common assessment of the Abbasid period and its civilization:

> All Muslims [meaning non-Arabs as well as Arabs] have had a part in [the shaping of] Islamic civilization, but Iranians have played a more prominent role than everyone else. This is not only because this people took charge of the main institutions of Islamic governance, but they were also direct promoters of science and literature or experts and teachers of learning (ma'lumat). As a result, the majority of the learned figures among the clerics, philosophers, and poets who wrote in Arabic during this period of Islamic civilization were Iranians.[40]

Iranian historians' views on Islam tended to focus on its secular aspects: governmental administration, worldly literature, and Hellenistic philosophy. The related project of crafting a genealogy for Iranian Shiʿism was similarly meant to highlight a unique and distinctive sense of identity, not articulated against Islam, but within it.

Employing a nationalist frame of thought, Iranian historians were more interested in tracing the legacy of Shiʿism in Iran rather than understanding it as a sect on its own terms. Two moments in Iranian Islamic history were of particular importance for these historians: first, the influence of the Iranian Shiʿi bureaucratic family, the Nowbakhtis; and second, the establishment of the Shiʿi Safavid state.

The Nowbakhti family attracted the attention of the professional Iranian historian ʿAbbas Eqbal, who wrote the earliest scholarly monograph on the topic in Persian.[41] He often appealed to ethnic/racial difference as part of a category of historical explanation. The Nowbakhtis were initially a family of Zoroastrian astrologers in the service of the Abbasid Caliph Al-Mansur (d. 775). They converted to Islam and later to Shiʿism. Eqbal emphasized their contribution to patronizing translations of Sasanian Pahlavi texts into Arabic in addition to rationalistic and theological defenses of Shiʿism. Unlike pious histories of the Shiʿi Imams and popular Shiʿi rituals and narratives that posited the truth of Shiʿism, Eqbal stressed the centrality of Shiʿism in differentiating Iranians historically from Sunni Muslims. He collapsed Iranian and Shi'i identities into one another by stressing the continuities between pre-Islamic Zoroastrianism and Shi'ism:

> [T]hose who pay careful attention to Iranian history know that just as before Islam, Iranian and Zoroastrian was synonymous with foreigner, likewise after Islam until contemporary times, Iranian and Shi'i have one meaning. The enemy of Shi'ism means the enemy of Iran and the opponent of Iran means the enemy of Shi'ism. . . . [T]he service of the Iranian Nowbakhti family in defending Iranian independence and saving them from transforming [into] a Sunni society is among the greatest services rendered which must be mentioned and appreciated as an entrusted obligation of every nationalist Iranian.[42]

The Nowbakhti contribution to Islamic administration and intellectual production—both hallmarks of "civilization"—were meant to foreshadow the fundamentally Shi'i identity of the majority of the Iranian population under the Safavid dynasty when the majority of the population underwent Shi'ization.[43]

In discussing the spread of Shi'ism in Iran, Iranian nationalist historians spoke of this process as part of a natural teleology. Iranians were supposedly always Shi'i in temperament. The Safavids, in their eyes, merely formalized the inevitable. Operating within a nationalist framework, Iranian nationalists praised Shi'ism for having brought about national unity to Iran after a long period of political fragmentation and regionalism. Connected to this idea, for Iranian historians, was the notion that the conversion to Shi'ism helped Iran differentiate itself from its Sunni neighbors: "The Safavids also strengthened the general and official religion of Iran, which is Shi'ism, and thereby distinguished this country from other Islamic countries [mainly the Sunni Ottomans]."[44] As the Pahlavi state embarked on a program of national homogenization and centralization, the Safavids were seen as worthy predecessors.[45]

So far these examples point to a largely secular appreciation for Islam as a civilization and Shi'ism as a force of national unity. More difficult to explain, however, is the pietistic tone adopted in history textbooks that presumed an exclusively Shi'i Muslim audience. Describing the Sunni-Shi'i split, one historian stated, "Abu Bakr became the Caliph and usurped the right of 'Ali bin Abi Talib, peace be upon him, who *according to the belief of us Shi'is* [emphasis added] is the immediate successor of the Prophet."[46] Hasan Taqizadeh, adopting a similarly pietistic tone, referred to the biography of the Prophet

Muhammad as "the biography of his holiness the noblest prophet (*sirat-e hazrat-e rasul-e akram*)."[47] 'Abd Allah Razi, in the late 1930s—during the supposed height of rabid anti-Arab and anti-Islamic sentiment—wrote, "Before mentioning the names of the learned figures of Shi'ism, we thought that we would mention the names of the blessed Imams (*a'emeh-e athar*), peace be upon them all, in order to bless and consecrate the pages of this short book."[48] The persistence of pietistic language in such history textbooks suggests the need for a more nuanced appreciation of the place of religion in interwar Iranian nationalism.

Beyond the assumption of an Iranian Shi'i readership of these textbooks, most authors championed an orthodox version of religion against heterodox movements in Iran, including the Manicheans, Mazdakites, Isma'ilis, and more recently, Babis and Baha'is. 'Ali Asghar Shamim, whose late-1930s textbook on eighteenth- and nineteenth-century Iran was used well into the 1960s, described the uprisings of the Isma'ili Agha Khan, the Naqshbandi Sufis of Khurasan and the Babi movement as "new seditious uprisings" (*fetnehha-e jadid*).[49] Heterodoxy was cast as a political threat to national unity and as an artificial and inauthentic expression of religiosity. Ironically, supposedly tolerant secular Iranian historians discussed heterodoxy—past and near present—with no less disdain than mainstream Shi'i *'ulama*.

Conclusion

Iranian historians played a crucial role in redefining the meaning and category of Islam by historicizing and nationalizing the category itself. Contrary to prevailing wisdom, the interwar Iranian state did not overwhelmingly focus on pre-Islamic Iranian history at the expense of the history of Iran after the rise of Islam in its official curriculum. Rather than rejecting religion as a source of backwardness, historians considered orthodox religion, in both its Zoroastrian and Islamic forms, as complementary to a successful Iranian state. In writing about early Islamic history, they blamed the Arab Umayyad dynasty for its exclusionary policies toward ethnic Iranians, but carefully distinguished between Arabs and Islam. Iranian historians indigenized the religion by arguing Iranians made unique contributions to Islamic civilization, administration, literature, and philosophy, particularly during the reign of the Abbasids. For these historians, Shi'ism became synonymous with Iranian Islam, distinguishing it from Sunni Arabs and Turks. The case of Iran—even during the supposed height of enthusiasm for secularism—demonstrates that, contrary to secularization theories that predict the demise and steady disappearance of religion with the rise of Westernizing elites, religion can and often did retain a crucial significance in secular narratives of history, albeit in novel and complex configurations.

Notes

An earlier version of this chapter was presented at the University of Arizona Center for Middle Eastern Studies lecture series and the "Rethinking Iranian Nationalism" conference at the University of Texas at Austin. I would like to thank Susan Crane, Yaseen Noorani, and Charles Smith for their comments and feedback. Kamran Aghaie, Aomar Boum, Aslı Iğsız, and Afshin Marashi read drafts of the chapter and made helpful suggestions.

1. Recent historians have tackled the issue of periodization in relation to nationalist discourses of decline and revival. See, in particular, Mohamad Tavakoli-Targhi, *Refashioning Iran: Orientalism, Occidentalism, and Historiography* (New York: Palgrave, 2001), 78; Afshin Marashi, *Nationalizing Iran: Culture, Power, and the State, 1870–1940* (Seattle: University of Washington Press, 2008), 54.

2. Nikki R. Keddie, *Iran: Religion, Politics, and Society: Collected Essays* (London: Cass, 1980), 99.

3. M. Reza Afshari, "The Historians of the Constitutional Movement and the Making of the Iranian Populist Tradition," *International Journal of Middle East Studies* 25, no. 3 (1993), 477–494; Touraj Atabaki, "Agency and Subjectivity in Iranian National Historiography," in *Iran in the 20th Century: Historiography and Political Culture*, ed. Touraj Atabaki (London: I. B. Tauris, 2009), 69–92.

4. See, for instance, Reza Zia-Ebrahimi, "'Arab Invasion' and Decline, or the Import of European Racial Thought by Iranian Nationalists," *Ethnic and Racial Studies* (November 2012), 1–19.

5. For a useful overview of both thinkers and their contribution to literary criticism, see Iraj Parsinejad, *A History of Literary Criticism in Iran: 1866–1951* (Bethesda: Ibex Publishers, 2002), 39–94.

6. Homa Katouzian, *Sadiq Hedayat: The Life and Literature of an Iranian Writer* (London, New York: I. B. Tauris, 1991); Paul Sprachman, "BEHRŪZ, DABĪḤ," in *Encyclopaedia Iranica* (Costa Mesa, CA: Mazda, 1990), Vol. IV, 111–113.

7. Michael Apple and Linda Christian-Smith, "The Politics of the Textbook," in *The Politics of the Textbook*, ed. Michael Apple and Linda Christian-Smith (New York: Routledge, 1991), 1–21. For a pioneering study of late Qajar and early Pahlavi Iranian textbooks, see Firoozeh Kashani-Sabet, *Frontier Fictions: Shaping the Iranian Nation, 1804–1946* (Princeton: Princeton University Press, 1999), 180–215. Kashani-Sabet focuses on the geographical notion of Iran found in textbooks more generally.

8. Kamran Aghaie makes a similar argument in his fine study of Islam in Pahlavi-era nationalist historiography: Kamran Aghaie, "Islam and Nationalist Historiography: Competing Historical Narratives of the Iranian Nation in the Pahlavi Period," *Studies in Contemporary Islam* 2, no. 2 (2000), 21–47. In the field of Ottoman history, Benjamin Fortna has questioned teleological narratives about the progressive "secu-

larization" of the Ottoman educational system in *Imperial Classroom: Islam, the State, and Education in the Late Ottoman Empire* (Oxford: Oxford University Press, 2002), 9.

9. Afshin Marashi, "The Nation's Poet: Ferdowsi and the Iranian National Imagination," in *Iran in the 20th Century: Historiography and Political Culture*, ed. Touraj Atabaki (New York: I. B. Tauris, 2009), 93–111.

10. On the use of the *Shahnameh* by the Safavids, see Stuart Welch, *A King's Book of Kings: The Shah-nameh of Shah Tahmasp* (New York: Metropolitan Museum of Art, 1972). For a discussion of how Nader Shah "imagined" a community in the absence of print technology, see Ernest Tucker, *Nadir Shah's Quest for Legitimacy in Post-Safavid Iran* (Gainesville, FL: University Press of Florida, 2006).

11. See Kishwar Rizvi, "Art History and the Nation: Arthur Upham Pope and the Discourse on 'Persian Art' in the Early 20th Century," *Muqarnas: Journal of Islamic Art and Architecture* 24 (2007): 45–66; Talinn Grigor, "Recultivating 'Good Taste': The Early Pahlavi Modernists and Their Society for National Heritage," *Iranian Studies* 37, no. 1 (March 2004), 17–45.

12. Mostafa Vaziri, *Iran as Imagined Nation: the Construction of National Identity* (New York: Paragon House, 1993).

13. Monica Ringer, "Iranian Nationalism and Zoroastrian Identity: Between Cyrus and Zoroaster," in *Iran Facing Others: Iranian Identity Boundaries and Modern Political Cultures*, ed. Abbas Amanat and Farzin Vejdani (New York: Palgrave Macmillan, 2012), 267–277.

14. David Menashri, *Education and the Making of Modern Iran* (Ithaca: Cornell University Press, 1992), 96.

15. Maryam Ekhtiar, "The Dar al-Funun: Educational Reform and Cultural Development in Qajar Iran" (PhD dissertation, New York University, 1994); John Gurney and Negin Nabavi, "DĀR AL-FONŪN," in *Encyclopaedia Iranica* (Costa Mesa, CA: Mazda, 1993), vol. VI, 662–668.

16. Abbas Amanat and Farzin Vejdani, "JALĀL-AL-DIN MIRZĀ," in *Encyclopaedia Iranica* (Costa Mesa, CA: Mazda, 2008), vol. XIV, 405–410; Abbas Amanat, "Pur-e Khaqan va Andisheh-e Bazyabi-ye Tarikh-e Melli-ye Iran: Jalal al-Din Mirza va Nameh-e Khosravan," *Iran Nameh* 17, no. 1 (Winter 1999), 5–54.

17. Monica Ringer, *Education, Religion, and the Discourse of Cultural Reform in Qajar Iran* (Costa Mesa, CA: Mazda Publishers, 2001), 145–186.

18. Farzin Vejdani, "Purveyors of the Past: Iranian Historians and Nationalist Historiography, 1900–1941" (PhD dissertation, Yale University, 2009), 199–252.

19. Roy Mottahedeh, *The Mantle of the Prophet: Religion and Politics in Iran* (New York: Pantheon Books, 1985); Marashi, *Nationalizing Iran.*

20. Vejdani, "Purveyors of the Past: Iranian Historians and Nationalist Historiography, 1900–1941," 251.

21. For a good series of essays comparing "authoritarian modernization" under the rule of these two military strongmen, see Touraj Atabaki and Erik Jan Zürcher, eds., *Men of Order: Authoritarian Modernization under Atatürk and Reza Shah* (London and New York: I. B. Tauris, 2004).

22. Speros Vryonis, *The Turkish State and History: Clio Meets the Grey Wolf* (Thessaloniki [Greece]: Institute for Balkan Studies, 1991). Umut Özkırımlı and Spyros A. Sofos, *Tormented by History: Nationalism in Greece and Turkey* (London: Hurst Publishers, 2008).

23. Yoav Di-Capua, *Gatekeepers of the Arab Past: Historians and History Writing in Twentieth Century Egypt* (Los Angeles: University of California Press, 2009).

24. Charles D. Smith, "The 'Crisis of Orientation': The Shift of Egyptian Intellectuals to Islamic Subjects in the 1930s," *International Journal of Middle East Studies* 4 (1973), 382–410.

25. For a detailed biography and analysis of his major works, see Lida Andisheh, "'Abbas Iqbal Ashtiyani (1897–1956): A Study in Modern Iranian Intellectual History" (PhD dissertation, University of Utah, 1982).

26. For a study of curricular developments in Iran from the constitutional period to the end of Reza Shah's reign, see Mahmud Taher Ahmadi, "Sayr-e Tahavvol-e Barnameh-e Tahsili az Mashruteh ta Payan-e Saltanat-e Reza Shah," *Ganjineh-e Asnad* 9, nos. 35–36 (1378 Sh./1999), 30–46.

27. Ibid., 41–42.

28. For the full text of the program, see Marziyeh Yazdani, "Ta'sis-e Dar al-Mo'allemat (Daneshsara-ye Dokhtaran) va Tahsilat-e Banuvan," *Ganjineh-e Asnad* 9, nos. 35–36 (1378 Sh./1999), 70–71.

29. *Dastur-e Ta'limat-e Shesh Saleh-e Motevaseteh-e Madares-e Zokur* (Tehran: Rowshana'i, 1307 Sh./1928).

30. Ibid., 9.

31. Kemal Karpat traces the genealogy of the modern notion of civilization in the Ottoman context to reformers who used the term *medeniyet* to mean "refinement, grace, order, respect for set rules, a higher form of living" instead of the more traditional Arabic meaning of "city and city dweller." Kemal Karpat, *Ottoman Past and Today's Turkey* (Leiden: Brill, 2000), 4. The main term used in modern Arabic initially to mean civilization was also *tamaddun*, although *hadarah* and *turath* came to be more prevalent later. Joseph Massad, *Desiring Arabs* (Chicago: University of Chicago Press, 2007), 53.

32. Jurji Zaydan, *Tarikh al-Tamaddun al-Islami*, 5 vols. (Cairo: Al-Hilal, 1901–1906). For an analysis of Zaydan's historiography, particularly as it pertains to the history of the Arabs and Islam, see Thomas D. Philipp, "Approaches to History in the Work of Jurji Zaydan," *Asian and African Studies* 9, no. 1, 63–85.

33. Jurji Zaydan, *Tarikh-e Tamaddon-e Eslami*, trans. 'Abd al-Husayn Dawlatshah (Tehran, 1911). The work was translated into English four years earlier. Jurji Zaydan, *Umayyads and 'Abbasids, Being the Fourth Part of Jurji Zaydan's History of Islamic Civilization*, trans. D. S. Margoliouth (Leiden: E. J. Brill, 1907).

34. For a penetrating discussion of literary transactions, see Kamran Rastegar, *Literary Modernity between Middle East and Europe: Textual Transactions in Nineteenth-century Arabic, English, and Persian Literatures* (London: Routledge, 2007). For a discussion of the impact of Jurji Zaydan's historical novels in Persian translation, see Kamran Rastegar, "Literary Modernity between Arabic and Persian Prose: Jurji Zaydan's Riwayat in Persian Translation," *Comparative Critical Studies* 4, no. 3 (2007), 359–378.

35. Ernest Dawn, "The Formation of Pan-Arab Ideology in the Interwar Years," *International Journal of Middle East Studies* 20, no. 1 (1988), 67–91.

36. Zaydan called the period from the Caliphat al-Saffah to Mutawakkil the "Persian period," giving the following explanation: "We call this period Persian, although it comes within the 'Abbasid age because the dynasty of the time, though Arabian in

respect of its sovereigns, language, and religion, was Persian in respect of its politics and administration. The Persians won the victory for it, maintained it, organized its government, and administered its offices. Persia provided its viziers, governors, scribes, and chamberlains." Zaydan, *Umayyads and 'Abbásids, Being the Fourth Part of Jurjí Zaydán's History of Islamic Civilization*, 142.

37. Orit Bashkin, "'When Mu'awiya Entered the Curriculum'—Some Comments on the Iraqi Education System in the Interwar Period," *Comparative Education Review* 50, no. 3 (2006), 346–366.

38. 'Abd al-'Azim Qarib, *Akhbar-e Baramakeh* (Tehran: Majles, 1312 Sh./1933).

39. Mohammad 'Ali Forughi argued that classical Arabic texts by Iranian authors were part of Iranian literature. Mohammad 'Ali Forughi, *Payam-e man beh Farhangestan* (Tehran: Dabirkhaneh-e Farhangestan, 1316 Sh./1937).

40. 'Abbas Eqbal, *Dowreh-e Tarikh-e 'Omumi* (Tehran: Matba'eh-e Sa'adat, 1343 H./1925), 125.

41. 'Abbas Eqbal, *Khandan-e Nowbakhti* (Tehran: Majles, 1311 Sh./1932).

42. Ibid., yeh-dal.

43. Rula Abisaab, *Converting Persia: Religion and Power in the Safavid Empire* (London and New York: I. B. Tauris, 2004).

44. Mohammad 'Ali Forughi and Mohammad Hosayn Forughi, *Dowreh-e Ebteda'i Az Tarikh-e 'Alam* (Tehran, 1318 H./1901), 393–394.

45. Nasr Allah Falsafi, who was an active composer and translator of textbooks during the interwar period, eventually published a four-volume study of Shah 'Abbas. Nasr Allah Falsafi, *Zendegani-e Shah 'Abbas Avval*, 4 vols. (Tehran: Daneshgah-e Tehran, 1332 Sh./1953). The place of the Safavids in early Pahlavi historiography has yet to be properly studied.

46. Eqbal, *Dowreh-e Tarikh-e 'Omumi*, 105.

47. Hasan Taqizadeh, *Az Parviz ta Changiz* (Tehran: Majles, 1309 Sh./1930), 32–39.

48. 'Abd Allah Razi, *Tarikh-e Iran* (Tehran: Eqbal, 1317 Sh./1938), 343.

49. 'Ali Asghar Shamim, *Tarikh-e Iran dar Qarn-e Davazdahom va Sizdahom-e Hejri Shamel-e Dowran-e Padeshah-e Afshariyeh va Zandiyeh va Qajariyeh* (Tehran: Markazi, 1316 Sh./1937), 270–275.

CHAPTER 11

Contesting Marginality: Ethnicity and the Construction of New Histories in the Islamic Republic of Iran

TOURAJ ATABAKI

It was a dominant paradigm in the 1950s and 1960s among social scientists that modernization breaks down traditional loyalties and confronts the individual with new opportunities, depending on individual achievements in harmony with universal criteria. "As people come to desire the same goals and rewards, they become more similar. Occupational and class differences become the salient social differentiators, displacing traditional solidarities that lose their utility and are reduced to innocuous cultural vestiges; loyalties are transferred from parochial to more encompassing national symbols produced by powerful and irreversible nation-building processes."[1] Consequently, "modernization, by socially mobilizing large segments of the population, would increase both the likelihood and tempo of their assimilation."[2] According to such arguments, urbanization, industrialization, schooling, communication and transportation would lead to ultimate assimilation in the multi-ethnic societies. "A decisive factor in national assimilation or differentiation was found to be the process of social mobilization, which accompanies the growth of market, industries, and towns, and eventually of literacy and mass communication. The trends in the underlying process of social mobilization could do much to decide whether the existing national trends in particular countries would be continued or reversed."[3] However, the validity of this doctrine could be challenged if one only examines the lengthy history of practicing modernization in today's most advanced industrialized societies. Communal solidarity and ethnic particularism and cultural awareness in these societies have not vanished with the high degree of social mobilization, technological and economical integration, but rather have been modernized, articulated, and intermingled with individualism and individual autonomy, both being indispensable parts of modern man's perception of civility.

The age of modernity began with a new era when the basic unit in the structures of modern society was the individual, rather than, as with agrarian or peasant society, the group or community. Accordingly, the individualism that was embodied in the liberty and autonomy of the individual provided a new definition embracing the new association between the individual and the polity. According to this new association, the individual in a modern society, in principle at least, was no longer the subject and agent of a particular king or priest, sultan, shah, or sheikh, endowed with divine or prescriptive authority. The individual, rather, acted according to rational and impersonal precepts formulated in laws. The investiture of new juridical and political rights, including the right of representation, was indeed the conclusion of this new association. The emerging commercial and industrial urban middle class was inextricably linked to this individualism.

However, if in European society the process of modernization was associated with the gradual development and expansion of critical reason incorporated in the gradual embodiment of individual autonomy and with the emergence of a civil society, in Iran the reverse was true. There, modernization was embraced by an intelligentsia composed of bureaucrats and military officers, who identified their own interests with those of the state. The rights of the individual and his relationship with the state were of marginal rather than central significance in the eyes of Iranian modernizers, and critical reason and individual autonomy seemed to have little relevance. The main reason for such a discrepancy lay in the fact that the development of modern European societies was synchronized with, and benefited from, the age of European colonialism and imperialism and wars against the Orient. Modernization in the Middle East was a defensive reaction.

The practice of authoritarian modernization in post–First World War Iran was embedded in the perceived failure of the earlier attempts at introducing modernization from below, as well as from above, in the country. After all, the efforts of the reformers of the nineteenth century and early twentieth century had not protected the country from occupation by European powers. The setback that the Iranian Constitutional Revolution (1905-1909) suffered in the years before the outbreak of the First World War, including the political disintegration and partial occupation of Persia during the war, left the middle classes and the intelligentsia in Iran no other option than to look for a man of order, who, as an agent of the nation, would found a centralized, powerful (though not necessarily despotic) government capable of solving the country's growing economic as well as political problems, while at the same time safeguarding the nation's unity and sovereignty.

Where social egalitarianism, liberalism, and romantic territorial nationalism had inspired the earlier generations of intellectuals in their efforts to initiate change and reform throughout the country, for the postwar intelligentsia more preoccupied with the ideas of modern and centralized state-building, political authoritarianism and linguistic and cultural nationalism became the indispensable driving forces for accomplishing their aspirations.

Despite the diversity of their political views, what distinguished them from the previous educated or learned individuals was the model of society, which they took for granted. The European model of society presupposed a coherent entity, by definition organized around the distinctive concepts of nation and state. They were convinced that only a strong centralized government would be capable of implementing reform, while preserving the nation's territorial integrity. Likewise, they believed that modernization and modern state-building in Iran would require a low degree of cultural diversity and a high degree of ethnic homogeneity. Along with ethnic and linguistic diversity, the existence of classes, too, was rejected.

Reza Shah's policy of centralizing government power and implementing modernization was in a sense a reaction to this widely felt need for authoritarian reform. During his twenty-year rule (1921–1941), Reza Shah performed with stupendous consistency the realization of most of the demands voiced by such intellectuals as Kazemzadeh, Taqizadeh, and Afshar. His policy of authoritarian modernization gradually changed Iran's traditional social and political makeup. New institutions were founded, among them a national standing army based on a program of universal male conscription and extensive reserve units, a secular education curriculum and a literacy program (reading and writing in the dominant language, Persian, reducing linguistic differences), a secularized juridical system, and a national monetary system. Moreover, a centralization policy that included such harsh and disruptive measures as the forced transfer and settlement of tens of thousands of nomads was pursued to achieve greater national uniformity. However, within a couple of years of his accession, Reza Shah's dictatorship was evolving toward autocracy, and soon afterward it turned into arbitrary rule. While some intellectuals were forced to accept political retirement, there were others who were imprisoned or executed. Only a few could find a refuge in exile, unable to witness the fulfilment of their aspirations.

Reza Shah's policy of authoritarian modernization during the 1920s and 1930s, with the motto "one country, one nation," was quite similar to attempts by previous monarchs to rewrite the parameters of ethnic identity in Iran. Forced migration and resettlement of nomadic tribes continued with even greater force, this time in order to eradicate the power of tribal chieftains who posed a threat to Reza Shah's modernization program. Encouraging a homogeneous urban society was seen as the formula for modelling the image of a modern Iranian citizen. Constructing the modern nation-state was based on the assumption of unity and homogeneity, and the nation-state itself gradually became a viable entity.

Furthermore, the well-known enduring social mobility, a characteristic of Iranian social dynamics, remained in place alongside growing anti-ethnic/anti-tribal social policies, contributing to a rapid growth of economic mobility in society. Therefore, a new meritocracy was gradually formed in Iran. Every citizen, regardless of his or her ethnic origin, enjoyed the right of personal achievement in the newly established administration, as long as he or she appreciated the state's definition of Iran as a modern integrated nation-state. There was no dominant ethnic group that held all key positions at the others' expense. The country's cultural unity was considered to be paramount in Reza Shah's brand of nationalism. As a result of the Shah's educational reforms, the traditional religious *maktab-khaneh* was transformed into the modern primary schools with a curriculum taught in Persian, now Iran's national language.

Meanwhile, it was not permitted to publish books and newspapers in any language other than Persian. Moreover, to achieve greater national uniformity, Reza Shah at a later date ordered the setting up of a government office called *Sazman-e Parvaresh-e Afkar* (Department for Fostering Thought), with the task of guiding and directing the younger generation toward service to the homeland.[4] As a result, a new Iranian "high culture"—to use Gellner's phraseology—was gradually recast. Here, too, the influence of economic imperatives determined cultural and national norms. A modern economy depends on mobility and communication between individuals at a level that can only be achieved if these individuals have been socialized into high culture (i.e., the official culture of the state and its ruler), so as to be able to communicate properly. This can only be achieved by a fairly monolithic educational system. Thus, culture, not community, provides the inner sanctions. The requirements of a modern economy inevitably result in the new idea of the mutual relationship of modern culture and state.[5]

Iranian Azerbaijan and Iranian Kurdistan

In 1945, during the Second World War, the Iranian Azerbaijani Democrats, backed by the Soviet Union, called for an autonomous government and ruled the province for one year. The existence of the Soviet Socialist Republic of Azerbaijan, bearing the same name as the Iranian province of Azerbaijan, made many Iranians concerned that what really lay behind the Soviet policy was nothing less than the desire eventually to annex Iranian Azerbaijan. In the face of this lurking suspicion, many politically active Iranians who were generally in favour of greater autonomy for the provinces were reluctant to lend their unconditional support to the Azerbaijani Democrats. In their minds, the Azerbaijan Democrats' call for regional autonomy was associated with the nightmare scenario of Azerbaijan's secession from Iran.[6]

Almost simultaneously with the activities of the Azerbaijani Democrats, the Iranian Kurds launched their own campaign for establishing an autonomous state in Iranian Kurdistan, which paradoxically called itself the Republic of Kurdistan.[7] In view of the deeply rooted tribal nature of society in the region, the campaign for autonomy in Kurdistan was based more on ethnotribal loyalties than on a purely ethnic identity, as in Azerbaijan. The destiny of the Republic of Kurdistan was no different from that of its neighbors in Azerbaijan. After one year of rule, by the time of the withdrawal of the Soviet Army from Iran, both provinces returned to the Iranian central government, which practiced the utmost viciousness in castigating the provinces for their local political activism.

In the years following the Second World War, as Iran's geopolitical location and national resources made the West aware of the importance of its territorial integrity, the country went through a major socioeconomic transformation. The process of rapid urbanization and industrialization caused some degree of ethnic dislocation throughout Iran. In the capital, Tehran, as in almost all of the country's big cities, Azerbaijanis formed a strong community, dominating the local economy. Tehran's Azeri population even exceeded in size that of Tabriz, the most populous Azerbaijani city. Furthermore, the expansion of education and communication for the most part contributed to a more homogeneous culture in Iran. This tendency towards homogeneity on the social, political, and cultural level may be seen to have culminated in the Islamic Revolution of 1979.

The Islamic Revolution and the Question of Ethnic Minorities

Social and political unrest with an ethnic flavor was common during the 1978–1982 revolution, which finally ended with the founding of the Islamic Republic in Iran. The revolts in Kurdistan and Turkmensahra in early 1979, which in the case of Kurdistan lasted for another six years, the political unrest in Khuzestan and Baluchistan in mid-1979, and the political uprising in Azerbaijan in late 1979 and early 1980 were the major cases of ethnic unrest that the new regime faced in its early days of formation. However, all these rebellions were exclusively founded and organized by local political activists affiliated with local or national political organizations, and there were barely any references to nonorganized elite participation.

The early stance of the Islamic government on the question of ethnicity and ethnic diversity was heard during the vociferous debates over the country's new Constitution in the Assembly of Experts (*Majles-e Khobregan*). Article 15 of the Constitution acknowledges Iran's ethnic diversity and the ethnic communities' fundamental rights to preserve their distinctive identities and cultures: "The official language and script of Iran, the lingua franca of its people, is Persian. Official documents, correspondence, and texts, as well as textbooks, must be in this language and script. However, the use of regional and tribal languages in the press and mass media, as well as for teaching of their literature in schools, is allowed in addition to Persian."[8] Following the ratification of the Islamic Republic's Constitution, Ayatollah Khomeini in a statement addressed the ethnic minorities' question in Iran in the following words:

Sometimes the word minorities is used to refer to people such as the Kurds, Lurs, Turks, Persian, Baluchis, and such. These people should not be called minorities, because this term assumes that there is a difference between these brothers. In Islam, such a difference has no place at all. There is no difference between Muslims who speak different languages, for instance, the Arabs or the Persians. It is very probable that such problems have been created by those who do not wish the Muslim countries to be united. . . . They create the issues of nationalism, of pan-Iranism, pan-Turkism, and such isms, which are contrary to Islamic doctrines. Their plan is to destroy Islam and the Islamic philosophy.[9]

The outbreak of the eight-year war with Iraq in 1980 had far-reaching consequences for cultural harmony in Iran. Forced migration and population dislocation on a large scale, unknown in modern Iranian history, refashioned Iranian identity within the national territory. While for the Iranian Islamic establishment the dominant ideology of war was the contest between devotion and desertion (*haq va batel*), for the majority of Iranians, especially those elites outside the Islamic establishment, the war with Iraq was nothing but the repetition of a foreign invasion of the kind they remembered from their past, i.e., the irredentist policy practiced by alien powers threatening the country's territorial integrity. Consequently, national unity and Iranian territorial identity were given priority over the nation's ethnic diversity and their distinctive identities and rights. During the eight-year war with Iraq, with the exception of a few ethnically oriented armed groups based beyond the western Iranian frontiers and functioning in the border regions, one finds no traces of any references to the ethnic challenges threatening Iranian territoriality, or any call for preserving or promoting ethnic identities in an individual or collective form.

However, by the end of the war in 1988, and during the period of "reconstruction" and partial liberalization of the presidency of Rafsanjani (1989–1997), the notion of ethnic rights gradually entered into the general discourse of individualism, individual autonomy, and citizenship, which was the preoccupation of the reforming circles. This pattern became even more vivid during the reign of President Khatami (1997–2005), exposing the interconnections between the question of citizenship and individual rights, including the rights of ethnic minorities in contemporary Iran.

The most articulated manifestation of such interconnectedness was the rapid increase in the number of books and periodicals published in ethnic languages since 1990. According to my own survey, during the presidencies of Rafsanjani and Khatami the number of books published in Azeri Turkish reached 460 titles with a circulation of up to 920,000 copies, while during the same period there were 78 periodicals published either in Azeri-Turkish or in Azeri-Persian bilingual form. For the Kurdish language, these figures increased to 708 book titles, with a total circulation of 1,416,000 copies, as well as 21 periodicals.

It was, indeed, during this period that writing on ethnic groups' distant past gradually became an intellectual enterprise engaging a large number of ethnic minorities' intellectuals. Writing ethnic history has developed into a persuasive political project, shaping a significant and unbroken link with each ethnic group's constructed past, aiming to fill the gap between the ethnic group's origin and its actuality. Books on local geography and ethnic history comprise the majority of these publications. Discovering and constructing both the immediate and distant past has become the preoccupation of large segments of the intelligentsia, whose aim was to refer to history in order to legitimize their call for autonomy and equal rights for their corresponding ethnic groups. However, the most concerted steps taken by certain ethnic groups, such as the Azeris, was the endeavor of a local intelligentsia to link their scholarly efforts with the political culture, and to refashion the latter accordingly.

Rewriting Ethnic-Local Histories

In 1999, Muhammad Taqi Zahtabi (1923–1998), an Azerbaijani linguist, published his two volumes of *The Ancient History of Iranian Turks* (*Iran Turklerinin eski tarikhi*). Zahtabi, as a follower of the Azerbaijan Democrat Party

(Azarbayjan Dimokrat Firqasi), fled to the Soviet Union in 1948, following the fall of the Party's one-year rule (1945–1946) in Azerbaijan. On arrival in the Soviet Union, he was arrested, charged with illegal border crossing, and sentenced to jail. After spending three years in a Siberian prison camp, he finally reached Baku, where he studied Turkic philology. During the 1978–1982 Iranian Revolution, he returned to Tabriz and lived there until his death in 1998. Zahtabi published a number of books on Azerbaijani philology and literature; however, his main publication was *The Ancient History of Iranian Turks*.

In this work, Zahtabi covers the history, geography, and philology of the northwestern region of Iran and the region north of the Araxes River from the "earliest time" to the Islamic period. The first volume, in 880 pages, covers the "earliest time to Alexander"; the second volume, in 696 pages, the "Alexander era to Islam." In the first volume, by criticizing the prevailing Iranian historiography, Zahtabi argues that, in ancient times as well as today, three groups of people lived on the Iranian plateau: "the Turks, the Aryans and the Semitic peoples"[10] and "during the pre-Islamic period, as well as in the Islamic time, the majority of rulers of the plateau were Turks."[11] The ancestors of the Turks lived in "southern and northern Azerbaijan before the arrival of the Aryans."[12] Subsequently, he adds that, by gradual migration of the Altaic people from Central Asia, the local Turks were able to consolidate their distinctive identity, and finally formed the Parthian dynasty.[13] However, the "Sassanian dynasty, by practicing Persian chauvinism, wiped out all sources relating to the culture and history of Turks in Iran."[14] Moreover, the Sassanian kings in general, and Khosraw Anushirvan in particular, by adopting a "mandatory migration policy, deporting Persian communities to Azerbaijan and driving out the Azerbaijan local population from Azerbaijan" endeavored to change the demography of Azerbaijan.[15] While praising Parthian rule for political tolerance and acknowledgment of local and ethnic autonomy, Zahtabi accuses the Sassanian rulers of "adopting and sustaining the most authoritarian and vicious rule," imposing "the superiority of Persians," and denying "the national rights of non-Persians."[16] Nevertheless, contrary to all these measures, according to Zahtabi, in the Sassanian period, "while the state languages in Azerbaijan remained Persian, the people's language stayed on as Azeri Turkish, the father of today's Azeri of Azerbaijan."[17] Zahtabi extends all his arguments not only to the region south of the Araxes River, but also to the Caucasian Albania and Arran, which he often refers to as "Northern Azerbaijan."[18]

Ultimately, while Zahtabi blames the Persians for their incompetence in upholding Iranian sovereignty, he praises the Azerbaijan Turks for leading the peoples of the Iranian plateau, including the Persians, to secure the country's integrity whenever it was occupied by neighboring empires.[19] His pre-Islamic example is the "Parthian Turks," who put an end to the rule of Macedonian Seleucids, and for the Islamic period he names Babak Khurrami, who stood against Baghdad and "demonstrated the susceptibility of the Islamic Caliphate."[20]

In the conclusion of his work, Zahtabi, by labeling Ahmad Kasravi, the Azerbaijani historian, as a pan-Iranist, accuses him of founding the theoretical ground for the Pahlavis' Persian chauvinism and imposing the superiority of Aryans to the non-Aryan inhabitants of Iran. According to Zahtabi, one even could see the continuity of the Pahlavis' national policy in the present Islamic Republic of Iran.[21]

Construction Memory and Selective Amnesia in Ethnic-Local Historiography

Zahtabi in his historical claims shows reluctance in giving sources for his arguments, except for the Parthian period. His reference to the Parthians is heavily dependent on narrative accounts given by Muhammad Hasan Khan E'temad al-Saltaneh. In *Durr al-Tijan fi Tarikh bani Ashkan*,[22] first published in Tehran in 1891 and 1892, during the reign of Naser al-Din Shah Qajar, E'temad al-Saltaneh argues that the Parthians, being of Turkic origin, pioneered the establishment of Turkic rule on the Iranian plateau, which, according to E'temad al-Saltaneh, persisted until the Qajar dynasty. Zahtabi, by referring to E'temad al-Saltaneh's book, shares his argument and conclusion.

With regard to other periods, or the geography of the region of north and south of the Araxes River, Zahtabi's study suffers from referential deficiencies. For example, he never refers to the accounts of renowned historians and travelers such as Ibn Faqih, Ibn Hawqal al-Muqaddasi, Ibn al-Nadim, Masudi, or al-Istakhri. On the geography of Azerbaijan, contrary to the claim of Zahtabi that Azerbaijan always lay both south and north of the Caucasus, the geographer Ibn Faqih describes Azerbaijan as being bounded to the south by Zanjan and to the east by Diylamistan, Tarum, and Gilan. To the west lay Varasan or Varadan, and the Araxes River formed the northern limit of the region.[23] Moreover, the anonymous tenth-century geographical work *Hudud al-Alam* refers to the region north of the Araxes as Arran.[24] The Araxes River is clearly taken to be the northernmost limit of Azerbaijan. Likewise, Ibn Hawqal considers the Araxes River to form the southernmost border of the region of Arran.[25] To this, one may add the remark of another tenth-century traveler, al-Muqaddasi, who divides the land of Iran into eight regions (including Arran and Azerbaijan).[26]

On the early language of the inhabitants of Azerbaijan, there are references in sharp contradiction to Zahtabi's claim that the language of Azerbaijanis in the early Islamic period was Turkish. However, the early reference to the language of Azerbaijan in the Islamic period dates back to the eighth century. Ibn al-Nadim, quoting Ibn al-Muqaffaʿ, refers to the language of Azerbaijan as Fahlawi (al-fahlawiya).[27] Fahlawi was related to Fahla or Pahla, a region comprising Azerbaijan, Ray, Hamadan, Mah, Nahavand, and Isfahan. In the tenth century, Masʿudi, who visited Tabriz in 926, refers to Azeri as a language belonging to the Iranian language family.[28] Another traveler of the tenth century, al-Istakhri, refers to the language of the Azerbaijanis as "Persian and Arabic," but he adds that "the people of the outlying districts of the Barda'a north of the Araxes River speak Arrani."[29] In the thirteenth century, six centuries after the conquest of Azerbaijan by the Muslim Arabs, according to Yaqut, along with Persian and Arabic the inhabitants of Azerbaijan spoke a language that was called *Azariyyah*.[30] The gradual disappearance of Azeri as a major Iranian language spoken by the population of Azerbaijan was the consequence of the penetration of Turkish into the region.

The Turkic language entered the region of Azerbaijan as a result of the great migration of Turks into Asia Minor in the eleventh century. The first group of Oghuz Turks arrived in 1029. Again in 1044, some 5,000 Turkmens returned to Azerbaijan from Mesopotamia through Diyarbakir and Armenia and occupied the town of Khoy. However, what may be considered as the conclusive event took place in 1054 when Tughrul Beg, the eminent Seljuk warlord, arrived in Azerbaijan and Arran to receive the submission of the local rulers. The language that these newcomers brought with them was that of the southwestern (Oghuz) group of Turkic languages. The new language, though strongly influenced by its close encounter with the language of indigenous Azeri, gradually replaced the latter and came to be the dominant language of Azerbaijan.

Zahtabi finishes his work with some remarks on the early "Turkish rebellion" against the Islamic Caliphate. He singles out Babak Khurramdin as the most renowned leader of such rebellions. The Muslim Arab conquest of Azerbaijan dates back to the seventh century when the Arab army, following its victories on the western frontier of Persia during the caliphate of ʿUmar, marched toward the north and between AD 639 and 643 succeeded in conquering Azerbaijan. However, ruling Azerbaijan soon became an intricate task for the new army. In *Futuh al-Buldan* there are references to a number of uprisings when the people of Azerbaijan resisted the Arab Muslim rule in the region. In one of these uprisings, which ended with the conclusion of a peace treaty between the Arab commander representing the Caliph and the Azerbaijani satrap, the Arab army had guaranteed to refrain from demolishing the fire temples in the province and acknowledging the right of Azerbaijanis to practice their religious and communal ceremonies and to celebrate with festivals.[31]

Following the Arab conquest, some Arab commanders ruled different parts of Azerbaijan; however, they all remained loyal to the Caliphate of Baghdad. It was only after the revolt of Babak Khurramdin, a neo-Mazdakite leader, against the Abbasid Caliphate, which started in 816 and 817 and lasted over twenty years, that the rule of the Baghdad Caliphate gradually diminished in Azerbaijan. For the next two centuries, until the arrival of the Seljuk Turks in the eleventh century, Azerbaijan was mostly ruled by local dynasties, and, with semi-autonomous status, from Baghdad.

Babak's somewhat sensational and legendary campaign has been discussed extensively in some well-known classics such as Ibn al-Nadim's *al-Fihrist*, al-Muqaddasi's *Ahsan al-Taqasim fi Ma'rift al-Aqalim*, Nezam al-Mulk's *Siyasat-nameh*, Abd al-Qahir Baghdadi's *al-Farq bayn al-Firaq*, Mas'udi's *Al-Tanbih wa al-Ishraf* and *Muruj al-Zahab*, Ya'qubi's *Tarikh Ya'qubi* and Abu Hanifeh Dinvari's *Akhbar al-Taval*, a work by a contemporary of Babak. One of the most detailed accounts of Babak's revolt may be found in *Akhbar Babak* by Waqid Ibn-'Amr Tamimi, which is quoted by Ibn al-Nadim's *al-Fihrist*.[32] However, while in none of these accounts is there a reference to Babak being a Turk, there are frequent references to there being many Turkic commanders in the army of the Abbasid caliph fighting against Babak.

From Historiography to Political Culture

It was during the first term of Mohammad Khatami's presidency that a tradition was invented in Azerbaijan known as praising and revering the Fort of Baz (Qal'eh-e Baz). Kalibar is a mountainous township one hundred and fifty kilometers northeast of Tabriz. In the south of Kalibar are the remnants of the ruins of an ancient fort, known as the Fort of Baz. According to Islamic historians, the fort was the bastion of Babak and his followers, who fought over twenty years in the early ninth century against the Abbasid Caliphate (750–1258 AD).

It was Mohammad Taqi Zahtabi who, by revealing Babak's identity as an Azeri Turk, inspired the Azerbaijanis to celebrate his memory by honoring and revering the Fort of Baz, now called the Fort of Babak, every year during the first week of summer. Gradually, the worship turned into a kind of public picnic or carnival when a large number of Azerbaijanis from all parts of the province started to congregate in the Fort of Babak to celebrate his alleged birth date. Although the leisure aspect of this congregation has been dominant, nevertheless, the amplified performance of Azeri music and dances not only dispenses with the government's general ban on the public performance of music and dance, but also it fashions a type of communal solidarity underscored more than anything else by a new sense of Azeriness. In other words, such festivities have developed into a manifestation of the juxtaposition of the individual and individual autonomy with the aspiration of promoting a collective identity distinguishing the Azeris from the neighboring peoples. Surely, through this event one could also trace unambiguous political schemes demanding the right of Azeris to have access to education in their mother tongue or for greater autonomy for the regional administration. Sometimes in presenting such a political scheme one could see a link to the status of the neighbouring Republic of Azerbaijan, which has been enjoying sovereignty following the fall of the Soviet Union.

In the early twentieth century, and following the process of crafting Iranian national identity, Babak's affiliation to Zoroastrianism and his strong anti-Arab and anti-Islamic attitude made him an icon of Iranian national awareness. However, it was during the reign of the ayatollahs that Babak was championed for the cause he might never have even fought for: shielding Iranian territorial integrity by promoting Iranian pre-Islamic cultures and values. Furthermore, Babak's attachment to Azerbaijan made him not only an agent of the Iranian motherland, but also a guardian of Azeri ethnicity. It was indeed the latter facet of Babak's crafted celebrity that made him an icon of Azeri desire for collective recognition.

Conclusion

Twentieth-century Iran has mostly succeeded in avoiding the fate which befell the Ottoman and Tsarist, and later the Soviet, empires. Its territorial integrity was sustained, and its different ethnic groups more or less got along. Nonetheless, in postrevolutionary Iran, calls for reform in the country's political structure to secure individual rights as well as collective rights in nondiscriminatory inclusion and access to economic opportunities and political participation have been associated with the call by ethnic minorities for equal cultural status and language recognition through some pattern of group proportionality. The recent local historiography to a large extent aims to address this call.

Notes

1. Milton J. Esman and Itamar Rabinovich, eds., *Ethnicity, Pluralism, and the State in the Middle East* (Ithaca: Cornell University Press, 1988), 14–15.

2. Walker Connor, "Nation-Building or Nation-Destroying?" *World Politics* 14 (1972), 323.

3. Karl Wolfgang Deutsch, *Nationalism and Social Communication; an Inquiry into the Foundations of Nationality* (Cambridge, MA: The Technology Press of MIT, 1953), quoted by Connor, "Nation-Building," 323.

4. Hossein Makki, *Tarikh-e bist saleh-e Iran*, vol. 6 (Tehran: Nashr Nashr, 1983), 412–413.

5. Ernest Gellner, *Nation and Nationalism* (Oxford: Blackwell, 1983), 140.

6. For a detailed study of the Autonomous Government of *Azerbaijan, see Touraj Atabaki, Azerbaijan: Ethnicity and the Struggle for Power in Iran* (London and New York: I. B Tauris, 1993).

7. On the history of the Kurdish autonomous movement in the post–Second World War period, the best study available in English is still William Eagleton, *The Kurdish Republic of 1946* (London: Oxford University Press, 1963). See also A. Roosevelt, "The Kurdish Republic of Mahabad," *Middle East Journal* 1 (1947), 247–269.

8. The Constitution of the Islamic Republic of Iran (Tehran: Islamic Consultative Assembly, no date), 33.

9. British Broadcasting Cooperation (BBC), Summary of World broadcasts, Middle East and Africa, 19 December 1979.

10. Muhammad Taqi Zahtabi, *Iran Turklerinin Eski Tarikhi*, 2 vols. (Tabriz: Kargah Sabz, 1999)

11. Ibid., vol. I, 7.

12. Ibid., vol. I, 171.

13. Ibid., vol. II, 57–72.

14. Ibid., vol. I, 28–29, vol. II, 622.

15. Ibid., vol. II, 468–469.

16. Ibid., vol. II, 470–471, 619–620, 632.

17. Ibid., vol. II, 627.

18. Ibid., vol. II, 628, 631, 651.

19. Ibid., vol. II, 570.

20. Ibid., vol. II, 570–571.

21. Ibid., vol. II, 674.

22. Muhammad Hasan Khan Eʿtimad al-Saltanah, *Dorr al-Tijan fi Tarikh bani Ashkan* (Tehran: Atlas, 1992).

23. Ibn Faqih, Abu Bakr Ahmad b. Muhammad b. Ishaq Hamadani, *Kitab al-buldan* (Tehran: Bonyad Farhang Iran, 1970), 128.

24. Anonymous, author, M. Sotudeh, ed., *Hudud al-ʿAlam min al-Mashriq ila al-Maghrib* (Tehran: Daneshgah Tehran, 1962), 50.

25. Ibn Hawqal, author, J. Shoʿar, ed., *Surat al-Arz* (Tehran: Bonyad Farhang Iran, 1966), 82.

26. Shams al-Din b. Abi ʿAbdullah Muhammad b. Abi Bakr al-Muqaddasi, author, M. J. de Goeje, ed., *Ahsan al-Taqasim fi Mʿarifat al-Aqalim* (Leiden: Brill, 1906), 259.

27. Ibn al-Nadim, *al-Fihrist* (Cario: n.p., n.d), 13.

28. 'Ali Ibn Hussein al-Mas'udi, author, M. J. de Goeje, ed., *Al-Tanbih wa al-Ishraf* (Leiden: Brill, 1893), 78.

29. Abu Ishaq al-Farsi al-Istakhri, author, M. J. de Goeje ed., *Kitab al-Masalik wa al-Mamalik* (Leiden: Brill, 1927), 191–192.

30. Abu 'Abdullah Yaqut, author, F. Wüstenfeld, ed., *Mu'jam al-Buldan*, I (Leipzig: Brockhaus, 1866), 173.

31. Ahmad b. Yahya Baladhuri, *Futuh al-Buldan* (Cairo: Maktab al-Nahda al-Misriyya, 1956), 400–406.

32. Ibn-Nadim, Muhamamd Ibn-Ishaq, *al-Fihrist*, Tajaddod Mazandarani, Mohammad Reza, trans., 2nd ed. (Tehran: Ibn Sina, 1967), 611. For the other references, see Shams al-Din b. Abi 'Abdullah Muhammad b. Abi Bakr al-Muqaddasi, author, M. J. de Goeje, ed., *Ahsan al-Taqasim fi Ma'rifat al-Aqalim* (Leiden: Brill, 1906); Nizam al-Mulk, Hasan Ibn-'Ali, *Siyasat-Nameh* (Tehran: Asatir, 1996); Abd al-Qahir al-Baghdadi, *al-Farq bain al-Firaq*, Mashkour, Muhammad Javad, trans. Title changed to *Tarikh Mazaheb-e Islam* (Tehran: Amir Kabir, 1965); 'Ali Ibn Hussein al-Mas'udi, author, M. J. de Goeje, ed., *Al-Tanbih wa al-ishraf* (Leiden: Brill, 1893), Mas'udi, Abulhasan 'Ali Ibn-Hussein, *Muruj al-zahab*, Abolqasim Payandah, trans., 3rd ed. (Tehran: Entesharat 'Elmi va Farhangi, 1986); Ahmad Ibn-Ishaq Ya'qubi, *Tarikh Ya'qubi* (Leiden: Brill, 1883); Abu Hanifeh Ahmad Ibn-Davud Dinvari, *Akhbar al-Taval*, Mahmud Mahdavi Damghani, trans., (Tehran: Nashr Now, 1986).

CHAPTER 12

Return of the Avant-Garde
to the Streets of Tehran

TALINN GRIGOR

Beginning in the early 1920s, under the auspices of the Pahlavi Dynasty, the tombs of selected historical figures were systematically destroyed to make way for a new kind of architecture that signaled secular nationalism. Initiated during the reign of Reza Shah, all but two of the projects were implemented under Mohammad Reza Shah. The monuments were ideologically inscribed commemorations of the political elite of the 1920s, who not only made up the first Pahlavi government, but also founded, in 1922, the Society for National Heritage (SNH, *anjoman-e asar-e melli*) with the aim of preserving and propagating Iran's cultural patrimony.[1] Within a matter of a few years, they managed to conceive and define the political as well as cultural parameters of modern Iran as a nation-state that upheld a particular ideology of nationalism. Architecture, from the outset, was a pivotal aspect of this complex undertaking. It not only reflected, but projected a specific secularist, modernist, and nationalist conception of the Iranian nation. The nation-state that the political elite left behind, despite cosmetic modifications, has remained unchanged to the present day. The endurance of a particular kind of nationalism formulated in the late nineteenth and early twentieth centuries by a small group of secular reformists, and the association of that nationalism with a particular (avant-garde) aesthetic, is at the heart of my argument.

During the six decades that followed, these men and their successors proceeded to construct forty mausoleums, carried out sixty preservation projects, tabulated an index of historical heritage, abolished the French monopoly over Iran's archeological sites, and established a national museum and a public library. The major architectural projects undertaken by the SNH included the mausoleum of the poet Ferdowsi in Tus (1934), designed by French archeologist and architect André Godard; the tomb-garden of the poet Hafez in Shiraz (1938), designed by French architect Maxime Siroux; the burial and museum complex of philosopher-scientist Ibn Sina (Avicenna) in Hamadan (1952), by Iranian architect Houshang Seyhoun; the tomb-memorial of poet Omar Khayyam in Neshapur (1934 and 1963), again as per Seyhoun's proposal; and the joint tombs of American art historians Phyllis Ackerman and Arthur Upham Pope in Isfahan (1972), designed by Iranian architect Mohsen Forughi. The mausoleums of Sa'di, Nader Shah, Reza Shah, Shaykh Farid al-Din Attar, Mohammad Ghaffari Kamal al-Molk, Shah Shoja', Imam Mohammad Mahruq, and Baba-Taher were also erected or renovated under the auspices of the SNH over the decades. The unprecedented scope, diversity, and systemacity of these activities were bolstered by numerous publications, lectures, exhibitions, and the invention of a tourist trade, as well as the very idea of national patrimony. Avant-garde architecture, despite political shifts, remained tied to this secularist and modernist conception of the nation. After the Iranian Revolution of 1978–1979, this association had deep ramifications both in the domains of art and culture and the politics of identity and power.

The significance of Pahlavi architecture lay not only in the way it instigated fundamental strategies of modernization, but also in the way that it formulated a discourse on the secular national domain of temporal "befores" and "afters." Despite their simplicity, the monuments incorporated a complex range of state-imposed civic practices, whereby architecture became a vital aspect of public instruction and middle-class leisure. Autopsies of remains stood as proof of the racial superiority of the nation, while the adjoining museums validated the logic of its display. The construction process harbored technically sophisticated documentation, categorization, and homogenization of the public sphere. Each monument's presence in provincial towns not only instigated superficial revitalization of otherwise minor cities, but also dictated secular social behavior in overwhelmingly religious regions. These projects also provided a platform for Western scholars, among whom were German archeologist and architect Ernst Herzfeld as well as Godard and Pope, to negotiate their conflicting personal and colonial ambitions as well as their quarrels over techniques of preservation, authenticity of heritage, and ownership of archaeological sites. Above all, what these monuments did was to present to Iranians a new national map upon which the old Shi'a routes of *ziyarat* (pilgrimage) were utilized and obscured by the new secular sites of national pilgrimage.[2] Religious pilgrimage became national tourism.

Proper modern behavior and forms of sociability previously not tolerated in these sites, which included former middle-of-nowhere locations like Ferdowsiyeh, former cemeteries like Hafeziyeh, or former *emamzadehs* like Khayyam's tomb-garden, now became the privileged norm. For the growing middle class that adhered to a modernistic aesthetic in their taste and looks, to pose and be photographed in these secular spaces was not only to feel and be modern, but was also to contribute to the modernity of the nation (figs. 12.1 and 12.2). The court and the state endorsed these social behaviors and taste in practice and in looks. While none of these tomb projects were "modernistic" in style or iconography, at least not in the strict art-historical definition of the term, they did serve modern structures of knowledge, organization, and experience. They each aimed to work as national heritage, which had to be read as venerable and timeless like the image of the monarchy that they re-flected and enhanced. Whereas they were implemented as a part of the larger project of modernization—in fact, they *were* the project of modernity—they were not intended to be deciphered as modernistic. The Pahlavi state compen-sated for this in other areas of architectural practice. Key structures, such as the White Palace (1936) by Khorsandi and Tatevosian, the House of Senate (1955) by Heydar Ghiaï, the Mehrabad Airport (1958) by Mohsen Forughi, the Museum of Contemporary Art (1977) and the Namaz Khaneh (prayer house, 1978) by Kamran Diba, were a handful of examples of the kind of avant-garde that was sponsored by the state, modernistic and minimalistic in temperament and intent (fig. 12.3 and fig. 12.4). Pahlavi architecture thus fashioned novel ways to map civic space, national time, and secular identity, in that it not only reflected but affected sociopolitical developments until the dawn of the Iranian Revolution of 1978–1979.

When in June 1978 Empress Farah decreed the allocation of $2 million for the squatters of southern Tehran, it was already too late, despite some liberal royalists who continue to believe that her regency could save the monarchy.[3] A week later, she made another attempt to demonstrate the monarchy's com-mitment to both Islam and Iran by first making a "pilgrimage to Imam Reza Shrine" and then inaugurating the fourth festival of Tus, where, for a last time, "efforts were made to revive the Persian language, Iranian nationalism, and . . . forgotten traditions."[4] To legitimize its existence, the royal house, it seems, was turning to both Imam Reza and Ferdowsi through the mediation of their resting places, for these had been pivotal sites around which so much of Pah-lavi history had revolved. Nevertheless, by then, no amount of urban planning or cultural engineering, however avant-garde, could prevent the toppling of the regime. The (re)presentation of a harmonious marriage between the Shiʻi shrine and the poet's mausoleum in Tus, as signifiers of Iranian identity, was belated. Any subsequent attempt to stop a revolution through architecture ended in failure. Not only had the people chosen revolution over architecture; they had co-opted architecture in their revolution.

Much of what really happened to official architecture during the fervor of the revolution is based on ruminations without much evidence: Bulldozers

Figure 12.1. An Iranian tourist on the steps of the new mausoleum-garden of Hafez, Shiraz, 1954. Courtesy of Seda Hovnanian.

Figure 12.2. A group of local tourists in front of the modern mausoleum of Sa'di, Shiraz, 1950s. Courtesy of Farah al-Moluk Fazel al-Araghi.

were at the gates of Persepolis, the Golestan Museum was raided, and the SNH's mausoleums were vandalized. As had not been the case in either either the French or the Russian revolutions, the deposed ruling family's palaces, museums, and important sites of national heritage had remained practically intact throughout the revolutionary upheaval. As violence erupted in the streets in September 1978, Mohammad Reza Shah ordered his armed forces to protect all such establishments throughout the country. After his departure four months later, the king's last prime minister, Shahpur Bakhtiar, the first prime minister of the Islamic Republic, Mehdi Bazargan, and Imam Khomeini himself upheld the same policy towards these sites until civil order was restored. Art belonged to the nation and had to be protected; nor was the civilian population much prone to violence toward artworks and edifices, except toward statues and portraits of the king and the royal family. Despite their animosity toward other visions of the nation, these men and their followers agreed on the sanctity of Iran's cultural heritage as a national wealth. When the Islamic Republic established itself as the sole successor to the revolution, the imam pushed for the reestablishment of the rule of law and public ordinance. By 1982, the Cultural Revolution intended to replace the "Pahlavi man" with the "Islamic man" was in full swing. It was an aesthetic project

Figure 12.3. Khorsandi and Tatevosian, White Palace, Sadabad Royal Complex, Tehran, 1936. Photo by author.

Figure 12.4. Kamran Diba, Namaz Khaneh, Farah Park, Tehran, 1978. Photo by author.

of representational replacement; the replacement of the Pahlavi avant-garde with a populist kitsch that could speak to the masses. While the government marginalized Iran's pre-Islamic artistic traditions as both an ideological reaction to and a methodological imitation of the shah's regime, it conducted an active policy of neglect toward Pahlavi sites. The pre-Islamic history, along with the Pahlavi era, was portrayed as the "age of ignorance," "time of despotic kings," and "era of plunder."[5] Both historical and modern edifices were (re)read as reminders of royal excess and class oppression.

The first generation of avant-garde artists and architects, even those who had participated in the revolutionary struggle, was marginalized. Any former association with Pahlavi culture was detrimental. The avant-garde was to be shunned. The core of Iranian modern and contemporary art was thus severed, precisely because the boundaries of avant-garde art and the Pahlavi construct of monarchy and modernity was indistinguishable. Despite his conservative and often regressive style of rulership, Mohammad Reza Shah projected the image of a revolutionary monarch at the vanguard of social change. His 1963 White Revolution (also known as the Shah-People Revolution) that included his many corps (i.e., Literacy, Health, and later Religion), his Worker's Act, his Women's Suffrage Act, his free and compulsory education for all, and his generous patronage of modernistic megaprojects were aspects of this avant-garde image making. While in the Russian case, the steady decline of the Romanov dynasty had opened up a public space between the 1905 and the 1917 revolutions for the avant-garde to come to fruition, in Iran the Pahlavi dynasty fell abruptly. Supported by the Pahlavi state, Iranian avant-garde art reached its zenith in the late 1960s. However, by the early 1970s, it was pressured to conform to Pahlavi ideological limits. In light of the centralization of power in the hands of a few throughout the 1970s, there was neither an ideological nor a public space for the maturation of the avant-garde that would instigate or, at the very least, represent political revolt. Therefore, when the revolutionary momentum began, the avant-garde, with a few sporadic exceptions in poster design, was unable to muster a dissenting philosophy and aesthetic of its own. Nor did the empress's personal commitment to avant-garde art help the revolutionary intentions of individual artists. In 1978 and 1979, when the intelligentsia, the professional middle class, the students, the ʿulama, and even the Pahlavi bureaucrats and army rose against the monarchy, the avant-garde's time had lapsed. With only a handful of exceptions, well-known artists and architects followed the royal family into exile.

The destruction of the Pahlavi ethos, one that both kings and their cultural institutions such as the SNH had meticulously cultivated since 1922, and the replacement of it with an Islamic-Shiʿi cultural aesthetic was one, if not the most significant, goal of the Iranian (Cultural) Revolution. Imam Khomeini was clear about this from the outset. He was the first among his peers, as Afsaneh Najmabadi notes, to remark on the collision course that the project of nation-building and Islamic institutions was set against.[6] As early as 1941 in his *Kashf al-asrar* (Uncovering the Secrets), he voiced concern over cultural decadence as a cause of moral corruption and the erosion of Iranian identity. He held Reza Shah's Ministry of Culture and Art responsible for this malaise. The anxiety over cultural decadence was reflected in the persistent urgency he placed on control over cultural self-representation throughout his long political life. In his September 1964 speech in Qom, the imam warned the Pahlavi court that without cultural autonomy no political reform would be possible, concluding with a characteristic ultimatum, "You should create an independent culture" or "give us [*ulama*] control over culture."[7]

When the Cultural Revolution was initiated, however, Imam Khomeini's statements revealed that his understanding of "culture" was anthropological, rather than art-historical. The policies to Islamize Iran—the mandatory Islamic dress code, the segregation of the sexes, the state's encouragement of religious pilgrimage (*ziyarat*) that the Pahlavis had discouraged, the diminished role of women in public and private life, the new marriage regulations, and the conversion of non-Muslims to Islam—are characterized by an anthropological understanding of culture, while the banning of Western music, dance, and art were coincidences of an anticolonial agenda integral to the larger revolutionary goals. His April 1980 speech at Tehran University, entitled "The Meaning of the Cultural Revolution," rendered this distinction plain.[8] Imam Khomeini explained to the students that "Islamization of the university" meant the pursuit of knowledge in such a manner as to strengthen the "needs of the nation," not, as many rumored, the Islamization of subject matter. It aimed to build cultural and educational institutions "autonomous, independent of the West" and "the East."[9] Science was to remain scientific. While elsewhere he encouraged artists to produced "committed art" and while the arts were the first to be affected by this second wave of revolution, the strictly art-historical definition of culture seems to have been absent from Imam Khomeini's philosophy and vision of an Islamic and a republican Iran.[10] This ambiguity pushed the visual to the center of power politics and at once created a chasm between kitsch and avant-garde art. For without any guidelines, nor even an art-historical definition of culture, art's role, function, and form in this new republic were left to others to negotiate. This was often done literally. Diba's Namaz Khaneh in Farah Park, for instance, was replaced by another, Islamized Namaz Khaneh in the renamed Laleh Park. As in all

Figure 12.5. Architect unknown, Namaz Khaneh, Laleh Park, Tehran, ca. 1985, destroyed in the 1990s. Photo by author.

things kitsch, the architecture was a formulaic recreation of an established style, and the architect was nameless (fig. 12.5).

The rejection of the avant-garde and the official adoption of a populist kitsch aesthetic had an important sociopolitical role. Throughout the 1980s, the revolution and the Iran-Iraq War had given the public propaganda art of the street a purpose: without the successful mobilization of the masses to the frontline, Iran might have fallen into pieces or, worse, been overrun by Saddam Hussein, or by the Soviets, or by the Taliban, etc. The propaganda art also effectively perpetuated the revolutionary spirit and validated the Islamic Republic (figs. 12.6 and 12.7). In the Second Republic, President Ali Akbar Hashemi Rafsanjani pushed for the expansion of the economic private domain and the historicization of the Iran-Iraq War (fig. 12.8). The appeal to beauty, rather than truth, by the Rafsanjani administration was a step toward the institutionalization of kitsch as the official visual language of the Islamic Republic. The projects of *baz-sazi* (reconstruction) and later *ziba-sazi* (beautification) were both aimed to normalize life after the war through an intense beautification of the visual and built environments. Rafsanjani's reconstruction plans thus endowed kitsch with a new sense of mission. In both cases, national sovereignty and variations of Iranian nationalism underpinned that image.

Figure 12.6. Payman Zadiri, *Shahid* (martyr), east side of Modaress Highway, Tehran, 2006. Photo by author.

The mercantile oligarchy that backed Rafsanjani's agenda, and for which kitsch had a particular appeal, was eager to consume it in part because the mercantile oligarchy needed to distinguish itself from its equally capitalist and oligarchic Pahlavi predecessor, and in part because kitsch projected a fitting picture of its populist background and practices of sociability. Kitsch articulated and normalized a coherent vision of otherwise contradicting new agendas: the mercantile bourgeoisie's insistence on looking just like everyone else, despite its newfound wealth and power; the state's resolve to institutionalize power and stabilize life under the Second Republic while continuing to create "the Islamic man" on orthodox Shi'a ideals; and the constitutional commitment to private property within the increasingly centralized formations of the nation-state. The potential for class conflict caused by this shift was "displaced onto relations among things" through a new ethos of mass consumption.[11] For Benjamin, this "cluttered 'kitsch'" was predicated on "the overproduction of commodities" that deferred the dream of the revolution onto consumer fetishism and urban consumption. In this effort, an appeal to God and to God's love of beauty was and remains pervasive. Next to the image of a bouquet of pink roses—a fake flower iconic of kitsch—many billboards and murals reproduced the Koranic verse that affirms that "God is beautiful and [he] loves beauty."[12] The (fake) flower is juxtaposed to the power of the divine.

Figure 12.7. Martyrs Foundation, artist unknown, west side of Taleghani Avenue, Tehran, September 1996. Photo by author.

Figure 12.8. One of the numerous memorials to the victims of the Iran-Iraq War, cemetery of Behesht-e Zahra, Ray, 1990s. Photo by author.

Whereas, in the 1980s and 1990s, the public domain saw an explosion of popular art, the private domain experienced the birth of a new avant-garde. In his analysis of kitsch, American art critic Clement Greenberg insisted that that the avant-garde transpires precisely because kitsch has taken over, for "where there is an avant-garde, generally we also find a rear-guard."[13] This sharp divide between the private and the public, the exclusivity of the official kitsch and the closeted avant-garde, is exacerbated by private property laws that protect, at least in principle, home studios and home showrooms. In the 1990s, these were the main spaces of avant-garde art that evolved into a highly active culture of exhibition opening, gallery going, and art consumption. After the election of the conservative government of President Ahmadinejad in 2005, even if artists are pressured and galleries are closed down, the constitution enables the ownership and running of private show rooms, the production of avant-garde art, the selling and buying of that art, the establishment of institutions preoccupied with artistic discourses and agendas, the publication of art journals and magazines, the teaching and learning of art, and above all the flourishing of artists' studios wherein the nude in its most fascinating and disturbing, its most tender and vulgar form, is ever present.

The transfer of the privileged status of avant-garde architecture in Pahlavi Iran to the avant-garde art in the Islamic Republic was not a mere coincidence. The tension between the public kitsch and the private avant-garde, as well as the public nature of architecture, had everything to do with this paradigm shift. Historically speaking, artistic patronage under Reza Shah was predominantly architectural. The Fine Arts Faculty at Tehran University was conceived, constructed, and run from 1938 on by a group of architects, including André Godard, who provided its curricular program and directed it until 1949. After his departure, all the subsequent deans of the faculty were prominent and practicing architects: Mohsen Foroughi (1949–1962), Houshang Seyhoun (1962–1968), Mohammad Amin Mirfendereski (1968–1971), and Mehdi Kowsar (1971–1979).[14] Architecture dominated the artistic field well into the 1970s; in and out of the university, the visual arts—painting, sculpture, graphic design, industrial design, and art education—while separate, were subordinate to the architecture department, structurally, pedagogically, and in terms of status. In the modernist context of Pahlavi Iran, to be an architect, a builder, and an engineer was more prestigious than any other discipline in the humanities. The best-known architects, including Seyhoun and Diba, were also recognized painters in avant-garde circles of the 1960s and 1970s.[15]

In analyzing the transformation of residential buildings, Diba notes that "architects brought modernism to Iran" by giving birth to new spaces that fostered the nuclear family: Reza Shah's modern middle class who would go on to base its class identity on the appreciation of avant-garde taste.[16] Along the same lines, it was Seyhoun who first used calligraphy to decorate as a form of an artistic search for a local modern on Omar Khayyam's modern mausoleum in Neshapur. Begun in 1959, it was inaugurated by Mohammad Reza Shah in April 1963, exactly a year before the Fourth Tehran Biennale, during which Persian calligraphic paintings proliferated.[17] By then, Empress Farah, who promoted local artists by seeing their works at the Café Shahrdari, "first started talking about the idea of building a permanent *architectural space* for modern art in Iran."[18] The Tehran Museum of Contemporary Art— the first, and thirty years on still the best, collection of Western modern and contemporary art outside the West—was conceived.[19] After setting up the physical and institutional infrastructure of modern art in Pahlavi Iran, architects vacated their privileged position to painters after the revolution, for only then did painting become more prestigious and prolific than building. The postrevolutionary substitution of painting as the representative of the new avant-garde over and above Pahlavi architecture speaks directly to the fact that architecture is conditioned by larger, sociopolitical concerns. Its location and patronage belongs to the public domain. Therefore, where the kitsch has taken over the streets, architecture can no longer prevail as the expression of the avant-garde. The chasm between the public kitsch and the private avant-garde since 1979 has endowed (closeted) painting with a place of honor at the vanguard of the desire for change.

Therefore, when President Mohammad Khatami came to power in 1997, his agenda for civil-society formation was directly linked to a generation of cultural norms that would align itself against the kitsch of the mercantile bourgeoisie. In his push to cultivate a professional middle-class foundation to his civil society programs, the arts were placed at the center of power politics.

During Khatami's tenure, the SNH's sites, as well as other major cultural and artistic institutions, were reorganized under the administration of the Ministry of Culture and Islamic Guidance, which now pursued an official policy of guidance, rather than persecution of artistic expression and artists. Most of the Pahlavi monuments, neglected during the first two decades of the revolution, were revamped and placed at the center of national tourism. In official narratives about Iranian culture, they often served as important markers that defined and administered high culture with a peculiarly nationalist undertone. These spaces, away from mosques and madrassas, enabled the reformist government to hone its version of national history and culture that would reinforce the agenda of civil society based on the professional middle class.

The SNH's tombs were an excellent means of finding a new angle of showing the pinnacle of Iranian culture to the public, even the illiterate. Their power resides in the spiritual claims and connections that the tombs enable while being linked to the Pahlavi secularist version of Iranian nationalism. In this matrix, a prominent place is reserved for Hafez, his work, his life, and death; and it is, as well, his resting-place.[20] When I asked Pegha, "Why do you go there every week?" she disclosed, "[F]or me, there is a big difference between going to Qom or Mashhad for *ziyarat* and going to Hafeziyeh, because he [Hafez] was not a *mollah*. He was an Iranian." UNESCO declared 1988 "The Year of Hafez," and the Islamic Republic celebrated it with enthusiasm. Various national newspapers as well as architectural journals published articles on the events; paramount was the image of Hafez's tomb-pavilion.[21] The state has continued to express its reverence ever since.[22] While Iranians continue to come to Hafeziyeh to read the *Divan* as devoutly as the Qur'an, they do not perform the Muslim practices of prayer, ablution, and *salavat*. Instead, they make a wish and take photographs of each other (figs. 12.9 and 12.10). At Hafeziyeh, a malleable line seems to be drawn between Shi'a religious and national secular behavior in the minds of those who visit.

The central place of visual culture—this intimate link between versions of nationalism and the wide spectrum of aesthetic appropriation—in Iranian

Figures 12.9 and 12.10. Iranian tourists in the courtyard of the mausoleum-garden of Hafez, Shiraz, 2007. Photos by author.

Figure 12.11. Election campaign banner stating "Youth, come aboard/Mir Hosayn Musavi," 8 June 2009, Vali Asr Avenue, Tehran. Photo by author.

politics was conspicuous during the June 2009 presidential election, when Tehran, along with other major urban centers in Iran, turned into a color-coded city. The green (Mousavi), red (Ahmadinejad), white (Karoubi), and yellow (Rezai) of the campaigners revealed not only the importance of the urban space in public life, but also the pivotal role of the visual in its operation. Each color imparted a highly symbolic historical and ideological meaning. It is precisely the official appeal to the divine love of beauty that was re-appropriated in many pre-election presidential campaign visual productions, in particular this one (fig. 12.11). Here, Michelangelo's finger of God touching that of Adam at the Sistine Chapel is reconfigured to encourage the young to vote. The combination of the green-stained fingertips of the election banner held by a campaigner with her meticulously French-manicured nails speaks to Nicholas Mirzoeff's point that "visual culture does not depend on pictures themselves but the modern tendency to picture or visualize existence." In the case of Iran, this is not just about visualizing one's own culture and history but about appropriating the Other's as an act of postmodernist claim to the world—visual and otherwise. The iconographic contradiction, fusion, and ap-propriation are multilayered and deeply meaningful: the green color of the Prophet and Mousavi's campaign, the fingers of God and Adam, the green fingerprints of the most classical signifier of democratic election, and the ring on God's finger are encapsulated in one Western image, thereby embracing the West in its own orbit of signs and signifiers, making it her own. The Iranians seem to have not moved away from the traditional institutions of avant-garde art—the structured museum and gallery—but rather have brought these sites into their sociopolitical struggle as important arenas of visual culture and its unpacking.

To attend a gallery opening and look at art is in fact an act of resistance, of protest. The avant-garde seems to be a renewed form of nationalism. Within the boundaries (*chahar-chub*) of the Islamic Republic, Mir Husayn Mousavi represents the avant-garde and tries to mend the chasm between kitsch and avant-garde, the public and the private domains. It comes as little surprise then that in May 2010, on the social media site Facebook, all those who "like Mir Husayn Mousavi" also have given thumbs up to Sohrab Sepehri, one of the best representatives of the Iranian avant-garde movement of the 1960s and 1970s in painting and poetry. The Iranian art community, who endorsed Musavi's candidacy in June 2009, portrayed him as "the architect of tomorrow"—not unlike Mohammad Reza Shah hovering over his white modernist city in many late Pahlavi-era posters. Mousavi's modern-left political career, combined with the fact that, since the late 1960s, he had been involved with the artistic avant-garde movement, made him the perfect candidate.

The Society of Iranian Painters demanded two things from his administration: protection of the artists and the widening of art appreciation among the masses. In effect, they asked for the avant-garde to be let out of its closet. That art community, just like Mousavi himself, is one that does not want to do without the nation-state; the Iranian state is one that cannot do without representation. Both are interlocked into a mutual agreement about the sanctity of the nation, of the territorial integrity and historical validity of a holistic Iran and Iranian identity as one. Both are also committed to the political sovereignty and cultural independence of that entity. While seemingly hegemonic and unreachable, the kitsch of the public domain is contested, like anything else in the Islamic Republic, both by different factions within the leadership as well as by ordinary people.[23] The commercial appropriation and nuanced perpetuation, while opportunistic, contributes in no small way to the endurance of a particular kind of national resistance (fig. 12.12). There ultimately seems to be a direct correlation between definitions of beauty, of culture, and of heritage, and the various colorings of Iranian nationalism. The ties between Pahlavi appropriation of avant-garde aesthetics and a solidification of the definition of nationalism must have a pivotal effect on this remanifestation of that specific conception of Iranian nationalism, as well as of its renewed aesthetics.

Figure 12.12. An advertisement for a Kenwood dishwasher on Vali Asr Avenue, northern Tehran, June 2009. Photo by author.

Notes

Parts of this article are drawn from my forthcoming book *Contemporary Iranian Art: From the Street to the Studio* (London: Reaktion Books, forthcoming in the spring of 2014) and a few of the images from my fieldwork in Iran in June 2009. I would like to thank Kamran Aghaie and Afshin Marashi, as well as the participants of the conference for their thought-provoking comments.

1. See Talinn Grigor, *Building Iran: Modernism, Architecture, and National Heritage under the Pahlavi Monarchs* (New York: Periscope/Prestel, 2009).

2. See Afshin Marashi, *Nationalizing Iran: Culture, Power, and the State, 1870–1940* (Seattle: University of Washington Press, 2008) and Grigor, *Building Iran*.

3. See "Sur instruction de SMI la Chahbanou: 2150 millions de rials pour le Sud de Téhéran," *Le Journal de Téhéran* 12.847 (29 June 1978), 1.

4. "SMI la Chahbanou au 4e Festival de Tous: Célébration de l'épopée de l'immortel Ferdowsi," *Le Journal de Téhéran* 12.853 (8 July 1978): 1–2. As late as 19 October 1978, the empress continued with her inaugurations of various cultural centers and exhibitions; see "Inauguration officielle du Centre Farahnaz Pahlavi," *Le Journal de Téhéran* 12.936 (19 October 1978): 1.

5. See, for example, publications such as R. Kaykhosrovai, *The Age of Ignorance: The Pillage of Iranian Cultural Heritage* (Tehran, 1984). Alternatively, see the introductions to the Iran National Archives Organization publications: *Ganjineh Asnad* 21 and 22 (Spring and Summer 1996); M. Delfani, ed., *Culture during Reza Shah* (Tehran, 1997); National Archives, *Iran and German Experts Immigrants 1931–1940* (Tehran, 1995); National Archives, *Records on the Archeological Missions in Iran 1875–1966* (Tehran, 2001).

6. Afsaneh Najmabadi, "Iran's Turn to Islam: From Modernism to a Moral Order," *The Middle East Journal* 41/2 (Spring 1987): 202–17, at 210.

7. Quoted in Shiva Balaghi, "Art and Revolution in the Islamic Republic of Iran," *The Middle East Institute Viewpoints* (Washington, DC, n.d.), 49–52, at 49. See also Ruhollah Khomeini, *Dar justeju-ye rah az kalam-e imam* ["In search of the path in the discourse of the imam"] vol. 16 (Tehran, 1363/1985), 435.

8. Hamid Algar, trans., "The Meaning of the Cultural Revolution," 26 April 1980, in *Islam and Revolution: Writings and Declarations of Imam Khomeini* (Berkeley: Mizan Press, 1981), 295–299.

9. Algar, *Islam and Revolution*, 298.

10. On Imam Khomeini's "committed art," see Hamid Keshmirshekan, "Discourses on Postrevolutionary Iranian Art: Neotraditionalism during the 1990s," *Muqarnas* 23 (2006), 131–157, at 135.

11. Susan Buck-Morss, *The Dialectics of Seeing: Walter Benjamin and the Arcades Project* (Cambridge, MA: MIT Press, 1989), 283–284.

12. Hadith, *Sahih Muslim* 1:275, *Kitab al-Iman*.

13. Clement Greenberg, "Avant-garde and Kitsch," in *Art and Culture*, ed. Clement Greenberg (Boston: Beacon Press, 1961, [original text 1939]), 3–21, at 9.

14. See M. Momayyez, "Faculties of the University of Tehran ii. Faculty of Fine Arts" and Nader Ardalan, "Architecture viii. Pahlavi, after World War II," *Encyclopedia Iranica Online*, no dates, available at www.iranicaonline.org.

15. Tehran Museum of Contemporary Art owns both of their paintings; see Mohammad Hassan Esbati, ed. *Iranian Modern Art Movement: The Iranian Collection of the Tehran Museum of Contemporary Art* (Tehran, 2006), 178, 206–207. President Mohammad Khatami's aim to broaden the middle class had important ramifications for the arts. He harnessed the arts to reform the political system and the avant-garde, until then formed of a small group of privileged upper class artists, now was envisioned as an important part of the civil society and of the same professional middle class that Reza Shah had forcibly begun to create.

16. Quoted in Hossein Amirsadeghi, ed., *Different Sames: New Perspectives in Contemporary Iranian Art* (London: TransGlobe Publishing Ltd, 2009), 113.

17. See Karim Emami, "Art in Iran XI Post-Qajar," in *Encyclopedia Iranica*, vol. ii, ed. Ehsan Yarshater (London and New York: Mazda Pub, 1987), 640–646.

18. Quoted in Amirsadeghi, *Different Sames*, 237, my emphasis.

19. For a critical account of TMoCA's early history, see Sarah McFadden, "Tehran Report: The Museum and the Revolution," *Art in America* (October 1981): 9–16. On Pahlavi history of TMoCA, see John Morris Dixon, "Tehran Museum of Contemporary Art: Cultural Hybrid," *Progressive Architecture* 59 (April–June 1978), no pages; Hengameh Fouladvand, "Art; Art, Diaspora; Art, Visual; Art Exhibitions," in *Iran Today: An Encyclopedia of Life in the Islamic Republic*, vol. i, eds. Mehran Kamrava and Manochehr Dorraj (Westport, CT, and London: Greenwood, 2008), 44–45; Kim Murphy, "Tehran Contemporary Art Museum has Picassos in Basement," *Los Angeles Times*, 26 September 2007; and Pierre Restany, "DAZ Planners: Museo Imperiale," *Domus*, February 1978, 14–17.

20. Postrevolutionary publications include N. T. Homayoon, "Dar Hashi-e Congre-e Bozorgdasht-e Hafez," *Sakhteman* 7 (November 1988) 36–39; S. Manoukian, "The City of Knowledge: History and Culture in Contemporary Shiraz" (Ph.D. dissertation, University of Michigan, 2001); Society for National Heritage 48, *Iqlim-e Pars: Asar-e Bastani va Ebni-e Tarikhi-e Fars* [Climes of Pars: Fars' Historic and Archeological Heritage] ed. Muhammad Taqi Mostafavi (Tehran, 1375/1996); Society for National Heritage 105, *Tarikh-e Baft-e Ghadim-e Shiraz* [The Old Fabric of Shiraz] ed. K. A. Afsar (1374/1995); H. Zedehdel, *Series of Guide Books to Iran: Fars Province* (Tehran, 1998); and P. Ziaian, *Shiraz: the Colorful Dream of Pars* (Tehran: Gooya, 2001).

21. N. T. Homayun, "In the Margin of the Congress in Honor of Hafez," *Sakhteman/Building* 7 (Azar 1367/November 1988): 36–39; and M. Nuri, "Report on the Congress in Honor of Hafez," *Soroush* 456 (19 Azar 1367/10 December 1988), 24–26.

22. On 11 and 12 October 2003, the celebrations took place in Hafeziyeh with a two-part program of poetry reading and concert, focused around the tomb of Hafez. The newspapers announced the "bozorgdasht-e rooz-e jahani-e Hafez bar gozar mi shavad." The first part of the program consisted of a scientific program (*elmi*) in the hall of Tehran University, and the second part, a cultural and artistic (*farhangi va honari*) segment at Hafeziyeh. The podium placed behind the marble tomb of Hafez was facing the hundreds of chairs filling the rest of the garden. The *talar* (portico) and the steps were occupied. A large screen in the southern garden permitted those who had not managed to get into the northern garden to view the program.

23. See, for instance, "The Presidents and the Mural," *The Guardian*, 5 February 2008, www.guardian.co.uk.

CHAPTER 13

Construction of Iran's National Identity: Three Discourses

SUSSAN SIAVOSHI

"Natarsid, Natarsid, Ma Hameh Ba Ham Hastim" (Do Not Fear, Do Not Fear, We Are All Together). This chant was heard again and again during the protest demonstrations against the questionable official result of the 2009 presidential election in Iran. The declared large margin of victory for incumbent President Mahmud Ahmadinejad, along with the manner and timing of the counting of the votes, convinced a large number of people that the election had been rigged. Iran was shaken for the next few weeks as hundreds of thousands, and at times millions, poured into the streets to protest the result and to demand a recount. The participants in these demonstrations consisted of young and old, male and female, rich and poor, religiously oriented and secular. The diverse character of the demonstrators raises several questions about the nature of this "we." Who were the participants, what shared interests and demands allowed them to think of themselves as a community, and how was this community and its demands perceived/labeled by the state as well as by exiled groups? As it turned out, these time-specific inquiries brought to the fore the broader, more enduring, and at the same time heatedly contested questions about Iranian national identity and its relation to the form and function of the state that presides over it.

Modern Iran has witnessed the development of several distinct discourses on the problem of national identity. In this study, I will compare the narratives constructed by the Iranian ruling elite, by the exiled monarchists,[1] and by the Green Movement. Since the most recent articulations of national identity by both the ruling class and the monarchists address the position of the Green Movement, I will pay special attention to these two competing versions of national identity. Based on these comparisons, I will make two points: one, that despite the fact that the ruling elite and monarchists consider each other as the classic *other*, their narratives on national construction have a great deal in common, especially in comparison to that of the Green Movement. And, two, that the Green Movement's construction of national identity is much more dynamic, open, and inclusive than those of either the ruling elite or the monarchists.

In order to make my argument, I was tempted to use the classic dualistic ethnic/cultural vs. civic approach to analysis of nation and nationalism for my comparative framework. The approach is based on an assumption that civic nationalism is blind to attributes such as race, religion, and ethnicity, and is, therefore, inclusive, universalistic, and generally liberal. Ethnic/cultural nationalism on the other hand is based on a conception of nationhood that is particularistic, illiberal, and therefore exclusivist.[2] It appears that the present Iranian ruling elite and a large segment of the exiled monarchists look at their community of reference primarily through cultural lenses of religion, ethnicity, or language, all of which are ascriptive attributes with exclusionary consequences. The Green Movement, on the other hand, seems to approach the concept of nation by an appeal to the political dimension of the nation-state, such as constitutionalism, republican rules of the game, and citizenship, and thus seems more inclusive. However, the critique of this neatly dichotomous approach is too great to ignore.[3] There are related cases particularly revealing for this study. For example, French nationalism today and Turkish nationalism under Ataturk, both labeled as civic nationalism, have demonstrated exclusive tendencies—with regard to their Muslim "citizens" in the case of France and Islamists in the case of Turkey. Muslims or Islamists in both of these cases have been denied the freedom to express certain aspects of their identity in the public sphere (e.g., forbidden to wear the veil). More importantly, the example of French and Turkish nationalisms demonstrates the difficulty of making neat and dualistic conceptual categorization, due to the fact that, at their base, each of these nationalisms rests on either certain cultural mores or ethnicity. The same problem of neat categorization exists in the case of Iran, as the boundaries of ethnic versus civic nationalisms prove to be much more porous and complicated than they at first appear.[4] All three groupings, to varying degrees, appeal to both ethnic/cultural and civic concepts and referents in order to legitimize their preferred political system in the eyes of the public.

If the classic ethnic versus civic approach falls short in providing the analytical framework for this study, how can we better understand the differences among the three narratives? I suggest the analysis should be based less on the differences *between* ethnic/cultural category on the one hand and the civic one on the other (although I am not completely ignoring it), than on the differences *within* the ethnic/cultural category. Understanding what type of ethnic/

cultural quality is chosen by each entity to construct its corresponding nation might tell us more about their inclusivity/exclusivity than whether their narrative is civic or cultural. For example, while the ruling elite in Iran appeal to Islam, and the monarchists look toward a pre-Islamic history for inspiration, the Green Movement prefers to talk about an Iranian identity that is inclusive of both Islam and Persian identities. And finally, I will argue that there is one other characteristic of each discourse that should be taken into consideration when we analyze the inclusivity/exclusivity divide, and that is whether the construction is static (a static version of Islam or a petrified version of Persian ethnicity), or whether it is dynamic and fluid (with an emphasis on the process of *becoming* and allowing the parameters of the national framework to change as events and forces unfold).

Nation: A Contested Concept

The ruling elites of both the Islamic Republic and the monarchist groups insist that their construction of Iranian identity is the authentic one. While the former emphasizes religion (Shi'ism) and the latter ethnicity (Persian identity), they both attempt to deny the other's marker as, at best, irrelevant, and, at worst, antithetical to true Iranian identity. But does history support the clear demarcation made by these two discourses? Have Iranians imagined themselves differently in different periods of their history? What role did religion and ethnicity play in that act of imagining? Do Islam and Persian identities reinforce and complement each other, or are they in conflict? And, finally, what roles have people in power played in directing/manipulating Iranian identity?

It would not be easy to imagine a harmonious and complementary role for Islamic and Persian identities—or rather, an undifferentiated notion of these identities—if one focused on the last few decades of Iranian history. However, Islam and Persian ethnicity, as identity markers, came into open conflict only in the nineteenth century. Many factors, such as the increasing intrusion of foreign powers in Iran, Western ideas of the Enlightenment and post-Enlightenment, and the despotic and corrupt rule of the Qajar kings, propelled some of Iran's intellectuals to search for a solution to the problem of the country's inferior world standing. In their diagnosis of the problem, many, particularly those educated in Western philosophy and methods, saw Islam and Islamic culture as the source of all ills, and attempted to solve the problem by constructing an Iranian history whose value lay in its independence from, and opposition to, Islam. In their view, the reason that Iran in the nineteenth century was an embarrassingly backward country had to do with the seventh-century "savage" Arab invasion, an invasion that replaced the "peaceful and civilized" Persian culture with one of "vulgarity," "violence," "superstition," and "backwardness." To rescue Iran from such a legacy, pre-Islamic Iran had to be returned to the limelight. The Qajar Prince Jalal al-din Mirza, the Azarbaijani playwright Mir Fathali Akhundzadeh,[5] and the Babi author Mirza Agha Khan Kermani[6] were among the most active participants in constructing a history of Iran that idealized the pre-Islamic period as the period of prosperity, glory, and progress.[7] A return to their vision of pre-Islamic identity would allow Iranians to follow harmoniously the requirement of the modern world and allow Iran to become a respectful member of the global community.[8]

While intellectuals were important for providing the theoretical tools for the development of Persian nationalism, it was the state that had the resources to disseminate these ideas among large segments of the population. This task began in earnest during the reign of Reza Shah Pahlavi (1925–1941). The mobilization of social forces, particularly during the Constitutional Revolution (1905–1911) was the harbinger of sociohistorical changes that eventually ushered Iran into a mass-politics society, and compelled the state to seek consent for their rule from new social forces. Manipulation of nationalist symbols, similar to the experience of European states in the eighteenth century, with its appeal to new social forces, was thought to be one method of ensuring political legitimacy.[9] It was mostly in the early 1930s that Reza Shah, partly in an attempt to eradicate the power of the clergy, began a series of policies, which were continued and expanded by Mohammed Reza Shah, to promote Persian at the expense of religious identity. To the Pahlavi kings, particularly Mohammed Reza Shah, modernization of Iran, based on the Western model (but without democracy), required the eradication of traditional/Islamic norms, attitudes, customs, and symbols. In pursuing this goal, a series of educational, cultural, legal, and economic policies were adopted. The Pahlavi state was serious in making Persian identity the authentic identity of Iranians.[10]

However, the autocratic rule of the Pahlavi regime with its modernist/Westernist, secularist, Persian-focused nationalism produced its own intellectual and political challengers. One important catalyst that compelled a significant portion of socially conscious Iranian intellectuals to reevaluate their position toward the West, modernity, and Iranian identity was the Western-engineered coup against Mohammad Mussadiq's government in 1953. Ever since the fall of Mussadiq's administration there were calls for finding the authentic self, this time defined by its Islamic/Shi'i component by men such as Jalal Al-Ahmad,[11] and later Ali Shariati.[12] The political manifestation of this shift was first demonstrated in the uprising of 1962, led by Ayatollah Ruhollah Khomeini. Khomeini made a frontal attack on the Pahlavi regime for its "betrayal" of Islamic Iran when the Iranian Parliament passed the "capitulation law," which gave American military personnel and their dependents immunity from Iranian laws in 1964.[13] Khomeini's appeal to the Islamic character of the nation as a way to recover a dignified and independent Iran resonated with many Iranians. However, it was the triumph of the 1979 revolution and the establishment of the Islamic Republic that forced a retreat of the Persian nationalist discourse. Similar to the prerevolutionary state, the Islamic Republic harnessed its ideological and financial tools to create an identity suitable for its goals. But this time it was Islam in general, and Shi'ism in particular, that constituted the essential ingredient in defining Iranian national identity. A notable intellectual expression of this effort was a mid-1980s book by a university professor and supporter of the Islamic Republic, Reza Davari.[14]

Davari asserted that modern nationalism is a European phenomenon and as such, and despite its initial liberating impact, is of no benefit for non-European, ex-colonized countries. The problem of nationalism, for Davari, lies in its modern/Western/secular character: nationalism as a phenomenon which is based on a social contract among individuals independent of any other entity, including God, is by nature secular[15] and liberal.[16] Davari argues that in the era of neocolonialism, where Western *este'mar* (colonialism) is replaced by Western *estekbar* (arrogance), a phenomenon whose central weapon is cultural, nationalism has ceased to be liberating. The ideological dependence of nationalism on the cultural values of *mostakberin* (arrogant powers) for Davari explains the transformation of nationalism from a liberating force to a subjugating one devoid of any revolutionary substance.[17] According to him, third-world nationalists, including Iranian/Persian nationalists, are caught in a harmful, useless, and contradictory game of promoting a hollow and mythical past with its "unique" ethnic customs and traditions, on the one hand, and mindlessly mimicking the *mostakberin* on the other.

This view of nationalism, however, does not prevent Davari from speaking of Iran as a community of people with common values and common historical memories, a community that deserves an independent and sovereign state. The glue for this community, however, is not Persian ethnicity but the religion of Islam.[18] In a mirror argument of the "pre-Islamic Persian" nationalists, who advocate the promotion of "authentic" Persian identity as necessary for Iran to get out of its state of decline, Davari argues for the promotion of a religious identity, a return to the "authentic" Islamic self "*bazgasht-e beh khishtan*" as the necessary step in the struggle against Western domination, or the cause of backwardness.[19] However, this "authentic self" is not an autonomous and self-referential individual, but a self that finds salvation in acknowledging his/her dependency on God. Like a good theocrat, Davari leaves the task of recovering this self to be performed "by those who are not only experts in the knowledge and practice of religious laws, but whose eyes, ears, tongues, and hands, in their closeness to the Truth have become His eyes, ears, tongues, and hands."[20] In the case of Iran, the task is left to the Supreme Leader, whose guidance will deliver the community from injustice and the oppression of world arrogance.

Even though the voices of those who see Iran as either Persian or completely Islamic may be the loudest, there exists another voice, one that belongs to those intellectuals who have acknowledged the existence of both Persian and Islamic components as legitimate or authentic parts of Iranian identity. Ehsan Naraghi is a representative of such a voice. In his book *Ancheh Khod Dasht* (What the Self Had), he analyzes and regrets the intellectual process that led to the bifurcation of Iranian identity. What follows is a summary of his analysis. The intellectual process started in the nineteenth century, when European scholars attempted to study Iran using the methods of natural sciences. These studies, complicated by the material interest of colonial powers, ultimately led to a body of literature in which Iranian history was rigidly divided into distinct categories, leaving no space for the elements of continuity in that history. Iranian intellectuals of the nineteenth century themselves imitated and added to the narrative of Western observers of Iran, and ended up constructing an Iranian identity which was based on a superficial separation of pre-Islamic Iran from its Islamic history, calling the former history authentically Iranian and the latter false, an aberration forced on Iran by alien Arabs.[21] Naraghi rejects this reading of Iranian identity and offers another, which combines religion (Shi'ism), Persian language, and the heritage of pre-Islamic Iran into one.[22] As we will see, it is such a view of national identity—one that believes in reconciliation of ethnicity with religion in constructing national identity—that appears in the narrative of the Green Movement.

The Ruling Elite Discourse

The present ruling elite of the Islamic Republic consists of individuals, organizations, and institutions with control over almost all levers of power. Among them are the supreme leader's office, the office of the president and its cabinet, the military establishment (including the Revolutionary Guard and the paramilitary groups of the Basij), the Guardian Council, much of parliament, a large number of Friday-prayer imams, and organizations such as Jame'eh-e

Ruhaniyat Mobarez (JRM). Among the most forceful supporters of the regime are its affiliated media: Kayhan, Saharnews, Raja, Vatan, Javan, and Fars News Agencies. How does this ruling elite frame the question of identity and community?

What is noteworthy about the ruling elite's construction of the nation is the supremacy of the state over the nation. Despite the popular/populist appeal of the Islamic revolution, and the frequent reference to the government as the servant of the people, the relation between the people and the state is more like that of children and parents. In this case, it is up to the state (particularly the wise leader) to decide what the interest of the people is and how to provide for it. The legitimate members of the community are only those who accept the supreme leader as the final protector of the nation's independence,[23] progress, and the overall well being of the community.[24] It is not difficult to conclude, then, who is, or should be, outside the community, and why. In this view, not only non-Muslims are potential/logical "others," but Shi'a who do not believe in the office of supreme leader, or rather in the absolute and arbitrary judgment of the supreme leader, run the risk of being labeled as either a traitor or hostile *other*.[25] But since the Islamic Republic is confined to the geographical area of modern Iran, the next question is whether and how the elite deal with the totality of Iranian history, including its pre-Islamic part. There have been sporadic references to a pre-Islamic Iran as part of the identity of the members of the community; for example, Ali Khamenei, the supreme leader, has acknowledged the pre-Islamic Iranian identity. His depiction of that identity, however, is based on a projection of the Islamic identity, one that fits the moral values of Islam as interpreted by the authoritarian segment of the Islamic Republic.[26] Ahmadinejad, the former president, has also made references to pre-Islamic Iran. In one of his speeches to Iranians living abroad, he praised Iran's ancient history and its prominent place among the cultures of the world. However, when it came to elaborating on characteristics of such a culture, the pre-Islamic part of the mix lost its distinction and disappeared into the Islamic (or more specifically Shi'i) part of Iranian history.[27]

Since the ruling elite attempts to base its legitimacy on providing for the Shi'is, anyone who challenges the elite must be proven to be an enemy of the Shi'i nation. Therefore, since the election crisis of 2009, the Green Movement, despite the fact that many of its representatives are prominent Shi'is, including from the high clergy, has been depicted as Yazidi, followers of the most hated enemy of Shi'ites in the latter's historical memory. Such a charge would automatically exclude the followers of the Green Movement from membership in the Shi'i community. In their effort to exclude the Green Movement from the nation, the ruling elite has appealed not only to long-standing historical memory, but also to the modern narrative of national security. The Green Movement's activists are not part of the nation, because they are either agents or appeasers of the hostile governments of the United Kingdom and the United States. There have also been attempts to connect the Green Movement leaders to the hated Pahlavi regime. A cursory review of statements by people in power and the government-affiliated media demonstrates this effort of portraying the Green Movement as an alien force. Soon after the beginning of the protests, Khamenei gave a speech that set the tone. In that speech, similar to what Davari said, Khamenei considered Islam, and more specifically Shi'i Islam, the only effective force in liberating the Middle East from the yoke of "World Arrogance." Based on his judgment, then, anyone who challenges the state, and specifically the office of the supreme leader, is, consciously or not, helping the *arrogance*, and thereby hurting the cause of liberation and the well-being of the Muslim community—and is, therefore, outside the nation.[28] And, of course, the reason for the effectiveness of religion in this battle against world arrogance lies in a cultural explanation. In a speech to the Basijis, Khamenei refers to the cultural weapon of the "arrogance" as the primary means in what he labels the "soft war" of this crisis,[29] which, to him, provides the opportunity for "the enemies within" to get involved in illegal and destructive behavior. Here is an excerpt from his speech:

> Everybody knows that Estekbar [World Arrogance] has changed its methods in confronting the regime of the Islamic Republic. Today it uses a method called "soft war," which means war through cultural tools, lies, and rumors. With the developed communication tools the World Arrogance tries to create doubts in people's hearts and minds . . . to create division. For example, these postelection events were all its [the outside enemies'] instruments to create disunity among people, by enabling the enemies within to do illegal acts. . . . All these are part of the major plans of the arrogance.[30]

Still, in none of his speeches does Khamenei refer to a particular individual leader of the Green Movement as a foreign collaborator or traitor, a restraint that has not been shown by many other members of the ruling elite. For example, Mohammed Yazdi, the former head of the Judiciary and the present member of the Guardian Council, accused the leaders of the Green Movement of activities that are not only against the Islamic Republic but are anti-Islam acts.[31] Still others have implied collaboration between the U.S. government and these leaders.[32] The elite's depiction of the Green Movement's oppositional activities (which, particularly in its early phase, could have been construed as the constitutional rights of loyal members/citizens) as acts of conspiracies and sedition against the nation and the state highlights the major elements of the elite's version of the Iranian nation.

In this construction of the community, the present ruling elite are restrictive in both the ethnic/cultural and civic dimensions. By privileging the authoritarian aspects of the constitution—or rather, by the nonrecognition of its republican articles—the ruling elite has virtually dismissed any civic notion in the construction of the nation. But beyond that, they have not only narrowed membership of the nation to mostly Shi'a, but to their own version of a good Shi'a, one whose character has no discernable difference from a seventh-century follower of the Prophet and the Imams.

The Monarchist Discourse

Who are the exiled monarchists, and how do they construct the identity of Iranians? It is difficult to paint an accurate picture of the Iranian monarchists,[33] because they consist of several scattered groups with no unifying umbrella organization.[34] For this study, I have chosen three of these monarchist organizations. One is the prominent and moderate Constitutional Party of Iran (CPI),[35] founded by Dariush Homayoun, the prerevolution minister of information. The other two, with more radical perspectives, are the Rastakhiz Organization of Iran (ROI),[36] founded by Masoud Khoshnood, and Anjoman-e Padeshahi-e Iran (API),[37] founded by Frood Fouladvand.[38] API has an overt military wing, the Tondar Organization, which took responsibility for a fatal bombing in a mosque in Shiraz.[39] Recently, API has received the most attention from the Western media, due to the execution of two of its alleged members in January 2010 in Iran.

Despite their lack of unity, almost all monarchists are faithful heirs of the Pahlavi policy to promote Persian identity. They pay homage to the Persian language[40] and in varying degrees to the pre-Islamic heritage and civilization. They also believe that Persian identity has been historically suppressed by forces of alien cultures and religion. They praise Reza Shah Pahlavi, the founder of the Pahlavi dynasty, and consider him to be a heroic figure who did his utmost to bring back dignity and independence to Iran by rejuvenating Iranian identity. They differ from each other, however, in what that identity entails. Homayoun, as we will see, believed in a model set by Enlightenment ideals, while ROI and API look back at the pre-Islamic time for inspiration. This difference also provides different rationales for their support for the monarchy. Homayoun, who labeled himself first and foremost a liberal democrat,[41] stated that his support for the monarchy was based on a utilitarian rationale.

He believed that, for historical reasons, a system of constitutional monarchy is best suited to protect an enlightened liberal democratic polity in Iran.[42] For the ROI and API, however, the support for the monarchy is based on organic, emotional, and romantic elements.[43]

Similar to that of many exiled political oppositional groups, the monarchists' effort has been to highlight the illegitimacy of the Islamic Republic. In the eyes of the monarchist opposition, the Islamic Republic from its inception was a usurping force and, thus, illegitimate. However, their attack on the *behavior* of the Islamic Republic does not shed much light on the monarchists' attitude toward national identity. What is helpful in understanding their attitude is a focus on their narrative on Islamic *essence* and its association with the Islamic Republic. For example, the ROI in the last point of its eleven-point section on "Political Ideology of Iran's Rastakhiz Organization" offers this judgment about Islam: "[We believe] that the religion of Islam is appropriate for Arab lands and that it has no connection with Iranians."[44] In one of API's postings, the author states that the fundamental problem faced by Iran is not the regime of the Islamic Republic or the problem of human rights abuses or the matter of economic hardships; the root of Iran's problem is in the fourteen hundred years of "shameful Islamic tradition."[45] The API characterizes Islam not only as an alien but as a violent religion, a religion suited only for *tazian*, i.e., Arabs.[46] By using the concepts of *tazian* in direct opposition to Persians, some of these organizations make race/ethnicity a focal point for community inclusion/exclusion.

It is not difficult to dismiss these radical, fringe groups of monarchists as irrelevant. But what about the more mainstream monarchists, such as the CPI? With a few exceptions,[47] the CPI has not been as upfront in rejecting Islam, but in its critique of the Islamic Republic it, too, sometimes reveals a position on Islam that is not too far from the more radical organizations. Their difference lies in the conceptual framework that each uses. The radical monarchists' conceptualization is, to a great extent, racially informed. These groups are also more emphatic in drawing a hard line between Persian ethnicity and Islamic identity. The CPI, or more accurately, Homayoun, on the other hand, was more circumspect in drawing a distinction between Persian and Islamic identities. In fact, he was critical of the kind of Persian nationalism that, he contended, is based on a static and prideful view of pre-Islamic Iran.[48] Again, unlike radical monarchists, Homayoun acknowledged the fact that Islam is the religion of the majority of Iranians,[49] and that the collapse of the Islamic Republic would not result in the collapse of Islam in Iran. His critique of Islam, unlike the racially conceived critique of radical groups, came from a mixed perspective of the Enlightenment and Persian nationalism.

He saw Islam as unable to serve Iran in its path toward progress, because in Islam the notion of an individual *right* is severely undermined by an emphasis on human *responsibility*. Freedom, liberty, and dignity of the individual appeared frequently in Homayoun's narrative as values that informed his political design. However, Persian nationalist discourse raised its head when Homayoun analyzed the problem further. Reminiscent of the ideas of the nineteenth-century orientalists such as those of Ernest Renan,[50] Homayoun implied that the roots of everything that is worthy in the Islamic period of Iranian history should be found in the non-Islamic, and specifically non-Arabic past.[51] Homayoun acknowledged the shining progress in Islamic science in the medieval period. But, again similar to orientalist philologists' views that Arabs, due to the limitation of their language, were unable to promote science or liberty or any of the requirements of progress, Homayoun argued that the medieval progress owed itself to non-Arabs, Persians in particular, who enriched the Arabic language by bringing into it some words of their own. He further surmised that, ever since the invasion of Iran by Arabs, the only glimmer of enlightenment and hope, even among Muslims such as Ibn Sina, has had Zoroastrian[52] and, more importantly, Greek roots.[53] Considering these judgments about Islam, how did Homayoun conceive of a progressive Iran with its Muslim majority? To him, Islam had to be transformed from its current form into one suitable for a progressive and Western-oriented society. Such an Islam, like Western Christianity, should be compatible with the Enlightenment project; it should belong to the private domain, and it should be stripped of all superstitious rituals and beliefs. This transformation would allow the Muslim majority of Iran to be counted as proper citizens of a liberal democratic society. The identity of the citizens of this new Iran, whose survival and stability depends on a constitutional monarchy, is not static, like that of the radical monarchists, but is inspired by a secular and individualistic model that dates back to eighteenth-century Europe.

All monarchists share the view that the Islamic Republic is the obstacle toward actualization of their ideal Iranian nation. Considering the strong anti–Green Movement rhetoric of the people in power in Iran, one would expect that all monarchists would welcome the emergence of the Green Movement. That is not the case, however; even though all monarchists wish for the Islamic Republic to be opposed, they do not share the same view about what constitutes an "authentic/national" opposition. The CPI, and particularly Homayoun himself, were more cognizant of the plurality of the movement, and its demands. For example, Homayoun praised the movement, and paid homage to both Mir Husayn Mousavi and Mehdi Karrubi as its leaders. He acknowledged their increasing distance from their past association with the Islamic revolution and the postrevolutionary state.[54] He was also open to the idea of a peaceful and gradual dissolution of the Islamic Republic. He saw in the Green Movement a certain democratic and liberal aspiration, and thus considered it to be the voice of the *nation*. He did not, however, agree with its leaders on the future form of the political system. For him, secularization of politics was a must, if Iran was going to be a viable country in the twenty-first century.

On the radical side, the ROI and API judge anyone who was or has been associated with the Islamic Republic, no matter how briefly, a betrayer of the *nation* and of the *national interest*. To them, there is no difference between reformists or hardliners in the Islamic Republic;[55] they are all anti-Iranian aliens. In addition, neither the ROI nor the API is sympathetic to the message or the method of resistance of the Green movement. The ROI paints the movement as a chimera, a lie, a play to deceive the "real" Iranians.[56] The API depiction is no more flattering. To the API, the fact that the Green Movement does not assume a "pure" Persian identity is problematic. The API's military wing, Tondar, also does not approve of the Green Movement's nonviolent methods. It calls it a deviated movement if it allows itself to be led by people who espouse nonviolence. Overall, neither the ROI nor the API considers the Green Movement a genuine oppositional movement and part of the authentic nation, because its demands are not pure (no one in the movement has made an overt call for a return of monarchy, or a return of a pre-Islamic Persian identity), and its method would lead nowhere except to appease the mortal enemy of Iran, the Islamic Republic. A true member of the Iranian community for these monarchist organizations is one who not only identifies with pre-Islamic Iran but also accepts a monarchy, modeled after Reza Shah's, as the proper political system.[57] The ROI and API are similar to the ruling elite of the Islamic Republic in their narrow and static conceptualization of the nation.

On the face of it, it seems that Homayoun's conception of the nation was all-inclusive on both cultural/ethnic and civic perspective. But a careful look reveals a more complicated picture. On the cultural/ethnic level, despite some ambiguities, Homayoun ultimately revealed his affection for the pre-Islamic, and his dismay at the Islamic, parts of Iranian identity. Not only Al-Ahmad and Shariati, but even someone like Naraghi, would accuse him of emptying Islam of its content and leave it as a shell, making Muslims who did not accept his notion of "reformed Islam" unworthy members of the community. As for civic aspects, his attachment to Western Enlightenment made him suspicious of nonsecular actors in the public sphere. The fact that he denied religion, and therefore religious groups, a role in politics, whether one approves of it or not, placed restrictions on elements of citizenship. His preferred nationalism, though based on different criteria than those of the radical monarchists or the ruling elite of the Islamic Republic, had its own inflexibility, through its un-critical attachment to an eighteenth-century European model of citizenship. His nationalism in cultural/ethnic and civic terms was more restrictive and static than it otherwise appeared. These facts become clearer as one looks at the Green Movement's narrative.

The Green Movement's Discourse

What is the character of the Green Movement, and who represents it? What was most evident, particularly in the early days of post-election upheaval, was the movement's diversity in terms of age, gender, social class, or by ap-pearance of religiosity. Such diversity made assigning the role of leadership to a specific individual or individuals a difficult task, especially when certain segments of the protesters became radicalized. Now that the street protests have ended, it is clear which individuals, groups, and organizations are con-sistently and continuously representing the concerns and demands associated with the early days of the massive and peaceful Green protestors. Among the individuals, the most obvious are Mir Husayn Mousavi, Mehdi Karrubi, and, to a lesser degree, Mohammed Khatami. These leaders have come from the heart of the revolution and have been its loyal supporters. Mir Husayn Mou-savi (who founded an association called the Green Path of Hope in August 2009) was prime minister of the Islamic Republic for eight years, until the abolition of the office in 1989. Mehdi Karrubi is a founder of the Associa-tion of Combatant Clerics (ASC), a former head of the parliament, and the founder of the relatively new political party National Trust. He was chosen by Khamenei to be a member of the Expediency Council, a position from which he has now resigned. Mohammed Khatami, another founding mem-ber of ASC, is the popular former two-term (1997–2005) President of the Islamic Republic. However, despite, or maybe because of, their dedication to the revolution, all three became critics of an authoritarian reading of Islam and of the Constitution of the Islamic Republic. The institutional support for these personalities comes from groups such as the ASC, the university stu-dents' organization of Daftar Tahkim Vahdat (The Bureau for Consolidation of Solidarity), a minority group of parliamentary representatives, and political parties and groupings such as the Mosharekat Party and Mojahedin Inqelab-e

Islami. There are also associated, or sympathetic, media outlets, some operating inside Iran, such as Parlemannews and Kaleme.org, and some such as Jaras, operating outside Iran.[58]

The discourse of the Green Movement on national identity is telling, due to its general lack of defining and limiting parameters. When there is a reference to national identity, it always has both Iranian and Islamic characteristics. There was some early tackling of the concept of nationality and identity by Khatami while he was the president of the Islamic Republic. Khatami saw Iran's identity as inexorably connected with Islam, but he did not deny the non-Islamic part of the identity. In one of his speeches during his presidency, Khatami challenged both the advocates of a purely pre-Islamic identity[59] as well as those who deny it. Instead, he declared that "our identity is Iranian-Islamic."[60] Khatami's reference is clear, in his delineation of a unique identity for Iranians as opposed to the rest of the Islamic world. In his insistence on Iranian-Islamic identity, he also acknowledged the right of other ethnic and religious minorities (albeit with a deafening silence about the Baha'is) to be considered part of the nation.[61] More recently, the notion of "Iranian-Islamic" as a descriptive label for Iranian identity has also been invoked in Mousavi's 18th Statement. What has been emphasized in this statement is an acknowledgment of women's equal rights, and, therefore, their inclusion as equal citizens. It also expresses more emphatic support for the rights of religious and ethnic minorities:

> The secret to preserving the Islamic-Iranian culture and solidarity is [to maintain] the coexistence of our long-lived national and religious values. . . . The Green Movement is an Iranian-Islamic movement that seeks a truly free and advanced Iran. Thus, any Iranian who acts in pursuit of a better tomorrow for her/his nation, counts as an activist of the Green Movement. . . . Respect for human dignity and human rights independent of ideology, religion, gender, ethnicity, and social status is one of the Green Movement's primary demands. . . . The Green Movement fully supports the women's movement, denounces any discrimination based on gender, and fully supports the rights of ethnic minorities.[62]

Generally, the discourse of the Green Movement has consistently expanded the number of groups who must be considered as part of the nation, and thus has become consistently more inclusive. In the narrative of Mousavi, inclusiveness has been extended even to those who have attacked the supporters of the Movement.[63] Probably most important is the changed attitude towards Baha'is. The reformist Shi'a Islamic discourse on freedom and equality has its Achilles' heel in relation to Baha'is. However, there came a significant declaration on the civil and human rights of Baha'is in 2008 by none other than the late Grand Ayatollah Husayn-Ali Montazeri, the spiritual leader of the Green Movement.[64] Of course, this statement does not provide for total equality for Baha'is, but, coming from a grand ayatollah, it opens the door for further change.

The Green Movement's approach is nonbinary, not only in its construction of the nation but also in its view of the political system. The question of who is included within the nation is well connected to the Green Movement's political vision. The representatives of the movement, along with their supportive media, have remained faithful to a call for peaceful resistance, asking for reform of the system rather than for its destruction.[65] Many of their demands, such as the elimination of the approbatory power of the Guardian Council,[66] or a call for the transparency and accountability of the political system,[67] are procedural. At the substantive level, the discourse of the Green Movement has been consistently in favor of promoting liberty and tolerance, with an emphasis on the republican aspects of the constitution, and against its authoritarian tendencies.[68] They see peaceful means as the proper approach, as they believe in the compatibility of democracy with Islam.[69]

There might be legitimate doubt as to whether the inside representatives of the opposition can express themselves freely, considering the obvious risks to their lives. Therefore, it might be useful to address also the discourse of individuals who, even though situated outside Iran, are associated with the Green Movement and its leaders. Noteworthy among them are Ata`ollah Mohajerani,[70] the former minister of culture in Khatami's administration; Mohsen Kadivar,[71] the reformist clergyman; Abdol-Ali Bazargan,[72] the son of the late Mehdi Bazargan, the first Prime Minister after the establishment of the Islamic Republic; and Akbar Ganji, the famous journalist whose resistance against the hardline factions landed him in jail, where he almost lost his life. The last mentioned is probably the most confrontational among this group.[73] The nature of the demands of most of these exiled representatives is not too far from that of the internal leaders. The materials that appear on the internet news and analysis site, Jonbesh-e Rah-e Sabz (JARAS) (The Movement of Green Path), which operates outside Iran and has Mohajerani, Kadivar, and Bazargan on its editorial board, supports the above assertion. JARAS describes itself as "an independent, projustice, profreedom, democratic, Islamic, antiviolence and pro-human rights organization."[74] In its stated goals, the site includes achievement of legal equality for all citizens of Iran, regardless of religion, gender, political ideology, and lifestyle, and it denounces the assignment of privilege or the imposition of discrimination upon people on the basis of their religious affiliation. JARAS also states that the Green Movement is against any kind of dictatorship, including religious dictatorship, i.e., absolute supreme leadership. Citizens as a whole are sovereign, and the legitimacy of the state is exclusively based on the people's consent and support. In addition, it declares that the necessary component of democracy is protection of the rights of minorities based on universal human rights. However, the site does not espouse secularism or the complete separation of religion and politics. It states that the Green Movement believes in democracy and in a public reformist Islam to compensate where there is a moral void.[75]

As for the specific demands for political reform, the most discussed document of the Green Movement was one signed by five exiled reformers (Mohajerani, Kadivar, Bazargan, Ganji, and Abdolkarim Surush, the famous religious reformer). This document followed another of Mousavi's statements (#17). Mousavi's five-point statement demands accountability of the executive power; an overhaul of the election laws, so that free and fair elections can be guaranteed; the release of political prisoners, and the restoration of their dignity; and freedom of press and assembly.[76] The five exiled reformers paid respect to Mousavi's demands, but considered them to be minimal, and added another five significant points. Much more bluntly than Mousavi, they included demands such as the resignation of Ahmadinejad and a call for new elections, abolition of the Guardian Council's discretionary power, punishment of agents of torture, removal of the military from all political, economic, and cultural arenas, and last but not least, for the "election, accountability, openness to criticism, and term limit for all the highest echelon of the country's leaders."[77] Even though this last demand, which applies also to the office of supreme leader, is the most radical, it still does not constitute a call for the destruction of the Islamic Republic. A liberal reading of the first postrevolution constitution of the Islamic Republic could allow for all of these demands; in fact, at one time or another, all of these demands (the last point more implicitly than explicitly) have been discussed within the reformist circles and their associated media during the previous decade in Iran. But more important for the purposes of this study is how these statements for reform of the state shed light on the movement's implied construction of its ideal community.

The movement's civic discourse allows for inclusion—through its emphasis on rights of citizens and responsibilities of the state, its push for dialogue, its call for reconciliation of forces and of positions that might seem mutually exclusive—and tolerance for plurality. The Green Movement acknowledges both Iranian and Islamic dimensions of identity, and in doing so it wishes to distort neither. There is not much in the discourse of the Green Movement that points to limitations or conditions that color the other two rival discourses when it comes to membership in the community. As statements on gender issues and the status of Baha'is show, the movement's discourse on nationhood is an evolving discourse, hinting at its possibility to be inclusive of hitherto unrecognized groups.

Conclusion

When the Islamic Republic was established in 1979, it put an end to a state policy that for almost a quarter of a century had promoted Persian identity. Instead, the revolutionary state attempted quickly and earnestly to Islamize Iranian identity. Similar to Pahlavi monarchs, the leaders of the Islamic Republic chose the educational system as one of its most important tools to inculcate values necessary for "re-creating" men and women as suitable members of an Islamic (Shiʻi) community. For some, the ideal Islamic community was that of the seventh century. The present authoritarian segments of the ruling elite have remained, to a large measure, faithful to that idea of a static identity.

In contrast, the exiled monarchists, heirs to the Pahlavi desire to Persianize Iranian identity, continued to build on, with varying degrees of subtlety, a narrative that not only privileged a pre-Islamic Iran, but made it the only "authentic" part of Iranian history. They considered most of the Islamic period, with the exception of the Pahlavi era, a hijacked history of a traumatized people kept backward by Arab-Muslim aliens whose latest manifestation is the Islamic Republic. To them, the only way to get rid of this alien force is through purging the Iranian identity from the Islamic culture by either *returning* to the "ancient authentic self" as the ROI and API would argue, or by *creating* a "new" one modeled after the Enlightenment version of an individual, as advocated by Homayoun.

Neither of these two narratives, despite the claims of some of their adherents to inclusivity and universality, constructs an identity that allows for the majority of Iranians to be true and complete citizens of the country. It is in the Green Movement's narrative that one detects a different kind of formation of national identity, an identity that is cognizant and respectful of the diversity of all Iranians, and one that allows for the inclusion of more and more people as equal member of the nation. The Green Movement's discourse is articulated by activists and intellectuals who came out of the womb of the revolution but along the way became disillusioned by many of its exclusionary and authoritarian excesses. It is partly this complex experience of the Green Movement's leaders that made it possible for their narrative to be fluid and dynamic, and therefore open to the inclusion of both old and new social forces.

Notes

1. For this study, I have chosen monarchist organizations because of their emphasis on national identity. Many other groups of the opposition, even those who advocate the total annihilation of the Islamic republic, its institutions, and leadership, stay away from national construction arguments, while many monarchists, in their attack on the Islamic Republic, frequently address the concept of nation and national identity.

2. Hans Kohn's work on nationalism and its categorization inspired many theorists of later generations to add and refine the basic premises of ethnic vs. civic distinction. See Hans Kohn, *The Idea of Nationalism: A Study of Its Origin and Background* (New York: Macmillan, 1944.)

3. For a critique of this approach, see, for example, Roger Brubaker, "The Manichean Myth: Rethinking the Distinction Between 'Civic' and 'Ethnic' Nationalism," in *Nation and National Identity: The European Experience in Perspective*, eds. Hanspeter Kriesi, Klaus Armington, Hannes Siegrist, Andreas Wimmer (Zurich: Verlag Rüegger, 1999), 55–71. As Brubaker observes, the use of civic and ethnic categories has been such that ethnic nationalism is coined as exclusive, and civic nationalism has been accorded a status of inclusiveness, even though in actuality all nationalisms are simultaneously inclusive and exclusive. See 64.

4. This problem is particularly true for the monarchist organization of Constitutional Party of Iran.

5. See, e.g., Akhundzadeh, *Alefba-e Jadid va Maktubat*, ed. Hamid Mohammadzadeh (Tabriz: Ehya Publications, 1978) and Baqer Mo'meni, ed. *Maqalat* (Tehran: Ava Press, 1972).

6. See, e.g., Mirza Agha Khan Kermani, *Seh Maktoub*, ed. (with an extensive introduction by) Bahram Choubin (Essen: Nima Press, 2000.) Accessed and downloaded in December 2012 from http://www.esnips.com/doc/1d9e2888-1dcf-4d5e-930e-99 d2b157ed55/3-Maktoob-Mirza-Agha-khan-kermani.

7. For a thorough examination of the nature of the thought of many of these intellectuals, see Afshin Marashi, *Nationalizing Iran: Culture, Power, and the State, 1870–1940* (Seattle: University of Washington Press, 2008). See, in particular, 49–85.

8. It is important to note that the actual redressing of Iran's semicolonial status and governmental despotism at the end of the nineteenth and the beginning of the twentieth centuries fell into the hands of intellectuals and activists who defied the dualistic approach and forged alliances among the revolutionary activists of religious and secular brands during the constitutional-revolution era.

9. Afshin Marashi argues that such manipulation of symbols started in the nineteenth century, during the reign of Nasser Din Shah. See Marashi, *Nationalizing Iran*, 15–39.

10. After the ousting of the Pahlavi dynasty and the establishment of the Islamic Republic, the exiled monarchist groups continued the discourse of Persian nationalism with even less inhibition than the Pahlavi state. For an example of such sentiment, see Khanak Eshghi-Sanati, *Nationalism va Regime-e Terror va Jonoon dar Iran* (Ottawa: Ava-e Iran, 1989).

11. Even though Al-Ahmad is most famous for his book on *Gharbzadegi*, it is in his later work *Dar Khedmat va Khianat-e Roshanfekran* (Tehran: Kharazmi Press, 1978)

that he presents Shi'i identity and the role of the clergy in promoting a healthy and authentic society.

12. See Ali Shariati, *Bazgasht-e Beh Khish* (Tehran: Hoseynieh Ershad, 1978). Even though Shariati was critical of the established clergy and its associated Islam, he still saw in Islam and Islamic discourse a potent tool for liberation.

13. Text of Khomeini's speech, accessed in December 2012 from http://www2.irib .ir/worldservice/imam/speech/16.htm.

14. Reza Ardakani Davari, *Nationalism va Inqelab* (Tehran: Daftar-e Pajouhesh-ha va Barnameh Rizi-e Farhangi, 1986).

15. Ibid., 164–165.

16. Davari defines liberalism here not as a belief in existence of private space or a series of freedoms, but as a belief that "humans are in charge of lawmaking and are the possessors of power, and anyone who disagrees with them should not be tolerated." See ibid., 170–171.

17. This argument has also been put forth by Morteza Motahhari, one of the most important religious thinkers in Iran, who was assassinated shortly after the revolution.

18. Davari, *Nationalism va Inqelab*, 20–21.

19. In fact it was Ali Shari'ati who first brought the notion of "Bazgasht-e be Khishtan" into the discourse of identity, from a religious point of view, as a remedy to alienation. Even though his notion of authentic identity was a call for rescuing ourselves from the yoke of the Western enchantment, he was also critical of traditional and static Shi'i notions of identity as the mirror image of enchantment with the West. See Ali Shari'ati, *Ensan-e bi Khod* (Tehran: Qalam Press, 1982), and Ali Shari'ati, *Bazshenasi Hoveyat-e Irani-Eslami* (Tehran: Elham Press, 1983).

20. Reza Ardakani Davari, *Inqelab va Vaz'e Kununi-e 'Alam* (Tehran: 'Alame Tabatabai Center for Culture, 1982), 254.

21. Ehsan Naraghi, *Ancheh Khod Dasht* (Tehran: Amir Kabir Publications, 1976), 155–159.

22. Ibid., 170–173.

23. For example, Kamran Daneshjoo, the minister of science, research, and technology, considers acceptance of a supreme leader as a necessary condition for any person to be a true member of the community, because it is only this adherence that shields an individual from an enemy's design for subjugation of the nation. See his statement at http://www.farsnews.com/newstext.php?nn=8812031060.

24. See the speech given by Heydar Moslehi, the minister of information, accessed in December 2012 from http://saharnews.ir/view-8954.html.

25. Of course, there are Sunnis, Christians, Jews, and Zoroastrians who are citizens of Iran but they, too, have to operate within the parameters set by the Islamic Republic, and have to accept the institutions of the Islamic Republic, including the office of the supreme leader.

26. See, e.g., Khamenei's reference to chastity as the determining characteristic of pre-Islamic Iranian society at http://farsi.Khamenei.ir/speech-content?id=9694.

27. See Ahmadinejad's speech to Iranians Living Abroad, 17 November 2007, in http://www.president.ir/fa/.

28. See http://farsi.khamenei.ir/speech-content?id=8485.

29. See http://farsi.khamenei.ir/speech-content?id=8430.

30. http://farsi.khamenei.ir/speech-content?id=8430.

31. See statements by Mohammed Yazdi, the former head of judiciary and present member of the Guardian Council, at http://www.rahesabz.net/story/5417/.

32. See http://www.kayhannews.ir/880925/2.htm#other206.

33. Most of the information about monarchist groups is provided by these groups on their own websites, in their pamphlets, and on their associated radio and television stations. The dearth of scholarly work about the monarchist groups makes verifying the claims of these organizations about their viability difficult. For a sample of scholarly works where there are some mentions of exiled monarchists, see Kathryn Spellman, *Religion and Nation: Iranian Local and Transnational Networks in Britain* (Oxford, Berghahn Books, 2004), Hamid Naficy, *The Making of Exile Cultures: Iranian Television in Los Angeles* (Minneapolis: University of Minnesota Press, 1993) and Sreberny-Mohammadi and Ali Mohammadi, "Post-Revolutionary Iranian Exiles: a Study of Impotence," *Third World Quarterly*, vol. 9, no. 1 (1987): 108–121.

34. In fact, many of these organizations are in bitter disagreement with each other. A concrete example is their disagreement about who should be the future king when the Islamic Republic falls. At least two of the more radical monarchical organizations are either not in favor of Reza Pahlavi to be that person, or are critical of him, due to their belief that he is not tough enough to fight the Islamic regime or that he flirts with people associated with the Islamic Republic. See, e.g., https://tondar.org/content/2010/08/701.html, and a four-part essay by Mas'oud Behnood in *Azarpaad*, accessed in December 2012 from http://www.rastakhiz.org/azarpaad/6/6.pdf.

35. On its platform [http://www.irancpi.net/menshor/menshor.htm] the party considers constitutional monarchy, in general, and the Pahlavi dynasty in particular, as the best political system for Iran, but for the most part its emphasis is on liberal democracy.

36. See http://www.rastakhiz.org/.

37. See http://www.tondar.org.

38. In 2007, he disappeared somewhere along the Turkish/Iranian border. There are several rumors about what might have happened to him. Some within the API, including his own son, believe that he has been killed, while Tondar maintains that he is somewhere in Iran and therefore cannot reveal himself.

39. See https://www.tondar.org/index.php?catid=9&blogid=1.

40. There have been attempts by all the monarchist groups, judging by their official websites, to purify the Persian language of Arabic words. This effort is particularly evident in the official site of the ROI.

41. Dariush Homayoun, *Pishtaz-e Hezareh Sevvum* (Hamburg: Talash Press, 2009), 81–86.

42. See an interview with Homayoun at http://www.iranian.com/Bayegan/2003/October/Homayoun/index.html.

43. See a sample of statements. For articles and essays in the publications of the ROI in this regard, see http://www.rastakhiz.org/rastakhiz/ri/prog/2.html, as well as a four-part essay by Mas'oud Behnood, the founder of the ROI in Azarpaad, the organization quarterly, accessed in December 2012: http://www.rastakhiz.org/azarpaad/6/6.pdf. For an API's representative statement, see https://tondar.org/content/2010/07/657.html, where the Achaemanid and Sasanid rules are considered as providers of laws and justice forever.

44. See http://www.rastakhiz.org/rastakhiz/ri/arman.html.

45. See the 30 January 2010 entry at https://tondar.org/.

46. In fact, Frood Fouladvand, the now-disappeared founder of the API, devoted a series of TV and radio programs called *Tazinameh*, aimed at refuting Islam. See https://www.tondar.org/tndoc/doku.php, accessed in December 2012.

47. See, e.g., a diatribe against Islam written by Ahmad Panahandeh on the CPI website. In his article titled "Islam, a Murderous Religion," Panahandeh states that Islam, in all its colors and sects, is a product of a temperament associated with desert, highway robbery, murder, pillage, and destruction, where humans and their dignity have no place: http://www.irancpi.net/digran/matn_3693_0.html. For another article by the same author and about the same subject, see http://www.irancpi.net/digran/matn_3610_0.html.

48. Dariush Homayoun, *Sad Sal Keshakesh ba Tajadod* (Hamburg: Talash Press, 2006), 206–208.

49. For an elaboration of Homayoun's view of Islam and Shi'ism, see Homayoun, *Pishtaz-e Hezareh Sevvum*, 265–302.

50. Ernest Renan, "Science and Islam," *Journal des Débats*, 19 May 1883: 1–24.

51. Homayoun, *Sad Sal Keshakesh ba Tajadod*, 203–240.

52. Ibid., 265–302.

53. Ibid., 206–208.

54. See http://www.irancpi.net/digran/matn_4057_0.html.

55. For several examples, see https://www.tondar.org/index.php?catid=3&blogid=1, accessed in December 2012.

56. See, e.g., Azarpaad, No. 7, Fall 2009, http://www.rastakhiz.org/azarpaad/7/7.pdf, accessed in December 2012.

57. These organizations have paid some lip service to the notion of civic construction of the polity in their constitutions. But such a notion pales in comparison to their praise for the strong rule of Reza Shah and, to some extent, of Mohammed Reza Shah.

58. In constructing the discourse of the Green Movement, I have used statements, announcements, and commentaries of these individuals, groups, and media outlets.

59. Mohammed Khatami, speech in Mas'ud La'li, ed., *Khatami az Che Miguyad* (Tehran: Ekhlas Press, 2000), 112.

60. Ibid., 114.

61. Ibid., 115–116.

62. See http://khordaad88.com/?p=1691.

63. In a detailed speech to university students, Mir Husayn Mousavi laid out the overall character of the movement, which included his views on this matter. See http://www.kaleme.com/1388/11/19/klm-11036.

64. See http://www.iranpresswatch.org/post/21.

65. See http://www.kaleme.com/1388/11/19/klm-11036.

66. See an article by Sadeq Zibakalam, a university professor and a reformist, on the internet site of Kalemeh: http://www.kaleme.com/1388/12/04/klm-12120.

67. See, e.g., Mohammad Khatami's statements during his meeting with a group of Tehran university students, in which he called for an overhaul of the election process in Iran: http://www.payvand.com/news/09/nov/1186.html.

68. See Mir Husayn Mousavi's 18th Statement, op. cit.

69. See Ayatollah Hossein-Ali Montazeri, *Hokumat-Dini va Hoquq-e Ensan* (Qom: 2007), in which he addresses the compatibility of the people's actual sovereignty/democracy with Islam. See, in particular, 13 and 34–35.

70. For Mohajerani's views see http://mohajerani.maktuob.net/.

71. For Kadivar's views, see http://www.kadivar.com/Index.asp, accessed in December 2012.

72. For Bazargan's views, see http://www.bazargan.com/Abdolali/.

73. For Ganji's views, see http://www.akbarganji.org/, accessed in December 2012.

74. See http://www.rahesabz.net/about/.

75. Ibid.

76. See the full translated text of the statement at http://www.uruknet.info /?p+61712.

77. See the full text at http://news.gooya.com/politics/archives/2010/01/098533 .php.

CHAPTER 14

Relocating a Common Past and the Making of East-centric Modernity: Islamic and Secular Nationalism(s) in Egypt and Iran

HANAN HAMMAD

Inspired by postcolonial theories, recent scholarship has studied the construction of Iranian and Egyptian modernity—including nationalism and identity—by focusing on the national engagement with European modernity or the *organic local* roots of modernity.[1] Leaving the Iranian engagement with Eastern cultures out of the inquiry, and limiting the discussion on the Iranian disengagement from the Arabo-Islamic legacies, oversimplifies and distorts the complex dynamics of the making of Iranian modernity. The limitation of this scholarship resulted in a misperception that Iranians in the late nineteenth and early twentieth centuries totally turned their backs on the Arab East, and that Arab cultural production was never a resource for Iranian modernity.[2] Recent scholarship on modern Egyptian intellectual history has done justice to the importance of Eastern culture, broadly speaking.[3] Yet the focus has been limited to the Arabo-Islamic culture, while the influence of Persian culture has been ignored, which led to a similar misperception that Iran had no place in modern Egyptian intellectual history, and that Egyptian intellectuals did not pay attention to, or even were hostile to, Iranian culture. In an attempt to de-center the West and to bring the East to its rightful place in the making of Iranian and Egyptian modernity, this article examines how the desire to *authenticate modernity* influenced the mutual perception of religious and secular intellectuals in Egypt and Iran in the first half of the twentieth century. I shift the focus to the East–East interaction to argue that reforming intellectuals in modern Egypt and Iran considered, influenced, and benefited from each other's historical experiences as a source of inspiration and a model for imitation. In their endeavor to construct national identities as *authentic* but modern, genuinely Eastern-Muslim but "almost European," Iranian reformists were interested in contemporary Egypt, while Egyptian intellectuals were infatuated with medieval Iran. Iranians sought contemporary Egypt as a modern Middle Eastern society, and Egyptians invested in medieval Iran as a source of Islamic-Eastern pride and achievement. Secular and religious intellectuals in both countries downplayed sectarian differences between Shiʻi Iranians and Sunni Egyptians, and contained the centuries-long Islamic polemics and disunity to combine "Eastern spirituality" with "Western advancement."

Egyptianness, Iranianness, and Relocating the Past(s)

Equipped with modern education, Iranian and Egyptian intellectuals claimed the mission of national modernization and reform.[4] Building a national identity was a core question in their project of modernization. To construct an authentic, but modern and almost European national identity, secularists in both countries were committed to Western-oriented territorial nationalism, and claimed that their societies were continuations of "authentic" pre-Islamic entities.[5] They based their cultural identities on their beliefs in the distinctiveness of the Egyptian and Iranian minds and cultures. The pre-Islamic pasts of both nations were well suited for the construction of Iranianness and Egyptianness. How Iranians employed the Zoroastrian-Sasanian past, and how Egyptians utilized the pharaonic heritage, to boost their respective territorial nationalisms has received efficient treatment in the historical inquiry. Here I deal only with how nationalists in both countries constructed the years when Egypt was part of the ancient Persian Empire, between 525 and 323 BC. Although they were on the opposite sides of this *colonial* experience, modern intellectuals in both nations employed it to generate national pride, and to project contemporary national sentiments onto that past. In his monumental multivolume *Iran-e Bastan*, on ancient Iran, Moshir al-Dowleh, known later on as Hassan Pirniya (1873-1935) gave readers a highly patriotic account of pre-Islamic Persia.[6] Hence, incorporating Pharaonic Egypt in the Persian Empire was part of constructing glorious ancient Iranian history. Pirniya emphasized that the Persian invaders were respectful to the Egyptians, their religion, and their culture.[7] According to this account, the Egyptian revolt that lasted six years, between 460 and 454 BC, during Ardashir's reign, was attributed to the Greeks' intervention and their tireless efforts to bring Egypt under their influence and away from Persian control.[8]

The *colonization* of ancient Egypt by the Persians afforded intellectuals of colonized Egypt historical capital to generate nationalist resistance against the British occupation. Poets and writers sought to express, and were influenced by, patriotic sentiments that were bolstered by foreign domination in the nineteenth and twentieth centuries. Thus, they recalled the *colonization* of Egypt by the Persians as an episode of the continuing Egyptian nationalist struggle against foreign colonizers. Egyptian revolts against the Persians provided the neoclassical poet Ahmad Shawqi (1868-1932), well known as the Prince of the Arab Poets, with a focal event around which he constructed a historical Egyptian patriotism.[9] Taha Husayn employed the Egyptian resistance against Persians to claim that Egypt was always apart from the Eastern mindset, and emphasized that the Egyptian mind was in rivalry with the Persian Eastern mind.[10] Interestingly, in his infatuation with the West and mastery of the medieval Arabic literature, Husayn playfully gave himself the liberty to change a poem by the Abbassid poet al-Buhturi, replacing the Sasanids with the Greeks.[11]

Mohamad Tavakoli-Targhi rightly argues that the selective remembrance of things pre-Islamic made possible the articulation of a new national identity and political discourse.[12] Yet it did not make the dissociation from Islam and Arabic culture possible mostly because, as Vejdani puts it concerning Iran, intellectuals demonstrated admiration for Islam as a civilization, and played a crucial role in redefining the meaning and category of Islam by historicizing and nationalizing the category itself.[13] Current scholarship focuses on how Iranian intellectuals since the nineteenth century have articulated a secular nationalist discourse and identity that glorified the pre-Islamic past, blamed Arabs and Islam for Iran's "decadence," and interposed the desirable attributes of Europeans on the pre-Islamic Self.[14] Similarly, the literary and intellectual history of Pahlavi Iran amplifies the continuation of that intellectual trend by focusing on particular authors such as Sadeq Hedayat and Bozorg Alavi, who explicitly scorned Arabs and Islam and voiced xenophobic nationalist sentiments.[15]

Those authors fit neatly into the construction of the intellectual history of modern Persia as part of the emergence and continuation of what Kamran Rastegar precisely calls the ideological project of "Persianism."[16] Hedayat, more than any other writer of the Pahlavi period, became the icon in the Iranian literary canon.[17] Praised by orientalist scholars and European literary figures, his impressive literary talent, proliferation in multiple genres, and expression of blatant mockery of Islam and Arabs, along with his dramatic death, all provide spectacular elements for a towering figure, or—to use Homa Katouzian's assessment—a *legend*, in Iranian culture.[18] The tendency to celebrate his influential literary legacy in the nationalist scholarship overlooks Hedayat's racism, not only against Arabs but also against Jews and Africans.[19] Of course, Hedayat was not alone among Iranians in his anti-Arab attitude. The Nazis' theory of the superiority of the Aryan race lent itself to this anti-Arab racism.[20] Yet, focusing exclusively on that anti-Arab intellectual trend distorts a complex cultural process in which Arab culture, particularly that which was produced in Egypt, actually enjoyed a strong position. Cultural interaction between Egypt and Iran during the late nineteenth and early twentieth centuries provides evidence that Arabic culture continued as an important source of modern Persian culture, as much as Persian culture provided Egyptian intellectuals with a source of pride and spiritual assurance.

In Search of the *Authentic* Modernity

With the spread of modern education beyond the elite classes, authenticity became a social capital that could be used politically by the newly emerged modern educated middle and lower-middle classes. Only a modernity backed up by a simultaneous claim of "authenticity" represented *the correct modernity*.[21] Propagating a constructed "traditionalism," in which the East, Arabism, and Islam enjoyed a central position, became a crucial element of the localized Middle Eastern modernity. Far from the misperception that Iranian intellectuals since the nineteenth century were collectively hostile to the Arabs and their culture, medieval and modern Arab cultural productions thrived in modern Iran. Prominent Iranian nationalists, such as Mohammad 'Ali Forughi, included Arabic texts within the national canon, and saw Arabic prose composed by ethnic Persians as part of Iranian literature.[22] The failure of the Farhangestan, the Persian Language academy, to purify the Persian language of Arabic words is equaled by the failure of Egyptian attempts to alter the Arabic alphabet and to omit some classical Arabic grammar from the curricula.[23] Classical Arabic texts and medieval authors continued to attract attention among modern Iranian intellectuals. They attended and wrote about major cultural events in the Arab world, such as the festivals of the millennium of the Arab poet Abu al-'Ala' al-Ma'arri in Damascus in 1944.[24] The Persian translation of *The Thousand and One Nights* by 'Abd al-Latif Tasiji during the reign of Mohammad Shah, and the translation of Jurji Zaydan's novels by 'Abd al-Hosayn Mirza Qajar in the 1900s, left us with monumental works of Persian literature that impacted the Iranian literary taste and Persian compositions.[25] In the nineteenth and twentieth centuries, many translations of European texts into Persian were made from Arabic or Turkish, not from the original language, a practice that Iraj Afshar calls "translation by proxy."[26] For example, Ali Dashti translated Edmond Demolins's *A quoi tient la supériorité des Anglo-Saxons?* into Persian from an Arabic translation that had been published in Cairo by the Egyptian Fathi Ahmad Zaghlul.[27] Translation of

Arabic texts and of works from Arabic translations shows that looking down on Arabs and the Arabic language and culture was far from being a universal attitude among Iranian intellectuals. Translations from Arabic, particularly Egyptian works, continued under the Pahlavis. Translated books ranged from religion to history and finance and financial laws authored by secular and religious scholars.[28]

Egypt was not a mere secondhand source of knowledge of the West, as a prominent Iranianist scholar claimed.[29] Egyptians provided their Iranian counterparts with an Eastern model of modernization. To put it differently, Egypt offered Iranians a model of authentic modernity, or an Eastern-tried modernity that might not be as alien as the European model, and consequently was more appealing for, and easier to adopt by, Iranians. Iranian scholars participated in scientific conferences held in Egypt, such as the International Conference of Geography and Race in 1925 and the International Conference of Medicine in 1938.[30] These participations and activities gave Iranian modernizers the opportunity to consider the Egyptian experience. Egypt had a longer history of adapting Western institutions and European thought.[31] It was no surprise that the Egyptian experiences in the fields of health, education, technology, etc., were frequently pointed to in Iranian scientific discourses.[32] Contemporary Egyptian cinema, art, literature, tourism, and cultural institutions attracted Iranian interest. There was also interest in Egyptian sociopolitical issues, such as the capitulations, labor laws, and social reform.[33]

Iranian students attended Egyptian institutes of higher education to study modern disciplines that were not available in Iran, and Cairo life attracted many Iranians who settled in Egypt instead of pursuing their intended journeys to Europe and the U.S.A.[34] The most notable example is Mohammad Mahdi Tabrizi, who befriended the Islamic modernist Muhammad 'Abduh while studying medicine in Cairo.[35] Upon finishing his studies, he founded the first Persian newspaper in Cairo, *Hekmat*, in 1892.[36] *Hekmat* was almost the Persian equivalent to the Arabic periodicals *al-Muqtataf* and *al-Hilal* in Egypt. It appeared every ten days for more than fifteen years, and was interested in technical and industrial innovations, science and medicine in particular, in addition to literature and politics.[37] Like the editor of *Hekmat*, Mirza abd al-Mohammad Mo'addab al-Soltan Esfahani Irani, the founder of the longest lived Iranian newspaper in Cairo, *Chehrenama*, and Ali Mohammad Kashani, the editor of *Soraya* and *Parvaresh*, settled in Cairo on their way to Europe.[38] *Soraya* appeared in October 1898, and *Parvaresh* appeared in June 1900. *Chehrenama*, which was established first in Alexandria and then moved to Cairo the following year, survived from 1904 until 1966. Although all these periodicals were partly geared to the Iranian community in Egypt, their major circulation was in Iran, and they attracted readers among Iranians in Turkey, Iraq, and India.[39] *Chehrenama* and other emigrant papers were banned in Iran under Mohammad Ali Shah (1907–1909). Beyond serving as mere community papers, Iranian periodicals in Cairo advocated Islamic unity to ward off aggressive foreign intervention, boycott foreign aggressors, promote a sound educational system, and adopt reforms to prevent "bloody revolutions."[40]

Cairo not only provided Iranian intellectuals with mass-communication technology, but also with freedom of expression. That would explain the proliferation of Persian publications printed in Cairo during the troubled years on the eve of the Constitutional Revolution. Even after the introduction of printing in Iran, Persian books were printed in Egypt, and the Bulaq Press in Cairo published many Persian books in the nineteenth and early twentieth centuries.[41] The oldest Persian book printed in Cairo and registered in the Egyptian archive was entitled *Tohfat Vahbi* and dates back to 1827.[42] A vibrant cultural life and freedom of expression in Cairo attracted Iranian intellectuals. Yusuf Ashtiani (E'tesam al-Molk) and Hajji Zayn al-'Abedin Maraghehi visited Egypt to explore its intellectual life.[43] Not surprisingly, Maraghehi published the first volume of his dissenting book *Seyahatname-e Ebrahim Beg* (*The Travel Diary of Ebrahim Beg*) in Cairo on the eve of the Constitutional Revolution. That book, which was venomously critical of the despotic Iranian government, was secretly circulated, and the regime arrested anybody who was found reading it; a number of people were arrested on suspicion of having written it.[44] Abd al-Rahim Taliboff, who was accused of atheism, and had his writing forbidden by the religious leaders of Tabriz, published his last work, *Masalek al-Mohsenun* (*The Way of the Charitable*), in Cairo in 1905.[45]

Religious and secular Egyptian periodicals of the first half of the twentieth century were circulated in Iran. The Egyptian press attracted wider readership among Iranians when some of its articles were translated into Persian and republished in major Iranian newspapers such as *Ettela'at* and *Keyhan*.[46] Iranian intellectuals read, translated, and adapted works of Egyptian intellectuals who were engaged with reformist thought and social critique. It was the works of the Egyptian Qasim Amin *Women's Emancipation* (1899) and *The New Woman* (1900) that triggered the debate over the issue of women's education in Iran. Only one year after their Arabic publication in Cairo, Yusuf Ashtiani (E'tesam al-Molk) published a partial translation entitled *Tarbiyat-i nesvan* (*The Education of Women*).[47] The following year. he published the first translation of Amin's second book, *The New Woman*, in 1901.[48] In the preface, E'tesam al-Molk noted that famous Egyptian writers such as Amin and Murqus Fahmi, as well as European thinkers, had written extensively on women's rights, including the right to education.[49] A fuller translation of Amin's *Women's Emancipation* was published by Muhazzib in 1937 under instructions from the Ministry of Education under the title *Zan va azadi* (*Woman and Liberty*). Under instructions from the Ministry of Education, Muhazzib also translated Amin's second book *al-Mar'a al-jadida*, under the title *Zan-e emruz* (*Today's Woman*).[50] A series of articles on the rights and liberties of women in the journal *Habl al-Matin* in 1905 considered Qasim Amin a pioneer of women's education, and reviewed the attacks against him, and the debates of that time, in the Egyptian press.[51] Iranian reformers shared Amin's conviction that the status of women is inseparably tied to the status of a nation, and the progress of a nation to the progress of women. The position of women in ancient Egypt, and the contemporary Egyptian feminist movement, continued to be admired by Iranian modernizers, who ignored the fact that Egyptian women were denied suffrage.[52] Other Egyptian authors were admired by Iranian intellectuals. The most notable example is Taha Husayn, whose books were translated into Persian, including two different Persian translations of his autobiography, *Days*. In a comment on Taha Husayn, an Iranian intellectual wrote:

> No compliment will do justice to his eloquence of speech and fluency of language and charm of rhetoric and clarity of words and unique rhythm in reciting the poems. Those who had read all of Dr. Taha Husayn's texts and deemed him worthy of the title "the dean of Arabic literature," after having seen him present a speech and heard him speak, found him two hundred times more eminent than they had imagined, especially because Mr. Dr. Taha Husayn is far more thoughtful than to concern himself with ethnic or linguistic prejudices.[53]

Against the misperception that Iranian intellectuals were disengaging from Islam, Egyptian works on Islamic history and philosophy were deemed worthy of translation into Persian. Interestingly, most of these translated books were authored by Egyptian liberal secularists such as Husayn Haykal, Taha Husayn and Tawfiq al-Hakim. In the late nineteenth and early twentieth centuries, many Egyptian books were circulated in Iran only a few months after their printings in Cairo.[54] The historical novels of Jurji Zaydan provided Egyptians, as well as Arabs and Iranians, with a sense of authenticity and pride. Eight of his historical novels were translated into Persian and enjoyed high popularity among both common and elite readers.[55] Egyptian scholars on modern Iranian literature argue that Zaydan's writing had a huge influence on early Iranian historical novels after the Constitutional Revolution: for example, the writings of Mohammad Baqer Kasravi and San'atzadeh Kermani.[56] After prolonged neglect of Zaydan's influence on modern Iranian culture by both

Iranian and Western scholars, a recent study argues that these writings played an important role in the process of innovating literary practices in order to conform to the needs and imperatives of the modern world.[57] Zaydan's multi-volume *Tarikh al-tamadun al-Islami* (*History of Islamic Civilization*), which was translated into Persian by ʿAbd al-Hosayn Mirza Qajar in 1911, signifies pan-Islamic solidarity across national boundaries.[58] This translation may have been intended as a textbook, since it was commissioned by a member of the Iranian parliament and approved by the Ministry of Education.[59] Zaydan's historical fiction and nonfiction highlight and praise the role of Persians in the Abbasid Caliphate.[60] The fact that Zaydan was an Arab Christian induced Iranian nationalists to celebrate his writings as acknowledgment from the *other*.[61] Zaydan's narratives were also sympathetic to the Shiʿa perspective of this history, while faithfully following Sunni themes as well, which contributed to the popularity of the books both in the Arab world and in Iran.[62] In that sense, Zaydan was a forerunner of the Egyptian secularists who wrote intensively on Islamic history and many of whose works were translated into Persian.

Egyptians were not less interested in translating from Persian. Egyptians focused mostly on medieval Persian literature and philosophy, and paid much less attention to contemporary Iranian politics and culture. Contemporary Egypt offered Iranian reformists a Muslim experience with modernization, while Egyptians profiled the heyday of *Islamic* Iran looking toward the glorious days of Islam and Islamic achievement in the arts, literature, and philosophy.[63] Egyptian secularists tended to overlook contemporary Iran and to focus on the "good old days." In a comment that revealed interest in Iran and Persian culture, Taha Husayn expressed his desire to learn Persian, because the Abbasid poet al-Mutanabbi's Shiraz verses possessed a certain freshness.[64] Thanks to the establishment of the Institute of Oriental Studies in Cairo in 1939, medieval Persian literature attracted intense attention. The founder of that program, ʿAbd al-Wahhab ʿAzzam, achieved the first complete Arabic translation of Ferdowsi's *Shahnameh* in 1932,[65] and published his book on Farid al-Din al-ʿAttar in 1945.[66] In the same year, Yahya al-Khashshab published his Arabic translation of Naser Khosrow's *Safarnameh*.[67] Although Persian language and culture were taught in Fuad, Faruq, and Ibrahim universities (now, respectively, Cairo, Alexandria, and ʿAyn Shams universities), Egyptian scholars of Persian culture did not pay much attention to modern Persian literature or contemporary Iranian society until the last decades of the twentieth century.[68] A bibliography of scholarly books on Iran published in Egypt until 1968 and containing eighty-one items in different disciplines did not list one book on modern Iranian literature or contemporary social debates.[69]

Another list of important scholarship produced in Egyptian universities until 1975 reveals that only medieval Persian literature and philosophy constituted Persian studies in Egypt.[70] Not one title indicates an interest in contemporary Iranian society. Aside from a translation of a very few short stories that were published by Amin 'Abd al-Majid Badawi in *al-Adab* magazine during the 1960s, Egyptian readers did not get to read the works of Sadeq Hedayat or his contemporary Iranian authors until Ibrahim al-Dusuqi Shita translated a collection of Hedayat's short stories in 1975.[71] Shita published the first Arabic translation of Hedayat's seminal novella *Buf-e Kur* the following year.[72] That interest in medieval Iranian intellectuals as preserved in archival manuscripts by successive generations of Egyptian Persianist scholars is consistent with the Western orientalist approach. It could be explained that from its inception, Persian studies in Egypt was affiliated with Oriental Studies departments, whose focus was mostly on Islamic Studies. Professors, both Egyptians and Europeans, were trained according to the orientalist academic traditions. On the other hand, pioneering intellectuals who championed Persian Studies, such as 'Abd al-Wahhab 'Azzam, had a strong inclination toward pan-Islamism and Arabism.[73] In their view, studying a shared Islamic history, rather than contemporary divided societies or divisive politics, served their cause of achieving Islamic unity and empowerment. In essence, they were not different from the secularist modernizers. Both borrowed Orientalist traditions to empower the Oriental self in opposition to the West. The state of Iran under the Pahlavis encouraged that approach by sponsoring academic activities and public commemorations of medieval Persian writers as part of its nation-building project.[74] Egyptian scholars were invited to these events and were praised for mastering classical Persian. For example, the state of Iran sponsored a two-week conference on Ferdowsi and his *Shahnameh* in Tehran in October 1934. Orientalists from forty-two countries, including the Egyptian Abd al-Wahhab 'Azzam, were hosted at the conference.[75] The state of Iran also frequently funded publications of Egyptian Persianists.[76] Musaddiq and the oil crisis attracted public attention and sympathy in Egypt in the early 1950s. This is when we see press coverage, publications, and translations for European works on modern Iranian history and contemporary politics.[77]

Easternists, Egyptianized Iranians, and the Road to the Islamic Rapprochement

The historical Islamic writings in interwar Egypt by secularist intellectuals such as Husayn Haykal, Taha Husayn, Abbas al-'Aqqad, and Ahmad Amin, paved the road to the call for rapprochement between Sunnis and Shi'is, giving rise to the Easternist discourse, and hence enjoyed popularity among Iranian readers. Through critical reading and questioning the authenticity of medieval Sunni sources and incorporating Shi'i sources, those authors provided a revisionist construction of the first Islamic century. Although they did not endorse any of the esoteric Shi'i dogmas, the Sunni Egyptian authors propagated views close to, but not identical with, the Shi'i views of many major developments leading to the split in the first Muslim community.[78] Easternist discourse in Egypt attracted staunch secularists such as Muhammad Husayn Haykal and others, who employed rich discursive practices, including rhetoric, symbols, terminology, representation, and historical narrative.[79] In a similar context, Islam enjoyed a strong presence in the interwar Iranian nationalist historiography, along with the Westernization drive.[80] Although many of the Easternists were educated in the West, or received western education locally, they criticized the blind imitation of the West and legitimized their calls for modernization without annulment of *authenticity* or traditions in both Egypt and Iran. The Sorbonne-educated Egyptian author Zaki Mubarak criticized Iranian intellectuals who were disengaging the Iranian culture from the Arabo-Islamic legacies.[81] The Iranian Ghasem Ghani, who admired Reza Shah and never criticized his Westernizing policies, was disturbed that the Lebanese upper classes "have adopted the loose lifestyle and manners of the French, their dancing and their debauchery. Almost all aspects of Arab and Eastern culture have disappeared."[82] During his ambassadorship in Cairo, he suffered a sort of alienation and depression because, as he put it, "[I]n recent years one has heard much about national and individual rights, and the words 'independence' and 'liberty' are on everyone's lips, but intellectual and spiritual freedom have declined."[83] However, he was at ease with secular scholars in Egypt, and developed a close friendship with Tahah Husayn, to the extent that he was the witness at the marriage of Husayn's daughter, and Husayn wrote a book chapter on their friendship.[84]

Easternist discourse was not a mere representation of an intellectual trend. It was the ideological expression of the socioeconomic needs of the rising Egyptian bourgeoisie and Iranian and Arab expatriates in Egypt. The Egyptian bourgeoisie were seeking the surrounding Eastern markets to export manufactured products, expand investments, and find jobs for the unemployed educated classes.[85] Those who got professional and bureaucratic jobs in Arab states *discovered* the East, and expressed their aspiration for Egyptian progress and independence as part of the progression of what they called "the Eastern Question." They redefined commonalities and differences between Egypt and the surrounding East, including the sectarian division between

Shi'is and Sunnis. After some of them—the Egyptian author Ahmad Amin in particular—recklessly stepped into the minefield of sectarianism in Iraq, they joined the call for Islamic rapprochement. That call incorporated Iran into the Egyptian vision of the Eastern Question.[86] While working in Iraq and witnessing the Iraqi-Iranian agreement on the Shatt al-'Arab borders in 1937, Zaki Mubarak called for reaching out to fellow Muslims in Iran, and wished for a settlement based on Islamic unity.[87] The rising Egyptian diplomacy after the cozy independence in 1922 encouraged the openness towards the East, particularly Iran, to strengthen the Eastern bond.[88] Iran was among the first nations to open an embassy in Cairo, and in 1928 signed an agreement that gave Iranians in Egypt property rights equal to those of Egyptian citizens. Interestingly, Egyptian diplomats explicitly expressed their discontent with their assignments to serve in Tehran, because they considered living in Tehran to be too harsh and backward.[89] The fact that two diplomats had died there made Tehran "a bad omen."[90]

The assimilation of the Iranian community in Egypt was substantial in propagating Easternism and Islamic rapprochement beyond religious and scholarly circles. Since the late nineteenth century, Iranian communities had grown up in Egyptian cities such as Cairo, Alexandria, al-Mahalla al-Kubra, Tanta, and al-Mansura. Benefiting from the economic boom and legal protection of the capitulation system, Iranian merchants in Egypt traded mostly in carpets, tobacco, and dried fruits and nuts. Their trade was large enough to justify the formation of the Iranian Chamber of Commerce in downtown Cairo in the first half of the twentieth century.[91] That chamber was so effective that it pressed its demand not to renew the Egyptian-Iranian Agreement, because it made Iranians in Egypt subject to the local Egyptian courts and relinquished their capitulation rights.[92] Iranians who had enjoyed the leverage of the Mixed Courts complained that the local Egyptian court system was too slow, and harmful to their interests.[93] The Iranian community was large and wealthy enough to form and support different social and cultural organizations. There were the Iranian Charity Association in Cairo, the Iranian Tikkiya in Alexandria, in which the community commemorated Muharram and other occasions, and the Iranian-Egyptian Youth Association in Cairo.[94] The community also supported several publications, as previously mentioned.

It is difficult to assess to what extent these publications were a cultural bridge between the two nations. They were in Persian, and did not target any Egyptian readership. Contrary to Iranian travelers, the community was settled in Egypt, and kept a *remote* connection with Iran. At the same time, we cannot underestimate the possibility of being fluent and influential on both cultures. Their publications traveled, carrying their ideas to Iranians in Iran and

in the diaspora. Their settlement in Egypt allowed the opportunity for interaction with the surrounding society and to influence some students of Persian
language and culture. In his memoir, the prominent Egyptian scholar of Oriental studies Husayn Mujib al-Misri gives a very strong positive account of
his friendship with the Egyptian-based Iranian intellectual Mo'addabzadeh.
Mo'addabzadeh was a second-generation Iranian living in Egypt; he inherited
his father's Persian magazine *Chehrenama*, which he edited until its closure in
1966. In addition to his work in journalism, he taught at the American University in Cairo.[95] The friendship that started when al-Misri was a student of
Persian in 1938 and continued until the death of Mo'addabzadeh in the early
1990s rendered great favors to al-Misri's scholarly career. It helped him to
master spoken Persian and the language of the Persian press, which he considered different from the language of literature, in addition to giving him access
to Iranian diplomats in Egypt and a sustainable source of new Persian books
and periodicals.[96] Yet al-Misri's published works were mostly concerned with
religious themes in Iranian literature.[97]

In the sphere of popular culture, Iranian commemoration of Muharram
was known among people of Cairo, particularly those who lived and worked
in the old city around the al-Azhar, al-Hakim, and al-Aqmar mosques.
These religious Shi'i events were called Zaffat al-'Ajam, the Iranian proces-
sion. While this name amplifies the presence of the Iranian ethnicity, it di-
minishes its association with Shi'i Islam and consequently understates the
participation of Arab, and maybe Egyptian, Shi'is. The mutual influence of
these processions and religious- and nonreligious-based folklore celebrations
in Egypt needs further research. However, the name Zaffat al-'Ajam draws
boundaries between those who participated and funded these events and the
Egyptian public, who deliberately or accidentally watched it or participated
in its festivities. It not only labels these practices as foreign, but also stresses
their connection to medieval times, calling them 'Ajam, rather than Persian
or Iranian.[98]

In the interwar period, fewer Iranians came to reside in Egypt; many members of the Iranian community were Egyptian-born and thus were more assimilated into Egyptian life, especially those who were born from intermar-
riages with Egyptians.[99] Arabic became predominant among them to the
point that the Iranian ambassador Ali Akbar Bahman addressed an Iranian
gathering in the embassy in Arabic so as not to have to use an interpreter, as
would have been necessary if he had spoken in Persian.[100] This generation was
socially and culturally hybridized. They were Egyptianized in many ways, but
they were also Iranians and Shi'is. They needed the Egyptian surroundings
to accept and understand their Shi'ism, and highlighted the shared Islamic

and Eastern civilization. In this context, cultural institutions championed by Iranians and Egyptians, mostly with Easternist intellectual orientations, flourished. An Iranian émigré in Egypt named Aqa Mirza Mahdi Beg Rafiʿ Meshki funded Jamʿiyyat al-Rabita al-Sharqiyya, the Eastern Bond Society, an organization composed of Egyptians and expatriates in Egypt in 1922. The Society was a collation of secular and religious intellectuals, orientalist scholars, merchants, and royal-family members, and functioned as a cultural club rather than as a political platform.[101] In October 1928, it started publishing an Arabic periodical called *al-Rabita al-Sharqiyya*, propagating Eastern cooperation and unity beyond pan-Islamism or Arab nationalism.[102] Meshki, whose family was prominent among the Iranian community in Egypt, was a major businessman, and chaired both of the Iranian Chamber of Commerce in Cairo and the Iranian Charity Organization for many years. Despite his high profile in the Iranian community, he represents a generation of Egyptian-born Iranians that were gradually assimilated into Egyptian social culture. He was a good Arabic poet and his poetry was well received.[103] Another Iranian émigré who was involved in the Eastern Bond Society is Muhammad Reza Qazvini. He chaired the Persian subcommittee that was designated to reach out to Persian-speaking intellectuals and to discuss issues related to Persia, Afghanistan and Baluchistan.[104] Among the most important activities of the Eastern Bond Society were the commemoration of Jamal al-Din al-Afghani in 1924, a reception for the Indian poet Rabindranath Tagore during his visit to Egypt in 1926, and another for the Afghani King Amanullah in 1927. The Iranian community in Egypt, particularly those who were active in the Eastern Bond Society, drew the attention of the Iranian government to the importance of Tagore's visit to Egypt as an Asian elder statesman bearing a message of "cultural revival."[105] This message impressed the Iranian officials in the Pahlavi regime, and, following suggestions from Iranians in Cairo, and inspired by Tagore's visit to Egypt, the officials at the foreign ministry and the Ministry of Education concluded that Iranians, like their Egyptian counterparts, would respond well to such a message.[106]

The marriage of the Iranian Crown Prince Mohammad Reza and the Egyptian Princess Fawziya at the end of the 1930s was an occasion to reconstruct cultural differences and commonalities between Egyptian and Iranian societies.[107] The compatibility of the marriage between the Shiʿi prince and the Sunni princess with the Islamic Sunni *Fiqh* jurisprudence triggered a debate in the press. The debate was decided in favor of the marriage, with a fatwa by al-Azhar rector Sheikh Abu al-ʿAziz al-Maraghy.[108] Several Egyptian periodicals, including *al-Manar*, welcomed the fatwa and emphasized that there is no Islamic rule that prevents intermarriage between Shiʿis and Sunnis.[109]

The royal marriage triggered a mutual interest in both directions. Dr. Ghasem Ghani commented on the denigration Iran received in the Egyptian press, and showed bitterness over the revival of hostile rumors and prejudices about Iranian Shi'i heresies.[110] However, this negative assessment was not the only view. Many intellectuals expressed admiration for Iranian civilization and its rich culture, and highlighted the "deep-rooted connections between Egypt and Iran."[111] In praise of Iran and Reza Shah, Ahmad Mahmud al-Sadati, who was a state employee at the Egyptian archive, *Dar al-Kutub*, published a book calling Reza Shah Pahlavi the founder of the Iranian renaissance.[112] The Iranian press was equally celebratory of Egypt and its royal family.[113] Due to the iron fist of Reza Shah, we can expect to see only those comments that were compatible with the marriage plan. Around that time, we see an increasing interest in ancient and contemporary Egypt, and how ancient Egyptians enjoyed scientific sophistication and advancement.[114] The Iranian press also welcomed the royal marriage as a step toward Islamic unity.[115] The Iranian regime employed the rhetoric of Islamic unity to counter Fawziyya's demand for divorce a decade later.[116]

In this atmosphere, a group of Iranians and Egyptians formed Jama'at al-ukhuwwa al-Islamiyya, the Islamic Brotherhood Society, which attracted members from inside and outside the religious establishments in forty-six countries.[117] The pioneer Persianist scholar 'Abd al-Wahhab 'Azzam, who had worked in Iraq and later became the first General Secretary of the Arab League, was the chairman. The main goals of the society were introducing Muslims of different countries to each other, easing the sectarian issues and avoiding fanatical discussions, protecting Islamic beliefs, coordinating curriculums of religious and moral education in Muslim countries, facilitating cooperation between Muslim students and helping them to join the Egyptian universities, and building and operating a dormitory based on Islamic moral codes.[118] The fact that 'Abd al-Wahhab 'Azzam, who was very close to the Royal Palace in Egypt and had direct influence on King Faruq's regional policies, chaired the society indicates that the society was an official endeavor to contain the antagonism provoked by the royal marriage.

Islamic reformers and Easternists in Egypt and Iran succeeded in achieving their far-reaching aims, i.e., to further Islamic ecumenism through the Dar al-Taqrib Bayna al-Madhahib al-Islamiyya, the Center for Rapprochement of Islamic Sects.[119] The center was founded in Cairo in 1948 exclusively for religious and social purposes, and issued a quarterly magazine called *Risalat al-Islam* (*The Message of Islam*).[120] The Iranian émigré Mohammad Taqi al-Qommi was instrumental in founding the center, and became its first general secretary.[121] The coalition between Egyptianized Iranians and Easternist Egyptians influenced the activities of the center to a large extent. It tried very hard to strike a balance between informing the public about Shi'ism and not angering regional Sunni regimes. Although the bylaws of the center never explicitly excluded any Muslim sect, its activities and publications show that it aimed only at rapprochement between Sunnis and Twelver Shi'is.[122] The center did not risk the anger of regional Sunni governments, particularly the Saudis who were hostile to Shi'is. Upon its establishment, the center contacted the Saudi king, Abdul-Aziz al-Saud, assuring him that the group did not intend to review Islamic jurisprudence, merge *madhhabs*, or endorse people of incorrect beliefs. Yet the Center propagated Shi'i scholarship and published Abu al-Fadl bil-Hassan al-Tabarsi's *Majma' al-Bayan li-'Ulum al-Qur'an*, which it considered the most acceptable interpretation of the holy book among both Sunnis and Shi'is. Shaltut and al-Qommi cooperated to collect *hadiths* that were agreed upon by Sunnis and Shi'is, a project that was never completed. The most important achievement of the center was teaching Shi'i jurisprudence in al-Azhar, and Shaltut's fatwa to legitimize worshipping according to the Shi'i Imami and Zaydi *madhhabs*.

The center emphasized its commitment to fighting fanaticism and ignorance by allowing only knowledgeable scholars of each sect to provide correct and accurate information about their *madhhabs*. The only Sunni scholar who claimed misrepresentation and took advantage of the center's platform to correct the public image of his sect was the Saudi Abd al-Karim Bin Juhayman from Najd. He rejected the term "Wahhabi," insisting that followers of Muhammad bin Abd al-Wahhab were "Hanbalis," and attributed their misrepresentation to their rivals.[123] On the other hand, defending the Shi'is intensively and highlighting Shi'i jurisprudence repeatedly made contemporary Shi'i and Sunni Egyptian authors consider the Center of Rapprochement a sort of center for Shi'i missionary work in Egypt.[124]

Conclusion

Rather than focusing on the imitation or adaptation of Eurocentric modernity in the nineteenth- and twentieth-century Middle East, this article focuses on how intellectuals in two linguistically and geographically disconnected countries considered each other's modernity. Tracing the mutual perception of secular and religious intellectuals in Egypt and Iran sheds light on an overlooked aspect of the complex process of *making, localizing*, and *authenticating* modernity in the Muslim East. There is a widespread misperception that Iranian intellectuals throughout the late nineteenth century and the first half of the twentieth looked down upon Arab culture and sought to eliminate the Arabo-Islamic legacies, and that their Egyptian counterparts were hostile to

Persian culture. In reality, both religious and secular intellectuals in Egypt and Iran showed a rigorous mutual interest. Cultural interaction between Egypt and Iran during the first half of the twentieth century provides a good case for the strong presence and the continuation of the Arabo-Islamic influence on modern Iran, and the revival of the Egyptian interest in Persian literature and philosophy. Around their concepts of being modern and authentic, intellectuals in modern Egypt and Iran mapped their cultural rapprochement and selectively considered how each culture could add to and aid the other. Intellectuals in both countries were very similar in many ways, particularly in their spontaneous aspiration to mimic Europe and to localize modernity. In engaging the European model, both Iranians and Egyptians were localizing Europe and Europeanizing the self. Simultaneously, to authenticate *their* modernity, intellectuals focused on Eastern civilization and Eastern spirituality, and grew critical of the Eastern mimicry of the West. They took pride in the Islamic past, advocated Islamic unity, and undermined the sectarian division between Sunni Egyptians and Shi'i Iranians in order to resolve the Eastern Question.

Notes

1. To name a handful of examples, see Stephen Sheehi, *Foundations of Modern Arab Identity* (Gainesville: University Press of Florida, 2004); Ussama Makdisi, *The Culture of Sectarianism: Community, History, and Violence in Nineteenth-century Ottoman Lebanon* (Berkeley: University of California Press, 2000); Keith Watenpaugh, *Being Modern in the Middle East: Revolution, Nationalism, Colonialism, and the Arab Middle Class* (Princeton: Princeton University Press, 2006); Afshin Marashi, *Nationalizing Iran: Culture, Power, and the State, 1870–1940* (Seattle: Washington University Press, 2008), and Mohamad Tavakoli-Targhi, "Refashioning Iran: Language and Culture during the Constitutional Revolution," *Iranian Studies*, vol. 23, no. 1/4 (1990), 77–101.

2. The notable exception in that respect is Kamran Rastegar, *Literary Modernity Between the Middle East and Europe: Textual Transactions in 19th Century Arabic, English and Persian Literatures* (Hoboken, NJ: Taylor & Francis, 2007).

3. See Israel Gershoni and James P. Jankowski, *Redefining the Egyptian Nation, 1930–1945* (Cambridge: Cambridge University Press, 1995); Ralph M. Coury, *The Making of an Egyptian Arab Nationalist: The Early Years of Azzam Pasha, 1893–1936* (Reading: Ithaca Press, 1998), and Michael Gasper, *The Power of Representation: Publics, Peasants, and Islam in Egypt* (Stanford: Stanford University Press, 2009).

4. For Egypt, see Gasper, *The Power of Representation*, and Lucie Ryzova, "Efendification: The Rise of Middle Class Culture in Modern Egypt" (Ph.D dissertation, Oxford University, 2009). For Iran, see Cyrus Schayegh, *Who Is Knowledgeable Is Strong: Science, Class, and the Formation of Modern Iranian Society, 1900–1950* (Berkeley: University of California Press, 2009).

5. For a broad discussion on territorial nationalism in Egypt, see Gershoni and Jankowski, *Egypt, Islam, and the Arabs: The Search for Egyptian Nationhood, 1900–1930*

(Oxford: Oxford University Press, 1987), Part II. For the decline of this intellectual trend after 1930s, see Israel Gershoni and James P. Jankowski, *Redefining the Egyptian Nation, 1930-1945*, 98 ff. For the discursive formulation of territorial Iranian nationalism, see Tavakoli-Targhi, "Refashioning Iran," 77-101. For authenticating modernity based on pre-Islamic heritage, see Marashi, *Nationalizing Iran*, 55.

6. Ervand Abrahamian, *A History of Modern Iran* (Cambridge: Cambridge University Press, 2008), 48.

7. Hassan Pirniya, *Iran-e Bastan: Kurosh-e kabir*, vol. 2 (Tehran: sazman-e ketabha-ye Gjibi, 1962/63), 484-486 and 566.

8. Hassan Pirniya, *Iran-e Bastan: Ardeshir-e Derazdast ta Ardeshir-e sevvom*, vol. 4 (Tehran: sazman-e ketabha-ye jibi, 1963/1964), 929.

9. Ahmad Shawqi, Kambiz, in *al-A'mal al-kamilah: al-masrahiyat*, authenticated by Sa'd Darwish (Cairo: al-Hay'ah al-Misriyah al-'Ammah lil-Kitab, 1984).

10. Taha Husayn, *Mustaqbal al-thaqafa fi Misr*, in *al-Majmu'a al-Kamila li-Mu'alafat al-Duktur Taha Husayn*, vol. 9 (Beirut: Dar al-Kitab al-Lubnany, 1973), 18 and 28.

11. Taha Husayn, *Rihlat al-Rabi'* (Cairo: Dar al-Ma'arif, 1948), 15.

12. Tavakoli-Targhi, "Refashioning Iran," 77-101.

13. Farzin Vejdani, "The Place of Islam in Interwar Iranian Nationalist Historiography," this volume.

14. Mohamad Tavakoli-Targhi, "Contested Memories: Narrative Structures and Allegorical Meanings of Iran's Pre-Islamic History," *Iranian Studies*, vol. 29, no. 1/2 (Winter–Spring 1996), 149-175.

15. For early writings that express this view, see their collective volume named *Aniran (Non-Iran)*, 1931. See also Michael Hillmann, "Literature East & West," *Major Voices in Contemporary Persian Literature*, vol. XX, nos. 1-4, (January-December 1976), 32.

16. Kamran Rastegar, "Literary Modernity between Arabic and Persian Prose: Jurji Zaydan's Riwayat in Persian Translation," *Comparative Critical Studies*, vol. 4, issue 3 (2007), 359-378.

17. See Hassan Kamshad, *Modern Persian Prose Literature* (Cambridge: Cambridge University Press, 1966), part 2; Michael C. Hillmann, ed., *Hedayat's "The Blind Owl" Forty Years After* (Austin: University of Texas Press, 1978); Iraj Bashiri, *The Fiction of Sadeq Hedayat* (Lexington, KY: Mazda Publishers, 1984); Homa Katouzian, *Sadeq Hedayat: The Life and Literature of an Iranian Writer* (London and New York: I. B. Tauris, 1991), and Homa Katouzian, ed., *Sadeq Hedayat: His Work and His Wondrous World* (London and New York: Routledge, 2008).

18. Homa Katouzian, *Sadeq Hedayat: The Life and Legend of an Iranian Writer* (London and New York: I. B. Tauris, 2002).

19. For numerous examples of Sadeq Hedayat's anti-Arab and anti-Jewish racism, see *Parvin Dokhtar-e Sasan va Isfahan Nesf-e Jehan*, 3rd ed., (Tehran: Mo'ssaseh-e chap va entesharat-e amir kabir, 1964); "Talab-e Amorzesh" and "Dash Akol," in *Seh Qatreh Khun* (Tehran: Mo'ssasih-e chap va entesharat-e amir kabir, 1964), 73-57, 43-62. For anti-African racism, see his satirical fiction: *Karavan-e Islam: al-Ba'satu al-Islamiyyah ila al-Bilad el-Ifranjiyyah*, 2nd ed. (Paris: Entesharat Sazman-e Jonbish Nationalisti Daneshgahiyan va Danesh Pajuhan va Rowshan Binan-e Iran, 1983), 13. For a discussion of that theme, see Leonard Bogle, "The Khayyamic influence in the Blind Owl,"

in *Hedayat's "The Blind Owl" Forty Years After*, ed. Michael Hillmann (Austin: University of Texas Press, 1979), 89.

20. Joya Blondel Saad, *The Image of Arabs in Modern Persian Literature* (Lanham: University Press of America, Inc., 1996), 33.

21. For more on this notion, see Ryzova, "Efendification: The Rise of Middle Class Culture in Modern Egypt," the Introduction in particular.

22. Vejdani, "The Place of Islam."

23. The collection of ʿAbdin Archive in Dar al-Wathaʿiq al-Qawmiyya, Mahfazat Abhath.

24. For detailed coverage of that event and the Iranian and Arab participants, see ʿAbbas Iqbal, *Yadgar* 3/1 (1944).

25. Iraj Afshar, "Book Translations as a Cultural Activity in Iran 1806-1896," *Iran* 41 (2003), 279-289; and Kamshad, *Modern Persian Prose Literature*, 28. For a discussion on the impact of Jurji Zaydan's historical novels in Persian translation, see Rastegar, *Literary Modernity between Arabic and Persian Prose*.

26. Afshar, "Book Translations as a Cultural Activity in Iran."

27. Kamshad, *Modern Persian Prose*, 73. Fathi Ahmad Zaghlul, trans., *Sirr takadum al-Ingiliz wal-Saksuniyin* (Cairo: 1899).

28. For a brief list of the most important modern Arabic books translated into Persian, along with names of the translators, see Badiʿ Muhammad Jumʿah, "al-ʿAlaqat al-thaqafiyya bayna al-ʿArab wa Iran fi al-ʿassr al-hadith," in *al-ʿAlaqat al-ʿArabiyah al-Iraniyah*, Jamal Zakariya Qasim and Yunan Labib Rizq, eds. (Cairo: Maʿhad al-Buhuth wa al-Dirasat al-Arabiyah, 1993), 335-361.

29. Nikki R. Keddie, *Iran and the Muslim World: Resistance and Revolution* (New York: New York University Press, 1995), 99.

30. Idarah-i Intishar-i Asnad-i Tarikhi: Daftar-i Mutalaʾat-i Siyasi va Bayn al-Milali, *Gozideh-e asnad-e ravabet-e khareji-e Iran va Mesr*, vol. II (Tehran: Moʾassaseh-i Chap va Entesharat-e Vezarat-e Omur-e Khareeh, 1996), 166-178 and 217-226.

31. For differences between Egyptian and Iranian experience with Western models of modernization, see Keddie, *Iran and the Muslim World*, 95-111.

32. Cyrus Schayegh, "Who is Knowledgeable is Strong: Science, Class, and the Formation of Modern Iranian Society, 1900-1950." (Paper presented at University of Texas-Austin, 1 May 2009). See also "Daneshkadeh Tebb va bimarestanha-e Mesr," *Ettelaʿat*, 19 July 1938.

33. "Eslahat-e Ejtemaʿi dar Mesr: Raport hayʾat-e Eʿzami bayn al-milali mashaghel," *Ettelaʿat*, 14 January 1933; Tawfiq Nasim Pasha, "Vaz ʿiyyat-e Ajaneb dar Mesr," *Ettelaʿat*, 19 and 20 February 1935.

34. Mohammad Yadegari, "The Iranian settlement in Egypt as seen through the pages of the community papers Chihrinimi, 1904-1966," in *Modern Egypt: Studies in Politics and Society*, Elie Kedourie and Sylvia Kedourie, eds. (London and Totowa, NJ: F. Cass, 1980), 98-114.

35. Muhammad al-Saʿid Jamal al-Din, "al-Shaykh Muhammad ʿAbdu wa al-thaqafa al-Farisiyya," in *Jawanib min al-silat al-thaqafiyya bayna Misr wa Iran*, Nur al-Din Al-Ali, ed. (Cairo: Dar al-Thaqafa lil-Tibaʾa wal-Nashr, 1975), 281-301.

36. Jamal al-Din, "al-Shaykh Muhammad ʿAbdu wa al-thaqafa al-Farisiyya."

37. Jahangir Sulhʾju, *Tarikh-e matbuʾat dar Iran va jahan* (Tehran: Kitabha-e

Simurgh, 1969), 168–170; and Jamal al-Din, "al-Shaykh Muhammad ʿAbdu wa al-thaqafa al-Farisiyya."

38. Yadegari, "The Iranian Settlement in Egypt."

39. Ibid.

40. Ibid.

41. Murtaza Ayatollahzadeh al-Shirazi, "Jawlah hawla al-rawabit al-maʿnawiyya bayna Iran wa Misr wa al-kitab al-Misri fi Iran al-Kitab al-Irani fi Misr," in *Jawanib min al-silat al-thaqafiyya bayna Misr wa Iran*, 169–179.

42. Sulh'ju, *Tarikh-e matbuʾat dar Iran*, 176.

43. Jumʿah, "al-ʿAlaqat al-thaqafiyya bayna al-ʿArab wa Iran."

44. Kamshad, *Modern Persian Prose*, 17.

45. Kamshad, *Modern Persian Prose*, 16.

46. Ayatollahzadeh al-Shirazi, "al-kitab al-Misri fi Iran al-Kitab al-Irani fi Misr."

47. Camron Michael Amin, *The Making of the Modern Iranian Woman: Gender, State Policy, and Popular Culture, 1865–1946* (Gainesville: University Press of Florida, 2002), 36–37.

48. Jumʿah, "al-ʿAlaqat al-thaqafiyya bayna al-ʿArab wa Iran."

49. Afsaneh Najmabadi, *Women with Mustaches and Men without Beards: Gender and Sexual Anxieties of Iranian Modernity* (Berkeley: University of California Press, 2005), 193 and 291.

50. Najmabadi, *Women with Mustaches and Men without Beards*, 291.

51. Ibid., 197 and 292.

52. "Vaziʾyat-e Ejtemaʿi Zan dar Mesr," *Ettelaʿat*, January 9, 1932 and "Azadi-e Zanan-e Mesr," *Ettelaʿat*, December 18, 1935.

53. Abbas Eqbal Ashtiani, "Jashn-e hezar saleh-e Abo al-ʿAlaʾ al-Maʿarri," *Yadgar* 3, 1–12.

54. Ayatollah zadeh al-Shirazi, "al-kitab al-Misri fi Iran al-Kitab al-Irani fi Misr" and Jumʿah, "al-ʿAlaqat al-thaqafiyya bayna al-ʿArab wa Iran."

55. Rastegar, "Literary Modernity between Arabic and Persian Prose."

56. Jumʿah, "al-ʿAlaqat al-thaqafiyya bayna al-ʿArab wa Iran." See also footnotes of Ibrahim al-Dusuqi Shita on his translation of Kamshad, *Modern Persian Prose*: Hassan Kamshad, *al-Nathr al-fani al-Farisi al-muʿasir*, trans. Ibrahim al-Dusuqi Shita (Cairo: al-Hayʾa al-ʿAmma lil-Kitab, 2005).

57. Rastegar, "Literary Modernity between Arabic and Persian Prose."

58. Farzin Vejdani, "Historical Transactions: Translating Histories into Persian in Late Nineteenth- and Early Twentieth-Century Iran" (unpublished paper, 2009).

59. Farzin Vejdani, "Historical Transactions."

60. Jurji Zaydan, *Abu Muslim al-Khurasani: riwayah tarikhiya* (Cairo: Matbaʾat al-Hilal, 1905); Zaydan, *al-ʿAbbasah ukht al-Rashid, aw Nakbat al-Baramikah: Riwayat tarikh al-Islam* (Cairo: Matbaʾat al-Hilal, 1960), and Zaydan, *Tarikh al-tamaddun al-Islami* (Cairo: Matbaʾat al-Hilal, 1902–1906).

61. Vejdani, "The Place of Islam."

62. Rastegar, "Literary Modernity between Arabic and Persian Prose."

63. Among many examples, see Qadri Hafiz Tuqan, *Turath al-ʿArab al-ʿilmi fi al-Riyadiyyat wa al-falak* (Cairo: al-Muqtataf, 1941); Zakin Muhammad Hassan, *al-Funun al-Iraniyya fi al-ʿasr al-Islami* (Cairo: Matbaʿat Dar al-Kutub, 1940), and Zakin

Muhammad Hassan, *al-Tasswir fi al-Islam 'inda al-Furs* (Cairo: Lajnat al-Ta'lif wa al-Tarjama wa al-Nashr, 1936).

64. *A Man of Many Worlds: The Memoirs and Diaries of Dr. Ghasem Ghani*, Cyrus Ghani, trans. (with Paul Sprachman) and ed. (Washington, DC: Mage Publishers, 2006).

65. Farh bin 'Ali bin Muhammad al-Bindari al-Isfahani, who was born in Isfahan and died in Damascus in 1245, did an incomplete Arabic translation of *Shahnameh*. 'Abd al-Wahhab 'Azzam, introduction to *Shahnameh* by Ferdawsi (Cairo, 1932), 1–15.

66. 'Abd al-Wahhab 'Azzam, *al-Tasawwuf wa-Farid al-Din 'Attar* (Cairo: 'Isa al-Babi al-Halabi, 1945).

67. Nasir Khusraw 'Alawi, *Safarnamah*, trans. and ed. Yahya al-Khashshab (Cairo: Ma'had al-Lughat al-Sharqiyah, Kulliyat al-Adab, 1945).

68. The former Iranian diplomat in Cairo, Dr. Ghasem Ghani, mentioned in his memoir that Dr. Abd al-Wahhab 'Azzam, who was then the head of the Faculty of Literature, had selected one of his books to translate from Persian into Arabic. Ghani, *The Memoirs and Diaries of Dr. Ghasem Ghani*, 222.

69. For the complete bibliography, see Nasrallah Mubashshir al-Tirazi, "al-Kitab al-Irani fi Misr," in *Jawanib min al-silat al-thaqafiyya bayna Misr wa Iran*, 129–167.

70. For that list, see Tal'at Abu Farha, "Adwa' ala al-Dirasat al-Farisiyya fi Misr," in *Jawanib min al-silat al-thaqafiyya bayna Misr wa Iran*, 199–226.

71. Sadiq Hidayat, *Qisas min al-adab al-Farisi al-mu'asir*, trans. Ibrahim al-Dasuqi Shita, reviewed by Muhammad Rashad Isma'ili Zadah and introduced by Yahya al-Khashshab (Cairo: al-Hay'ah al-Misriyah al-'Ammah lil-Kitab, 1975).

72. Sadiq Hedayat, *al-Bumah al-'amiya'*, trans. Ibrahim al-Dusuqi Shita (Cairo: al-Hay'ah al-Misrīyah al-'Amah lil-Kitab, 1976).

73. For 'Azzam's career in propagating pan-Islamism and Arab nationalism, see Ralph M. Coury, "Who 'Invented' Egyptian Arab Nationalism?" *International Journal of Middle East Studies* 14, no. 3 (Aug. 1982), 249–281.

74. See a good discussion on employing these events by the state in Afshin Marashi, *Nationalizing Iran: Culture, Power, and the State*, 1870–1940, 110–132.

75. Abd al-Wahhab 'Azzam, *Rahalat* (Cairo: Matba'at al-Risala), 113–135.

76. Examples of these publications include Husayn Mujib al-Misri, *Iran wa Misr 'Abra al-Tarikh* (Cairo: Maktabat al-Anglo al-Misriyya, 1972), and the collection of studies published in *Jawanib min al-silat al-thaqafiyya bayna Misr wa Iran*.

77. See Muhammad Hasanayn Haykal, *Iran fawqa burkan* (Cairo: Dar Akhbar al-Yum 1951); Donald Wilber, *Iran Madiha wa hadiriha*, trans. 'Abd al-Na'im Hasanyn (Cairo: Maktabat Misr, 1958), and Ahmad 'Abd al-Qadir al-Jammal "Mawqif Iran mina al-sira' al-'alami" in *Mushkilat al-Sharq al-Awsat* (Cairo: Maktabat al-Anjlu al-Misriyya, 1955).

78. For detailed discussion on how those authors treated the early split in the first Muslim community, see Hanan Hammad, "Shi'ism in the Egyptian Liberal Age" (unpublished paper, 2009). For a broad discussion on the Islamic writings in the liberal age in Egypt, see Gershoni and Jankowski, *Redefining the Egyptian Nation*.

79. Israel Gershoni, "The Return of the East: Muhammad Husayn Haykal's Recantation of Positivism," in *Middle Easter Politics and Ideas: A History from Within*, ed. Moshe Ma'oz and Ilan Pappé (London: I. B. Tauris, 1997), 59.

80. Vejdani, "The Place of Islam."

81. Zaki Mubarak, *Layla al-Marida fi al-ʿIraq*, vol. 1 (Cairo: Matbaʿat al-Risala, 1939), 226–227.

82. Ghani, Man of Many Worlds: *The Memoirs and Diaries of Dr. Ghasem Ghani*, 215.

83. Ibid., 236.

84. Ibid., 240–243.

85. See Coury, "Who 'Invented' Egyptian Arab Nationalism?"

86. Ahmad Amin used derogatory language against Shiʿa, which provoked a dialogue with Shiʿi scholars. See Ahmad Amin, *Fajr al-Islam*, edition 5 (Cairo: Lajnat al-Taʾlif wa al-Tarjamah wa al-Nashr, 1945), 276, and Muhammad al-Husayni Kashif al-Ghataʾ, *Asl al-Shiʿa wa usulaha*, 10th ed. (Cairo: 1958), 73.

87. Zaki Mubarak, *Layla al-Marida fi al-ʿIraq*, 226–227.

88. Yunan Labib Rizq, "al-ʿAlaqat al-Iranyah bi-Misr wa al-ʿIraq ʿala ʿAhd al-usrah al-Bahlwiyah 1925–1979," in *al-ʿAlaqat al-ʿArabiyah al-Iraniyah*, 103–128.

89. Rizq, "al-ʿAlaqat al-Iranyah bi-Misr wa al-ʿIraq."

90. Hassan Yusuf, *Mudhakkirat Hasan Yusuf: al-Qasr wa dawrih fi al-siyasa al-Misriyya*, 1922–1952 (Cairo: Markaz al-Dirasat al-Siyasiyah wa-al-Istiratizhiyah bi-al-Ahram, 1982), 25.

91. Saʿid al-Sabbagh, *al-ʿAlaqah bayna al-Qahirah wa-Tihran tanafus am taʾawun? al-muhaddidat wa-al-asrar* (Cairo: al-Dar al-Thaqafiyah lil-Nashr, 2003), 20.

92. *Gozideh-ʾe asnad-e ravabet-e khareji-e Iran va Mesr*, vol. III.

93. Ibid., vol. II, 319–326.

94. Al-Sabbagh, *al-ʿAlaqah bayna al-Qahirah wa-Ttihran tanafus am taʾawun?*, 20.

95. Husayn Mujib al-Misri, *Ayyami bayna ʿahdayn: Sira zatiyya* (Cairo: al-Dar al-thaqafiyya lil-nashr, 1999), 32.

96. Al-Misri, *Ayyami bayna ʿahdayn*, 32–33.

97. For a full list of al-Misri's published books between 1948 and 1996, see al-Misri, *Ayyami bayna ʿahdayn*, 264–267.

98. "Bilad al-ʿAjam," rather than "Iran," continued to be frequently used in the Egyptian government documents throughout 1930s.

99. Yadegari, "The Iranian Settlement in Egypt."

100. *Chehrenema*, vol. 37, no. 8, December 1940, 9.

101. For more on the Eastern Bond Society, see Awatif Abd al-Rahman, *Misr wa Falastin* (Kuwait: ʿAlam al-Maʿrifah, 1980), 51–58, and Gershoni and Jankowski, *Egypt, Islam, and the Arabs: The Search for Egyptian Nationhood, 1900–1930*, 255–270.

102. Abd al-Rahman, *Misr wa Falastin*, 57.

103. Yadegari, "The Iranian Settlement in Egypt."

104. Abd al-Rahman, *Misr wa Falastin*, 54.

105. I thank Afshin Marashi for drawing my attention to the role that the Iranian community in Egypt played in bringing about Tagore's visit to Iran in 1932, after they witnessed his visit to Egypt in 1926.

106. Afshin Marashi, "Imagining Hafez: Rabindranath Tagore in Iran, 1932," *Journal of Persianate Studies* 3 (2010), 46–77.

107. For the political employment of that marriage in the nationalist and feminist Iranian discourse, see Camron Michael Amin, *The Making of the Modern Iranian*

Woman: Gender, State Policy, and Popular Culture, 1865–1946 (Gainesville: University Press of Florida, 2002), 135–139.

108. Rizq, "al-'Alaqat al-Iranyah bi-Misr wa al-'Iraq."

109. Ibid.

110. Ghani, *The Memoirs and Diaries of Dr. Ghasem Ghani*, 205.

111. Husayn Fawzi, *al-Ahram*, 16 June 1938.

112. Ahmad Mahmud al-Sadati, *Rida Shah Bahlawi: Nahdat Iran al-Haditha* (Cairo: Maktabat al-Nahda al-Misriyya, 1939).

113. "Nazar-e ijmali bitarikh Jadid-e Misr: Mahbobiyat khandeh saltanati-e Misr," *Ettela'at*, 31 July, 1938.

114. *Ettela'at*, 4 September 1938, 10 and 14 March 1939, and 12 April 1939.

115. "Etehad-e Eslam bevasileh-e Iran va Mesr mishavad mohaqaq," *Ettela'at*, 209 March, 1939.

116. Ghani, *The Memoirs and Diaries of Dr. Ghasem Ghani*, 217–231.

117. 'Abd al-Wahhab 'Azzam, *Rida Shah Bahlawi: Nahdat Iran al-Haditha*, L-N.

118. Muhammad Hassan al-A'zamy, "Bahth 'ann al-Shi'ah," in Ahmad Mahmud al-Sadati, *Rida Shah Bahlawi: Nahdat Iran al-Haditha*, 163–202.

119. For a comprehensive history of the group, see Rainer Brunner, *Islamic Ecumenism in the 20th Century, The Azhar and Shiism between Rapprochement and Restraint* (Leiden: Brill 2004).

120. *Risalat al-Islam*, 1, year 1, January 1949, 96.

121. See Mahmoud Shaltout, "Introduction," an appendix published in *Risalat al-Islam*, issues 55 and 56, June 1964, 5–6.

122. To undermine differences among Sunnis, Zaydis, and Twelvers, the center published a booklet during the hajj season of the year 1949 on the hajj rituals in the three madhhab.

123. *Risalat al-Islam*, 3, first year, July 1949, 277–280.

124. For contemporary anti-Iran and Shi'ism writing in Egypt, see Nabil Muhammad Rashwan, *al-Islam al-Farsi* (Cairo: Matba'at al-Sharq, 1992). For pro-Iran and Shi'ism, see Salih al-Wirdani, *al-Shi'ah fi Misr min al-Imam Ali hatta al-Imam al-Khomeini* (Cairo: Maktabat Madbuli al-Saghir, 1993).

CHAPTER 15

"East Is East, and West Is West, and Never the Twain Shall Meet"? Post-1979 Iran and the Fragile Fiction of Israel as a Euro-American Space

HAGGAI RAM

On August 1, 2003, U.S. immigration authorities, in tandem with the Department of Homeland Security, issued new regulations requiring U.S. consulates to interview many more foreigners before letting them into the United States. These new regulations were planned to help prevent terrorists, such as those who carried out the 9/11 attacks, from entering the country. The stringent regulations have since been modified, but from then on all Israelis seeking an entry visa to the U.S. were required, as part of the screening process, to show up for personal interviews at their nearby U.S. consulates. The increased scrutiny of Israeli travelers caused severe bottlenecks and long delays in their visa approval process. Whereas in the past Israelis were allowed to apply for a visa by mail, they now had to go to U.S. consulates weeks, and even months, before their trip.[1]

The Israeli government might have found this policy tolerable if it were applied evenly. But it was not: Nationals from twenty-seven countries faced no interviews or background checks for visits up to ninety days, because the U.S. exempted them from all visa requirements. Significantly, the visa-waiver countries included the United States's strongest *Western* allies and trading partners, such as the U.K., Germany, and France, but not Israel. Enraged, the Israeli government soon dispatched its representatives, including the foreign minister and the ambassador to the U.S., to lobby against Israel's exclusion from the Visa-Waver Program (VWP).[2] "Does anyone really think an Israeli national is going to be involved in terrorist attacks?" an Israeli Embassy spokesman protested.[3] In response, U.S. officials laconically reminded these officials that, with all due respect, Israel, unlike the U.K. or Germany or France, was not located in Europe but in the Middle East. Thus, in addition to the more than one million Palestinian Arabs living inside Israel, "Israeli Jews [will] also draw scrutiny from increasingly watchful U.S. consular officers

if they were born in countries such as Yemen, Saudi Arabia [*sic*], and Iran—
facts noted on Israeli passports."[4] In other words, where homeland security is
concerned, the U.S. will regard Israel as a Middle Eastern country—even if,
as one of Israel's staunch congressional supporters put it, "many Israelis have
felt it to be insulting."[5]

I begin with this anecdote in order to exemplify my main concern in this
article: The duress under which we Israelis habitually find ourselves whenever and wherever we are confronted with the daunting realization that realities do not always fall in line with, and are therefore injurious to, our self-
image, which historically has helped us to view ourselves as extensions of
Euro-America. In recent decades, this fiction of Israel as a Euro-American
space received severe, some would say irreparable, blows, due to a convergence of numerous domestic *and* external trends and circumstances. Indeed,
Palestinian and Mizrahi histories and politics of identity within the Jewish
state have always produced rifts in this fiction, and I will say more about these
later on. But as Israeli Jews entered the twenty-first century, they have had
plenty of additional reasons to cast doubt on this fiction. "As Israeli demog-
raphers continued to warn of rising Arab birthrates, the growing community
of foreign workers, and the magnitude of the Russian Christian immigration
inside the state—this proved a particularly fragile fiction that required vigi-
lant making and remaking in the face of its dissolution."[6] The string of anti-
democratic legislations—such as the "Nakba Law"[7]—passed in 2011 by the
Israeli right-wing government of Benjamin Netanyahu has been yet another
cause of the Israelis' disenchantment with their Euro-American self-image,
as well as the growing international debate about whether or not Israel is in
reality an intransigent "rogue state."

Here I intend to discuss one particular aspect in the "making and remaking" of this fiction within Israeli public culture, which is concerned with
an unlikely external actor—post-1979 Iran. Previous scholarship on the topic
has traced this fiction's dissolution to domestic circumstances, mainly politics of identity *within* the Jewish state: To wit, they have shown how the
emergence of subversive internal forces of ultrareligious (*haredi*) and ethnic
(Mizrahi) politics since the 1970s have progressively produced ruptures in the
foundations (shaky to begin with) of the Israeli ethnocratic regime, which
historically had buttressed the dominance of the Ashkenazi (European) Jewish ethnoclass.[8]

In this article, I acknowledge the contribution of this scholarship to the
ongoing debate on the history of Jewish-Israeli nationalism and its discontent.[9] Still, I also intend to complement and add to this debate by drawing on
works by historians and anthropologists who have read metropolitan and colonial cultures together, or contrapuntally, thereby illuminating the porous and

contingent nature of the supposedly rigid boundaries separating "the local" from "the foreign," "here" from "there." In doing so, I hope to be able to show that the battle over the nature and identity of the Jewish state was/is not determined by domestic forces alone, but also by the ways in which Israeli public culture has come to visualize and understand the Islamic Republic of Iran, the ultimate alien force in Israeli contemporary imagination. More precisely, I demonstrate that Israeli perceptions of post-1979 Iran have been connected to domestic notions of identity and politics within the Jewish state and fashioned on the basis of what Israelis believed to be the (dis)ordering of their society at home. In many ways, then, the story told here is a story of disenchantment, the disenchantment of many Israeli Jews who, by analogizing and adapting Iranian realities to their own realities, have come to realize that their ascribed "modernity *is* crisis, not a finished ideal state seen as the culmination of a majestically plotted history."[10]

Lastly, as mentioned, the following discussion joins an increasing body of critical literature on Israeli identity, society, and politics. At the same time, this discussion is equally pertinent to this volume's immediate subject of inquiry—rethinking Iranian nationalism. Indeed, it goes without saying that nationalism cannot be studied in isolation, or that scholars engaging with the topic can no longer content themselves with viewing the "nation" as the sole, given, and inevitable terrain of analysis. This awareness is especially important in the study of the Middle East, where so many phenomena appear exceptional, as though they can be observed nowhere else in the world. In my study I will propose a correction to these bogus, self-contained understandings. Although my study's main focus is Israeli society and politics, its comparative engagement with Israeli and Iranian nationalisms demonstrates the extent to which each one of the two is at once the condition and the effect of the other. The two nationalisms are shown to be woven together in an intricate design that, in turn, disentangles Iranian nationalism from its association with radical otherness.

But before I proceed any further, I should lay out—in the following two sections—the context in which this study has been conceived and written, and situate myself, as an *Israeli* historian who teaches and writes about modern Iranian history, within that context.

The Unthinkable, Part 1: Integrating Israel into the Middle East

In March 1996, I gave an interview to *Haaretz Weekly Supplement* (http://www.haaretz.com/). Titled "The Demon Is Not So Terrible,"[11] the interview immediately sparked a public uproar that nearly cost me my academic career. In that interview, I essentially suggested (a) that the Israeli government, academia, and media were disseminating distorted images of Iran that are informed by the state's security and ethnocentric concerns; (b) that Israeli scholarly research on the Middle East and Iran has remained impervious to innovative analytical tools and paradigms used in other disciplines of the humanities and the social sciences, in ways that are reminiscent of the epistemic self-sufficiency of Orientalism as a mode of knowledge production; and (c), that in spite of Israeli insistence to the contrary, Iran and Israel were, in fact, much more similar than some would have us believe. As a young and admittedly conceited (but untenured!) faculty member at the newly established Department of Middle East Studies in Ben Gurion University, Israel, I was completely unprepared for the devastating backlash that would soon follow. A barrage of condemnations coming from various academic and political sources appeared in the printed and electronic media, questioning my "intellectual integrity and basic knowledge of facts."[12] Prof. Avishai Braverman, the university president (now turned Labor Party politician), demanded my head and let it be known that he would be content with nothing short of my dismissal. Save a handful of colleagues who hailed my "daring attempt to challenge the accepted perceptions of the [Israeli] Middle East Studies establishment,"[13] the message coming from virtually everywhere was loud and clear: "Dr. Ram doesn't represent us."[14]

Fortunately (for me) I survived the backlash. More to the point, however, it appears that what prompted the scathing outrage against me was not my charge that the boundaries between the Israeli state and Israeli Middle East studies were dangerously porous; many of Israel's Middle East scholars would see nothing wrong with that.[15] Rather, it was my contention that the Israeli and Iranian polities deserve to be studied comparatively or contrapuntally. Consider, for example, how David Menashri—Israel's most prominent expert on Iran and my former teacher at Tel Aviv University—responded to this call of mine:

> Dr. Ram's main original contribution is a comparison of Zionism and Khomeinism. I see no fault in such intellectual drills, but we must distinguish between what is important and what is marginal. It is, of course, possible to compare many things, even a mosquito to a helicopter, or a fish to a submarine. But are the two really essentially similar? Compared from the perspective of their ideational substances, the similarities between Khomeinism and Zionism are marginal. It suffices to read Herzl and Khomeini in order to appreciate how different the two are. Has Zionism aspired to establish a theocratic state (*medinat halacha*)?[16]

In this paper, I take issue with this type of contemptuous dismissal of the value of a comparative study of "Zionism" and "Khomeinism." As will become apparent later on, my interpretive perspective on the benefits of such a comparative undertaking is not merely an "intellectual drill," a creation of my interpretive imagination. Rather, it was born in the interstices between my own research agenda *and* the accepted cultural practices in the Israeli polity. As such, it is based on a "double hermeneutic," to use Anthony Giddens's useful term;[17] or, in other words, on my attempt to read the meaning of "lay" or everyday concepts by reappropriating them into my own scholarly discourse.[18]

Much has already been said and written about the discursive and physical partitions and enclosures that formed the Israeli self-image as a "villa in the jungle," to use Ehud Barak's revealing formulation. I will say more about these partitions and enclosures later on. I should mention here, though, that efforts to mark clear borders of identity between Jews as Westerners, on the one hand, and Arabs and Muslims as Easterners, on the other hand, have permeated Israeli institutions of higher learning, in which a clear-cut institutional division of labor has been introduced between "Israel (and Jewish) studies" and "Middle East studies." In both cases, rarely will one come across any attempt to incorporate Israel into the larger Middle East in teaching and research agendas.

One of the answers to the question of why Israeli scholars have shunned incorporating Israel into their research on Middle East societies is to be found in the disciplinary, coercive role of the politics of Western modernity within the Jewish state. "Nation-states," as Dipesh Chakrabarty reminds us, "have the capacity to enforce their truth games, and universities, their critical distance notwithstanding, are part of the battery of institutions complicit in this process."[19] Embedded as they are in various institutional practices that invoke the nation-state at every step, Israeli scholars of the Middle East have, therefore, been predisposed to insist on Western modernity. This insistence becomes particularly manifest (and occasionally even violent) in times when trends and circumstances within the Israeli polity seem to challenge the hegemony of Israeli ethnocracy.

As I will demonstrate in Section Three, Israeli anxieties about Iran are linked to, and cannot be examined in isolation from, these *domestic* (ethnic and religious) challenges to the nature and outlook of the Jewish state. Still, because these challenges might imperil neat and homogenous conceptualizations of Israel as a "Europe in the Middle East," many Israeli scholars insist on examining them in relation to the countries of Euro-America. By leapfrogging over the immediate Middle East, they have in effect joined, intentionally or unintentionally, the enterprise of calibrating an insurmountable gap between the Jewish state and its Arab and Muslim neighbors. Israeli historian Benny Morris provides a striking example of this, contending that the Middle East is in reality "a world whose values are different [from ours]. A world in which human life doesn't have the same value as it does in the West, in which freedom, democracy, openness and creativity are alien."[20]

The Israeli media, too, have been anxious to consign Israeli realities to an imaginative Europe—or "a hyperreal Europe."[21] In a panel on the set of Channel 1's late-night television news show dedicated to the publication of the Hebrew edition of Samuel Huntington's *The Clash of Civilizations*, the host, Emmanuel Halperin, was concerned not with the validity of Huntington's thesis, which he uncritically embraced, but rather with the question, "Where are *we* [i.e., Israeli Jews] located" civilization-wise? The foreign-affairs commentator, Oren Nahari, did not pause for one second: the Jewish state, he proclaimed, is "the rampart . . . the emissary of Western civilization in the Middle East." Or take Channel 10 News megameteorologist Danni Rop, who joyfully announced on one particularly stormy day (in February 2007) that "the snowiest place in all of *Europe* today was Mount Hermon." (Significantly, Rop was not concerned with the fact that Mount Hermon, snowy as it might have been, is part of the Golan Heights, which was occupied from Syria in 1967.)

Of course, one cannot address Israel's drive to constitute itself as Euro-America without referring to the continuous "wall"—or "fence" or "barrier"—with which it has surrounded itself in recent years. The barrier, it is true, was designed as a buffer against horrific terrorist bombings by Palestinians in Israeli cities, and it may have contributed to a reduction in the penetration of Israel by Palestinian bombers. Still, as Ian Lustick recently commented in a highly instructive essay,

> [T]he effect of the barrier, and perhaps more of its purpose than is commonly acknowledged, is not to keep Middle Easterners out of Israel, but to physically and psychologically remove Israel from the Middle East. The iconic formula, offered originally by Yitzhak Rabin, picked up by Ehud Barak as his campaign slogan, but used now by virtually all supporters of the barrier to describe its purpose most succinctly, is *"Anachnu po, hem sham"* ("Us here, them there"). . . . It is undeniable that a continuous barrier separating Israel from the Palestinian territories . . . greatly reduces the amount of contact Israelis have with the only part of the Muslim/Arab Middle East to which they have had direct access. In these ways the barrier contributes directly to an Israel separation or escape from the Middle East.[22]

Clearly, in and by itself the "wall" does not, and cannot, remove Israel to Europe (or Euro-America) in any concrete or tangible way. But it does endow Israelis with the mental capacity to *imagine* that it does, which is perhaps why, contrary to the domino effect akin to the fall of the Berlin wall and the collapse of communism, "the only wall in sight—Israel's apartheid wall—pointedly stays up."[23]

The Unthinkable, Part 2: Are "Zionism" and "Khomeinism" Really Two Worlds Apart?

And so, are Israel and Iran—"Zionism" and "Khomeinism"—really two worlds apart, as a mosquito stands in relation to a helicopter, or a fish to a submarine? As mentioned above, I don't share this view. However, many an Israeli Jew would like to *think* that Israel and Iran are not only worlds but galaxies apart. A flagrant illustration of this was provided in the wake of the devastating earthquake that leveled the Iranian town of Bam in December 2003. Asked about the earthquake in a television interview with Channel 1, Menashe Amir, a leading Israeli media expert on Iran, put it most succinctly and frankly: "Human life has no value there." In Amir's mind, "there" is diametrically opposed to *here*, Israel's world, the putative abode of Western, *Judeo-Christian* humanity, even if the footage running in the background as Amir was making his ludicrous allegation actually told an entirely different story: mothers lamenting their children who were buried under the rubble, rescue teams spraying corpses to prevent epidemics, and physicians in makeshift hospitals trying to save lives with the paltry means at their disposal. Still, no one in the studio cared to challenge the expert's assertion. On the contrary, they remained resoundingly silent about his allegation, thus accepting it as an immutable fact of nature—even while the background pictures showed the exact opposite.

Another telling example of how Israelis have been adamantly reluctant to bring down the physical and mental barrier that separates the Jewish state from the Islamic republic is the controversy surrounding a handshake exchange between Iran's and Israel's past presidents, Muhammad Khatami and Moshe Katsav, during Pope Paul II's funeral in spring 2005. Reportedly, the two dignitaries had also exchanged a few words in their native Persian centering on their shared city of provenance, Yazd.[24] These gestures, I argue, had the potential of destabilizing the principle of difference upon which Israelis imagine themselves in relation to Iran, because they demonstrated that the two leaders shared a linguistic-cultural foundation and common childhood memories. By exchanging a handshake and a few words in their shared native tongue the two leaders called the lie of Iran's radical alterity, showing that Israelis and Iranians were tied together in ways that defied simple unraveling. And yet, the backlash against Katsav which soon followed clearly indicated that Israelis were not prepared to cast a friendly, familiar, and human limelight upon anything Iranian: "Katsav disgraced Israel"—such was the knee-jerk reaction by "senior state officials" to their own president's seditious act.[25] Even Katsav himself, apparently with an eye to public opinion, tried to undo his terrible wrongdoing by declaring that the gestures had "no meaningful significance whatsoever."[26]

This overall aversion to the Katzav-Khatami encounter serves as yet another indication that Israelis are generally unprepared to come to terms with the idea that Iranians and Israelis might not be so different from each other. Take, for example, the literary editor of *Haaretz* Benny Ziffer's impressions from a screening event of an Iranian movie that took place at a Cairo film festival in December 2006. Ziffer was particularly astounded by the fact that the Iranian guard who let him into the theater was "exceptionally friendly." At the end of the movie, as Ziffer recounted with bewilderment, the guard even "gave me a friendly wink and asked me if I enjoyed the movie." Although Ziffer had serious misgivings about the quality of the film—it "was not . . . exemplary in any sense; it was just a comedy"—he was struck by its protagonists who, lacking horns, swastikas, sacred rage, and a penchant for martyrdom and jihad, were "just like everyone else in the world: fathers who wanted to marry off their children, and children who wanted to be modern . . . by using computers and all sorts of technological gadgets."[27] Similarly, when it was reported in January 2008 that the performance of Israeli pupils in mathematics was poorer than that of their Iranian counterparts, Israelis took this finding as a grave offense. This came out most clearly in many a television talk show and news program, with the then-opposition leader Benjamin Netanyahu crying out in clear exasperation, "*Even* Iran surpassed us."

As mentioned, my 1996 interview with *Haaretz* had earned me the wrath of the Middle East studies community precisely because I claimed in the interview that "one of the best ways to understand the Islamic Revolution in Iran is to compare it to the history of Zionism."[28] I would now like to expand on this supposedly blasphemous argument, and explain how and why it bears direct relevance to this article's subject of inquiry. According to Martin Riesebrodt, a phenomenon such as the one we call "fundamentalism" should be "placed in a larger context, [so that we may] attempt to compare its ideologies, adherents, or causes of mobilization with those of secular movements."[29]

No doubt, the term *fundamentalism* does not quite capture the gist of post-1979 Iranian realities—not the least because the "tradition" that Khomeini discovered had actually never existed. Still, scholarly research over the past three decades has amply demonstrated that Iran's "fundamentalist" project bears close affinity to secular movements in different geographies and in different temporalities—"Western," "Eastern," fascist, populist, nationalist, and Third World anti-imperialist.[30] Thus, to the extent that "the white man takes his own mythology, Indo-European mythology . . . for the universal form of that he must still wish to call Reason,"[31] "fundamentalism," too, should be considered an essential part of that mythology.

Within this context, the Jewish state offers us something of dramatic resonance for thinking about messianic politics in the modern world: "a nation vested in, at times struggling with—but repeatedly failing to discard—the mantle of God."[32] Clearly, the genealogies of many a Euro-American and postcolonial nationalism have been entwined with religion, as religion served, and still does serve, as an unrivaled basis for mobilization, and a component of national identity virtually everywhere, in the West and in the non-West. Yet the danger of religious messianism feeds into the very heart of modern and (ostensibly) secular Jewish nationalism, as the illustrious philosopher, historian, and founder of the scholarly study of Jewish mysticism, Gershon Scholem, warned some time ago. "They think," as Scholem wrote his friend Franz Rosenzweig in 1926, "they have made Hebrew into a secular language, that they have removed its apocalyptic sting." But, he continues, every word "taken from the treasure house of well-worn terms is laden with explosives."[33] In other words, messianism colors Zionism, including secular Zionism, at every turn. As Jacqueline Rose forcefully observes,

> [There is a] line that runs from messianism to the heart of Zionism, including secular Zionism—that is, to the heart of Zionism *even when, or perhaps especially when, it does not know it is there.* We cannot therefore relegate messianism to the religious Zionists and Orthodox Zionists, any more than we can to Gush Emunim or indeed the even more fervently fundamentalist and ruthlessly messianic movement of [Rabbi Meir Kahane's] Kach. We are talking about the "*slow but steady*" penetration of the civic culture by a vision that many of Israel's citizens do not explicitly embrace. . . . Messianism, as unconscious inspiration, is in the air and soil of Israel.[34]

In light of this brief examination, one can no longer be sure if a statement concerning the "contradiction between God's rule and man's" or, if you will, between "religious and democratic rule," which originally appeared in a "survey on Iran" in the *Economist*,[35] provides a faithful description of Zionism *or* of Khomeinism, of Israeli or Iranian realities. I'm not suggesting, of course, that the two cases are identical—after all, Khomeinism means a range of things, from a doctrine embedded in a (certain) modernist interpretation of Shi'ite teachings to what Ervand Abrahamian defined as a form of Third-Worldist populism,[36] and so does Zionism. Yet, for the narrow concerns of my inquiry, I argue that messianism and the interpenetration of the sacred and the profane have been crucial for imagining the modern nation in Israel and Iran, and should be considered a fundamental cause of the respective tensions, contradictions, and exclusionary practices inherent in both societies and political systems.

An additional parallel between Khomeinism and Zionism, also centering on the issue of messianic expectation, will further illustrate this point. In most general and schematic terms, both *secular* Zionists and *Islamist* Iranians, respectively, in their endeavor to break with the past, differed from the old, religious, Jewish and Shi'ite messianic varieties, in that they moved salvation from the heavens to the plains. In both cases, redemption was to be realized not by miraculous, transcendent intervention; rather, both assigned human activity a crucial role, if not *the* crucial role, in the purification of history.

Zionism and Khomeinism usurped the divine prerogative, which made human agency redundant, and engaged in the tasks of the world, thus, in effect, forcing "the end," albeit little by little. In both cases, redemption would not come suddenly, with divine succor, but through human hands. In secular Zionism, redemption was—will be?—realized through the progressive settlement of the Land of Israel—"we shall have to build houses, dig wells, and plant vines and olive trees," as one of Zionism's "Harbingers," Yehuda Alkelai, surmised;[37] and in Islamist Iran, it would be realized through progressive revolutionary action for the elimination of injustice and tyranny anywhere, as explained in June 1980 by Tehran's Friday-Prayer Leader (and today's Supreme Leader) Ali Khamenei: "The same [Iranian] people who waged a revolution and have [therefore] drawn themselves one step closer to the Imam of Our Time, are able . . . to take a step, and another step, and yet another step, in bringing themselves closer to the Imam of Our Time."[38] Despite respective differences, *secular* Zionism has accorded the same role to human agency in bringing about messianic redemption to the Jewish people:

> Zionism called for Jewish immigration to the Land of Israel, just as messianism promised the return to Zion and the ingathering of the exiles. As the former movement sought to attain political independence for the Jewish people, the latter hoped for the liberation of the Jews from "subjugation to

the great powers." Zionism worked to make the land fruitful, to "conquer the waste places"; it even spoke explicitly of "redeeming the land." Employing a somewhat different idiom, messianism taught (in the words of the Talmud) that "there is no revealed End than this, as it is said, 'but you, O mountains of Israel, shall yield your produce and bear your fruit, for their return is near.'"[39]

Both undertakings, then, were conditioned on the active creation, by means of human agency, of what can be described as a "favorable environment" for the imminent return/coming of the Hidden Imam/Messiah. Both Zionism and the Islamic Revolution seized the initiative from History, thrusting the task of redemption into the hands of human beings, thereby vehemently coming out, perhaps in an act of pure sacrilege, against previous Jewish and Shiite conceptions of messianism as expectant and passive.

What all this seems to suggest is that *theological* concepts or ways of thinking underlie political, social, economic, and cultural discourses in contemporary Israel and the Islamic Republic of Iran. Indeed, if central concepts of modern politics are, in effect, secularized versions of older theological concepts, it is then possible to argue that political theology serves as a comparable paradigm in the histories and constitutions of both polities.

The Imaginable: "We Are Not Only on Our Way to Becoming a State of Ayatollahs, We're Already in Its Midst"

As mentioned, despite the apparent structural and ideological affinities between Israel and Iran, in the past three decades, Israelis have generally opted to talk and write about the two polities on the basis of a politics of difference—as a manifestation of a putative opposition between a backward, Islamic, religious, and Oriental dictatorship, on the one hand, and a modern, Jewish, secular, and Western democracy on the other hand.[40] However, a closer look at the ways in which Iran has been debated in Israeli public culture reveals a more nuanced and complex picture, one in which the articulation of difference between the two polities appears simultaneously with the articulation of incorporation. In other words, the debate on Iran in Israeli public culture was at least as much about the replication of sameness and similarities as it was about the insistence on difference and divergence.

Indeed, my underlying argument in this section is that discussion about Iran in the Israeli public sphere was/is a projection of a moral panic directed at the Jewish state's "Iran-like" ethnic and religious forces, or "strangers from within." Consequently, this discussion expresses not only concern about a hostile Islamist "fanatic" and "irrational" government whose objective it is "to wipe Israel off the map," but also ethnocratic concerns about the current and future direction of secular-cum-Western Zionism. Talal Asad suggests that "the notion of horror has to do with the collapse of social and personal identity and thus with the dissolution of form."[41] Accordingly, Israeli anxiety about Iran is linked to a range of practices employed by members of the Israeli ethnocracy to protect their valued identities, beliefs, and forms of life in light of the challenges posed by Israel's religious and ethnic underclass.

To fully understand this point it is necessary to situate the 1979 revolution not, as one might expect, in its immediate Iranian context, but rather in the context of Israeli *domestic* politics since the latter part of the 1970s. Indeed, it is crucial to remember that the 1979 revolution happened to unfold in the streets of Iran at a particular moment when the Israeli ethnocratic regime was coming under direct attack from various directions. Two years before, in 1977, the Likud Party had won the national election, ending nearly thirty years of Labor Party rule. Personifying the antithesis to Labor's quasi-socialist ethos, Likud appealed to many Mizrahi Israelis, mostly first- and second-generation Jewish immigrants from Muslim countries who were continuously treated by members of Israeli ethnocracy as second-class citizens.

Yet the entry of the Mizrahim into Israeli politics as a force to be reckoned with was not the only serious threat posed to Israeli ethnocracy. So, too, were Likud's open embrace of "traditional" or "exilic" Judaism, and the rise of the religious Zionist settler movement since the mid-1970s. While the Mizrahim militated against the Euro-American Israeli self-image, thereby threatening to assimilate the Jewish state into the surrounding Arab and Muslim Middle East, forces of religion drove home the message that the Jewish state could not fully embody the separation between religion and secularity.

By virtue of its timing and its internal dynamics—and this is the crucial point I want to make here—the 1979 revolution concretized and dramatized these threats. Divisive politics of ethnicity, charismatic clerical leaders and their underrepresented "Oriental mobs," messianic politics, and the conflation of nation and religion and state and religion—all those features that had made their striking appearance in the 1979 revolution also seemed to represent and underline the domestic, ethnic, and religious threats to the dominance of Israeli ethnocracy. The expulsion of the post-1979 Iranian polity to the realm of radical alterity was driven, at least in part, by the Israelis' perception of radical, religious, and ethnic alterities operating in their own midst.

In what follows I substantiate this argument with several illustrations from the past three decades. In January 1979, while the Shah was still waging a battle of survival, Israelis already had noted a perceived resemblance between Khomeini's "religious reactionary regime" and the religious Zionist settlement movement. Yossi Sarid, then a Knesset Member from the center-to-left, secular Alignment (Labor) Party, lashed out at Hebron's religious Zionist settlers describing them as "Khomeini-style fanatics . . . gripped with convulsions."[42] At about the same time, Michael Harsegor, the late professor of European history, traced in the 1979 revolution the paradoxes of Jewish secularity. In an editorial bearing the suggestive title "Israel, Beware of the Ayatollah," Harsegor claimed that "Ayatollah Khomeini was not the only person . . . putting into practice the ideal of backwardness in the East." Participating in this endeavor, he alleged, were also ultra-orthodox and religious Zionist political parties: "their objection to theater plays, autopsy, abortion under medical supervision, [and] women [*sic*] rights . . . puts them in one front with the fanatic old man who is turning Iran upside down."[43] In short, for Sarid and Harsegor, two avid secular Zionists, Israel potentially faced a fate similar to that of Iran, given that a sizable portion of the population closely allied religious heritage with political Zionism.

In 1980 and 1981, while reports from Iran focused on the deterioration of that country into anarchy and civil war, Israelis were preoccupied with an election campaign that was rightly described at the time as "befittingly violent."[44] In early June 1981, nearly a month before the election, confrontations began between supporters of Menachem Begin, Likud Party's incumbent prime minister, and supporters of Shimon Peres, Alignment (Labor) party's candidate for the position. These confrontations soon transformed into serious street scuffles between Likud and Labor activists, and the very last election rallies were held under the heavy protection of Israeli police.

Whatever the significance of these events may be, it is clear that they "[s]ignaled for the first time the tensions between Mizrahim and Ashkenazim . . . as the real threat to the existence of Israeli society."[45] Indeed, expressing profound anxiety about this circumstance, and capturing the sentiments of paternalism and racism befitting large segments of Israeli ethnocracy, Amnon Dankner, the late journalist and novelist, related his impressions from an election rally held for Shimon Peres in the town of Petah Tikva:

We drove through the streets adjacent [to the rally], and all of the sudden we saw some people gathering and shouting things. I got out of the car and walked in their direction. From afar I could hear them shout: "Traitor! Maniac! Go fuck yourself, you communist!" I watched those people— scores of [Likud's] youth whose dark faces were twisted in hatred and their clenched fists raised high. The air was soaked with sweaty, savage violence and loaded with intense hatred. "Maniacs," the rioters screamed, "we will smash your face! Go away you son of a bitch! We'll kill you!" One of the rioters approached me and screamed to my face, "Shut up, you piece of shit!" As I looked into his eyes I got frightened. In them I saw hatred that could provide for an entire public rally in a central square in Baghdad. . . . Finally, members of the [Alignment Party's] security unit arrived. . . . I felt like someone participating in a scene from a Western movie, in which a fort is about to surrender to Indians and a unit of the cavalry suddenly shows up in gallops and trumpet blasts.[46]

Given such frightened backlash, it is not at all surprising that a parallel was immediately drawn between the political behavior of the Iranian people and that of Likud supporters; both were reduced to passive "Oriental" victims easily manipulated by cynical charismatic leaders, Khomeini on the one hand and Begin on the other. It is no coincidence, either, that when the term "Khomeinism" gained parlance in the Western media, the term "Beginism" came to evoke undemocratic and unruly political behavior in Israel: "This time you really must choose between Beginism and an enlightened government," read an Alignment Party election ad published in *Haaretz* (15 June 1981). Within this context, when Likud Party supporters interrupted the previously mentioned election rally arranged for Shimon Peres and threw tomatoes at him, he rebuked them as follows: "You are a Khomeini-like unruly mob! I'm not afraid of your tomatoes. Khomenists! Fascists! . . . Go back to Persia—that's where your future belongs."[47]

The routinization of the post-revolutionary Iranian state in the 1980s and 1990s redirected attention in Israel to the theocratic foundations of Iran's Islamic regime. But this, in turn, once again reinforced the understanding that the conflation of religion and politics also ruled out definitions of the Israeli polity as secular and enlightened. A typical example is the phrase "This is not Iran" (*kan lo iran*), which was penned by Meretz, the center-to-left secular Zionist party, as its slogan for the 1992 election campaign. In this slogan, Meretz obviously rejected Iran, but at the same time it also suggested that Israel was becoming an Iran-like state, treading a dangerous path that might culminate in the establishment of a Jewish theocracy.

The phrase "this is not Iran" is intimately related to the increasing alarm with which secular Israeli Jews from across the political spectrum have watched the ascendancy, since the 1980s, of the Shas Party to the center of the political and public stage in Israel. Shas is an ultra-orthodox party associated in the main with Israel's Mizrahi community. Support for the party was fueled in large part by the prejudicial treatment the Mizrahim bore from state institutions, as well as from ultra-orthodox Ashkenazi parties.[48]

Because Shas blended ultra-orthodox Judaism with Mizrahi politics of identity (hence ushering in the "Mizrahi-Haredi Revolution"), its electoral successes have unsettled and subverted the political and cultural status quo. "Whatever values it supports," writes an astute observer, "Shas provides and generates a collective identity, challenging the foundations of the dominant culture. [Shas] . . . has produced a critique of Zionism that focuses on the suppression of religion and Sephardic Jewish tradition."[49] The secular mainstream, in turn, mounted a campaign against Shas, charging that it aimed to institute an "Oriental" theocracy that would remove Israel from the progressive First World—a similar scenario that they scripted for Iran with the political domination of clerics under Khomeini and his successors. Accordingly, op-eds and editorials appearing regularly in the liberal press warned that if Shas were to continue operating freely, the ultra-orthodox Mizrahim would turn Israel into "an Iranian-style theocracy" (*medinat halacha*).[50] On other occasions, commentators argued somberly that Israel has already been lost to an Iranian-style Shas regime: "There are those among us who warn against the danger of making Israel a theocratic state. They are probably too late. We are not only on our way to becoming a state of the ayatollahs, we are already in its midst."[51]

It is important to note that the striking electoral successes of (the now defunct "secular" and "liberal") Shinui Party at the 1999 and 2003 elections, in which it gained six and fifteen out of one hundred and twenty parliamentary seats, respectively, stemmed in large part from similar concerns about an Iran-like ultra-orthodox Mizrahi regime taking over the country. Note, for example, the following statement by a businesswoman from Ramat Hasharon, a middle-class city that gave Shinui overwhelming support in the 1999 election: "When I watch [Shas supporters] on television, [that is] all those people [dressed in] black . . . I panic. Their appearance reminds me of Iran and [the] violent demonstrations in which the Shi'ites beat themselves until blood comes oozing out. Sometimes I say to myself: 'Good Heavens, they look exactly like them!' That's why I voted for [Shinui] at the parliamentary election."[52]

A final example of the complex ways in which images of Iran underscored a moral panic with respect to Israel's ethnic and religious "outsiders within" is taken from the 2001 prime-ministerial elections. On election eve, it became increasingly clear that Ehud Barak, the Labor Party's incumbent prime minister, would suffer a landslide defeat at the hands of his Likud Party rival, Ariel

Sharon. As a result, secular and liberal Israelis once again voiced their alarm over what Talal Asad described as "the potential entry of religion into space already occupied by the secular."[53] In their forecast, Sharon was to be elected prime minister, but would fail to entice secular Zionist parties to join Likud in a coalition government. Sharon would then have no other recourse but to seek the support of ultraorthodox and anti-Zionist factions. Submitting unconditionally to their sectarian demands, he would be forced to install a "fundamentalist" government that would make Israel a "Jewish Iran."[54]

Russian immigrants in Israel, many of whom support separation of religion from state and espouse anti-Mizrahi sentiments,[55] were particularly alarmed by this prospect. Yaakov Kedmi is a case in point. Kedmi, a Russian-born Israeli, was Barak's one-time confidant and the person who headed the Mossad's Russian Immigration Bureau. Probably better than anyone else at the time, he knew that, unlike in 1999, the majority of Israelis of Russian descent would not vote for Barak in the forthcoming election. Asked, therefore, if it was still possible for Barak to restore his credibility among Russians, he replied, "Yes," but only if these immigrants were to be told:

> You are not choosing between Ehud Barak and Arik Sharon, but between a democratic Israeli state, which is modern, free, and does not discriminate among Jews of types A, B, and C, on the one hand, and, on the other, a state dominated by a fundamentalist Jewish school in all respects. . . . This [latter] state will resemble Iran in terms of belligerency, aggressiveness, cruelty, and influence on the life of its citizens. Today we must choose between Jewish fundamentalism and a normal Jewish state. . . . On 6 February we shall vote either for a democratic state or for a fundamentalist state.[56]

Incidentally, here Kedmi reinforces a secular, albeit distinctly *Jewish*, definition of the Israeli collective, hence supplying one more testimony to the "pitfalls of religiosity"[57] inscribed in Jewish secularity. What is more, he assumes that "a democratic Israeli state, which is modern [and] free," is a state where no distinctions are to be made among "Jews of types A, B, and C." The overriding problem, of course, is that Kedmi excludes the non-Jewish, mainly Palestinian citizens from his imagined community, and does not view their exclusion as an obstacle to the kind of "democratic, modern, and free" state he is calling for.

As the foregoing discussion has shown, the debate over Iran in Israeli public culture stems in no small part from a perceived hegemonic imperative to exorcise the "Oriental," ethnic and ultrareligious (Iran-like) "demons" within Israeli society. The production of meaning about Iran is driven by a moral panic concerning the nature of Israeli identity no less than by any strategic or other rivalry between the two states. Even if some of Israel's concerns with the Islamic republic may be justified, the perceptions of Iran issuing from its public sphere should be examined within the context of heightened anxieties, lest Iran's post-1979 realities turn out to be the dark future of the Jewish state.

Conclusion

In her fascinating work on the relationship between domestic and foreign policies of American empire and their cultural manifestations, Amy Kaplan has demonstrated the link between domestic and foreign affairs in the manufacturing of such an imperial project. As Kaplan explains, "the concept of foreign policy depends on the idea of the nation as a domestic space imbued with a sense of at-homeness, in contrast to an external world perceived as alien and threatening. Reciprocally, a sense of the foreign is necessary to erect the boundaries that enclose the nation as home."[58] My analysis has likewise shown that perceptions of the Iranians as alien and threatening were fashioned and comprehended on the basis of what Israelis believed to be the (dis)ordering of their society at home. Consequently, these perceptions have turned into a defensive protection of the home front. This interpenetration of the "foreign" and the "domestic" belies the premise that "subversive" domestic forces are solely responsible for the continuing dissolution of the fiction of Israel as a Euro-America space. At the same time, it also challenges the entrenched conviction, which is shared by most scholars of Israeli-Iranian relations, and put forth most recently by Trita Parsi, that "internal developments . . .—while important—have little or no impact on [these states'] respective foreign policies."[59]

As I have argued elsewhere,[60] Israeli mainstream readings of Iran have much in common with their American counterparts, as analyzed in the literature.[61] However, they also bear distinctive qualities that can help us develop a "post-Orientalist" approach to Israeli politics, culture, and society. The Orientalist paradigm à la Said, as we know, presupposes the homogeneity of the "Occident" (or "Judeo-Christian civilization") and the "Orient" (or "Islam"), respectively, as well as the impenetrable gulf that separates "Occidentals" from "Orientals." However, Israeli readings of Iran contested such notions of homogeneity and difference—specifically because they were informed interchangeably by an acute awareness of cultural differences at home and of commonalities between Israelis and Iranians.

Nonetheless, many Israelis in positions of power continue to disseminate

Orientalist understanding of the (domestic and external) non-West with a view to silencing critical, ethnic, and religious reassessments of the Israeli polity. In so doing, they confirm the allegation that "Zionist Israel . . . reflects a contradictory unity, a democratic despotism, in a single space."[62] This Orientalism practiced by the Israeli state is thus in keeping with "the tendency of colonial regimes to draw a stark dichotomy of colonizer and colonized without themselves falling into such a Manichaean conception."[63] The Israeli case may also suggest, perhaps in another departure from the Saidian paradigm, that even producers of Orientalist representations know full well that these representations are not reliable and faithful reflections of reality.[64]

Finally, the Israeli case may also suggest that constructions of national identity do not depend solely on the production of difference. Rather, they also depend on the rejection of affinity with—or ambivalence toward—the Other, who is already included in the national self. Paradoxically, then, national identity becomes intelligible not only through a perception of threat that produces *difference*, but also through a perception of threat that is produced by *similarity*.

Notes

1. Thomas Frank, "Of Tourists and Terrorists: U.S. Visa Policy Irks Israelis," *Newsweek*, 22 July, 2003.

2. The countries included in the VWP are listed in the U.S. Department of State website: http://travel.state.gov/visa/temp/without/without_1990.html#countries.

3. Cited in Frank, "Of Tourists and Terrorists."

4. "Nobody wants to be the visa officer who lets a terrorist into the country," said a congressional aide close to the issue, recalling the outcry after revelations that all the 9/11 hijackers had been granted visas by U.S. consulates; cited in ibid.

5. Ibid.

6. Rebecca Stein, "The Ballad of the Sad Café: Israeli Leisure, Palestinian Terror, and the Post/colonial Question," in *Postcolonial Studies and Beyond*, eds. Annia Loomba, Suvir Kaul, Matti Bunzl, Antoinette Burton, and Jed Esty (Durham: Duke University Press, 2006), 327.

7. The Nakba Law legislates the withdrawal of state funding from any institution that commemorates the Palestinian day of mourning, and is recognized as discriminatory and threatening to Palestinians and Jews alike.

8. See, e.g., Ella Shohat's "The Invention of the Mizrahim," *Journal of Palestine Studies* 29/1 (1999), 7, which sums up the Israeli ethnocracy's predicament as follows: "The fact that the 'Orientals' have had closer cultural and historical links to the presumed enemy—the 'Arab'—than to the Ashkenazi Jews with whom they were coaxed and coerced into shared nationhood threatens the conception of a homogeneous na-

tion akin to those on which European nationalist movements were based, while it also threatens the Euro-Israeli self-image."

9. I will refer to particular studies within this body of scholarship as I proceed in my discussion.

10. Edward Said, *Reflections on Exile and Other Essays* (Cambridge, MA: Harvard University Press, 2000), 473.

11. Ronen Bergman, "The Demon is Not So Terrible," *Haaretz Weekly Supplement*, 15 March 1996.

12. Dayan Center's Meir Litvak and Joshua Teitelbaum, in a letter to the editor, *Haaretz*, 29 March 1996.

13. Haifa University's Ilan Pappé in a letter to the editor, *Haaretz*, 29 March 1996.

14. Ben Gurion University's Dror Zeevi in a letter to the editor, *Haaretz*, 5 April 1996.

15. E.g., Eyal Zisser, director of Tel Aviv University's Dayan Center for Middle East and African Studies at the time, and currently the Dean of the Faculty of Humanities at Tel Aviv University. Zisser sees no problem with the fact that, in addition to his senior university positions, he also holds "an important and sensitive position" in Israeli military intelligence. See Idan Ring, "We Have with Us Our Commander . . . eh, Our Analyst," *Haaretz Weekly Supplement*, 5 March 2008.

16. David Menashri, "In the Wake of a Conversation with a Former Student," *Haaretz Weekly Supplement*, 22 March 1996.

17. Anthony Giddens, *New Rules of Sociological Method* (London: Hutchinson, 1976).

18. Needless to say, in what follows I will not be suggesting that Israel and Iran are made of one cloth, as it were, or that Israel is heading toward the establishment of an Iran-like theocracy. Rather, I talk about the Israelis' imagination, which, though neither objective nor empirical, is emblematic of their concerns and fears about the domestic sphere.

19. Dipesh Chakrabarty, *Provincializing Europe: Postcolonial Thought and Historical Difference* (Princeton: Princeton University Press, 2000), 41.

20. Ari Shavit, "Survival of the Fittest," Haaretz, 9 January 2004.

21. Chakrabarty, *Provincializing Europe*, 45.

22. Ian Lustick, "Abandoning the Iron Wall: Israel and 'The Middle Eastern Muck,'" *Middle East Policy Council*, 2011: http://www.mepc.org/journal/middle-east -policy-archives/abandoning-iron-wall-israel-and-middle-eastern-muck.

23. Naomi Klein, "Can Democracy Survive Bush's Embrace?" *The Nation*, 9 March 2005.

24. Calling Katsav a "dignitary" would be somewhat outlandish, especially because he has been convicted of the rape and sexual harassment of several of his subordinates.

25. Itamar Eicher and Zvi Zinger, "Katsav Disgraces Israel," *Yedi'ot Ahronoth*, 10 April 2005.

26. The Katsav-Khatami encounter also caused a great deal of embarrassment to the Iranian government, and even Khatami denied this encounter took place. See www .nbcnews.com/id/7443548/ns/world_news/t/iranianpresident-deves-israeli-hand shake/.

27. Benny Ziffer, "The Voice of Thunder from Cairo," *Haaretz*, 7 December 2006.

28. Bergman, "The Demon Is Not So Terrible."

29. Martin Riesebrodt, *Pious Passion: The Emergence of Modern Fundamentalism in the United States and Iran*, trans. Don Reneau (Berkeley: University of California Press, 1993), 8.

30. See, e.g., Nikki R. Keddie, "Iranian Revolutions in comparative Perspective," *The American Historical Review* 88/3 (1983): 579–598; Said Amir Arjomand, "The State and Khomeini's Islamic Order," *Iranian Studies* 13 (1980), 147–164; Said Amir Arjomand, "Iran's Islamic Revolution in Comparative Perspective," *World Politics* 38 (1986), 383–414; Shahin Gerami, "Religious Fundamentalism as a Response to Foreign Dependency: The Case of the Iranian Revolution," *Social Compass* 36 (1989), 451–467; Sami Zubaida, *Islam, the People and the State: Political Ideas and Movements in the Middle East* (London: I. B. Tauris, 1993); Ervand Abrahamian, *Khomeinism: Essays on the Islamic Republic* (Berkeley: University of California Press, 1993); Houchang Chehabi, *Li Kulli Fir'awn Musa: The Myth of Moses and Pharaoh in the Iranian Revolution in Comparative Perspective* (Waltham: Brandeis University, Crown Center for Middle East Studies, 2010).

31. Jacques Derrida, *Margins of Philosophy*, trans. Alan Bass (New York: Oxford University Press 1982), 213.

32. Jacqueline Rose, *The Question of Zion* (Princeton: Princeton University Press, 2005), 8.

33. Cited in ibid., 42. On Gershom Scholem's ideas about the links between messianism and Zionism, see Amnon Raz-Krakotzkin, *Exil et souveraineté: Judaïsme, sionisme, et pensée binationale* (Paris: La Fabrique éditions, 2007), 131–157.

34. Rose, *Question of Zion*, 53–54. On the failure to effect a break between Zionism and Jewish messianism, or between religion and Jewish nationalism, see Aviezer Ravitsky, ed., *Shas: Cultural and Ideological Perspectives* (in Hebrew) (Tel Aviv: Am Oved, 1996); Baruch Kimmerling, "Religion, Nationalism and Democracy in Israel," *Constellations* 6 (1999): 339–363; Yossi Yonah and Yehuda Goodman, eds., *In the Whirlpool of Identities* (in Hebrew) (Tel Aviv: Hakibbutz Hameuchad, 2004); Yehouda Shenhav, *The Arab Jews: A Postcolonial Reading of Nationalism, Religion, and Ethnicity* (Stanford: Stanford University Press, 2006).

35. 18 January, 2003.

36. Abrahamian, *Khomeinism*.

37. Cited in Rose, *Question of Zion*, 36.

38. *Dar Maktab-e Jom'eh: Majmu`ah-e Khotbeh-e Namaz-e Jom'eh-e Tehran*, Vol. 2 (Tehran: Entesharat-e Chapkhaneh-e Vezarat-e Ershad-e Eslami, 1986), 202.

39. Aviezer Ravitsky, *Messianism, Zionism, and Jewish Religious Radicalism* (Chicago: University of Chicago Press, 1996), 37–38.

40. Others—and most prominently and recently Trita Parsi, in *Treacherous Alliance: The Secret Dealings of Israel, Iran, and the U.S* (New Haven: Yale University Press, 2007)—have come to view this enmity as a manifestation of a strategic rivalry for power and preeminence in the Middle East.

41. Talal Asad, *On Suicide Bombing* (New York: Columbia University Press, 2007), 3.

42. "Khomeini's Zealots in Kiryat Arba Exchange Blows with IDF Soldiers," *Haaretz*, 3 January 1979.

43. Michael Harsegor, "Israel, Beware of the Ayatollah," *Davar*, 12 January 1979.

44. See, e.g., Gabi Shefer, "Violence and Politics," *Haaretz*, 8 May 1981.

45. Dror Mishani, *The Ethnic Unconscious: The Emergence of "Mizrahiut" in the Hebrew Literature of the Eighties* (in Hebrew) (Tel Aviv: Am Oved, 2006), 12.

46. Amnon Dankner, "I Didn't Want to Write an Article, I Just Wanted to Return Home in One Piece," *Haaretz*, 19 June 1981.

47. "A Mob of Likud Supporters Goes Wild at a Rally with Peres," *Haaretz*, 15 June 1981.

48. The party won just four seats (out of 120) when it debuted in the 1984 elections, but in 1999, it won seventeen seats and became the third-largest Knesset faction. In the 2003 election, Shas gained eleven seats; in the 2006 election it gained twelve seats; and in 2009, it won eleven parliamentary seats.

49. Amnon Raz-Krakotzkin, "The Zionist Return to the West and the Mizrahi Jewish Perspective," in Ivan Davidson Kalmar and Derek J. Penslar, eds., *Orientalism and the Jews* (Waltham: Brandeis University Press, 2005), 173. For critical perspectives on the Shas phenomenon, see Yoav Peled, ed., *Shas: The Challenge to Israeliness* (in Hebrew) (Tel Aviv: Yedi'ot Ahronoth, 2001); Aviezer Ravitsky, ed., *Shas: Cultural and Ideological Perspectives* (in Hebrew) (Tel Aviv: Am Oved, 2006); David Lehmann and Batia Siebzehner, *Remaking Israeli Judaism: The Challenge of Shas* (London: Hurst, 2006).

50. Ran Kislev, "Shas Nevertheless," *Haaretz*, 25 May 1999.

51. Ran Kislev, "On the Way Towards a State of the Ayatollahs," *Haaretz*, 24 June 1998.

52. Daniel Ben-Simon, "Secular Fundamentalism in Ramat Hasharon," *Haaretz*, 28 May 1999.

53. Talal Asad, *Formations of the Secular: Christianity, Islam, Modernity* (Stanford: Stanford University Press, 2003), 199.

54. Elie Kamir, "Yaakov Kedmi: On 6 February We Shall Vote for a Democratic State or a Fundamentalist State," *Maariv*, 5 January, 2001.

55. Dimitry Shumski, "Post-Zionist Orientalism? Orientalist Discourse and Islamophobia among the Russian-Speaking Intelligentsia in Israel," *Social Identities* 10 (2004), 83–99.

56. Kamir, "Yaakov Kedmi."

57. Baruch Kimmerling, *Immigrants, Settlers, Natives: The Israeli State and Society between Cultural Pluralism and Cultural Wars* (in Hebrew) (Tel Aviv: Am Oved, 2004), 15.

58. Amy Kaplan, *The Anarchy of Empire in the Making of U.S. Culture* (Cambridge, MA, and London: Harvard University Press, 2002), 25.

59. Parsi, *Treacherous Alliance*, xii.

60. Haggai Ram, *Iranophobia: The Logic of an Israeli Obsession* (Stanford: Stanford University Press, 2009).

61. See, e.g., Elizabeth Shakman Hurd, "The International Politics of Secularism: U.S. Foreign Policy and the Islamic Republic of Iran," *Alternatives* 29 (2004), 115–138; Melani McAlister, *Epic Encounters: Culture, Media, and U.S. Interests in the Middle East, 1945–2000* (Berkeley and Los Angeles: University of California Press, 2001), 198–234; Hamid Naficy, "Mediating the Other: American Pop Culture Representation of Postrevolutionary Iran," in *The U.S. Media and the Middle East: Image and Perception, ed. Yahya R. Kamalipour* (Westport, CT: Greenwood Press, 1995); Edward

Said, *Covering Islam: How the Media and the Experts Determine How We See the Rest of the World* (London: Routledge and Kegan Paul, 1981).

62. Mahmood Mamdani, *Good Muslim, Bad Muslim: America, the Cold War, and the Roots of Terror* (New York: Pantheon Books, 2004), 247.

63. Ann Laura Stoler and Fredrick Cooper, "Between Metropole and Colony: Rethinking a Research Agenda," in *Tensions of Empire: Colonial Cultures in a Bourgeois World*, eds. Fredrick Cooper and Ann Laura Stoler (Berkeley and Los Angeles: University of California Press, 1997), 3.

64. Chakrabarty (*Provincializing Europe*, 27–28) offers a useful formulation of this issue: "Liberal-minded scholars would immediately protest that any idea of a homogeneous, uncontested 'Europe' dissolves under analysis. True, but just as the phenomenon of Orientalism does not disappear simply because some of us have now attained a critical awareness of it, similarly a certain version of 'Europe,' reified and celebrated in the phenomenal world of everyday relationships of power as the scene of the birth of the modern, continues to dominate the discourse of history. Analysis does not make it go away."

Bibliography

Government Archives

National Archives and Record Administration (U.S.)

U.S. State Department Records 891

British National Archives

WO 33
WO 106
WO 208
FO 248
FO 371
FO 460
FO 624

Books and Articles

'Alawi, Nasir Khusraw. *Safarnamah*. Translated by Yahya al-Khashshab. Cairo: Ma'had al-Lughat al-Sharqiyah, Kulliyat al-Adab, 1945.
'Azzam, 'Abd al-Wahhab. *al-Tasawwuf wa-Farid al-Din 'Attar*. Cairo: 'Isa al-Babi al-Halabi, 1945.
Abd al-Rahman, Awatif. *Misr Wa Falastin*. Kiewit: 'Alam al-Ma'rifah, 1980.
Abd al-Wahhab 'Azzam, Abd al-Wahhab. *Rahalat*. Cairo: Matba'at al-Risala, n.d.
Abrahamian, Ervand. *A History of Modern Iran*. Cambridge: Cambridge University Press, 2008.
———. *Iran Between Two Revolutions*. Princeton: Princeton University Press, 1982.
———. *Khomeinism: Essays on the Islamic Republic*. Berkeley: University of California Press, 1993.
———. *Tortured Confessions: Prisons and Public Recantations in Modern Iran*. Berkeley: University of California Press, 1999.

Adamiyat, Fereydun. *Ideolozhi-e Nehzat-e Mashrutiyat-e Iran (The Ideology of Iran's Constitutional Movement).* Tehran: Payam, 1976.

Afary, Janet. *Sexual Politics in Modern Iran.* Cambridge, UK, and New York: Cambridge University Press, 2009.

Afsar, K. A. *Tarikh-e Baft-e Ghadim-e Shiraz (The Old Fabric of Shiraz).* Tehran, 1374.

Afshari, Iraj. "Book Translations as a Cultural Activity in Iran 1806–1896." *Iran* 41 (2003).

Aghaie, Kamran Scot. "Islam and Nationalist Historiography: Competing Historical Narratives of Iran in the Pahlavi Period." *Studies on Contemporary Islam* 2, no. 2 (2000): 20–46.

———. "Islamist Historiography in Post-Revolutionary Iran." In *Iran in the 20th Century: Historiography and Political Culture*, edited by Touraj Atabaki, 233–263, 318–322. London and New York: I. B. Tauris, in association with the Iran Heritage Foundation, 2009.

Ahmadi, Wali. "The Institution of Persian Literature and the Genealogy of Bahar's 'Stylistics.'" *British Journal of Middle Eastern Studies* 31, no. 2 (2004).

Akhundzadeh. *Alefba-e Jadid Va Maktubat.* Tabriz: Ehya Publications, 1978.

Al-Ahmad, Jalal. *Dar Khedmat Va Khianat-e Roshanfekran.* Tehran: Kharazmi Press, 1978.

al-Baghdadi, Abd al-Qahir. *al-Farq Bain Al-firaq [Tarikh Mazaheb-e Islam].* Translated by Mohammad Javad. Tehran: Amir Kabir, 1965.

al-Din, Muhammad al-Saʿid Jamal. "Al-Shaykh Muhammad ʿAbdu Wa Al-thaqafa al-Farisiyya." In *Jawanib Min Al-silat Al-thaqafiyya Bayna Misr Wa Iran*, edited by Nur al-Din Al-Ali. Cairo: Dar al-Thaqafa lil-Tibaʾa wal-Nashr, 1975.

al-Ghataʾ, Muhammad al-Husayni Kashif. *Asl al-Shiʿa Wa Usulaha.* 10th ed. Cairo, 1958.

al-Jammal, Ahmad ʿAbd al-Qadir. *Mushkilat al-Sharq al-Awsat.* Cairo: Maktabat al-Anjlu al-Misriyya, 1955.

al-Masʿudi, ʿAli Ibn Hussein. *Al-Tanbih Wa Al-ishraf.* Edited by M. J. de Goeje. Leiden: Brill, 1893.

al-Misri, Husayn Mujib. *Ayyami Bayna ʿahdayn: Sira Zatiyya.* Cairo: al-Dar al-thaqafiyya lil-nashr, 1999.

al-Muqaddasi, Shams al-Din b. Abi ʿAbdullah Muhammad b. Abi Bakr. *Ahsan Al-taqasim Fi Mʿarifat Al-aqalim.* Edited by M. J. de Goeje. Leiden: Brill, 1906.

al-Sabbagh, Saʾid. *al-ʾAlaqah Bayna al-Qahirah wa-Tihran Tanafus Am Taʿawun? Al-muhaddidat Wa-al-asrar.* Cairo: al-Dar al-Thaqafiyah lil-Nashr, 2003.

al-Sadati, Ahmad Mahmud. *Rida Shah Bahlawi: Nahdat Iran al-Haditha.* Cairo: Maktabat al-Nahda al-Misriyya, 1939.

al-Wirdani, Salih. *al-Shiʿah Fi Misr Min al-Imam Ali Hatta al-Imam al-Khomeini.* Cairo: Maktabat Madbuli al-Saghir, 1993.

Alam, Muzaffar, and Sanjay Subrahmanyam. *Indo-Persian Travels in the Age of Discoveries, 1400–1800.* Cambridge: Cambridge University Press, 2007.

Algar, Hamid. *Religion and State in Iran, 1785–1906: The Role of the Ulama in the Qajar Period.* Berkeley: University of California Press, 1969.

Amanat, Abbas. *Pivot of the Universe: Nasir al-Din Shah and the Iranian Monarchy, 1831–1896.* Berkeley: University of California Press, 1997.

Amin, Ahmad. *Fajr al-Islam*. 5th ed. Cairo: Lajnat al-Ta'lif wa al-Tarjamah wa al-Nashr, 1945.

Amin, Camron Michael. "Selling and Saving 'Mother Iran': Gender and the Iranian Press in the 1940s." *International Journal of Middle East Studies* 33 (2001).

———. *The Making of the Modern Iranian Woman: Gender, State Policy, and Popular Culture, 1865–1946*. Gainesville: University Press of Florida, 2002.

Anderson, Bendict. *Imagined Communities: Reflections on the Origins and Spread of Nationalism*. Verso, New Edition Edition, 1991.

Anonymous. *Hudud Al-'alam Min Al-mashriq Ila Al-maghrib*. Edited by M. Sotudeh. Tehran: Daneshgah-e Tehran, 1962.

Aqeli, Baker. *Davar Va Adlieh*. Tehran: Elmi, 1990.

Arberry, Arthur. *Hafiz, Fifty Poems*. Cambridge: Cambridge University Press, 1953.

———. *Sufism: An Account of the Mystics of Islam*. London: George Allen & Unwin, 1950.

Ardakani Davari, Reza. *Inqelab Va Vaz'e Kununi-e 'Alam*. Tehran: 'Alame Tabatabai Center for Culture, 1982.

———. *Nationalism Va Inqelab*. Tehran: Daftar-e Pajouhesh-ha va Barnameh Rizi-e Farhangi, 1986.

Ardalan, Nader. "Architecture Viii. Pahlavi, After World War II." In *Encyclopedia Iranica*, n.d.

Arjomand, Said Amir. "Iran's Islamic Revolution in Comparative Perspective." *World Politics* 38 (1986).

———. *The Shadow of God and the Hidden Imam: Religion, Political Order, and Societal Change in Shi'ite Iran from the Beginning to 1890*. Chicago: University of Chicago Press, 2010.

———. "The State and Khomeini's Islamic Order." *Iranian Studies* 13 (1980).

Armirsadeghi, Hossein. *Different Sames: New Perspectives in Contemporary Iranian Art*. London: TransGlobe Publishing, 2009.

Arvidsson, Stefan. *Aryan Idols: Indo-European Mythology as Ideology and Science*. Chicago: University of Chicago Press, 2006.

Asad, Talal. *Formations of the Secular: Christianity, Islam, Modernity*. Stanford, CA: Stanford University Press, 2003.

———. *On Suicide Bombing*. New York: Columbia University Press, 2007.

Ashraf, Ahmad. "Historical Obstacles to the Development of a Bourgeoisie in Iran." *Iranian Studies* 2, no. 2 (1969).

Atabaki, Touraj. *Azerbaijan: Ethnicity and the Struggle for Power in Iran*. London and New York: I. B. Tauris Publishers; distributed the United States and Canada by St. Martin's Press, 2000.

Aubin, Jean. "Études Safavides. I: Shah Isma'il Et Les Notables De l'Iraq Persan." *Journal of the Economic and Social History of the Orient* 2 (1959).

———. "Révolution Chiite Et Conservatism. Lessoufis De Liahejian, 1500–1514." *Moyen Orient & Océan Indien* 1 (1984).

Babayan, Kathryn. *Mystics, Monarchs, and Messiahs: Cultural Landscape of Early Modern Iran*. Cambridge, MA: Harvard University Press, 2002.

Babayan, Kathryn, Afsaneh Najmabadi, and Sahar Amer, eds. "Cross-Dressing and Female Same-Sex Marriage in Medieval French and Arabic Literatures." In *Islami-*

cate Sexualities: Translations Across Temporal Geographies of Desire. Cambridge, MA: Center for Middle Eastern Studies of Harvard University. Distributed by Harvard University Press, 2008.

Babinger, Franz. *Die Geschichtsschreiber Der Osmanen Und Ihre Werke.* Leipzig: O. Harrassowitz, 1927.

———. "Einer Von Vielen." *Das Bayernland* 44, no. 19 (1933).

———. *Mehmed Der Eroberer Und Seine Zeit: Weltenstürmer Einer Zeitenwende.* München: F. Bruckmann, 1953.

Bakhash, Shaul. *Iran: Monarchy, Bureaucracy, and the Reforms Under the Qajars, 1858–1896.* London: Ithaca Press, 1978.

Baladhuri, Ahmad b. Yahya. *Futuh Al-buldan.* Cairo: Maktab al-Nahda al-Misriyya, 1956.

Balaghi, Shiva. "Art and Revolution in the Islamic Republic of Iran." *The Middle East Institute Viewpoints* (n.d.).

———. "Print Culture in Late Qajar Iran: The Cartoons of 'Kashkul.'" *Iranian Studies* 34, no. 1_4 (2001).

Balay, Christophe. "Orientalisme Et Occidentalisme." In *Rêver d'Orient, Connaitre l'Orient: Visions De l'Orient Dans L'art Et La Littérature Britanniques.* Paris: Éditions, 2008.

Banarasi, 'Ali Ebrahim Khan Khalil. *Sohof-e Ebrahim: Bakhsh-e Mo'aseran.* Edited by Mir Hashem Mohaddes. Tehran: Anjoman-e asar va mofakher-e farhangi, 1384.

Barker, Philip W. *Religious Nationalism in Modern Europe: If God Be for Us.* New York: Routledge, 2009.

Bashiri, Iraj. *The Fiction of Sadeq Hedayat.* Lexington, KY: Mazda Publishers, 1984.

Bauer, Otto. *The Question of Nationalities and Social Democracy.* Minneapolis: University of Minnesota Press, 2000.

Bayat, Kaveh. "Andishe-ye Siasi-ye Davar Va Ta'sis-e Dowlat-e Modern Dar Iran." *Goft-o-Gu* 2 (1993).

Baygdeli, Lutf 'Ali ibn Aqa Khan Azar. *Atashkadeh.* Edited by Hassan Sadat Nasiri. 4 vols. Tehran: Amir Kabir, 1336.

Behnam, Jamshid. *Berlaniha.* Tehran: Farzan, 2000.

Bell, Gertrude Lowthian. *The Hafez Poems of Gertrude Bell: With the Original Persian on the Facing Page.* Bethesda, MD: Iranbooks, 1995.

Bendix, Reinhard. *Kings or People: Power and the Mandate to Rule.* Berkeley: University of California Press, 1978.

Benton, William. "The Voice of America Abroad." *Journal of Educational Sociology* 19, no. 4 (December 1945).

Blüher, Hans. *Die Rolle Der Erotik in Der Mänlichen Gesellschaft.* Jena: E. Diederichs, 1919.

———. *Familie Und Männerbund.* Leipzig: Der neue Geist Verlag, 1919.

———. *Family & Male Fraternity: A Theory of the Eros.* Translated by Heinrich Hoffstiepel. Paris: Dioscures, 1994.

Bonnerot, Olivier H. *La Perse dans la littérature et la pensee francaises au XVIIIe siecle: De l'image au mythe.* Paris: Champion-Slatkine, 1988.

Boroujerdi, Mehrzad. "Contested Nationalist Constructions of Iranian Identity." *Critique: Journal for Critical Studies of the Middle East* 12 (Spring 1998).

Breuilly, John. *Nationalism and the State.* Chicago: University of Chicago Press, 1982.

Brockett, Gavin D. *How Happy to Call Oneself a Turk: Provincial Newspapers and the Negotiation of a Muslim National Identity*. Austin: University of Texas Press, 2011.

Brookshaw, Dominic Parviz. "Odes of a Poet-Princess: The Ghazals of Jahān-Malik Khātun." *Iran* 43, (2005).

Browne, Edward G. *A Literary History of Persia. Volume 4, Modern Times (1500–1924)*. Cambridge University Press, 1929.

———. *Press and Poetry of Modern Persia*. Los Angeles: Kalimat Press, 1983.

Brubaker, Roger. "The Manichean Myth: Rethinking the Distinction Between 'Civic' and 'Ethnic' Nationalism." In *Nation and National Identity: The European Experience in Perspective*, edited by Andreas Wimmer, Hannas Siegrist, Klaus Armington, and Hanspeter Kriesl. Zurich: Verlac Rüegger, 1999.

Buck-Morss, Susan. *The Dialectics of Seeing: Walter Benjamin and the Arcades Project*. Cambridge, MA: MIT Press, 1989.

Burleigh, Michael. *Confronting the Nazi Past: New Debates on Modern German History*. New York: St. Martin's Press, 1996.

Calhoun, Craig, ed. *Habermas and the Public Sphere*. Cambridge, MA: MIT Press, 1992.

Cannadine, David. "The Context, Performance, and Meaning of Ritual: The British Monarchy and the 'Invention of Tradition,' c. 1820–1977." In *The Invention of Tradition*, edited by Eric Hobsbawm and Terence Ranger. Cambridge: Cambridge University Press, 1983.

Carhart, Michael C. *The Science of Culture in Enlightenment Germany*. Cambridge, MA: Harvard University Press, 2008.

Cetinsaya, Gokhan. "Rethinking Nationalism and Islam: Some Preliminary Notes on the Roots of the 'Turkish-Islamic Synthesis' in Modern Turkish Thought." *Muslim World* 89, no. 3_4 (1999): 350–376.

Chakrabarty, Dipesh. *Provincializing Europe: Postcolonial Thought and Historical Difference*. Princeton, NJ: Princeton University Press, 2000.

Chatterjee, Partha. *Nationalist Thought and the Colonial World*. London: Zed Books, 1986.

———. *The Nation and Its Fragments*. Princeton: Princeton University Press, 1993.

Chehabi, Houchang. *Li Kulli Firʿawn Musa: The Myth of Moses and Pharaoh in the Iranian Revolution in Comparative Perspective*. Waltham, MA: Brandeis University, Crown Center for Middle East Studies, 2010.

Chittick, William C. *Sufism: A Short Introduction*. Oxford: Oneworld Publications, 2000.

———. *The Sufi Path of Love: the Spiritual Teachings of Rumi*. Albany: State University of New York Press, 1983.

Clermont, Betty. *The Neo-Catholics: Implementing Christian Nationalism in America*. Atlanta, GA: Clarity Press, 2009.

Connor, Walker. "Nation-Building or Nation-Destroying?" *World Politics* 14 (1972).

Constitution of the Islamic Republic of Iran. Tehran: Islamic Consultative Assembly, 1980.

Cooper, Fredrick, and Ann Laura Stoler. "Between Metropole and Colony: Rethinking a Research Agenda." In *Tensions of Empire: Colonial Cultures in a Bourgeois World*, edited by Fredrick Cooper and Ann Laura Stoler. Berkeley: University of California Press, 1997.

Coury, Ralph M. *The Making of an Egyptian Arab Nationalist: The Early Years of Azzam Pasha, 1893–1936.* Reading, England: Ithaca Press, 1998.

————. "Who 'Invented' Egyptian Arab Nationalism?" *International Journal of Middle East Studies* 14, no. 3 (August 1982).

Cronin, Stephanie, ed. *The Making of Modern Iran: State and Society Under Riza Shah, 1921–1941.* London: Routledge/Curzon, 2003.

Dadlani, Chanchal. "The 'Palais Indiens' Collection of 1774: Representing Mughal Architecture in Late Eighteenth-Century India." *Ars Orientalis* 39 (2010).

Daghestani, 'Ali Qoli Khan Valeh. *Tazkareh-e Riyaz Al-sho'ara.* Edited by Mohsen Naji Nasirabadi. Vol. 1. Tehran: Asatir, 1384.

Dalal, Ghulam Abbas. *Ethics in Persian Poetry: With Special Reference to Timurid Period.* New Delhi: Abhinav Publications, 1995.

Dar Maktab-e Jom'eh: Majmu'ah-e Khotbeh-e Namaz-e Jom'eh-e Tehran. Vol. 2. Tehran: Entesharat-e Chapkhaneh-e Vezarat-e Ershad-e Eslami, 1986.

Delfani, M. *Culture During Reza Shah.* Tehran, 1997.

Derrida, Jacques. *Margins of Philosophy.* Translated by Alan Bass. New York: Oxford University Press, 1982.

Deutsch, Karl. *Nationalism and Social Communication.* Cambridge, MA: MIT Press, 1969.

Dinvari, Abu Hanifeh Ahmad Ibn-Davud. *Akhbar Al-taval.* Translated by Mahdavi Damghani. Tehran: Nashr No, 1986.

Dixon, John Morris. "Tehran Museum of Contemporary Art: Cultural Hybrid, Progressive Architecture." *Progressive Architecture* 59 (June 1978).

Eagleton, Terry. *Literary Theory: An Introduction.* London: Blackwell, 1983.

Eagleton, William. *The Kurdish Republic of 1946.* London: Oxford University Press, 1963.

Eckl, Andreas E. *S'ist Ein Übles Land Hier: Zur Historiographie Eines Umstrittenen Kolonialskrieges.* Köln: Köppe, 2007.

Eley, Goeff. "Nations, Publics, and Political Cultures: Placing Habermas in Nineteenth-Century Germany." In *Habermas and the Public Sphere*, edited by Craig Calhoun. Cambridge, MA: MIT Press, 1992.

Eley, Goeff, and Ronald Grigor Suny, eds. *Becoming National: A Reader.* New York: Oxford University Press, 1996.

Emami, Karim. "Art in Iran XI Post-Qajar." In *Encyclopedia Iranica*, n.d.

Ernst, Carl W. "Between Orientalism and Fundamentalism: Problematizing the Teaching of Sufism." In *Teaching Islam*, edited by Brannon M. Wheeler. New York: Oxford University Press, 2003.

Esbati, Mohammad Hassan. *Iranian Modern Art Movement: The Iranian Collection of the Tehran Museum of Contemporary Art.* Tehran, 2006.

Eshghi Sanity, Khanak. *Nationalism Va Regime-e Terror Va Jonoon Dar Iran.* Ottawa: Ava-e Iran, 1989.

Esman, Milton J., and Itamar Rabinovich. *Ethnicity, Pluralism, and the State in the Middle East.* Ithaca, NY: Cornell University Press, 1988.

Faruqi, Shamur Rahman. "Unprivileged Power: The Strange Case of Persian (and Urdu) in Nineteenth-Century India." *The Annual of Urdu Studies*, 1998.

Ferdowsi, Abolqasem. *Shahnameh: The Persian Book of Kings.* Translated by Dick Davis. New York: Penguin, 2007.

Floor, Willem. *Industrialization in Iran: 1900–1941*. Durham: Durham Centre for Middle East and Islamic Studies, Occasional Papers Series, No. 23, 1984.

Floor, William. *Guilds, Merchants, & Ulama in Nineteenth-Century Iran*. Washington, DC: Mage Publishers, 2009.

Foran, John. *Fragile Resistance: Social Transformation in Iran from 1500 to the Revolution*. Boulder: Westview Press, 1993.

Foucault, Michel, and Robert Hurley. *The History of Sexuality*. New York: Vintage Books, 1988.

Fouladvand, Hengameh. "Art; Art, Diaspora; Art, Visual; Art Exhibitions." In *Iran Today: an Encyclopedia of Life in the Islamic Republic*, edited by Mehran Kamrava and Manochehr Dorraj. Westport, CT: Greenwood Press, 2008.

Gasper, Michael Ezekiel. *The Power of Representation Publics, Peasants, and Islam in Egypt*. Stanford, CA: Stanford University Press, 2009.

Gellner, Ernest. *Nations and Nationalism*. Oxford: Blackwell, 1983.

———. *Thought and Change*. London: Weidenfield and Nicholson, 1964.

Gelvin, James. "Nationalism, Anarchism, Reform: Political Islam from the Inside Out." *Middle East Policy* XVII, no. 3 (Fall 2010).

Gerami, Shahin. "Religious Fundamentalism as a Response to Foreign Dependency: The Case of the Iranian Revolution." *Social Compass* 36 (1989).

Gershoni, I., and James P. Jankowski. *Egypt, Islam, and the Arabs: The Search for Egyptian Nationhood, 1900–1930*. New York: Oxford University Press, 1986.

———. *Redefining the Egyptian Nation, 1930–1945*. Cambridge: Cambridge University Press, 2002.

Gershoni, Israel. "The Return of the East: Muhammad Husayn Haykal's Recantation of Positivism." In *Middle Eastern Politics and Ideas: A History from Within*, edited by Moshe Maoz and Ilan Pappe. London: I. B. Tauris, 1997.

Ghani, Cyrus. *A Man of Many Worlds: the Memoirs & Diaries of Dr. Ghasem Ghani*. Translated by Paul Sprachman and Cyrus Ghani. Washington, DC: Mage Publishers, 2006.

Ghanoonparvar, Mohammad. "Nineteenth-Century Iranians in America." In *Society and Government in Qajar Iran: Studies in Honor of Hafez Farmayan*, edited by Elton L. Daniel. Costa Mesa, CA: Mazda Publishers, 2002.

Gheissari, Ali. *Iranian Intellectuals in the Twentieth Century*. Austin: University of Texas Press, 1998.

Giddens, Anthony. *New Rules of Sociological Method*. London: Hutchinson, 1976.

Goldberg, Michelle. *Kingdom Coming: The Rise of Christian Nationalism*. New York and London: W. W. Norton, 2007.

Goodman, Yehuda, and Yossi Yonah, eds. *In the Whirlpool of Identities*. Tel Aviv: Hakibbutz Hameuchad, 2004.

Gottheil, Richard J. H. *Golestan in Persian and Japanese Literature*. Vol. 2. London: The Colonial Press, 1900.

Green, Nile. *Bombay Islam: The Religious Economy of the West Indian Ocean, 1840–1915*. Cambridge: Cambridge University Press, 2011.

Greenberg, Clement. *Art and Culture: Critical Essays*. Boston: Beacon Press, 1961.

Greenblatt, Stephen Jay. *Marvelous Possessions: The Wonder of the New World*. Chicago: University of Chicago Press, 1992.

Grigor, Talinn. *Building Iran: Modernism, Architecture, and National Heritage Under the Pahlavi Monarchs*. New York: Periscope Publishing, distributed by Prestel, 2009.

Grimm, Gerhard. "Franz Babinger (1891–1967) Ein Lebensgeschichtlicher Essay." *Die Welt Des Islams* 38 (1998).

Guha, Ranajit. *Dominance Without Hegemony: History and Power in Colonial India*. Cambridge, MA: Harvard University Press, 1997.

———. *Elementary Aspects of Peasant Insurgency in Colonial India*. New Delhi: Oxford University Press, 1983.

———. "On Some Aspects of the Historiography of Colonial India." In *Selected Subaltern Studies*, edited by Ranajit Guha and Gayatri Spivak. New York: Oxford University Press, 1988.

Günther, Hans F. K. *The Racial Elements of European History*. London: Methuen & Co. Ltd., 1927.

Habermas, Jürgen. *The Structural Transformation of the Public Sphere: An Inquiry into a Category of Bourgeois Society*. Cambridge, MA: MIT Press, 1991.

Haneda, Masashi. *Le Châh et les Qizilbāš: Le système militaire safavide*. Berlin: K. Schwarz, 1987.

Hanisch, Ludmila. "Akzentverschiebung—zur Geschichte Der Semitistik Und Islamwissenschaft Wahrend Des 'Drittes Reiches.'" *Berichte Zur Wissenschaftsgeschichte* 18 (1995).

Hasan Khan I'timad al-Saltanah, Mohammad. *Dorr al-Tijan Fi Tarikh Bani Ashkan*. Tehran: Atlas, 1992.

Hassan, Zakin Muhammad. *Al-Funun al-Iraniyya Fi Al-'asr al-Islami*. Cairo: Matba'at Dar al-Kutub, 1940.

———. *al-Tasswir Fi al-Islam 'inda al-Furs*. Cairo: Lajnat al-Ta'lif wa al-Tarjama wa al-Nashr, 1936.

Hau, Michael. *The Cult of Health and Beauty in Germany: A Social History, 1890–1930*. Chicago: The University of Chicago Press, 2003.

Haykal, Muhammad. *Iran Fawqa Burkan*. Cairo: Dar Akhbar al-Yum, 1951.

Hechter, Michael. *Internal Colonialism: The Celtic Fringe in British National Development*. Berkeley: University of California Press, 1975.

Hedayat, Sadeq. *Karavan-e Islam: al-Ba'satu al-Islamiyyah Ila al-Bilad el-Ifranjiyyah*. Paris: Entesharat Sazman-e Jonbish Nationalisti Daneshgahiyan va Danesh Pajuhan va Rowshan Binan-e Iran, 1983.

———. *Parvin Dokhtar-e Sasan Va Isfahan Nesf-e Jehan*. 3rd ed. Tehran: Mo'ssaseh-e chap va entesharat-e amir kabir, 1964.

———. *Seh Qatreh Khun*. Tehran: Mo'ssaseh-e chap va entesharat-e amir kabir, 1964.

Herman, Arthur. *The Idea of Decline in Western History*. New York: Free Press, 1997.

Hidayat, Sadiq. *Al-Bumah Al-'amiya'*. Translated by Ibrahim al-Dasuqi Shita. Cairo: Al-Hay'ah al-Misrīyah al-'Amah lil-Kitab, 1976.

———. *Qisas Min Al-adab al-Farisi Al-mu'asir*. Translated by Ibrahim al-Dasuqi Shita. Cairo: al-Hay'ah al-Misriyah al-'Ammah lil-Kitab, 1975.

Hillmann, Michael Craig. *Hedayat's "The Blind Owl" Forty Years After*. Austin: Center for Middle Eastern Studies, University of Texas at Austin, 1978.

Hinz, Walther. *Irans Aufstieg Zum Nationalstaat Im Fünfzehnten Jahrhundert*. Leipzig: Walter de Gruyter & Co., 1936.

Hobsbawm, Eric. *Nations and Nationalism Since 1780*. Cambridge: Cambridge University Press, 1990.

Homayoon, N. T. "Dar Hashi-e Congre-e Bozorgdasht-e Hafez." *Sakhteman 7* (November 1988).

Homayoun, Dariush. *Pishtaz-e Hezareh Sevvum*. Hamburg: Talash Press, 2009.

———. *Sad Sal Keshakesh Ba Tajadod*. Hamburg: Talash Press, 2006.

Hourani, Albert Habib. *Arabic Thought in the Liberal Age 1798–1939*. Cambridge: Cambridge University Press, 2009.

Hroch, Miroslav. *The Social Preconditions of National Revival in Europe*. New York: Columbia University Press, 2000.

Husayn, Taha. "Mustaqbal Al-thaqafa Fi Misr." In *al-Majmu'a al-Kamila li-Mu'alafat al-Duktur Taha Husayn*. Vol. 9. Beirut: Dar al-Kitab al-Lubnani, 1973.

———. *Rihlat al-Rabi'*. Cairo: Dar al-Ma'arif, 1948.

Hutchinson, John, and Anthony D. Smith. *Nationalism*. London: Oxford University Press, 1994.

Ibn al-Nadim. *Al-Fihirst*. Cairo, n.d.

Ibn Faqih, Abu Bakr Ahmad b. Muhammad b. Ishaq Hamadani. *Kitab Al-buldan*. Tehran: Bonyad Farhang Iran, 1970.

Ibn Hawqal. *Surat al-Arz*. Edited by J. Sho'ar. Tehran: Bonyad Farhang Iran, 1966.

Ibn Nadim. *Al-Fihrist, Tajaddod Mazandarani*. Translated by Mohammad Reza. 2nd ed. Tehran: Ibn Sina, 1967.

Idarah-i Intishar-i Asnad-i Tarikhi: Daftar-i Mutala'at-i Siyasi va Bayn al-Milali. *Gozideh-e Asnad-e Ravabet-e Khareji-e Iran Va Mesr*. Vol. 2. Tehran: Mo'assaseh-i Chap va Entesharat-e Vezarat-e Omur-e Khareeh, 1996.

Inalcik, Halil. *Essays in Ottoman History*. Istanbul: Eren, 1998.

Ishay, Micheline R., and Omar Dahbour, eds. *The Nationalism Reader*. Atlantic Highlands: Humanities Press, 1995.

Issawi, Charles. *The Economic History of Iran, 1800–1914*. Chicago: University of Chicago Press, 1971.

Javadi, Hasan. "James Morier and His Hajji Baba of Ispahan." In *Iran Society Silver Jubilee Volume*. Calcutta, 1970.

Jenning, Richard. "Introduction." In *The Adventures of Hajji Baba of Ispahan*. London: Cresset Press, 1950.

Juergensmeyer, Mark. *Global Rebellion: Religious Challenges to the Secular State, from Christian Militias to Al Qaeda*. Berkeley: University of California Press, 2008.

———. *Religion in Global Civil Society*. Oxford and New York: Oxford University Press, 2005.

———. *The New Cold War? Religious Nationalism Confronts the Secular State*. Berkeley: University of California Press, 1994.

Jum'ah, Badi' Muhammad. "al-'Alaqat Al-thaqafiyya Bayna al-'Arab Wa Iran Fi Al-'assr Al-hadith." In *al-'Alaqat al-'Arabiyah al-'Iraniyah*, edited by Jamal Zakariya Qasim and Yunan Labib Rizq. Cairo: Ma'had al-Buhuth wa al-Dirasat al-Arabiyah, 1993.

Kamshad, H. *Modern Persian Prose Literature*. Cambridge: Cambridge University Press, 2010.

Kaplan, Amy. *The Anarchy of Empire in the Making of U.S. Culture*. Cambridge, MA: Harvard University Press, 2002.

Kashani-Sabet, Firoozeh. *Frontier Fictions: Shaping the Iranian Nation, 1804–1946.* Princeton: Princeton University Press, 1999.

Kasravi, Ahmad. *Hafez Che Migoyad (What Is Hafez Saying?).* Tehran, 1943.

———. *Tarikh-e Pansad Salah-e Khuzistan.* Tehran: Dunya-e Kitab, 2005.

Katouzian, Homa. *Sadeq Hedayat: His Work and His Wondrous World.* London and New York: Routledge, 2008.

Katouzian, M. A. Homa. *Sadeq Hedayat: The Life and Legend of an Iranian Writer.* London: I. B. Tauris, 1991.

Kaykhosrovai, R. *The Age of Ignorance: The Pillage of Iranian Cultural Heritage.* Tehran, 1984.

Keddie, Nikki. "Pan-Islam as Proto-Nationalism." *Journal of Modern History* 41, no. 1 (March 1969).

Keddie, Nikki R. *Iran and the Muslim World: Resistance and Revolution.* New York: New York University Press, 1995.

———. "Iranian Revolutions in Comparative Perspective." *The American Historical Review* 88, no. 3 (1983).

Keddie, Nikki. "Religion and Irreligion in Early Iranian Nationalism." *Comparative Studies in Society and History* 4 (1962).

———. *Religion and Rebellion in Iran: The Tobacco Protest of 1891–1892.* London: Frank Cass, 1966.

———. "The Economic History of Iran 1800–1914 and Its Political Impact." *Iranian Studies* 5, no. 2 (1972).

———. "The Origins of the Religious-Radical Alliance in Iran." *Past and Present* 34 (July 1966).

Kedourie, Elie. *Nationalism.* London: Blackwell, 1994.

———. *Nationalism in Asia and Africa.* London: Weidenfield and Nicholson, 1970.

Keshmirshekan, Hamid. "Discourses on Postrevolutionary Iranian Art: Neotraditionalism During the 1990s." *Muqarnas* 23 (2006).

Khalidi, Tarif. *Arabic Historical Thought in the Classical Period.* Cambridge: Cambridge University Press, 1996.

Khomeini, Ruhollah. *Dar Justeju-ye Rah Az Kalam-e Imam (In Search of the Path in the Discourse of the Imam).* Vol. 16. Tehran, 1363.

———. *Islam and Revolution: Writings and Declarations.* Translated by Hamid Algar. Berkeley: Mizan Press, 1981.

Kia, Mana. "Accounting for Difference: A Comparative Look at the Autobiographical Travel Narratives of Muhammad 'Ali Hazin Lahiji and 'Abd al-Karim Kashmiri." *Journal of Persianate Studies* 2 (2009).

———. "Contours of Persianate Community, 1722–1835." PhD dissertation, Harvard University, 2011.

Kimmerling, Baruch. *Immigrants, Settlers, Natives: The Israeli State and Society Between Cultural Pluralism and Cultural Wars.* Tel Aviv: Am Oved, 2004.

———. "Religion, Nationalism and Democracy in Israel." *Constellations* 6 (1999).

Kinnvall, Catarina. *Globalization and Religious Nationalism in India: The Search for Ontological Security.* Routledge, 2006.

Kinra, Rajeev. "Make It Fresh: Time, Tradition, and Indo-Persian Literary Modernity." In *Time, History and the Religious Imaginary in South Asia*, edited by Anne Murphy. New York: Routledge, 2011.

Kohn, Hans. *The Idea of Nationalism: A Study in Its Origins and Background*. New York: The Macmillan Company, 1944.

Kolb, Eberhard. *The Weimar Republic*. New York: Routledge, 2005.

Kondo, Nobuaki. "Qizilbash Afterwards: The Afshars in Urumiya from the Seventeenth to the Nineteenth Century." *Iranian Studies* 32, no. 4 (1999).

Kontje, Todd. *German Orientalisms*. Ann Arbor: University of Michigan Press, 2004.

Kurt, Umit. "The Doctrine of 'Turkish-Islamic Synthesis' as Official Ideology of the September 12 and the 'Intellectuals' Hearth—Aydinlar Ocagi' as the Ideological Apparatus of the State." *European Journal of Economic and Political Studies* 3, no. 2 (2010): 111–125.

Lane, Barbara Miller, and Leila J Rupp. *Nazi Ideology Before 1933: A Documentation*. Austin: University of Texas Press, 1978.

Lustick, Ian. "Abandoning the Iron Wall: Israel and 'The Middle Eastern Muck.'" *Middle East Policy Council* (2011).

Maftun, Hajji 'Ali Mirza. *Zobdat Al-akhbar Fi Savaneh Al-asfar: Safarnamah-e Iran Qarn-e Nuzdahom-e Miladi*. Edited by Zakera Sharif Qasemi. New Delhi: Islamic Wonders Bureau, 2003.

ibn Mahmud "Mir Khvand," Mohammad ibn Khavandshah. *History of the Early Kings of Persia: From Kaiomars, the First of the Peshdadian Dynasty, to the Conquest of Iran by Alexander the Great*. Translated by David Shea. London: Oriental Translation Fund, 1832.

———. *Tarikh-e Rawzat Al-safa Fi Sirat Al-anbeya' Va Al-moluk Va Al-kholafa'*. Edited by Jamshid Keyanfar. 15 vols. Tehran: Asatir, 1380.

Mahrad, Ahmad. *Die Deutsch-Persischen Beziehungen Von 1918–1933*. Frankfurt, 1974.

Makdisi, Ussama Samir. *The Culture of Sectarianism: Community, History, and Violence in Nineteenth Century Ottoman Lebanon*. Berkeley: University of California Press, 2000.

Makki, Hossein. *Tarikh-e Bist Saleh-e Iran*. Tehran: Nashr Nashr, 1983.

Mamdani, Mahmood. *Good Muslim, Bad Muslim: America, the Cold War, and the Roots of Terror*. New York: Pantheon Books, 2004.

Manoukian, S. "The City of Knowledge: History and Culture in Contemporary Shiraz." PhD dissertation, University of Michigan, 2001.

Marashi, Afshin. "Imagining Hafez: Rabindranath Tagore in Iran, 1932." *Journal of Persianate Studies* 3 (2010).

———. *Nationalizing Iran: Culture, Power, and the State, 1870–1940*. Seattle: University of Washington Press, 2008.

———. "Performing the Nation: The Shah's Official Visit to Kemalist Turkey, June to July 1934." In *The Making of Modern Iran: State and Society under Riza Shah, 1921–1941*, edited by Stephanie Cronin, 99–119. London: Routledge, 2003.

Marchand, Suzanne L. *Down from Olympus*. Princeton, NJ: Princeton University Press, 1996.

Mash, Harold. *Enlightenment Phantasies: Cultural Identity in France and Germany, 1750–1914*. Ithaca, NY: Cornell University Press, 2003.

Massignon, Louis, and Herbert Mason. *The Passion of Al-Hallaj: Mystic and Martyr of Islam*. Princeton, NJ: Princeton University Press, 1994.

Massoudi, Abbas. *China: A Land of Marvels*. Tehran: Ettela'at, 1973.

Mas'udi, Abbas. *Ba Man Be-Amrika Biya'id: Sharh-e Haft Hafteh-e Siyahat Dar Sarasar-e Keshvarha-ye Mottahed-e Amrika.* Tehran: Sherkat-e Sahami-i Chap, 1949.

———. *Didari Az Shaykh Neshinha-ye Khalij-e Fars.* Tehran: Iran-e Chap, 1966.

———. *Didari-ye Tazeh Az Shaykh Neshinha-ye Khalij-e Fars Pas Az Khoruj-e Niruha-ye Ingelis.* Tehran: Entesharat-e Mo'assaseh-ye Ettela'at, 1969.

———. *Khalij-e Fars Dar Dauran-e Sarbolandi Va Shokuh.* Tehran: Entesharat-e Mo'assaseh-ye Ettela'at, 1973.

———. *Khāterat-e Mosafarat-e Chin (Taiwan). Jam'avari Az Ruznameh-e Ettela'at.* Tehran: Tehran, Edarat-e Entesharat-e Sefarat-e Kobra-ye Jomhuri-ye Chin, 1955.

———. *Posht-e Pardeh-e Ahanin Cheh Didam.* Tehran, 1952.

Mas'udi, Abulhasan 'Ali Ibn-Hussein. *Muruj Al-zahab.* Translated by Abolqasim Payandah. 3rd ed. Tehran: Entesharat 'Elmi va Farhangi, 1986.

Mas'udi, Farhad. *Piruzi-e Labkhand.* Tehran: Ettela'at, 1975.

Matthee, Rudi. "The Imaginary Realm: Europe's Enlightenment Image of Early Modern Iran." *Comparative Studies of South Asia, Africa and the Middle East* 30, no. 3 (2010).

Mcalister, Melani. *Epic Encounters: Culture, Media, and U.S. Interests in the Middle East, 1945–2000.* Berkeley: University of California Press, 2001.

McFadden, Sarah. "Tehran Report: The Museum and the Revolution." *Art in America* (October 1981).

Mehran, Golnar. "The Presentations of the 'Self' and the 'Other' in Postrevolutionary Iranian School Textbooks." In *Iran and the Surrounding World: Interactions in Culture and Cultural Politics,* edited by Nikki R. Keddie and Rudolph P. Matthee, 232–253. Seattle: University of Washington Press, 2002.

Meisami, Julie. "The Past in the Service of the Present: Two Views of History in Medieval Persia." *Poetics Today* 14, no. 2 (Summer 1993).

Menashri, David. *The Iranian Revolution and the Muslim World.* Boulder: Westview Press, 1990.

Milani, 'Abbas. *Eminent Persians: The Men and Women Who Made Modern Iran, 1941–1979. Volume 1 (Politics).* Syracuse, NY: Syracuse University Press, 2008.

Minorsky, Vladimir. "Review of Iran's Aufstieg Zum Nationalstaat Im Fünfzehnten Jahrhundert by Walther Hinz." *Bulletin of the School of Oriental Studies* 9, no. 1 (1937).

———. *Tadhkirat Al-muluk: A Manual of Safavid Administration (circa 1137/1725).* London: E. J. W. Gibb Memorial Series, 1943.

———. "The Aq-qoyunlu and Land Reforms (Turkmenica, 11)." *Bulletin of the School of Oriental Studies* 17, no. 3 (1955).

———. "The Poetry of Shah Isma'il I." *Bulletin of the School of Oriental Studies* (1942).

Mirsepassi, Ali. *Political Islam, Iran, and the Enlightenment: Philosophies of Hope and Despair.* Cambridge: Cambridge University Press, 2011.

Mishani, Dror. *The Ethnic Unconscious: The Emergence of "Mizrahiut" in the Hebrew Literature of the Eighties.* Tel Aviv: Am Oved, 2006.

Mitchell, Colin Paul. *The Practice of Politics in Safavid Iran Power, Religion and Rhetoric.* London and New York: Tauris Academic Studies. Distributed in the United States and Canada exclusively by Palgrave Macmillan, 2009.

Moallem, Minoo. "Cultural Nationalism and Islamic Fundamentalism: The Case of Iran." In *Antinomies of Modernity: Essays on Race, Orient, Nation*, edited by Vasant Kaiwar and Sucheta Mazumdar, 196–222. Durham: Duke University Press, 2003.

Mohammadi, Ali, and Sreberny Mohammadi. "Post-Revolutionary Iranian Exiles: A Study of Impotence." *Third World Quarterly* 9, no. 1 (1987).

Momayyez, M. "Faculties of the University of Tehran Ii. Faculty of Fine Arts." In *Encyclopedia Iranica*, n.d.

Montazeri, Husayn-Ali. *Hokumat-Dini Va Hoquq-e Ensan*. Qom, 2007.

Mosse, George. *Crisis of German Ideology: Intellectual Origins of the Third Reich*. New York: Grosset and Dunlap, 1964.

Mostafavi, Muhammad Taqi. *Iqlim-e Pars: Asar-e Bastani Va Ebni-e Tarikhi-e Fars (Climes of Pars: Fars' Historic and Archeological Heritage)*. Tehran, 1375.

Mubarak, Ibrahim b., and Jalal al-Din Amini. *Futuhat-e Shahi*. Tehran: Anjuman-i Asar va Mafakhir-e Farhangi, 2004.

Mubarak, Zaki. *Layla al-Marida Fi al-'Iraq*. Cairo: Matba'at al-Risala, 1939.

Nabavi, Negin. "Readership, the Press, and the Public Sphere in the First Constitutional Period." In *Iran's Constitutional Revolution: Popular Politics, Cultural Transformations and Transnational Connections*, edited by Houchang Chehabi and Vanessa Martin. London: I. B. Tauris, 2010.

Nafici, Hamid. "Mediating the Other: American Pop Culture Representation of Post-revolutionary Iran." In *The U.S. Media and the Middle East: Image and Perception*, edited by Yahya R. Kamalipour. Westport, CT: Greenwood Press, 1995.

———. *The Making of Exile Cultures: Iranian Television in Los Angeles*. Minneapolis: University of Minnesota Press, 1993.

Najmabadi, Afsaneh. "Iran's Turn to Islam: From Modernism to a Moral Order." *The Middle East Journal* 41, no. 2 (Spring 1987).

———. *Women with Mustaches and Men Without Beards*. Berkeley: University of California Press, 2005.

Naraghi, Ehsan. *Ancheh Khod Dasht*. Tehran: Amir Kabir, 1976.

Narin, Tom. *Faces of Nationalism: Janus Revisited*. London: Verso Books, 1997.

Nashat, Guity. *The Origins of Modern Reform in Iran, 1870–80*. Urbana: University of Illinois Press, 1982.

Nicholson, Reynold A. *The Mystics of Islam*. London: G. Bell and Sons Ltd., 1914.

Nizam al-Mulk, Hasan Ibn-'Ali. *Siyasat-Nameh*. Tehran: Asatir, 1996.

Omidvar, 'Isa, and 'Abdallah Omidvar. *Safarnameh-e Baradaran-e Omidvar*. Tehran: Entesharar-e Jomhuri, 1380.

Özel, Oktay. "Limits of the Almighty: Mehmed II's 'Land Reform' Revisited." *Journal of the Economic and Social History of the Orient* 42, no. 2 (1999).

Parsi, Trita. *Treacherous Alliance: The Secret Dealings of Israel, Iran, and the U.S.* New Haven, CT: Yale University Press, 2007.

Parsinejad, I. "Zeyn ol-'Abedin Maragheh'I." *Annals of Japan Association for Middle Eastern Studies* 2 (1987).

Parsinejad, Iraj. *A History of Literary Criticism in Iran, 1866–1951: Literary Criticism in the Works of Enlightened Thinkers of Iran—Akhundzadeh, Kermani, Malkom, Talebof, Maraghe'I, Kasravi, and Hedayat*. Washington, DC: Ibex Publishers, 2003.

Paul, Ludwig. "Göttingen, University of, History of Iranian Studies." In *Encyclopedia Iranica*. n.d.

Paxton, Robert Owen. *The Anatomy of Fascism*. New York: Knopf, 2004.

Peled, Yoav. *Shas: The Challenge to Israeliness*. Tel Aviv: Yediot Ahronoth, 2001.

Perry, John R. "The Banu Kaʿb: An Ambitious Brigand State in Khuzistan." *Le monde Iranien et l'Islam* (1971).

Pirnia, Hassan. *Iran-e Bastan: Ardeshir-e Derazdast Ta Ardeshir-e Sevvom*. Vol. 4. Tehran: sazman-e ketabha-e Gjibi, 1963.

———. *Iran-e Bastan: Kurosh-e Kabir*. Vol. 2. Tehran: Sazman-e ketabha-e Gjibi, 1962.

Pollard, Lisa. *Nurturing the Nation: The Family Politics of Modernizing, Colonizing, and Liberating Egypt, 1805–1923*. Berkeley: University of California Press, 2005.

Pollock, Sheldon, and Muzaffar Alam, eds. "The Culture and Politics of Persian in Precolonial Hindustan." In *Literary Cultures in History: Reconstructions from South Asia*. Berkeley, CA: University of California Press, 2007.

Prodan, Dan. *Franz Babinger En Roumanie, 1935–1943: Étude Et Sources Historiques*. Istanbul: Les Editions Isis, 2003.

Quinn, Sholeh Alysia. *Historical Writing During the Reign of Shah ʿAbbas: Ideology, Imitation, and Legitimacy in Safavid Chronicles*. Salt Lake City: The University of Utah Press, 2000.

Rahimi, Babak. *Theatre State and the Formation of an Early Modern Public Sphere in Iran*. Leiden: Brill, 2011.

Rahimieh, Nasrin. *Missing Persians: Discovering Voices in Iranian Cultural History*. Syracuse, NY: Syracuse University Press, 2001.

Rainer Brunner, Rainer. *Islamic Ecumenism in the 20th Century: The Azhar and Shiʿism Between Rapprochement and Restraint*. Leiden: Brill, 2004.

Ram, Haggai. *Iranophobia: The Logic of an Israeli Obsession*. Stanford, CA: Stanford University Press, 2009.

Ram, Haggay. "The Immemorial Iranian Nation? School Textbooks and Historical Memory in Post-Revolutionary Iran." *Nations and Nationalism* 6, no. 1 (2000).

Rashwan, Nabil Muhammad. *Al-Islam al-Farsi*. Cairo: Matbaʾat al-Sharq, 1992.

Rastegar, Kamran. "Literary Modernity Between Arabic and Persian Prose: Jurji Zaydan's Riwayat in Persian Translation." *Comparative Critical Studies* 4, no. 3 (2007).

———. *Literary Modernity Between Middle East and Europe: Textual Transactions in 19th Century Arabic, English and Persian Literatures*. London: Routledge, 2010.

Ravitzky, Aviezer. *Messianism, Zionism, and Jewish Religious Radicalism*. Chicago: University of Chicago Press, 1993.

Ravitzky, Aviezer, ed. *Shas: Cultural and Ideological Perspectives*. Tel Aviv: Am Oved, 1996.

Raz-Krakotzkin, Amnon. *Exil Et Souveraineté: Judaïsm, Sionisme, Et Pensé Binationale*. Paris: La Fabrique Éditions, 2007.

———. "The Zionist Return to the West and the Mizrahi Jewish Perspective." In *Orientalism and the Jews*, edited by Derek J. Penslar and Ivan Davidson Kalmar. Waltham, MA: Brandeis University Press, 2005.

Rehatsek, Edward. *Catalogue Raisonne of the Arabic, Hendustani, Persian and Turkish MSS in the Mulla Firuz Library*. Bombay: Managing Committee of the Mulla Firuz Library, 1873.

Renan, Ernest. "Science and Islam." *Journal Des Debats* 19 (1883).

Reynolds, Dwight Fletcher, and Kristen Brustad, eds. *Interpreting the Self: Autobiography in the Arabic Literary Tradition*. Berkeley: University of California Press, 2001.

Rice, Cyprian. *The Persian Sufis*. London: George Allen & Unwin Ltd., 1964.

Ridgeon, Lloyd V. J. *Castigator of Sufism: Ahmad Kasravi and the Iranian Mystical Tradition*. London: Routledge/Curzon, 2005.

Riesebrodt, Martin. *Pious Passion: The Emergence of Modern Fundamentalism in the United States and Iran*. Berkeley: University of California Press, 1993.

Roosvelt, A. "The Kurdish Republic of Mahabad." *Middle East Journal* 1 (1947).

Rose, Jacqueline. *The Question of Zion*. Princeton, NJ: Princeton University Press, 2005.

Ryzova, Lucie. "Efendification: The Rise of Middle Class Culture in Modern Egypt." PhD dissertation, Oxford University, 2009.

Saad, Joya Blondel. *The Image of Arabs in Modern Persian Literature*. Lanham, MD: University Press of America, 1996.

Sadr-Hashemi, Mohammad. *Tarikh-e Jarayed Va Majallat-e Īran*. Vol. 1. 2nd ed. Tehran: Kamal, 1363.

Said, Edward. *Covering Islam: How the Media and the Experts Determine How We See the Rest of the World*. London: Routledge, 1981.

———. *Reflections on Exile and Other Essays*. Cambridge, MA: Harvard University Press, 2000.

Savory, Roger. *Iran Under the Safavids*. Cambridge: Cambridge University Press, 1980.

———. "Ḳizil-bāsh." Edited by W. P. Heinrichs, E. van Donzel, C. E. Bosworth, Th. Bianquis, and P. Bearman. *Encyclopaedia of Islam*. Brill, n.d.

———. "Some Reflections on Totalitarian Tendencies in the Safawid State." *Der Islam* 53 (1976).

———. *Studies on the History of Safawid Iran*. London: Variorum Reprints, 1987.

Schayegh, Cyrus. *Who Is Knowledgeable, Is Strong: Science, Class, and the Formation of Modern Iranian Society, 1900–1950*. Berkeley: University of California Press, 2009.

Schimmel, Annemarie. *I Am Wind, You Are Fire: The Life and Work of Rumi*. Boston and New York: Shambhala, 1992.

———. *Islam in the Indian Subcontinent*. Leiden: Brill, 1980.

———. *Mystical Dimensions of Islam*. Chapel Hill: University of North Carolina Press, 1975.

Schmitt, Rüdiger. "Hinz, (A.) Walther." In *Encyclopedia Iranica*, n.d.

Schurtz, Heinrich. *Alterklassen Und Männerbünde*. Berlin: G. Reimer, 1902.

Schwab, Raymond. *The Oriental Renaissance: Europe's Rediscovery of India and the East, 1680–1880*. Translated by Victor Reinking and Gene Patterson-Black. New York: Columbia University Press, 1984.

Shakman Hurd, Elizabeth. "The International Politics of Secularism: U.S. Foreign Policy and the Islamic Republic of Iran." *Alternatives* 29 (2004).

Shaltout, Mahmoud. "Introduction." *Risalat al-Islam*, no. 55, 56 (June 1964).

Shani, Ornit. *Communalism, Caste, and Hindu Nationalism: The Violence in Gujarat*. Cambridge and New York: Cambridge University Press, 2007.

Shariati, Ali. *Bazgasht-e Beh Khish*. Tehran: Hoseynieh Ershad, 1978.

———. *Bazshenasi Hoveyat-e Irani-Eslami*. Tehran: Elham Press, 1983.

———. *Ensan-e Bi Khod*. Tehran: Qalam Press, 1982.

Sharma, Sunil. "From 'A'esha to Nur Jahān: The Shaping of a Classical Persian Poetic Canon of Women." *Journal of Persianate Studies* 2, no. 2 (2009).

————. "Redrawing the Boundaries of 'Ajam in Early Modern Persian Literary Histories." In *Iran Facing Others: Identity Boundaries in a Historical Perspective*, edited by Abbas Amanat and Farzin Vejdani. New York: Palgrave Macmillan, 2012.

Shawqi, Ahmad. *Kambiz, in al-A'mal Al-kamilah: Al-masrahiyat*. Cairo: al-Hay'ah al-Misriyah al-'Ammah lil-Kitab, 1984.

Sheehi, Stephen. *Foundations of Modern Arab Identity*. Gainesville: University Press of Florida, 2004.

Sheikholeslami, A. Reza. *The Structure of Central Authority in Qajar Iran, 1871–1896*. Atlanta: Scholars Press, 1997.

Shenhav, Yehouda. *The Arab Jews: A Postcolonial Reading of Nationalism, Religion, and Ethnicity*. Stanford, CA: Stanford University Press, 2006.

Shohat, Ella. "The Invention of the Mizrahim." *Journal of Palestine Studies* 29, no. 1 (1999).

Shumski, Dimitry. "Post-Zionist Orientalism? Orientalist Discourse and Islamophobia Among the Russian-Speaking Intelligentsia in Israel." *Social Identities* 10 (2004).

Shushtari, Mir 'Abd al-Latif. *Tuhfat Al-alam Va Zel Al-tuhfat*. Edited by Samad Muvahhid. Tehran: Ketabkhaneh-e Tahuri, 1363.

Siebzehner, Batia, and David Lehmann. *Remaking Israeli Judaism: The Challenge of Shas*. London: Hurst, 2006.

Smith, Anthony D. *The Ethnic Origins of Nations*. New York: Blackwell, 1986.

————. *The Ethnic Revival in the Modern World*. Cambridge: Cambridge University Press, 1981.

Smith, Matthew Chaffee. "Literary Courage, Language, Land, and the Nation in the Work of Malik al-Shu'ara Bahar." PhD dissertation, Harvard University, 2006.

Sorush, Abd al-Karim. *Razdani Va Rowshanfekri Va Dindari*. Tehran: Mo'assaseh-e Farhangi-e Serat, 1998.

Spellman, Kathryn. *Religion and Nation: Iranian Local and Transnational Networks in Britain*. Oxford: Berghahm Books, 2004.

Stein, Rebecca. "The Ballad of the Sad Café: Israeli Leisure, Palestinian Terror, and the Post/colonial Question." In *Postcolonial Studies and Beyond*, edited by Jed Esty, Antoinette Burton, Matti Bunzl, Suvir Kaul, and Annia Loomba. Durham, NC: Duke University Press, 2006.

Subtelny, Maria Eva. "Centralizing Reform and Its Opponents in the Late Timurid Period." *Iranian Studies* 21, no. 1/2 (1988): 123–151.

Sulh'ju, Jahangir. *Tarikh-e Matbu'at Dar Iran Va Jahan*. Tehran: Kitabha-e Simurgh, 1969.

Süssheim, Karl, Barbara Flemming, and Jan Schmidt. *The Diary of Karl Süssheim (1878–1947): Orientalist Between Munich and Istanbul*. Stuttgart: F. Steiner, 2002.

Tafazoli, Hamid. *Der Deutsche Persien-diskurs: Von Der Fruhen Neuzeit Bis in Das Neunzehnten Jarhundert*. Bielefeld: Aisthesis, 2007.

Taqi Zahtabi, Mohamm. *Iran Turklerinin Eski Tarikhi*. 2 vols. Tabriz. Kargah Sabz: 1999, n.d.

Taqizadah, Hasan. *Khatabah-e Aqa-e Sayyad Hasan Taqizadah*. Tehran: Mehregan, 1959.

Tavakoli-Targhi, Mohammad. "Contested Memories: Narrative Structures and Allegorical Meanings of Iran's Pre-Islamic History." *Iranian Studies* 29, no. 1/2 (Winter-Spring 1996).

———. "Refashioning Iran: Language and Culture During the Constitutional Revolution." *Iranian Studies* 23, no. 1 (1990).

———. "Tajaddod-e Ekhtera'i, Tajaddod-e 'ariyati, Va Enqelab-e Rohani" (Inventing Modernity, Borrowing Modernity)." *Iran Nameh* (Spring/Summer 2002).

Tavakoli-Targhi, Mohamad. *Refashioning Iran: Orientalism, Occidentalism and Historiography*. Basingstoke: Palgrave, 2001.

Tilli, Charles, ed. *The Formation of National States in Western Europe*. Princeton, NJ: Princeton University Press, 1975.

Tilli, Jouny. "An Interpretation of Finnish Religious Nationalism: The Four Topoi of Theological Depoliticisation." *Nations and Nationalism* 15, no. 4 (2009): 597–615.

Todorov, Tzvetan. *On Human Diversity: Nationalism, Racism, and Exoticism in French Thought*. Cambridge, MA: Harvard University Press, 1994.

Toprak, Binnaz. "Religion as State Ideology in a Secular Setting: The Turkish-Islamic Synthesis." In *Aspects of Religion in Secular Turkey*, edited by J. Malcolm Wagstaff. Durham: University of Durham, Centre for Middle Eastern and Islamic Studies, 1990.

Truesdell, Mathew. *Spectacular Politics: Louis-Napoleon Bonaparte and the Fête Impérial, 1849–1870*. New York: Oxford University Press, 1997.

Tuqan, Qadri Hafiz. *Turath al-'Arab Al-'ilmi Fi al-Riyadiyyat Wa Al-falak*. Cairo: al-Muqtataf, 1941.

Unowsky, Daniel. *The Pomp and Politics of Patriotism: Imperial Celebrations in Habsburg Austria, 1848–1916*. West Lafayette, IN: Purdue University Press, 2005.

Vaziri, Mostafa. *Iran as Imagined Nation: the Construction of National Identity*. New York, NY: Paragon House, 1993.

Veer, Peter van der. *Religious Nationalism: Hindus and Muslims in India*. Berkeley: University of California Press, 1994.

Waite, Robert. *Vanguard of Nazism*. New York: W. W. Norton, 1969.

Watenpaugh, Keith David. *Being Modern in the Middle East: Revolution, Nationalism, Colonialism, and the Arab Middle Class*. Princeton, NJ: Princeton University Press, 2006.

Wilber, Donald. *Iran Madiha Wa Hadiriha*. Translated by 'Abd al-Na'im Hasanyn. Cairo: Maktabat Misr, 1958.

Wittek, Paul. *The Rise of the Ottoman Empire*. London: The Royal Asiatic Society, 1938.

Ya'qubi, Ahmad Ibn-Ishaq. *Tarikh Ya'qubi*. Leiden: Brill, 1883.

Yadegari, Mohammad. "The Iranian Settlement in Egypt as Seen Through the Pages of the Community Papers Chihrinimi, 1904–1966." In *Modern Egypt: Studies in Politics and Society*, edited by Elie Kedourie and Sylvia Kedourie. London and Totowa, NJ: F. Cass, 1980.

Yaqut, Abu 'Abdallah, and F. Wüstenfeld. *Mu'jam Al-buldan*. Vol. 1. Leipzig: Brockhaus, 1866.

Yarshater, Ehsan. "Safavid Literature: Progress or Decline." *Iranian Studies* 7, no. 1/2 (Winter–Spring 1974).

Yonan, Gabrielle, and Bahman Nirumand. *Iraner in Berlin*. Berlin: Auslanderbeaufragate, 1994.

Yusuf, Hassan. *Mudhakkirat Hasan Yusuf: al-Qasr Wa Dawrih Fi Al-siyasa al-Misriyya, 1922–1952*. Cairo: Markaz al-Dirasat al-Siyasiyah wa-al-Istiratizhiyah bi-al-Ahram, 1982.

Zaghlul, Fathi Ahmad. *Sirr Takadum al-Ingiliz wal-Saksuniyin*. Cairo, 1899.

Zaydan, Jurji. *Abu Muslim al-Khurasani: Riwayah Tarikhiya*. Cairo: Matba'at al-Hilal, 1905.

———. *al-'Abbasah Ukht al-Rashid, Aw Nakbat al-Baramikah: Riwayat Tarikh al-Islam*. Cairo: Matba'at al-Hilal, 1902.

Zedehdel, H. *Series of Guide Books to Iran: Fars Province*. Tehran, 1998.

Zia-Ebrahimi, Reza. "Self-Orientalization and Dislocation: The Uses and Abuses of the 'Aryan' Discourse in Iran." *Iranian Studies* 44, no. 4 (July 2011).

Ziaian, P. *Shiraz: The Colorful Dream of Pars*. Tehran: Gooya, 2001.

Zirinsky, Michael P. "Imperial Power and Dictatorship: Britain and the Rise of Reza Shah, 1921–1926." *International Journal of Middle East Studies* 24, no. 4 (November 1992).

Zubaida, Sami. *Islam, the People and the State: Political Ideas and Movements in the Middle East*. London: I. B. Tauris, 1993.

Zubrzycki, Geneviève. *The Crosses of Auschwitz: Nationalism and Religion in Post-communist Poland*. Chicago: University of Chicago Press, 2006.

Contributors

KAMRAN SCOT AGHAIE received his PhD in history from the University of California, Los Angeles, in 1999. He is associate professor of Islamic and Iranian history at the University of Texas at Austin, and is currently serving as Director of the Center for Middle Eastern Studies. His main publications include *The Martyrs of Karbala: Shiʿi Symbols and Rituals in Modern Iran* (Seattle: University of Washington Press, 2004) and *The Women of Karbala: Ritual Performances and Symbolic Discourses of Modern Shiʿi Islam* (Austin: University of Texas Press, 2005).

CAMRON MICHAEL AMIN received his PhD in Near Eastern languages and civilizations from the University of Chicago in 1996. He is a professor of Middle Eastern history at the University of Michigan–Dearborn. His main publications include *The Making of the Modern Iranian Woman: Gender, State Policy, and Popular Culture, 1865–1946* (Gainesville, FL: University Press of Florida, 2002) and, as a contributing editor (with Benjamin C. Fortna and Elizabeth Frierson), *The Modern Middle East: A Sourcebook for History* (Oxford: Oxford University Press, 2006).

ALI ANOOSHAHR received his PhD in Islamic history from the University of California, Los Angeles, in 2005. He is an associate professor of comparative pre-modern Islamic history at the University of California, Davis, with a heavy emphasis on the Mughals and the Safavids. He is author of *The Ghazi Sultans and the Frontiers of Islam* (London and New York: Routledge, 2009).

TOURAJ ATABAKI graduated with a degree in theoretical physics and then completed his doctoral work in Oriental studies at Utrecht University in

1990. He holds the chair in the social history of the Middle East and Central Asia at Leiden University, and is the head of the Middle East and Central Asia Desk at the International Institute of Social History. His main publications include *Azerbaijan: Ethnicity and the Struggle for Power in Iran* (London: I. B. Tauris, 1993) and *Beyond Essentialism: Who Writes Whose Past in the Middle East and Central Asia?* (Amsterdam: Aksant, 2003). He has also edited and coedited numerous other volumes.

WENDY DESOUZA received her PhD in history from the University of California, Los Angeles, in 2010. She is PARSA Visiting Lecturer in Iranian Studies at the University of California, Davis. Her research examines modern notions of gender and sexuality in the writings of twentieth-century Iranian scholars of Oriental studies. Her dissertation, titled "Scholarly Mysticism and Mystical Scholars: Iranian Intellectuals at the Dawn of Modern Sexuality and Gender," is currently being edited for publication.

TALINN GRIGOR received her PhD in history, theory, and criticism of architecture from Massachusetts Institute of Technology in 2005. She is associate professor of modern and contemporary architecture at Brandeis University. Her main publications include *Building Iran: Modernism, Architecture, and National Heritage under the Pahlavi Monarchs* (New York: Prestel, 2009), and a volume coedited with Sussan Babaie titled *Persian Kingship and Architecture: Strategies of Power in Iran from the Achaemenids to the Pahlavis* (London: I. B. Tauris, 2012).

HANAN HAMMAD received her PhD in history from the University of Texas at Austin in 2009. She is assistant professor of Middle Eastern and Islamic history at Texas Christian University. Her publications include "Between Egyptian National Purity and Local Flexibility: Prostitution in al-Mahalla al-Kubra in the First Half of the Twentieth Century" in *Journal of Social History*, March 2011; "The Other Extremists: Marxist Feminism in Egypt, 1980–2000" in *Journal of International Women's Studies*, March 2011; and "Khomeini and the Iranian Revolution in the Egyptian Press: From Fascination to Condemnation" in *Radical History Review*, September 2009.

FIROOZEH KASHANI-SABET received her PhD in history from Yale University in 1999. She is associate professor of Middle Eastern history at the University of Pennsylvania and is currently serving as the Director of the Middle East Center there. She is author of *Conceiving Citizens: Women and the Politics of Motherhood in Iran* (Oxford: Oxford University Press, 2011) and *Frontier Fictions: Shaping the Iranian Nation, 1804–1946* (Princeton, NJ: Princeton University Press, 1999).

MANA KIA received her PhD in history and Middle Eastern studies from Harvard University in 2011. She also has an MA in Near Eastern studies from New York University (2001) and a BA from Vassar College in international studies (1997). She is assistant professor in the Department of Middle Eastern, South Asian, and African Studies at Columbia University. She has published articles on various aspects of the comparative and connective social and cultural histories of West, Central, and South Asia (eighteenth to twentieth centuries) and is currently finishing a book on transregional Persianate sensibilities of belonging before nationalism.

BRIAN MANN is a doctoral candidate in history at the University of Texas at Austin and is currently an assistant professor of Middle Eastern history at Eastern Illinois University. His main areas of research include the modern Middle East, nineteenth- and twentieth-century Iran, Khuzistan, nationalism, tribal groups and ethnic minorities, imperialism, urbanization, labor, and social movements.

AFSHIN MARASHI received his PhD in history from the University of California, Los Angeles, in 2003. He holds the Farzaneh Family Chair in Iranian Studies and is associate professor of history and international and area studies at the University of Oklahoma. He is author of *Nationalizing Iran: Culture, Power, and the State, 1870–1940* (Seattle: University of Washington Press, 2008).

AFSHIN MATIN-ASGARI received his PhD in history from the University of California at Los Angeles in 1993. He is professor of Middle Eastern history at California State University, Los Angeles, and is author of *Iranian Student Opposition to the Shah* (Los Angeles: Mazda, 2001).

HAGGAI RAM received his PhD in Near Eastern studies from New York University in 1992. He is an associate professor of Middle East studies at Ben Gurion University of the Negev, Israel. His main publications include *Myth and Mobilization in Revolutionary Iran* (Washington, DC: American University Press, 1994) and *Iranophobia: The Logic of an Israeli Obsession* (Stanford: Stanford University Press, 2009).

SUSSAN SIAVOSHI received her PhD in political science from Ohio State University in 1985. She is a professor and the chair of the Department of Political Science at Trinity University in San Antonio, Texas. She is the author of *Liberal Nationalism in Iran: The Failure of a Movement* (Westview Press, 1990).

INDEX

Note: Italic page numbers refer to illustrations.

CPSIA information can be obtained
at www.ICGtesting.com
Printed in the USA
FSOW01n1126101115
13196FS